Coleridge
and the Idea of Friendship, 1789–1904

Coleridge and the Idea of Friendship, 1789–1804

Gurion Taussig

Newark: University of Delaware Press
London: Associated University Presses

© 2002 by Rosemont Publishing & Printing Corp.

All rights reserved. Authorization to photocopy items for internal or personal use, or the internal or personal use of specific clients, is granted by the copyright owner, provided that a base fee of $10.00, plus eight cents per page, per copy is paid directly to the Copyright Clearance Center, 222 Rosewood Drive, Danvers, Massachusetts 01923. [0-87413-741-1/02 $10.00 + 8¢ pp, pc.]

Other than as indicated in the foregoing, this book may not be reproduced, in whole or in part, in any form (except as permitted by Sections 107 and 108 of the U.S. Copyright Law, and except for brief quotes appearing in reviews in the public press).

Associated University Presses
2010 Eastpark Boulevard
Cranbury, NJ 08512

Associated University Presses
16 Barter Street
London WC1A 2AH, England

Associated University Presses
P.O. Box 338, Port Credit
Mississauga, Ontario
Canada L5G 4L8

The paper used in this publication meets the requirements of the American National Standard for Permanence of Paper for Printed Library Materials Z39.48-1984.

Library of Congress Cataloging-in-Publication Data

Taussig, Gurion, 1971–
    Coleridge and the idea of friendship, 1789–1804 / Gurion Taussig.
      p. cm.
    Includes bibliographical references and index.
    ISBN 0-87413-741-1
    1. Coleridge, Samuel Taylor, 1772–1834—Friends and associates.
2. Coleridge, Samuel Taylor, 1772–1834—Views on friendship. 3. Male friendship—England—History—18th century. 4. Male friendship—England—History—19th century. 5. Authors, English—19th century—Biography. 6. Authors, English—18th century—Biography. 7. Friendship in literature. I. Title.
PR4483 .T38 2002
821'.7—dc21
                                                                                                  2002018094

PRINTED IN THE UNITED STATES OF AMERICA

To my family,
with love

Contents

List of Illustrations	9
Acknowledgments	11
Introduction	15
1 Transcendence and Its Limits: Friendship in the 1780s	50
2 Idea and Substance: Coleridge, Thomas Poole, and the Genderings of Male Friendship	87
3 Coleridge, Southey, and the Problem of Pantisocratic Friendship	116
4 Friends of Humanity: Coleridge, Southey, and *The Anti-Jacobin*	146
5 "They answer and provoke each other's songs:" Coleridge, Thelwall, and Oppositional Friendship	177
6 "It is a usual concomitant of persons of his character to explain a human sympathy by a divine impulse:" Coleridge, Charles Lamb, and Charles Lloyd, 1794–98	214
7 Coleridge and Wordsworth: Friendship and the Problem of "living with thyself / And for thyself"	246
8 Managing Friendship: Coleridge, Godwin, and Southey, 1799–1804	278
9 Postscript: "Our excellent transatlantic friend": Coleridge and Washington Allston, 1806–18	315
Notes	328
Bibliography	357
Index	368

List of Illustrations

"Friendship. *A principal Beard*" (1791)	76
"Enjoying a Friend" (1798)	79
"*You that walk in the light of your own fire; and in the sparks that ye have kindled, ye shall lie down in sorrow*" (1645)	144
"The Friend of Humanity and the Knife Grinder" (1797)	163
"Tears of Sensibility—Sympathy a Poem—Let's all be Unhappy together—^{ie} The Wig Club in Distress &c, &c" (1798)	165
"Copenhagen House" (1795)	180
"An Irish Hug alias A Fraternal Embrace. The Dearest Friends must Part" (1798)	181
The Marriage of Heaven and Hell, plate 3 (1790)	186
"The Wrangling Friends or Opposition in Disorder" (1791)	192
"Mutual Confidence in the Year 1799" (1799)	226
Washington Allston, *Portrait of Samuel Taylor Coleridge (unfinished)* (1806)	317
Washington Allston, *Self-Portrait* (1805)	318
Washington Allston, *The Sisters* (c. 1816–1817)	326

Acknowledgments

I WOULD LIKE TO THANK THE FOLLOWING PEOPLE AND INSTITUTIONS who in various ways have facilitated the writing of this book: Professor David Fairer for his generous supervision, support and friendship throughout; the British Academy for funding my research; the School of English, University of Leeds, for supporting my postgraduate studies; Lord Abinger, the National Library of Wales, Aberystwyth, the Museum of Fine Arts, Boston, the Syndics of Cambridge University Library, Cambridge, Fitzwilliam Museum, Cambridge, Harvard University Art Museums, the Houghton Library, Harvard, the British Library, London, the British Museum, London, the Pierpont Morgan Library, New York, the Bodleian Library, Oxford, the McHenry Library, Santa Cruz, Oxford University Press and Routledge Press for allowing me to reproduce manuscript and other materials; Christopher Atkins, Evelyn Bavier, Jenny Houghton, Winni Li, Tom Mayberry, Robert Parks, Jr., and Chantal Serhan for locating and reproducing manuscripts and prints; the staff at Cambridge University Library, the National Library of Ireland, Dublin, the Brotherton Library, Leeds, the British Library and the Bodleian Library; Daniel Alexander, Dr Pamela Clemit, Dr Eric Griffiths, Dr Ruth Morse, Dr John Mullan, Dr Seamus Perry, Dr Felicitas von Peter, Dr Elinor Shaffer, William St Clair, Dr Anya Taylor, Dr Benjamin Tipping, Dr John Whale.

Coleridge
and the Idea of Friendship,
1789–1804

Introduction

WHILE READING JEAN PAUL'S *GEIST* IN 1813, COLERIDGE CONFIDED TO his notebook a plan to compose an essay on a subject in which he was deeply versed, both through the devotion of considerable philosophic and poetical energy and through extensive personal experience:

"Ich finde alles eher auf der Erde, sogar Wahrheit und Freude, als FREUNDSCHAFT!" [I find everything on earth, even truth and joy, sooner than FRIENDSHIP] Jean Paul—
   This for the motto—to examine and attest the fact—and then to explain the Reason—first, the extraordinary Qualifications demanded for true Friendship—the multitude of causes that make men delude themselves & attribute to Friendship what is only a ~~sympathy~~ similarity of Pursuit, or even mere dislike of feeling one's self *alone* in any thing /—but supposing it as real as human nature ordinarily permits, yet how many causes are at constant war against it—violent irruptions, unobserved yet constant wearings away by dispathy &c—Exemplify this in Youth—& then in Manhood—/—The influence of wives, how frequently deadly to Friendship—~~of~~ by direct incroach, & perhaps intentional plans of alienation—by ~~of~~ families, by otherwise occupying the heart—and of Life in general, by the worldly-wise, chilling Effect of prudential anxieties—[1]

Jean Paul offers Coleridge the sobering insight that friendship represents an Idea whose realization is precarious in the extreme. This thought resonates with Coleridge's experience: knowing the lineaments of "true Friendship," he can only "suppose" (as if merely for the sake of argument) that it can exist in human relations. In documenting the many causes in individual psychology and contemporary life that undermine friendship, Coleridge points towards a culture where protestations and professions of friendship abound but where the relationship itself either proves elusive or easily destroyed.
   In beginning to catalogue the forces hostile to friendship, Coleridge offers a glimpse of the Idea and the conflict between the Ideal and its earthly embodiments. Where true friendship would encompass an unworldly, altruistic benevolence of spirit, in encountering

"human nature" it is easily marred by prudential self-interest. The ideal emerges here as a male bond whose Eden is threatened from several directions; although friends should focus their attention utterly on each other, in practice such intimacy founders on their conventional allegiance to marriage and the family. Where friendship's state would ideally be a perfect calmness, such stasis is undermined both by an ongoing organic process of "unobserved" erosion and the explosive force of "violent irruptions." In the light of Johnson's *Dictionary* definition, such "irruptions" might indicate a mysterious natural force breaking into the friend's bloodstream and suspending the affectionate beatings of his heart.[2] Moreover, Coleridge is confident that these conflicts are not merely personal to him, but are recognizable as a description of a more general experience.

Coleridge did not write his essay on friendship. But in several of his intimate male relationships, he had already traced a path from idealism to various levels of disillusionment. This book attempts to reconstruct these narratives in his correspondence and other writings. Coleridge's correspondence with men from diverse spheres—ranging from the political agitator John Thelwall to his Quaker pupil Charles Lloyd, from the tanner Thomas Poole to the more literary figures of Southey and Wordsworth—places him at the centre of a network of discourses on friendship, each of which takes on a subtly different character and articulates a clash of principle or interpretation. My main hypothesis is that Coleridge's personal experiences of friendship are shaped by a wider cultural preoccupation with friendship evident during the 1780s and 1790s, and are worked out in the interchange of correspondence and poetry between himself and his friends.

In this introduction, I situate my main arguments within the critical literature as it pertains to Coleridge's idea of friendship in the 1790s. My historicist approach differs both from traditional biographical criticism with its heavy reliance on psychology and from those studies that undervalue the biographical context in which Coleridge's views on human relations often originate. In his 1967 biographical study, Geoffrey Yarlott presupposes that Coleridge's enthusiasm for friendship reveals his "emotional and moral instability."[3] Self-sufficient men like Southey and Wordsworth provided Coleridge with a "sheet-anchor" for his unbalanced personality (p. 32). Thomas McFarland offers a Freudian formulation, arguing that Coleridge sought a warm mother and accepting brother, and assumed in his friendships "something of the situation of a child, for the neurotic nature of his needs froze him into certain infantile attitudes, as though (and Freud has emphasized the point) in the psychic arena where the problem originated, there must it forever be ministered to" (pp. 121–23). For Molly Lefebure, Coleridge's neuroses help explain why his relationships failed: his childhood experiences ("hopelessly spoiled" by his mother, suffering his father's death, sent to a "large and impersonal public school") together result in the "adult Coleridge having great difficulty in sustaining closely intimate relationships."[4]

However persuasive such psychologically grounded studies are, they tend to narrow the focus to the poet's psychological needs and insecurities. None of them takes into account the extent to which friendship was being analyzed during the late eighteenth century. What might be thought to have a purely psychological interpretation can be seen to be also part of a wider cultural preoccupation (often politically inflected) with the nature of the friend. Similarly, tensions in these relationships can be examined less as symptoms of the poet's psychopathology, and more in terms of conflicting ideas of friendship that these relationships negotiate. This kind of historicist analysis can qualify the points raised by Yarlott and McFarland. For instance, many of Coleridge's contemporaries regarded dependency upon a friend as vital to an individual's improvement and not necessarily symptomatic of a "neurotic malaise." As Charles Atkinson remarked in *The Mind's Monitor* (1793):

> A real Friend is the agreeable Moderator in all our Actions and inward Sensations. His Genius we carefully consult in all that concerns our Amusement and Interest. It is his principles which actuate our Motives. . . . The more learned our Friend, the greater his Value. By his superior Knowledge we are instructed to adhere to such Principles as will not only obtain for us a lasting Pleasure, but also render us of more Benefit to ourselves and to others.[5]

This view was shared by one of Coleridge's "sheet-anchors," Southey. He remarks on the advantage for any "young man entering the world": "To have a friend, dear enough & respectable enough to hold the place of a confessor."[6] In this context, Coleridge's dependence on male figures might not be so unusual, but a practical enactment of the latest theories of friendship. Coleridge's own mentoring during the 1790s has been underemphasized. In his relations with Lloyd, he is paid to become the guiding friend to a dependent, younger man entering into adult life.

My methodology also differs from the most extensive monographs on Coleridge's ideas of human relationship, Anthony Harding's *Cole-*

ridge and the Idea of Love (1974) and J. Robert Barth's *Coleridge and the Power of Love* (1988).[7] Both critics treat Coleridge's work in isolation, splicing together quotations from his letters and notebooks without considering fully the context of these remarks within individual developing relationships. This facilitates Harding's assertion that "an essentially coherent idea of human relationship did exist for Coleridge," which he summarizes axiomatically:

> the recognition of personality, rather than conduct, as the starting-point of morality; the essentiality of love, which is part of the striving of the individual towards the "one Life"; the origin of self-consciousness, morality and Reason itself in the individual's sense of "otherness;" and the vital function of religion and the developing social state in breaking through the individual's insular subjectivity. (p. 5)

Although Harding lists important Coleridgean axioms, his taxonomic view presents an overly confident picture of "what Coleridge thought." How Coleridge articulates his ideas of friendship is often contingent upon individual relationships and specific moments within them. Although various motifs recur, by restricting my focus to the 1790s a sharper and properly less coherent picture should emerge. In charting the trajectories of particular relationships, friendship reveals itself as an idea in process, changing with differing relationships, and as Coleridge and his friends reflect on the progress of a particular relationship.

Discussing friendship in moral rather than psychological terms, *The Universal Magazine* revealed a cultural uncertainty as to what kind of moral relationship friendship in 1793 represented:

> The words *friendship* and *friend* are used indeed in such a variety of senses, all different, that it is almost impossible to recognize the genuine features of that old fashioned thing called friendship, among such a group of unaccountables. A spendthrift, after various attempts to borrow money, complains with a sigh, that he has not a *friend* left in the world; . . . captain Swagger, of the guards, who has accepted a challenge, requests a brother-officer to go out with him as his *friend*, and see that he be *fairly* run through the body. Ladies, who prefer keepers to husbands, usually call them their *friends*; and a highwayman, who quarrels with his accomplices, concerning the distribution of the booty, wonders that there should be any bickerings among *friends*.[8]

For this anonymous writer ("Caius"), the "old fashioned thing" had been much abused in modern parlance. Caius bewails the casual usage of the term "friend" by morally reprehensible characters and its subsequent dissociation from an ethical discourse. Furthermore, the term is not only debased by some but is overdetermined by others. In more "romantic" discourse it designates an extraordinary relationship of transcendent virtue:

> There are, on the other hand, some persons, who entertain a notion of friendship, so very celestial and romantic, as is not to be expected from the frailty of human nature. . . . They expect *every* thing from a friend, and in this are as much in fault, as the others who expected *any* thing. Romantic notions of friendship are much cherished in novels and sentimental writings, but their tendency is often fatal, and at all times pernicious. A very short intercourse with the world of men convinces them, that they have been reading of ideal beings; and their tempers are apt to be soured; in consequence of which they entertain worse notions of men than they deserve. (p. 327)

Between the casual and metaphysical usages, Caius presents friendship as having a problem of definition at the end of the eighteenth century. In response to this, he offers his own concept of "the very essence, the life's blood, . . . of friendship," which reiterates Johnson's primary *Dictionary* definition of the relationship as one of "mutual benevolence" (p. 328).[9]

Johnson's authority, however, was itself uncertain, for his *Dictionary* admitted the multitude of meanings surrounding the term. Although "Friendship" can signify the "highest degree of intimacy," a "friend" is not necessarily a moral figure: it can refer negatively to "one without hostile intentions," or be merely a casual or "familiar compellation." Between these extremes a "friend" may signify "an attendant, or companion," or a "favourer."[10] Caius recognizes that appeals to authority are limited, conceding that "the original meaning, if it can be acquired, is of little use" (p. 326). This fear that friendship's meaning cannot be prescribed, indicates a degree of cultural anxiety surrounding the term's semantic range.

Coleridge's usage of the term "friend" in the 1790s encompasses many of the significations Johnson had noted. His awareness of such variation in meaning may be introduced by a poem, "The Three Sorts of Friends" (1801):

> Though friendships differ endless *in degree*,
> The *sorts*, methinks, may be reduced to three.
> *A*cquaintance many, and *Con*quaintance few;
> But for *In*quaintance I know only two—
> The friend I've mourned with, and the maid I woo![11]

Deriving from the Latin root "cognoscere," "*ac, con* and *in*quaintance" measure friendship in terms of each party's knowledge of the other. The highest category of "*In*quaintance" gestures at an interpenetration of soul, by which friends come mutually not only to understand but to participate in each other's inner emotional and spiritual life, whether this consists of sorrow or joy.

The variation Coleridge identifies in friendship itself has become apparent in two divergent critical assessments of Coleridge's ideas of friendship and love. Critics who stress the importance of "*In*quaintance" typically understand friendship as a Coleridgean expression of love, where in Barth's terms, "love is for Coleridge a completion of ourselves and therefore implies— . . . a commonality between ourselves and the object of our love."[12] Barth's emphasis on unifying subjectivity leads him to conclude that "Coleridge's preferred model" of love relationship is "'married friendship', for . . . it is only in marriage that friendship can come to its perfection. It is only in marriage that the longed-for union can take place on every level of one's being, including the physical" (p. 21).

Defining friendship as an expression of love, however, risks conflating the two concepts. Other critics have stressed how Coleridge theorizes an essential difference between love and friendship. Drawing on Coleridge's assertion that "All in a moment *Love* starts up or leaps in, and *takes place* of Liking," as well as his order to "Reverence the Individuality of your friend!," Laurence Lockridge argues:

> Friendship evolves out of the total recognition of the "thou" as "other," yet as equally conscious and worthy.
> The difference between friendship and love is that the latter seeks to deny that the "thou" *is* "other." . . . Love is the "yearning of the whole Being to be united with some one other Being."[13]

Unlike love, friendship constantly negotiates difference, and in respecting another's unique identity concerns itself both with the creation of closeness and the preservation of boundaries between friends. This view addresses Coleridge's first two sorts of friends, "*ac*quaintance" and "*con*quaintance." As a schoolboy, Coleridge confirmed Lockridge's distinctions, celebrating in "Nil Pejus Est Caelibe Vitâ" (1787) "Hymeneal bliss" (line 5) as "That more than friendship, friendship mix'd with love" (line 6).[14] Love is associated with familial attachments to a "child or tender wife" (line 7), without which the bachelor remains "A stranger to Affection's tye" (line 10). Friendship offers no compensatory hope that the bachelor will not die "forgot" (line 17). The variation in Coleridge's statements and modern commentaries reflects Coleridge and his culture's shifting idea of friendship's range of meaning.

This shifting informs many critical comments on Coleridge's usage of the term "friend." One particular area concerns Coleridge's construction of his reader. Often emerging as a "friend," the ideal Coleridgean reader is a figure of unity, exhibiting a perfect sympathetic understanding of the author. Lucy Newlyn traces Coleridge's anxiety as a writer to the problem of confronting a heterogeneous public, whose "intellectual capacities" might not meet "his *expectations* of readers."[15] Coleridge "replaced unknown readers whose tastes he could not anticipate with intimate reading-circles, frequently made up of family and friends" (p. 208). For Newlyn, Coleridge's appeal to friendship is driven less by psychology and more by his sensitivity to the uncertain reception facing the "man of letters" at this particular moment.

E. S. Shaffer has further revealed how, in constituting his reader as a friend, Coleridge was participating in the latest theories of textual hermeneutics as elaborated by Friedrich Schleiermacher.[16] For Schleiermacher, a friend enjoys a privileged, divinatory understanding of another's mental processes, which enables him

> to explore how my friend has moved from one thought to another or try to trace out the views, judgments, and aspirations which led him to speak about a given subject in just this way and no other. (p. 205)

In this scenario, friends also become the best readers and critics of each other's texts. Whether as listener or reader, Schleiermacher's actively sympathetic "friend" participates in the inner life of the speaker/author-friend, overcoming the usual barriers to an understanding of another's subjectivity. For Shaffer, Coleridge draws upon Schleiermacher in *Biographia Literaria* (1817), which is addressed to his friends "to whom he can 'open out his heart' because he knows or hopes them to be 'of like mind with himself'" (p. 212). Coleridge's fascination in the 1790s with being and finding a sympathetic friend was structured by similar ideas, but emphasized here is the influence upon Coleridge of English moral philosophy, in particular David Hume's theory of sympathy and personal identity.

Other critics, however, have highlighted the dangers of Coleridge's appeal to his reader's sympathetic understanding. Newlyn admits that "the collapsing of divisions between separate identities is a source of anxiety" and that this could explain why "Coleridge has reservations about allowing criticism to move from its secondary status; and why he evolves defence-mechanisms that keep the authorial imagination somewhat aloof" (p. 221). In *The Friend* (1808–1809), Coleridge represents the reader as a "Water Lilly in the midst of Waters" who "lifts up its' broad Leaves, and expands its' Petals at the first pattering of the Shower, and rejoices in the Rain with a quicker Sympathy, than the parched Shrub in the sandy Desart."[17] As Deirdre Coleman notes, the sympathetic reader is placed "at the bottom of an hierarchical structure, where even the highest form of response (that of the water lily) is nevertheless a response of the sustained to the sustainer." Coleman highlights how Coleridge feels he must defend himself against "the charge of arrogance" arising from his "insistence on authorial superiority."[18] The experience of the Coleridge circle in the 1790s confirms that the sympathizing friend can find himself in a subordinate position; chapter 7 explores how Coleridge's desire to enter into Wordsworth's identity can become self-abasement. Chapter 6, meanwhile, examines the hierarchical relations between Coleridge and his disciples Lamb and Lloyd.

The tension between Coleridge's hierarchical and sympathetic relations with his reader and his friends, is one aspect of a wider Coleridgean discussion of egotism's compatibility with friendship. In a notebook entry of 1801, Coleridge declares that those "who from prudence have abstain from Egotism in their writings, are still Egotists among their friends—/ It would be unnatural effort not to be so / & Egotism in such cases is by no means offensive to a kind & discerning man."[19] As Stephen Bygrave has argued, "rather than refute the charge of a disabling presence of self, [Coleridge] defines egotism precisely as an enabling quality for his own poetry and an affective quality in reading other poets."[20] This positive view of egotism underpins Lockridge's understanding of friendship as respecting each party's individuality. Such arguments are confirmed by Coleridge's relations with Thelwall, which thrive during 1796–97 upon the epistolary clash of distinct, even oppositional selves.

Coleridge's ambivalence regarding egotism's place within friendship is illustrated in a notebook entry from December 1803:

> Egotistic Talk *with me* very often the effect of my Love of the Persons to whom I am talking / My Heart is talking of them / I cannot talk continuously of them to themselves—so I seem to be putting into their Heart the same continuousness as to me, that is in my own Heart as to them.[21]

Ostensibly, Coleridge's talking about himself is intrinsic to what Newlyn calls the "collapsing" of "subject into object" (p. 221) within friendship. Often, however, his experience of relationship confirmed his fears: not only does he charge Poole, Southey, and Wordsworth with an undesirable excess of egotistical selfhood, but he is himself accused by Lamb and Lloyd of harming their friendship through the same vice.

In his "Preface" to *Poems on Various Subjects* (1796), Coleridge admits that "there is one species of egotism which is truly disgusting; not that which leads us to communicate our feelings to others, but that which would reduce the feelings of others to an identity with our own."[22] Several critics have emphasized that the unity to which Coleridgean friendship often aspires can mask a "disgusting" kind of egotism that fails to respect the boundaries separating personal vision from another's subjectivity. Often concentrating on the Conversation poems, such commentators revise a critical tradition emphasizing Coleridge's altruism towards his autonomous textual friends. Walter Jackson Bate typifies this older view in identifying Coleridge's "habitual role" as "benevolent and understanding usher":

> It was not he who could receive the "blessing." Hence the premise of some of the conversation poems . . . : the release, the happiness or confidence, the opportunity for insight, are either given or presumed to be possible only to another. What is involved here . . . is an act of "blessing," and in the older meaning of that term: a surrender, a giving, which assumes sacrifice.[23]

Eugene Stelzig has challenged this notion of Coleridge's altruistic self-effacement, arguing that both Wordsworth and Coleridge's verse is characterized by "the rhetorical co-opting or subordination of a person addressed in a poem to fit the poet's psychic needs or to reify his self-image."[24] Both poets indulge in "a metaphoric conversion of *alter* into *ego*, of writing to or about another as a cover or pretext for writing about oneself" (p. 26).

In a more sophisticated reading, Charles Rzepka argues that Coleridge's egotistic denial of his textual friends' autonomous existence arises from his dependence on the validation of an audience, "not just [for] his self-esteem" but "his very sense of manifest existence."[25] The power the poet's friends have over the fate of his ego is countered by Coleridge's presenting the poet "as a preternatural mesmerist, dominating, and resisting domination by his subject audience" (p. 109). The fear that he will not be "recognized and included among others" provokes him "to dilate the self as mind, stand outside the 'all', incorporate the world and its inhabitants in himself, and finally presume the acquiescence of other minds in the 'reality' of what his imagination alone has created" (p. 158). While acknowledging its force, my account qualifies Rzepka's argument by showing how benevolence and disabling egotism are both aspects of Coleridge's friendship rhetoric. The mesmeric relation Rzepka traces between poet and listener-friend in "The Nightingale" (1798) does not detract from Coleridge's espousal there of a less egotistic Humean self, capable of establishing sympathetic bonds with human beings and nature alike. The pathos of "Frost at Midnight" (1798), moreover, lies in the poet's acknowledgement that his solipsistic dream of friendship is precisely that—a dream.

Stelzig and Rzepka are primarily interested in questions of rhetoric. However, Coleridge's treatment of friendship can also be seen as participating in, and structured by, various contemporary modes of relationship. Mary Shelley's 1831 edition of *Frankenstein* shows how the different modes can be kept simultaneously in play so as to establish both a union of interest, and a preservation of difference. This is clear from the first encounter between Walton and Frankenstein:

> I spoke of my desire of finding a friend—of my thirst for a more intimate sympathy with a fellow mind than had ever fallen to my lot; and expressed my conviction that a man could boast of little happiness, who did not enjoy this blessing.
> "I agree with you," replied the stranger; "we are unfashioned creatures, but half made up, if one wiser, better, dearer than ourselves—such a friend ought to be—do not lend his aid to perfectionate our weak and faulty natures.["]26

In his desire for "intimate sympathy," Walton echoes Schleiermacher's celebration of the divinatory understanding possible between friends. By contrast, Frankenstein (like Charles Atkinson) celebrates the idea of a pefectionating friend who views his friend dispassionately, in order to "aid" a faulty nature. Often assuming an advisory or pedagogic role, the perfectionating model implies a hierarchy in which friends perform the roles of tutor and student, parent and child, or husband and wife. It recognizes that the desire for sympathy can represent an egocentric desire for affirmation, not improvement. The operation of these alternative, and at times conflicting, modes of friendship become prominent features of the Coleridge-Poole bond, examined in chapter 2.

By tracing these and other competing models of friendship operating within Coleridge's personal connections, I aim to develop Lockridge's view that

[the] Romantics verge on declaring friendship a paradigm in its own right, instead of a falling away from some greater intensity. . . . But the Romantics do not bring this possibility to the level of conscious articulation. They do not admit the possible superiority or distinctiveness of friendship relative to passionate love.²⁷

Lockridge underemphasizes how the Coleridge circle are intensely engaged in bringing the idea of friendship "to the level of conscious articulation." He identifies friendship as "the unacknowledged paradigm of human relations—a selfless, non-genital eros" (p. 446). However, the extent to which friendship could or should encompass erotic feeling, or an idealized altruism, are matters of debate in the Coleridge circle. Coleridge's relationships in the 1790s often negotiate a pair of conflicting contemporary ideas of friendship that inform the way these friends conceive their relationship. The tension between sympathy and advice is part of a larger debate as to whether male friends should address one another primarily in sentimental or more rationalistic tones. Questions as to friendship's capacity to transform itself into a familial bond inform several Coleridgean relationships, while Coleridge's intimacy with Lloyd and Lamb is riven by competing spiritual and economic modes of friendship. By the end of the decade, idealist conceptions of friendship are challenged by an increasing perception of the relation as an organic phenomenon, liable to disintegration.

Focusing on the ways the Coleridge circle articulate friendship may qualify some negative assessments of the poet's relationships. Lockridge has emphasized Coleridge's "notable tendency to befriend those whom he accuses of supermoralism: George Coleridge and Southey, for example."²⁸ Despite being "attracted to principles in principle," Lockridge's Coleridge "dislikes the censoriousness and literal-mindedness of those who invoke and act upon them. The problem with Southey, he writes to Godwin, is his moral purity itself" (pp. 115–16). Although convincing in general terms, this view understates the degree to which Coleridge, at least at the time of Pantisocracy, is attracted to Godwin's highly principled model of friendship, based on the premise: "All attachments to individuals, except in proportion to their merits, are plainly unjust."²⁹ Godwinian friendship becomes the concord of reasoning minds who discover in each other principles that are worthy of affection. This idea underpins Coleridge's intimacy with Southey during 1794–95, and qualifies Lockridge's view that Coleridge's attraction to his principled friend was driven merely by a "psychological need . . . to ingratiate himself with those upon whom he is dependent" (p. 115).

Lockridge, however, usefully highlights Coleridge's insistence that "a morality must be found that embraces more aspects of the human being than his rational capacity." This view applies to Coleridge's developing notion of friendship as a moral relation, which leads him to criticize Godwin in 1802 for "a total want of affectionate Enquiry."[30] For Coleridge, a moral affection attends to more mundane aspects of a friend's life—such as his physical health. Afflicted by "sickness" and "Disquietude," he confesses to Godwin that he has had

> little inclination to write to *you*, who have not . . . associated enough of that esteem, which you entertain for the qualities, you attribute to me, with *me myself me*, to be much interested about the carcase, Coleridge.—So of Carcase Coleridge no more.[31]

Coleridge's Pantisocratic friendship with Southey highlights the question whether friendship's moral union depends upon a mutual attachment to principle or upon a solicitous attention to the man-in-himself.

Coleridge's peevish demand that Godwin concern himself with *"me myself me"* illustrates his characteristically childlike desire for the unconditional loving kindness of a good parent. Analyzing Coleridge's "effort to get understanding, approval, and forgiveness" in his letters to Southey and brother George, Beverly Fields concludes:

> It is as though he found it impossible to define himself, to validate his identity, except through some submission to the glasses of someone else's eyes, like a child, whose only understanding of himself comes to him through parental responses to his behavior. . . . The reaction he appeared to want was a loving one; the judgment would then reflect a docile identity for him, the identity of a "good" child.[32]

Although Coleridge's relations with Southey and Poole often confirm this view, in the Coleridge-Poole bond Coleridge represents himself more variously than Fields allows, at times resisting his childlike identity, at others adopting a self-confident, "manly" persona. This variety of roles appears in other Coleridgean friendships during the 1790s, in which the poet can portray himself as an adult equal (with Thelwall and Southey), a brother, and even a parental figure (with Lamb and Lloyd).

Whereas Fields speculates on the psychoanalytic motivation driving Coleridge's desire for loving parents, Kelvin Everest emphasizes that this wish for "familial community," although beginning in "emotional insecurity," becomes an "intellectual commitment."³³ This amounts to a sociopolitical vision of universal familial belonging comprised of Unitarian, Hartleian, and Neoplatonic elements: "ideally, a Christian family of all mankind, united in prayer with a parent of intimate love" (pp. 54–55). Everest highlights Coleridge's attraction to realizing in microcosm this ideal within "a retired familial community" in America or Nether Stowey, which would embody "a number of related themes and images; friendship, family, marriage, the retired, self-sufficient 'dell' . . . providing an intimately known home in nature" (p. 41). Given the imperfect progress of Coleridge's personal relationships, Everest convincingly argues that his familial ideal forms a poignant contrast with the actualities of his life:

> The concern with family and friendship in Coleridge's poetry follows an ascending and then receding movement that parallels the unfolding of his private life. Idealisation against the background of deprivation develops into the secure, creative confidence of happy marriage and friendly community . . . ; this recedes into a nostalgic yearning for a lost or unattainable domestic paradise with Asra. (p. 46)

Many Coleridgean friendships, as well as his poetry, trace this path during the 1790s from idealization to disillusionment. Whether friendship is articulated as a familial, religious, rational, politico-sentimental, or oppositional idea, in each of his relationships realizing the Idea proves to be an uncertain process, often carrying unforeseen consequences that test the strength of a particular relationship.

Undoubtedly, family for Coleridge is an ideal to which friendship aspires. This premise qualifies Everest's contention that family and friendship are interchangeable terms, in that "friendship was as important to Coleridge as family, and he often describes one in terms of the other" (p. 50). Coleridge is often well aware that friendship offers a subtly different "sense of belonging" (p. 54) to familial bonds. In this respect, Charles Lloyd enunciates in his "Dedicatory Sonnet. *Ad Amicos*" (1795), a more pertinent idea of friendship that applies as much to Coleridge as to Lloyd:

> How would the soul unsatisfied, and cold,
> Pine all unconscious of its secret powers,
> Those powers did fostering Friendship ne'er unfold,
> Nor ward with fond attempt each storm that lowers.³⁴

Through "fostering Friendship," one friend consciously becomes a surrogate parent to another, and uses his nurturing affection to bring his foster child to a full realization of his potential. The extent to which Coleridge needed Poole and latterly Wordsworth to offer him such fostering friendship, is a subject of chapters 2 and 7.

Lloyd's verse points to a more general desire in the 1790s to place friends in a parental role, a fact overlooked by Fields's psychoanalytic account of Coleridge's relationships. "Fostering Friendship" also recognizes, however, that it is a substitute for original familial love, as does Lloyd's sense that a foster-parent-friend can only "attempt" to protect him from the storm. Despite Coleridge's claim that Lloyd had been "fostered in the bosom of my confidence,"[35] by 1798 any familial relationship between them had broken down irreparably. In his relations with Southey and Poole, Coleridge becomes aware of the difficulty in transforming a friend into a parent. With the Wordsworths, Coleridge recognizes the obstacles facing a friend who wishes to become incorporated into another's family.

Other critics have highlighted the religious significance of Coleridge's fascination with family affection. Timothy Fulford highlights how, during his lecture tour of the Midlands in 1796, Coleridge was

> moved almost to tears by the "picture of Heaven" that the hymn-singing daughters of Mr Barr created, uniting the family as if "in one melodious allelujah." . . . This association of familial harmony with holy language re-created domestic voices as those of angels. It was a potent association for Coleridge since it discovered in a community of religious voices the family love which he lacked.[36]

Coleridge's lecturing and political preaching were attempts to establish "a relationship with his audience in which such religious and emotional enchantment united all in one conviction" (p. 5). Among those enchanted during this tour of 1796 was Charles Lloyd, who rapidly became as desirous as Coleridge to create through friendship a spiritual fellowship.

An analysis of the religious ideals informing these two men's relations confirms Barth's elaboration of the religious basis to Coleridge's idea of friendship. Quoting Coleridge's comment in 1796 to Poole—"The Heart, thoroughly penetrated with the flame of virtuous Friendship, is in a state of glory"—Barth notes that "glory" is an "epithet used in the Old Testament to convey the presence of God" (p. 10). For Barth, "love of God and love of man are . . . inextricably bound up with one another," and the friends' love of God manifests itself in virtuous human relations. Friends thus imitate Christ, whom Coleridge sees as "the perfect image of God's love—

and at the same time the epitome of all human love" (p. 20). Coleridge's friendships with Poole, Lloyd, and Lamb exemplify how these religious notions helped to structure the experience and expectations of Coleridge's personal relationships.

These bonds also confirm Ronald Sharp's historicist argument that the spiritual function which friendship has increasingly taken on is a relatively modern phenomenon:

> Friendship has . . . appropriated to itself functions that traditionally have been understood as religious or spiritual in nature. We turn to friends for consolation in times of trial; we often act out a kind of confession with them, in which we share our deepest dreams and fears along with, in an earlier parlance, our sins; . . . friends have always been sources of consolation, meaning, and faith, but now they seem to be primary sources.[37]

This historical shift Sharp analyzes was becoming increasingly apparent in late-eighteenth-century English culture. The fervor that characterizes the friendships of Coleridge and many of his contemporaries is often indicative of a cultural elevation of friendship from a mundane to a spiritually charged mode of interaction.

Barth is troubled, however, by the possibility that friendship might remain a nontranscendent, quotidian connection. While affirming that the poet "never lost faith in the validity of those [religious] ideals," he sadly concedes that "Coleridge's life, as we know, did not realize all these ideals of love" (p. 23). Although there is certainly an uneasy transfer of spiritual ideals into embodied practice, it is misleading primarily to consider Coleridge's friendships as attempting to realize certain "ideals"—religious or otherwise. Although certain *ideas* of friendship often become *ideals*, it is the competing nature of the ideas that often creates tension within relationships. Despite its religious trappings, the Coleridge circle also present friendship through "worldly" discourses of pragmatism and self-interest. The uncomfortable coexistence of spiritual and Hobbesian discourses of friendship in Coleridge's relations may be introduced by briefly examining his decision to call his 1809–10 periodical *The Friend*. Deirdre Coleman explains how Coleridge used this self-image to appeal to Quakers and non-Quakers alike:

> When one Quaker speaks to another, the term Friend simply denotes a fellow member of the sect; but it is also used of non-Quakers, signifying a broad Christian fellowship where friendship is envisaged as the highest relationship possible between men. . . . Thus, the double aspect of the word "Friend" suited Coleridge's purposes exactly . . . ; whilst

happy to have Quakers respond to his title's special appeal, he was equally keen to insist that his periodical was written for all Christian believers. (p. 95)

In other words, Coleridge exploits the term's religious meanings specifically to maximize his potential subscribers. As Coleman notes, in the event Quaker expectations were disappointed: "Coleridge was bidding for the attention of Friends, and yet his Prospectus did not give so much as a hint of any commitment to Quaker doctrine" (p. 96). The ambiguous way in which Coleridge celebrates friendship as an exalted bond while also using it for self-interested, commercial ends becomes particularly apparent in his short-lived tutoring of Charles Lloyd.

Two further competing modes of friendship that impinge on the Coleridge circle are dependent on Platonic and organic conceptions of relationship. Recalling his birthplace in 1792, Coleridge depicts a spot "where Friendship's fixt star beams a mellow'd Ray" (line 50).[38] This image introduces Coleridge and his culture's fascination with friendship as a Platonic Idea, combining a perfect altruism with permanence (see chapters 1 and 8). The "fixt star," however, implicitly draws attention to the difficulty in practice of achieving this ideal. The Coleridge circle are equally aware of friendship as a dynamic mode of intercourse that subtly changes its character over time. Organic metaphors become used, especially by Southey, to account not only for the developing influence of friends upon each other but also for changes in one friend's feelings for the other, and the mutability of all earthly friendships.

Organicist modes of friendship have filtered into modern critical thinking on Coleridgean relationships, as in Thomas McFarland's influential discussion of Coleridge and Wordsworth's "symbiotic" relationship.[39] "Symbiosis" implies an exchange of life between two organisms that is contributive to the vital development of each, and McFarland finds this process enacted in the poets' intellectual interchange in the late 1790s, by which they "mutually fecundate" each other. The result is "a development of attitude so dialogical and intertwined that in some instances not even the participants themselves could discern their respective contributions" (p. 57). In this way, McFarland employs organic terminology to explain a friendship's transformative effect upon the individual character. *The Coleridge Connection* (1990) has extended McFarland's idea, exploring more generally "the various ways in which Coleridge impinged upon the creative lives of five other friends, and they upon him, in a complex pattern of ventriloquism and cross-insemination" (p. 10). To this end, it emphasizes Humphry Davy's fulfilment in his poetic works of "aspects of a Coleridgean recluse project" (p. 11), and Lamb's critical influence in "steering" Coleridge "towards the style of the 'conversation poems'" (p. 10). The methodology of these case studies resembles this study's to the extent that they examine the trajectory of Coleridge's connections as two-way, interactive phenomena, and which confirm Coleridge's dictum, "Man is truly altered by the co-existence of other men; his faculties cannot be developed in himself alone, & only by himself."[40]

Despite reiterating the romantics' penchant for organic terminology, however, neither Gravil nor McFarland analyze the organic discourse that accrues to the Coleridge circle's discussions of friendship itself. In this regard, M. H. Abrams's discussion of organicism in Coleridge's theory of imagination is more instructive:

> Coleridge's central problem . . . was to use analogy with organic growth to account for the spontaneous, the inspired, and the self-evolving in the psychology of invention, yet not to commit himself so far to the elected figure as to minimize the supervention of the antithetic qualities of foresight and choice.[41]

During the 1790s, a similar debate centres on friendship. Despite a frequent desire to will it into being, friendship is widely regarded as subject to inscrutable natural processes of growth and decay. In a 1794 essay in the periodical, *The Looker-On*, William Roberts (writing as the "Rev. Simon Olive-Branch") finds himself afflicted

> by a mournful conviction of the general decay of friendship among mankind: I felt too, that the case before me was more desperate than common; for friendship can be inforced neither by precept nor example, like a common duty of morality. It is not dependent on the will; and it were better not to feign, where there is not the heart to feel: it is dependent only on our most generous feelings, and softest sympathies: it must be produced, and not engrafted; born, and not adopted; and, ere we can hope to establish it in the mind, we must there first create a second nature, with a more favourable growth of habits, and a wholesomer progeny of interests and sensibilities.[42]

Men can do little more than create favorable conditions for friendship's growth. It develops of its own accord through an organic process of "production," and not through mechanical attempts to adopt and engraft heterogeneous materials. Roberts's criticisms help draw attention to the cultural urge in the 1790s to create friendship *ex nihilo* by an effort of will, exemplified in Coleridge and Southey's scheme of Pantisocracy. By the time of their second intimacy in 1799, however, both Pantisocrats share Roberts's pessimism regarding friendship's organic life, which resists rational control.

In discussing issues of organicism, this book draws upon John Beer's discussion of the multitude of quasi-scientific discourses circulating at the end of the century, which posit the existence of instincts and attractions binding people together below the surface of individual consciousness.[43] Influenced by doctrines of animal magnetism, Coleridge "began to think in terms of two levels of consciousness" (p. 78), a secondary consciousness referring to man's sense-governed relation to the external world, and a primary consciousness "which was in direct communication with the inner life-forces of the universe" (p. 86). For Beer, the existence of "inner life-forces" enabled Coleridge to imagine a deep-seated unity amongst men. My discussion in chapter 8 draws on this work, but instead emphasizes the Coleridge circle's awareness that the operation of natural energies and an organic principle of growth and decay may work to destroy as well as to create relationship.

Attention to the Coleridge circle's correspondence brings out their preoccupation with preserving particular friendships over time. In discussing the "intimacy convention" of the late-eighteenth-century familiar epistle, H. J. Jackson observes: "The familiar letter is generally a private communication and a tribute to friendship: it should evoke qualities both of the absent friend and of the friendship itself."[44] Letters, however, highlight temporality, and their expressions of affection seek to stave off the deleterious effects that time and absence can have on a relationship. William Dowling argues that "epistolarity itself" in the eighteenth century can be viewed "as a gesture toward community in a world where some preexisting order is threatened with decline or disintegration."[45] This tradition remains "perpetually mindful of the moment of loss or absence in which the letter originates," and carries through into the Coleridge circle's discussions of friendship. Coleridge and Poole demonstrate a particularly subtle attention to the state of their relationship, with the friends frequently testing the strength of one other's feelings, and in allaying anxiety generating additional effusions of affection.

Against the threat of decay, correspondence can construct friendship—implicitly or explicitly—in contractual terms. The epistolary exchange then polices and carries out the contract of friendship upon which friends set their seals. For Lockridge, Coleridge "fears that his sins of omission—his failure to answer letters promptly, for example—may be misinterpreted as positive violations of a bond," which leads him into the "elaborate and awkward" apologizing characteristic of his correspondence.[46] Such quasi-legal epistolary bonds express a broader cultural urge during the 1790s actively to instigate friendship and guarantee its permanence. This is apparent in a letter from Poole to Henrietta Warwick:

> You reproach me, Henrietta, I understand, for a breach of promise. It is true I agreed to write to you; but you will remember that no particular time was specified. . . . If you find me irregular even in answering your letters, I must implore you to attribute it to no want of inclination, or of interest . . . , but to such causes as you yourself, were I to trouble you by reciting them, would deem sufficient. Thus, you see, at the threshold of our intercourse *I am making terms for myself.* This I deem necessary, as I foresee it will in future prevent my blotting much of that paper with apologies for apparent neglect, which ought to be more profitably employed.[47] [my italics]

Poole constructs clear contractual parameters for friendship whereby both parties must adhere to a precise set of expectations and duties. Although he does not recite the "causes" that would exculpate a friend from the offence of non-correspondence, he assumes a shared set of criteria exists, one that is too obvious to need repeating. Poole and Coleridge similarly construct their relationship as a kind of marital contract, replete with vows expressive of some of the duties and expectations of a conventional married couple.

Furthermore, it is within correspondence that a friendship's terms are agreed upon and its character established. Poole tells Henrietta that "the main design of our correspondence is mutually to instruct and amuse each other, and not, as is too often the case, to exaggerate the value of any talents we may possess" (1:132). Each mode of relationship—whether political, spiritual, or gendered—has terms to which friends contract, tacitly or explicitly, within their correspondence. These dictate how a friend articulates friendship within his letter, whether through sympathy, advice, frankness, or reserve. Sincerity is a condition of Godwin's friendships, while in Coleridge's relations with Thelwall intellectual opposition is part of the epistolary contract. Correspondence thus binds friendship into specified modes of discourse: it "contracts" the relation in a limiting sense, establishing boundaries beyond which friends should not wander.

Furthermore, correspondence is a primary medium for the kind of mutual influence examined by McFarland and *The Coleridge Connection*. An unpublished letter from Godwin to Coleridge from

1800 helps to explain the importance of concentrating on the two-way correspondence between friends rather than on Coleridge's ideas of friendship in isolation. Godwin writes:

> I have abstained from writing to you ever since my return from Ireland, thinking it not improbable from day to day that I might have the pleasure of a letter from you, & feeling it as rather an undesirable circumstance that two letters, without relation to or acquaintance with each other, should cross on the road, instead of having those reciprocal bearings & friendly comments in their structure, which constitute the best sense of the word Correspondence.[48]

For Godwin, a familiar letter should highlight the dialogical "relationship" between correspondents. He does not wish their two texts to pass each other in the night without acknowledgement. Repeatedly, ideas of friendship circulate between Coleridge and his correspondents as matter for debate, as they reflect on the issues raised by a particular relationship.

In several ways, letter strives to realize idea. Godwin's wish that a correspondent respond in detail to the letter he has read, is part of what Thomas McCarthy identifies as "the blurring of the demarcation between the roles of reader and writer" in the Romantic period.[49] He argues that correspondence helps to realize an idea of friendship as a profound merging of identities: "What makes these letters so fascinating is that while they are concrete evidence of the distance separating the two correspondents, the emotion and intimacy which they manifest demonstrate a collapsing of boundaries" (p. 92). This dissolving of boundaries results from the correspondent's sympathetic reading of his friend's text, so that he strives to participate in his friend's joys and agonies. Other conventions of the familiar letter facilitate the Romantic correspondent's project of erasing the sense of distance—emotional and physical—between friends. For H. J. Jackson, "perhaps the most conspicuous" of these conventions is "that of spontaneity" (p. viii), which Coleridge confirms in a marginal note on one of John Donne's published letters: "A noble Letter . . . in which Friends communicate to each other the accidents of their meditations, and baffle absence by writing what, if present, they would have talked."[50] In order to "baffle absence," a familiar letter for Coleridge should imitate the expressiveness and informality of conversation.

Jackson and Griggs, editors of Coleridge's letters, have both praised him for his unselfconscious spontaneity: "Letter-writing was to Coleridge a means of self-expression," Griggs avers, "and his epistolary style, now sparkling with poetic language, now overflowing with amplifications and qualifications, varies with mood and subject."[51] In his marginal note, Coleridge himself argues that correspondence enables an unselfconscious expression of affection, declaring that "nothing can be tenderer" than Donne's observation: "I write very affectionately, and I chide and accuse my self of diminishing that affection which sends them, when I ask my self why" (2:232). As we shall see, however, Coleridgean affection does not just appear. It must be seen to manifest itself through a clearly recognizable system of signs. *The Complete Letter-Writer* (1792) advises that a familiar letter should "wear an honest, chearful countenance, like one who truly esteems, and is glad to see his friend; and not like a fop, admiring his own dress, and seemingly pleased with nothing but himself."[52] As such instructions show, representing a "chearful countenance" in correspondence may be a performative exercise, and the familiar letter's denial of artifice its greatest art.

The Coleridge circle repeatedly direct their correspondents to interpret their text as one of friendship. Grosvenor Bedford distinguishes between kinds of epistolary style in order to signify his writing's intimacy: "I do not correct what I write to you for I have no objection to your knowing my sentiments in their crude & original state. in my own opinion the only means of creating confidence between each other."[53] The friend is entitled to views of an authentic self that are not given out lightly, even in correspondence. In having "no objection" to Southey's gazing at his unformed thoughts, Bedford stresses that he could have written in a different style and presented himself in a more auspicious light. Bedford, however, invites Southey to read his text as a sign of friendship, one that renders irrelevant the unpolished nature of the material. For Bedford and Coleridge, the successful expression of friendship depends on being able to write and recognize an intimate style.

Both Coleridge and his friends, however, draw attention to the limitations of recreating friendly intercourse through correspondence. Coleridge laments to Godwin that "when I see how little I have *written* of what I could have *talked*, I feel with you that a Letter is but 'a mockery' to a full & ardent mind."[54] This sentiment is developed in a fascinating exchange between Southey and Bedford in 1801. Excusing himself for a lapse in his correspondence, Southey declares:

> If by any magic of the ear you could hear how often your name passes my lips—or could you see how often I see your figure in my walks—the

recollections—& the wishes—, but what are these?—an hundred times should I have begun a letter if these had been enough to fill it—if I could have sent you the exquisite laugh when I again saw St Augustine & his load—or the smile when I read Leanders death in the newspaper—but these are unwriteable things—the gossip & the playfulness & the boyness & the happiness.[55]

In reply, Bedford reflects that even a convincing epistolary style may in fact *distort* that intuitive communication that friends enjoy:

However free & unreserved correspondence by letter may be it never can convey that which is to be gained only by conversation, that truest means of knowledge of a man's heart. You have surely found how delightful the society of a friend may have been with whom perhaps no word may have been exchanged during a long space of time in which either thought may have been absent or intense—and yet there has been a communication of mind a reciprocity of sentiment which words could not have made more complete—Letters can not give this nor between the paragraphs of writing can you imagine what space what train of thoughts may have occurred which the mind of a present friend almost intuitively discovers.[56]

For Bedford, the familiar letter expresses and obscures friendship. It allows him to articulate his idea that friends enjoy an extralinguistic, Schleiermachian kind of sympathetic communication. However, he also feels that the letter presents artifice rather than authenticity, hiding the "real" thoughts in the space "between the paragraphs." At different points during the 1790s, Coleridge is also ambivalent whether correspondence aids or hampers him in expressing his affection for a particular individual.

Furthermore, ideas do not float free within correspondence from the specific rhetorical context in which they are produced. As Jackson notes, "the occasion of the letter needs to be kept in mind, as a context that often qualifies what is actually said" (p. x). This insight may be illustrated in a group of letters from Coleridge to Poole in December 1796, in which the former persuades his suddenly hesitant friend to let him settle at Stowey. On Monday evening, Coleridge vents his "Bitterness of Soul," dramatizing for his friend his immediate anguish:

Mrs Coleridge has observed the workings of my face, while I have been writing; and is intreating to know what is the matter—I dread to shew her your Letter—I dread it. . . . My God! what if she should dare to think, that my most beloved Friend is grown cold towards me![57]

Continuing next morning, Coleridge justifies such dramatization by appealing to the importance in epistolary friendship of a spontaneous sharing of one's private self:

> As the sentiments over Leaf came from my Heart, I will not suppress them.—I would keep a Letter by me, which I wrote to a mere acquaintance, lest any thing unwise should be found in it—but my friend ought to know not only what my Sentiments are, but what all my feelings were. (1:273)

Such self-expression is not, however, merely an unselfconscious effusion of feeling but a deliberate attempt to increase the pressure on Poole.

Coleridge's letters to Poole at this pivotal moment further demonstrate that his varying epistolary articulations of friendship frequently have a strategic purpose. Contemplating his move to Stowey, Coleridge desires in November "to see you daily, to tell you all my thoughts in their first birth, and to hear your's, to be mingling identities with you, as it were."[58] For McCarthy, "Coleridge's notion of 'mingling identities' aptly captures both the dangers and the opportunities generated by sympathetic reading [. . . in] that as both correspondents assume the dual role of reader and writer, their feelings and even identities overlap" (p. 103). Perceiving Poole's continued hesitation, however, Coleridge tries a different tack:

> I have never considered my settlement at Stowey in any other Relation than it's advantages to myself. . . . My objects (assuredly, wise ones) were to learn agriculture (& where should I get instruction except at Stowey) and to be where [I] can communicate in a literary way?[59]

In this scenario, Coleridge greatly reduces his emotional demands upon Poole, and in his letter written the following day he desires only:

> Instruction, daily advice, Society—every thing necessary to my feelings & the realization of my innocent Independance.—You know, it would be impossible for me to learn *every* thing myself—to pass across my Garden once or twice a day, for five minutes, & set me right, & cheer me with the sight [of] a friend's face, would be more to me than hundreds. (1:274)

Delimiting contact to "five minutes" a day, and declaring that "Independance" is his ultimate goal, Coleridge presents friendship as a more distant relation, grounded in advice-giving between two affectionate but unmingled individuals. Underlying his conflicting ideas of friendship, however, is a pressing need to find a mode of intercourse acceptable to Poole. In other Coleridgean correspondences, attention to a particular context reveals that articulations of friendship are often similarly rhetorical strategies for gauging the emotional load, increasing the pressure, or voicing an ultimatum.

In *Poems* (1796), Coleridge prefaces his collection of verse epistles with an anonymous quatrain linking correspondence, friendship, and poetry:

> Good verse *most* good, and bad verse then seems better
> Receiv'd from absent friend by way of Letter.
> For what so sweet can labor'd lays impart
> As one rude rhyme warm from a friendly heart?[60]

Ideally, a friendly letter will include poetry, which in turn becomes emblematic of the intimacy embodied in the correspondence. For the Coleridge circle, there are complex and profound connections between poetry and friendship. William Christie argues that friendliness is a key characteristic of the poetic style Coleridge developed during the 1790s. "Corrupt poetic diction or expression" represented for himself and Wordsworth

> an act of profound insincerity. It set up an opaque medium between the poet and the reader on the one hand, and Nature and God on the other. When in "To a Friend" Coleridge rejects the "elaborate and swelling" rhetoric of *Religious Musings*, therefore, he is also rejecting a way of relating to Man, to Nature, and to God. The conversational style and tone were essential to these new values of intimacy and "home-born Feeling" and are as symbolic of the altered consciousness as the new imagery and naturalistic detail.[61]

Informing such stylistic developments was Coleridge's long-held belief that poetry could be for him a friend. Bate explains Coleridge's youthful enthusiasm for Bowles's poetry thus: "It was *familiar*. It had in it the kind of thing one could associate with family or with friends. What was wrong with occasionally prizing literature when it was simply a 'friend'—a friend that could comfort while it informed and uplifted?" (pp. 9–10). The implications of Bate's insight are brought out by Coleridge's prefatory remarks to his privately published pamphlet, *Sonnets from various Authors* (1796), which he bound up with Bowles's sonnets.[62] There Coleridge celebrates the sonnet as a poetic form conducive to the friendly interpenetration of reader and writer:

> Easily remembered from their briefness, and interesting alike to the eye and the affections, these are the poems which we can "lay up in our hearts, and our soul," and repeat them "when we walk by the way, and when we lie down and when we rise up." . . . Hence they domesticate with the heart, and become, as it were, a part of our identity. (p. [1])

By encouraging such egotistic expression of feeling, sonnets provide a medium for collapsing separate identities within a unity of feeling, a state Coleridge associates with those domestic bonds between family and friends. The collection of sonnets itself strives to create community. For "Sonnet I," Coleridge chooses Bowles's "To a Friend" (p. 3), and on each page he lays out a single pair of sonnets, often by different authors (including Lloyd, Lamb, Bowles, Southey, Thomas Warton, and Charlotte Smith) but on a similar theme. In thus bringing separate poems into dialogical relation, Coleridge invites his reader to discover unifying points of sympathy between individual poets, whom he has suggestively grouped together as friends.

Such editorial procedure offers an example of Coleridge's attempts to employ poetry as a medium for generating and reflecting upon friendship. A Coleridgean friendship often results in poetic collaboration or the inclusion of poems in a friend's volume, and in doing so he invites a reader to consider issues of friendship. For instance, in placing Lloyd's "Lines Addressed to S. T. Coleridge" (1796) in *Poems* (1797) after his own poem, "To C. Lloyd, on his Proposing to Domesticate with the Author" (1796), Coleridge presents the former as a response to the latter. In doing so, he highlights poetry's privileged role not only in the private communication of feeling between friends but also in meditating upon general philosophical notions of friendship—in this case its spiritual aspect. For these reasons, it is important to examine the original published forms of Coleridge's poetry.

Coleridge's poetry is often specific to particular relationships and moments within them. George Mclean Harper was the first critic to draw attention to this aspect of the Conversation poems, when he declared that these "Poems of Friendship"

> cannot be even vaguely understood unless the reader knows what persons Coleridge has in mind. They are, for the most part, poems in which reference is made with fine particularity to certain places. They were composed as the expression of feelings which were occasioned by

quite definite events. . . . They require and reward considerable knowledge of his life and especially the life of his heart.[63]

This study attempts to scrutinize in more detail those issues of friendship that Coleridge and his friends debate in the Conversation poems. Although Coleridge's letters do not explicate the poetry, the poems incorporate many of the same concerns of his correspondence, offering spaces in which concepts of relationship are worked out or worried over. Coleridge expressed dissatisfaction with "To the Reverend George Coleridge" (1797) in that "the metaphor on the diverse sorts of friendship is *hunted down.*"[64] My concern is to hunt down these and other less explicit friendship metaphors in Coleridge's early poetry.

Single poems can touch on a number of issues and a variety of Coleridge's personal relationships. In this respect, "The Nightingale, A Conversational Poem; Written in 1798" is an important text. Stuart Curran has drawn attention to the way the poem self-reflexively analyses the idea of converse:

> The nightingales converse. The solitary nightingale whose song prompts Coleridge's poetic musings is, in fact, conversing with him. . . . Song draws forth song in conversation. The songs of nature prompt human art: conversation creates community, linking Coleridge with an unknown lady, linking her in turn with his inarticulate son, drawing both into a circle enlarged by the sympathetic receptivity of the Wordsworths.[65]

This study develops Curran's insights, contextualizing "The Nightingale" in chapter 1 with some contemporary poetry of friendship, in chapter 8 with theories of magnetic attraction, and in chapter 7 with the Coleridge-Wordsworth bond. Coleridge presents in the poem an idealized view of the two men's converse as characterized by their sympathetic responsiveness. However, he also represents the nightingales as articulating their affection through a mock-aggressive "skirmish" (line 59), an image that indirectly comments upon his oppositional converse with John Thelwall (see chapter 5).

Poetry has a further important role in the gendered dimension of Coleridge's male friendships. According to Richard Holmes, "the constant exchange of each other's poetry was central" to Coleridge's Romantic ideal of friendship as "an intimate masculine circle sharing thoughts and feelings and confidences which stretch across or beyond domestic boundaries" (pp. 125–26). A recurrent concern of this book is to question how far friendship affirms or undermines the "masculinity" of its participants. Most critics differ from Holmes in emphasizing Coleridge's attraction to men who are more "manly" than himself. "His relationship to Wordsworth," McFarland declares "is as a feminine principle to its masculine counterpart," culminating in "Coleridge's need to have his own identity flow into that of his friend" (p. 65). Friendship feminizes Coleridge, highlighting his tendency passively to subordinate himself to stronger male presences. He confesses: "The approbation & Sympathy of good & intelligent men is my Sea-breeze, without which I should languish from Morn to evening; a very Trade-wind to me, in which my Bark drives on regularly & lightly."[66]

From a historicist perspective, Coleridge's feminine roles, although psychologically motivated, are facilitated by a general cultural gendering of friendship as a feminine relationship, especially in its epistolary mode. Julie Ellison observes that "conversation and its historical correlative, the letter, permeated the romantic writings by men for which women provided models, audiences, and metaphors."[67] Late-eighteenth-century men idealized female subjectivity "as more authentic because it expresses itself in speech or its written equivalent, the epistle" (pp. 31–32). Coleridge understands that epistolary friendship encourages self-revelation, often through the confession of immediate feeling. He is aware, though, that by encouraging a "feminine" discourse of sensibility, friendship may destabilize the "manly" identity of a male friend.

However, neither Coleridge nor his contemporaries consistently conceive of friendship as a feminine mode. For Janet Todd, Coleridge participates in a fin de siècle attack on sensibility, doing so "not from a belief in a superior rational system but in part from a deeply gendered apprehension of human psychology."[68] Coleridge's criticism in *The Watchman* that "sensibility is not Benevolence" expresses his denigration of the feminine, and Todd notes that Coleridge uses "the common abusive gender terms for sensibility, terming it effeminacy and emasculation" (p. 140). Coleridge's scorn for a feminine mode of sentimental friendship lurks within his response to Southey's unhappiness at the "Nehemiah Higginbottom" sonnet, "To Simplicity" (1797). In declaring he had "no conception" how Southey "could apply to yourself a Sonnet written to ridicule infantine simplicity, vulgar colloquialisms, and lady-like Friendships,"[69] Coleridge invokes a manly nonsentimental mode of intimacy, one that affirms male friends' adult identities.

Again, Coleridge reflects a broader cultural consciousness. In his 1794 article on "Female Friendship" in *The Looker-On*, Roberts stresses that friendship is a masculine relationship. This arises from his report on "the present state of female friendship, in Great

Britain," at "the Society of Ladies" (4:294). Female intimacies reveal themselves as superficial, formed quickly and ruptured by trivialities. "Rev. Simon Olivebranch" tells the meeting why female friendship so often fails:

> Friendship and love require, each of them, a peculiar built of mind; structures agreeing perhaps in the nature of their materials, but differing altogether in their style and manner: . . . the one is the masculine strength of the Tuscan column; while the elegant loftiness and profuse decoration of the Corinthian pillar best expresses the delicacy, richness, and elevation, which characterise the passion of love. (4:310)

As a Tuscan rather than Corinthian pillar, friendship eschews the "profuse" gestures of feminine sensibility. Reverend Simon defines friendship as masculine, and open only to men:

> It seems as if Nature had severally committed to the male and the female, the maintenance of love and friendship in the world, as their respective trusts [. . . and] it may surely with safety be asserted, that modern love has not lost more of its original purity in the hands of the females, than modern friendship under the care of the men. (4:311)

In the 1790s, then, male friendship can represent either a feminine or masculine discourse. Coleridge uses these differing cultural modes to adopt manly and feminine personas, varying his gender role with different friends and at different times within particular relationships. However, the degree to which spiritual and sexual expressions of affection may fit these categories is unclear. Traditionally, male friendship has been identified as a spiritual brotherhood. According to Jeffrey Richards, David's love for Jonathan in the Second Book of Samuel provides the archetype for a "manly love" surpassing that of women:

> It is higher than and different from, rather than a substitute for, the love of women. The difference lies essentially in the fact that the love of women is sexual and therefore inferior; the love of a man for a man is spiritual, transcendent and free from base desire.[70]

Coleridgean friendship exemplifies and qualifies Richards's view. His pursuit of Sara Hutchinson at times confirmed to him that a higher love was not possible with a woman: in 1801 he has a vision of a man endeavoring to create a "virtuous & tender & brotherly friendship with an amiable Woman—the obstacles—the jealousies—the impossibility of it."[71] By contrast, he constructs his relations with Poole as a spiritual alternative to Coleridge's marital bond.

Nevertheless, Coleridge does not deny physicality a role within male friendship. This complicates C. S. Lewis's view that the "kingliness of Friendship" is its transcendence of, "not only our physical bodies but that whole embodiment which consists of our family, job, past and connections. . . . Eros will have naked bodies; Friendship naked personalities."[72] Coleridge's male friendships, however, are frequently concerned with the friends' embodied selves. Coleridge associates Poole's friendship with his attention to the poet's physical well-being, whether this entails raising a subscription, interesting himself in Coleridge's precarious health, or providing him with a place to live. For Coleridge and his culture, male friendship is often mediated through such physical activities as drinking and laboring, or through embraces and handshakes. Interpreting physical signs of affection, however, can be problematic. In the autumn of 1795, Southey accuses Coleridge of hypocrisy in giving him his "usual Shake of the Hand" on the street while carrying out his "plans in secrecy."[73] In defence, Coleridge suggests that Southey has misread his physical gesture:

> You gave me your hand—and dreadful must have been my feelings, if I had refused to take it. Indeed, so long had I known you, so highly venerated, so dearly loved you, that my Hand would have taken your's *mechanically*.—But is shaking the Hand a mark of Friendship?—Heaven forbid! I should then be a Hypocrite many days in the week—It is assuredly the *pledge of Acquaintance, and nothing more*. (1:167)

Coleridge exploits the ambiguities inherent in conventional physical expressions of affection, which enable him to deny that his "usual" vigorous handshake is an automatic sign of friendship. Chapter 5 examines the radical meanings encoded in images of men embracing in the 1790s, and argues that they inform the discourse of physicality operating in the Coleridge-Thelwall correspondence.

The homoeroticism of Coleridge's friendships has been widely noted, and this study focuses on the eroticized language informing his quasi-marital bond with Poole.[74] However, Ronald Sharp's caution that there are "reasons to be wary of placing too much importance on the issue of homosexuality in friendship" is applicable to Coleridge's relationships. This should lead us to qualify overstated views regarding Coleridge's latent homosexuality. Discussing "The Rime of the Ancyent Marinere" (1797–1798), Wayne Koestenbaum highlights the sexual meaning latent in the term "will," reading the Mariner's magnetic hold over his listener (in which "The Marinere hath his will" [line 20]) as "the act of sexual possession" and his narration as "a kind of rape."[75] According to Koestenbaum, the Mariner's "sadistic and inseminating" (p. 79) power symbolizes Coleridge's desire for domination over his collaborator, William Wordsworth. Koestenbaum's "outing" of Coleridge's homosexuality assumes a psychological pattern of repression, which he finds inherent in male poetic collaborations. But Romantic male friendship does not deny physicality only to find it returning as latent homoeroticism. It celebrates passionate feeling in order to create an ambience of physical intimacy, and to kindle a "manly," nonsexual relation. Metaphors of embowerment, in particular, offer Coleridge an innocent space in which erotic feelings can be articulated without fear of sin.

Friendship's gendered aspect is part of the term's private and personal meanings. However, a range of political discourses of friendship also affect Coleridge's private relationships. Within the highly charged political landscape of the 1790s the term "friend" loses its ideological innocence as it is appropriated by revolutionary and counter-revolutionary ideologies alike. Coleridge's relationships with Thelwall and Southey enable us to see how the political stage is illuminated by private language, and how the idea of friendship is itself changed by becoming public property. Shearer West has drawn attention to the development in the later eighteenth century of friendship's role in a public discourse of patriotism:

> Friendship suddenly emerged as a subject worthy of debate from the 1760s. Friendship came to be seen as an essential aspect of British liberty. Conversation was interpreted as an unequivocal symptom of "social freedom," and betrayal of friendship was equated with betrayal of country.[76]

West argues that in the late 1770s this concern with "natural social ties" (p. 97) informed the "republican solidarity" (p. 96) of drinking clubs such as the Society of Dilettanti. By the 1790s, however, equating friendship with British liberty had become appropriated by Anti-Jacobins to justify a continuation of the war as well as the preservation of Britain's unwritten constitution.

Nevertheless, the decade witnessed the rise of radical friendships, as evidenced by the rapid growth of Friendly and Corresponding societies. As Mary Favret points out, "the 'Friends of Liberty' became an umbrella term for the more than one hundred radical societies established in England between 1790 and 1797,"[77] and she examines the "new determination of friendship and familiarity" (p. 25) that developed within these groups. Often meeting in taverns, friendship between members was actively promoted: oaths were sworn of " 'inviolable friendship' and 'friendly dispositions, etc' to the French," and letters penned "between various 'friends of the people'," which "forged a sense of identity and political purpose throughout the British Isles" (p. 29). "Friendship," she concludes,

> denoted not just sympathy and understanding, but a political solidarity based on egalitarian principles and on correspondence itself. . . . "Friendly" correspondence drifted very close to notions of "universal fraternity." More significantly, it threatened to replace—not just reform—representative government in England. (pp. 28–29)

In tracing the impact of these public discourses upon Coleridge's writings, my methodology follows the historicist arguments recently developed by Paul Magnuson. He contends that "the meaning of a poem depends on the themes and figures that exist in the public discourse before the poem is written, on the allusive structure of its public language" as well as the "paratextual frame" created by poems with whom it is published.[78] I follow Magnuson in comparing "Coleridge's poems with other written material not often considered in traditional explication"—notably *The Anti-Jacobin; or, Weekly Examiner* (1797–1798)—"which implies that a Romantic lyric participates in the political rhetoric of the day" (p. 68). In terms of Coleridge's politics in the latter 1790s, his utilizing of both radical and conservative discourses of friendship confirms both Magnuson and Karl Kroeber's conclusions that in major political statements, in particular "Fears in Solitude" (1798), Coleridge "attempts through imaginative deployment of ordinary language to reconcile claims of nationalism with those of international amity, local loyalty with the brotherhood of man."[79]

The appropriation of friendship by radicals and conservatives alike is part of the greater politicization of sensibility in the period. A. R. Humphreys has described the radicalized sentimental character, known to the 1790s as the "Friend of Humanity," as "humane, charitable, opening at a hint the sacred source of sympathetic tears, . . . 'by nature an admirer of happy human faces',"[80] and who celebrates cross-rank and cross-cultural friendships. In charting Coleridge's progression from radical to more conservative modes of sensibility, I probe the extent to which he himself embodies during these years this radical persona. This should allow us to qualify more dismissive views of Coleridge's politico-sentimental discourse of affection as being merely nebulous. David Aers, Jonathan Cook, and David Punter analyse Coleridge's millenarian vision of universal Christian brotherhood in "Religious Musings" (1794–1797):

> [Coleridge] rejects contemporary individualism, yet fails to consider how much his own form of piety may be a reflection of what he rejects. The coveted universal community he now invokes is "one wondrous whole" which "fraternises man" and in it he finds, "self, that no alien knows." . . . But this transcendence of individualism and "alienation" ironically involves an utterly desocialized community, a metaphysical abstraction in which all conceivable human agencies, empirical differentiations and historical particulars are obliterated.[81]

These criticisms underemphasize Coleridge's awareness of the difficulty in transforming a sentimental friendship for humanity into social practice, and it is this problematic passage from idea to action that is examined here. Not only did Coleridge's politico-sentimental poetry come to be seen by *The Anti-Jacobin* as sufficiently significant to be satirized, but the radical idea of Pantisocracy sought to ground Coleridge's sentimental community within a more elaborated social theory than that presented in "Religious Musings."

Pantisocratic theory engages with a long philosophical tradition linking private friendship to the abolition of property. For Montaigne, there should ideally be between two friends a "complete fusion of the wills," with "everything being in effect common between them—will, thoughts, opinions, goods, wives, children, honour, and life."[82] In glossing this passage, Allan Bloom illuminates some of the assumptions underlying Pantisocratic aspheterism:

> There is simply an expansion of individual consciousness to a common consciousness of the pair. Therefore, there is a perfect communism of property, overcoming the deepest source of separation among men. This means that friendship implicitly denies the sacredness of private property and is supportive of the old dream of communism. . . . The longing for communism . . . is the precondition of a real community of persons.[83]

The Pantisocratic Coleridge concurs: not only does he assume that the Pantisocrat-friends will desire to live communally but also that friendship characterizes a just society that realizes "a perfect communism of property."

To an extent, this study confirms Everest's view that Coleridge's ideal of rustic retirement in the 1790s is politically radical, through its espousal of a select group perfecting their moral being within a communal life. Discussing Pantisocracy, Everest challenges Geoffrey Carnall's view that the scheme represented a retreat from political engagement:

> It is difficult to see how Pantisocracy, a theory of social organisation, could be regarded as "anti-political." It certainly assimilates Coleridge's stress on the values of friendship and familial community, but this argues for the politicality that developed in these values, rather than for Coleridge's resort to these values as an alternative, transcending social and political issues, to involvement in the life of his times. (p. 58)

Everest convincingly points out that this politicality of "friendship and familial community" "involved the differentiation between kinds of domesticity," in which the family, provided it developed "outside an existing social structure" (p. 69), could become an ideal social model for the generation of a radicalized benevolence. This necessitated, however, "a rejection of conventional domesticity," whose conservative self-interest represents "an effective agent of social pressure" militating against a radical sensibility. Everest underplays, however, the closeness of the Pantisocratic idea to radical and conservative modes of domesticity. The power Coleridge and Southey both ascribe to domestic friendship helps lead to their inability to leave their English friends and family.

Friendship in particular could be conceived as an alternative to political engagement. The "friend" differs from closely related terms, such as "brother" and "patriot." As Carl Woodring states, a "patriot" is for Coleridge "a man who acts with concern for the state," and he notes that in *The Watchman* (1796), Coleridge "uses the word *patriot* favourably, once as synonymous with 'the Friends of Freedom.'"[84] Unlike "patriotism," however, the discourse of friendship could be used to disown active engagement in matters of state. This potential is revealed even within Coleridge's unequivocally radical prose. In *The Plot Discovered* (1795), he denounces the Gagging Acts, complaining that:

> If even in a friendly letter or in social conversation any should assert a Republic to be the most perfect form of government, and endeavour by all argument to prove it so, he is guilty of High Treason: . . . It will be in vain to allege, that such opinions were not wished to be realized, except as the result of progressive reformation and ameliorated manners; . . . still he would be guilty of high Treason.[85]

The adjective "friendly" emphasizes the innocuousness of a familiar letter or "social conversation." Such converse is not "patriotic" for it does not imply any "realized" political action. On the contrary, it constitutes a quietist, nondisruptive domain of private intercourse.

Nevertheless, there remains during the 1790s deep uncertainty regarding the possible politicality of friendship, which in Coleridge's case becomes focused in the group of friends that gathered around him at Nether Stowey. The presence during 1797 of Wordsworth and Thelwall confirms C. S. Lewis's contention that friendship is easily perceived as subversive: "It withdraws men from collective 'togetherness' as surely as solitude itself could do; and more dangerously, for it withdraws them by two's and three's" (p. 72). In the "friendly letters" Coleridge and Thelwall exchange during 1796–1797, Coleridge struggles to reconcile his politicized alliance with the radical leader, with his growing wish to establish himself within a loving community at Stowey, integrate himself into English society, and retire from radical politics.

This study follows the trajectory of Coleridge's individual friendships in the 1790s. In each case I trace the dynamics of the relationship as articulated in letters and poems, which reveal diverse symbols and concepts of friendship. My account is two-sided, focusing on the articulations of friendship voiced by Coleridge's correspondents as much as his own. Coleridge's ideas of friendship are not developed in isolation but are part of a dialogue with his personal friends on the subject of relationship. Through this contrastive approach, Coleridge's ideas should gain greater definition as they become situated within wider cultural discussions on friendship. One difficulty in finding an appropriate form for this study is the need to highlight issues common to Coleridge's friendships, while remaining faithful to the complex trajectory of each individual relationship. Although certain problems recur with different figures, the most suitable format must keep intact a sense of a friendship's unique character and the specific issues it foregrounds. As Coleridge himself remarked in 1818, "a man may have and love *many* Friends / and but yet if indeed Friends, he lives with each a several and individual Life."[86]

Many issues raised in the preceding analysis were being discussed in 1792 in the *Encyclopædia Britannica*'s ten-page, double-column entry on "Friendship."[87] Ostensibly an exercise in definition, the article demonstrates that interest in friendship during the late eighteenth century was more than a local or private concern.

The *Britannica*'s various subsections illustrate the extent of this interest: "Definition of friendship" (7:467), "circumstances favourable to the rise and continuance of friendship" (7:468), "sex" (7:469), "relations of consanguinity," "laws of friendship" (7:470), "general view of the advantages of friendship," "mistakes in forming friendships, and consequent inconstancy" (7:473), "friendship countenanced by our Saviour's example" (7:475). An underlying theme is the degree of union or separation appropriate to friendship. These sections provide "laws for supporting the attachment and regulating the intercourse of friendship" (7:470) as an answer to the writer's related questions, "what degree of mutual confidence ought to take place between friends?" and "how far is an *union of interests* to take place between friends?" (7:472).

The *Britannica* legislates that "friendship must diminish neither our benevolence nor prudence: it must not seduce us from an honest attention to our private interests, nor contract our social affections" (7:470). It denies that friends can become as intimate as family members, and suggests they preserve their own individual property (7:472). In political terms, the encyclopedist is similarly conservative, arguing that "we cannot become citizens of the world . . . without becoming outcasts from every particular society" (7:475). But the *Britannica*'s determination to restrict the union of interest between individuals, families and nations testifies to the attempts of others at this time to expand the possibilities of friendship. The next chapter examines how, during the period of Coleridge's childhood and adolescence, friendship became associated with an enthusiastic sensibility that threatened to disrupt conventional allegiances to family, state, and church, and how conservative writers strove to limit friendship's new aspirations.

1

Transcendence and Its Limits: Friendship in the 1780s

"Repulsed alike in friendship as in love," the dejected poet Abraham Skelton suddenly finds himself in the midst of a vision, wandering "o'er a dreary plain, / Where tempests raged" and "ceaseless poured the rain:"[1]

> Here as I strayed, upon my raptured sight
> Burst a bright Form in all the blaze of light,
> No pomp she shewed, the emblem of the vain,
> Plain she appeared, but elegantly plain;
> A placid smile of sweet engaging grace
> Softened the awful glories of her face.
>
> (p. 2)

Appearing miraculously from an immaterial dimension, this Platonic "Form" is the "fair Goddess" (p. 11), "sunlike Friendship" (p. 27). Combining sublimity with beauty, her "awful glories" demand reverence, while her "sweet engaging grace" radiates sympathy. The Goddess's "elegantly plain" dress reveals the virtuous simplicity of a character devoid of selfishness. Enraptured, the poet follows this visionary Form towards the "peaceful dome" (p. 6) in which she presides.

On their journey, the poet emphasizes the gulf between the affection possible in the embodied and Platonic worlds. This becomes apparent as the Goddess passes over a vale populated by a "plumy throng" of birds who "To Love and Friendship swelled the willing song":

> But hark! how floating on the whispering gale
> Airs more exalted charm the listening vale;
> No more the feathered songsters strain their throats,
> But in soft silence drink th'extatic notes.
>
> (p. 7)

1: TRANSCENDENCE AND ITS LIMITS: FRIENDSHIP IN THE 1780S

The birds find themselves in the presence of a higher power, which has produced a song of friendship in excess of the birds' natural affections. These "exalted" sounds carried on the "whispering gale" do not embody the Goddess herself: transcribed by Skelton's "Muse" (p. 7), the song itself entreats the Goddess to "let us feel thy influence move, / Expanding o'er the mind," so "Connecting all Mankind" in "one golden chain of love" (p. 8). Articulating the desire for universal love indicates an indirect communication with the divine Idea, but as soon as the song ceases,

> the grove resounds,
> Each warbler strives to reach the rapturous sounds,
> In vain their music thrilled along the grove,
> In vain to reach the rapturous sounds they strove;
> Though Nature's self should pour the strains along.
> (p. 10)

The birds' transient communication with the transcendent messages of love draws attention to the gap between the embodied natural world and the higher Idea.

The Goddess finally leads the poet to her temple of "unadorned Doric columns" (p. 10) in which he gazes on a pantheon of classical and biblical exemplars of friendship. Although the vision fades, Skelton retains an idea of virtuous affection to which his embodied existence can now aspire, specifically through his friendship with "dear C—":

> Come then, dear C—, my resolution aid,
> Ere Folly's fickle band my breast invade;
> Lo! radiant Virtue here has deigned to smile,
> Teach me for her to meliorate the soil,
> Teach me to woo aright the Heavenly guest,
> And clasp her glowing beauties to my breast.
> (p. 27)

The aim of earthly friendship is to bring into being the transcendent Idea revealed briefly in the poet's vision, chiefly through the mutual moral influence of the two participants. Emphatically, though, Skelton's allegiance is to "Friendship" rather than "C—," and he represents his devotion in religious terms:

> To thee, to thee, I dedicate my youth,
> With every vow of unrepenting truth,
> And oh! benignant Goddess, kindly shed

> Each virtuous blessing on thy Votary's head.
> I spoke; the Goddess smiled upon my prayer,
> And the gay Vision melted into air,
> Yet the sweet Form still lives within my breast,
> And smoothes the wintry frowns of Care to rest,
> Still shall she live my bosom's gentle Queen,
> Till Death's chill curtain drop, and close this earthly scene.
>
> (p. 28)

The poet's "vow" indicates his initiation into a quasi-religious order that turns away from an impure world to embrace friendship's virtuous life. Despite the Goddess herself acknowledging that "Religion" (p. 6) is the ultimate moral authority, the speaker's devotion reveals that the "sweet Form" of "Friendship" has become for him virtue's primary source.

One poem that might be linked to Skelton's is Coleridge's "The Nightingale; A Conversational Poem, Written in April, 1798."[2] Coleridge's representation of the "gentle Maid" and the grove of nightingales is strikingly reminiscent of *The Temple of Friendship*. Coleridge describes how the girl,

> at latest eve,
> (Even like a Lady vow'd and dedicate
> To something more than nature in the grove)
> Glides thro' the pathways; she knows all their notes,
> That gentle Maid!
>
> (lines 71–75)

Like the "Votary" of Skelton's poem, Coleridge's "Maid" worships a supernatural presence. What links her devotion to friendship is her understanding of the birds' notes. Like Skelton's birds, Coleridge's nightingales possess "sweet voices, always full of love / And joyance!" (lines 42–43). This song (understood by the maid) is reminiscent of the divine music that passes over Skelton's birds. "With one sensation,"

> those wakeful Birds
> Have all burst forth in choral minstrelsy,
> As if one quick and sudden Gale had swept
> An hundred airy harps! And she hath watch'd
> Many a Nightingale perch giddily
> On blosmy twig still swinging from the breeze,
> And to that motion tune his wanton song,
> Like tipsy Joy that reels with tossing head.
>
> (lines 78–86)

In both poems, birds become possessed by the musical "air:" as Skelton's gale reveals the Platonic melody to his "plumy throng," so Coleridge compares the nightingales' intoxicated song to a "Gale" playing upon "airy harps." Reading "The Nightingale" against *The Temple of Friendship* suggests that Coleridge's harps express the divine music of friendship. Coleridge's poem works harder, though, to mediate the Neoplatonic and embodied worlds. Coleridge's setting for the birdsong is not a visionary dream but the everyday situation of friends taking an evening walk. For Skelton, the birds remain distinct from the exalted sounds. Coleridge's "airy harps," however, refer literally to the birds and metaphorically to the immaterial realm in which the music is created. For Coleridge, the nightingales' song itself expresses the divine spirit of love animating the universe, carried on the breeze, and understood by the "gentle Maid."

These connections between "The Nightingale" and *The Temple of Friendship* help to situate Coleridge within a broader cultural discussion of friendship in the 1780s and 1790s. In particular, this period of Coleridge's youth and early adulthood witnesses a vigorous debate regarding "transcendent" and "empiricist" articulations of relationship, an argument that helps shape Coleridge's private friendships in the 1790s. Empiricist positions include all those doctrines that value "knowledge gained by trial and practice."[3] As Jean H. Hagstrum notes of Samuel Johnson's anti-Platonic cast of mind, "all mental action, whether rational or imaginative, is always secondary to the direct experience of reality and is, apart from experience, seriously suspect."[4] Transcendentalist positions, to borrow Wendell Harris's terms, depend on "insight into a structure which is not only invisible but which cannot be deduced from the phenomena of experience," and encompasses

> those whose belief in a transcendent realm is the result of orthodox religious faith and those whose belief is philosophical or even mystical. It can include those who believe in universal innate ideas. . . . It can include those who believe in special revelation or vision as well as those who hold the main tradition of Natural Law.[5]

During the latter part of the eighteenth century, friendship became subject to vehement contestation by these opposing philosophical traditions. In the following pages, I aim to trace this debate across a range of genres including poetry, novels, periodical essays, and prints. In doing so, this chapter places Coleridge within a cultural argument in the 1780s regarding transcendent and empiricist notions of friendship.

Despite his attempts to symbolize the Idea in "The Nightingale," Coleridge admits the difficulty of translating divine music into human language. Although the gentle maid "knows all their notes," her knowledge highlights the poet's more limited capacity to articulate the meaning of the divine message. The problem is one inherent to Platonism: how to represent an order of reality that exists beyond the perceivable world. This dilemma particularly exercised the milkmaid poet, Ann Yearsley, who during 1795 resided in Bristol at the same time as Coleridge, and who throughout the 1780s and 1790s conceived of friendship as a Platonic Ideal. In "Remonstrance in the Platonic Shade, Flourishing on an Height" (1796), Yearsley characteristically declares "Love, friendship, virtue" to be a Platonic, "Trinomial pow'r."[6] However, she laments how

> These feeble sounds
> Give not my soul's rich meaning; or my thought
> Rises too boldly o'er the human line
> Of alphabets (misused).
>
> (pp. 69–70)

For Yearsley, friendship has a value that resists translation into human speech:

> O world! what hast thou in thy sounds
> So dear as silent memory when she leads
> The shade of the departed? Ask despair
> What renovation is, when friendship bends
> To kiss her tears away;—but ask her eyes;
> The pleasing anguish dwells not on her tongue.
>
> (p. 70)

Although the mysterious communication between friends' eyes offers a glimpse into this transcendent experience, it remains sealed off from further investigation, and is understandable only to the ecstatic friends themselves. Nevertheless, as Lucinda Cole and Richard Swartz note, it is Yearsley's "failure to articulate her 'rare' vision" that "becomes a sign of meanings which lie beyond the power of any language to articulate."[7]

In Yearsley's "Address to Friendship" (1785), friendship's higher love is suggested by its purifying the "soft flame" of passion that so bewilders "th'infatuated soul":

> Yet well refin'd
> By Virtue's brightening flame, pure it ascends,

> As incense in its grateful circles mounts,
> Till, mixt and lost, with Thee it boasts thy name.[8]

As for Skelton, "Virtue" is central to realizing transcendent forms of friendship, taking on the purifying role analogous to that of the Messiah, who also comes "like a refiner's fire."[9] As an expression of virtue, Yearsley's friendship represents a prelapsarian state of moral purity in which the individual is free from self-interest or bodily Eros. She follows a long tradition celebrating friendship as a spiritual alternative to bodily love. In "An Ode on Friendship" (?1740), Samuel Johnson similarly criticizes love as "a stranger to the blest, / Parent of thousand wild desires" (lines 5–6) and celebrates friendship's heavenly origin: "Thy lambent glories only beam, / Around the fav'rites of the sky" (lines 11–12).[10]

To articulate this idea, however, Yearsley requires a state of quasi-religious enthusiasm—a term literally meaning "possession by a God." Such is her experience in "On Being Presented with a Silver Pen" (1787).[11] Addressing her new pen, "Fair proof of Friendship," Yearsley wonders whether it will "Paint high her [Friendship's] raptures in thine artless Song; / Her beauties ask, Idea all divine" (p. 83). By using this gift, Yearsley hopes to induce a "willing transport" (p. 83) through which she can express the transcendent "Idea." Such ecstasy does not come from social interaction, however, but through the poet's solitary intercourse with the Idea. Unsurprisingly, this state of feeling is unstable. Yearsley suddenly complains that "Rapture dies" as her "valued Pen" can no longer "swell the glowing line" with friendship's "beauties" (p. 91), and the poem ends.

Yearsley's devotion to the Platonic Idea reflects her sense that terrestrial, embodied friends fail to mediate moral perfection. As she declares in "Address to Friendship":

> O, 'tis the deepest error man can prove,
> To fancy joys disinterested can live,
> Indissoluble, pure, unmix'd with self;
> Why, 'twere to be immortal, 'twere to own
> No part but spirit in this chilling gloom.
>
> (p. 84)

The embodied self that "lives" is defined by not manifesting "spirit." Where the material and spiritual worlds are radically disunited, earthly friendship becomes a logical impossibility. Nevertheless, Yearsley is driven emotionally to quest after this religious sublime, sustaining her faith in the existence of Platonic friendship somewhere in the world, if only it could be found:

> Thou unfound blessing! woo'd with eager hope,
> As clowns the nightly vapour swift pursue,
> And fain wou'd grasp to cheer their lonely way;
> Vain the wide stretch, and vain the shorten'd breath,
> For, ah! the bright delusion onward flies.
>
> (p. 80)

Despite her vision of a Platonic union of soul, she remains firmly aware of the difficulty in "grasping" the Idea.

Like Yearsley, Coleridge also believes enthusiasm to be intrinsic to friendship, lamenting to Thelwall in 1796 that "the *Enthusiasm* of Friendship is not with S. and me."[12] However, he is more successful in grounding his experience of the Idea, at least periodically, within embodied relationships. Coleridge's passion for friendship is part of a more general upsurge in confidence during the 1780s and 1790s that the Idea could be realized within the material world. This movement towards action is exemplified by a four-volume comic novel, *The Amicable Quixote; or, The Enthusiasm of Friendship* (1788), whose subtitle foreshadows Coleridge's letter to Thelwall.[13] Published anonymously, this text traces the social encounters and liaisons of its hero, George Bruce, and uses them to scrutinize a range of contemporary notions of friendship. George's key characteristic is his optimistic enthusiasm for a Platonic Ideal:

> One favourite propensity, the effect of a noble disposition, had often led him into ridiculous situations, by which he was exposed to the laughter of his acquaintance; this was the *enthusiasm of friendship,* which glowed in his heart with such uncommon rapture and such invariable philanthropy, that his whole study was to admire every one he knew of both sexes, and to bind himself to them by the strongest ties of inviolable attachment. (1:6–7)

Unlike Yearsley, the divine communication George experiences impels him to realize by his own efforts the transcendent Idea. "I was formed to friendship," he declares, "from my birth; or, indeed, I rather think, before it: I certainly enjoyed a kind of *pre-native* cordiality, which inspired me with just notions of esteem, e'er I found objects whereon to fix them" (3:5–6). Rejecting the Wordsworthian claim that "Our birth is but a sleep and a forgetting" (line 58),[14] a break in contact with Platonic Reality, George asserts that the friendship he enjoyed in his ethereal pre-existence can be continued in the material world.

At the same time, it is clear that the "friendship" he claims to enjoy with people is not dependent on any usual process of social intercourse with embodied "objects." George complacently claims to have "nineteen intimates in Russia, whom I never saw" (1:13). As he explains to Miss Dawkins:

> ["]Do you suppose me, then, Madam, so inconsiderable as to owe the possession of friendship to my existence! Do you imagine that none are my friends but those who know me?"—"Sir! you absolutely astonish me!"— . . . "Madam, I pride myself on the number and excellence of my friends; but, I should be sorry to have it taken for granted that they are partial to me, because they are my acquaintance; no, Madam, I hope their regard proceeds from a nobler source: it is the true friendship that I demand, unmingled with the subordinate and cautious considerations of acquaintance. Upon that principle, Madam, I am charmed with your noble, your hospitable, your munificent—I beg pardon, these are terms too paltry; I mean—your *friendly* invitation and partiality." (3:7–8)

The comic satire here depends upon debunking the Platonist's disregard for embodiment. George declares himself enamored of the Idea of friendship rather than any particular person. Indeed, "mingling" with human beings threatens to compromise the purity of the Idea. George does not, however, argue that the imperfection of the material world militates against realizing friendship. In refusing to ground his friendship on empirical knowledge of embodied selves, this idealist can assert his affection for anyone he likes, irrespective of whether he has met them.

The figure of George Bruce represents a larger cultural phenomenon. An article published in *The Universal Magazine* in 1791 gives popular expression to the desire of realizing an abstract principle of friendship in actual, earthly relationships. The humorous mediator here is "The Guardian Angel," an emissary from a celestial dimension:

> I should . . . shew but little acquaintance with the real sources of felicity in that blessed region of which I am a native inhabitant, if I did not occasionally embrace an opportunity of explaining the nature of genuine friendship to mankind, and of recommending the calm and amiable purity of this attachment to general cultivation among my terrestrial wards and pupils.[15]

Through friendship, claims the Angel, mankind imitates those from the "blessed region," in that the relationship provides a principal means of moral and intellectual progression: "the mind of man becomes expanded, and the sphere of his rational enjoyments enlarged," until he becomes able to enjoy "all that is noble, or intellectual, in the whole sphere of sublunary pleasures" (p. 14).

Like George, the Guardian Angel does not share Yearsley's pessimism that such virtuous intercourse depends on first finding a person of transcendent moral worth. The Angel admits that "pleasures, like these, can only be enjoyed by virtuous, feeling, and enlightened souls." However, he also declares it to be

> equally true, that entering into a friendly association, with a well-selected few, for the purpose of cultivating pleasures of this description, will imperceptibly, yet rapidly, increase the virtue, the feelings, and the intelligence of the parties.
>
> Convinced as I am of the truth of these observations, what can I do better than recommend to mankind, especially to the generous and the young, to cultivate, with social ardour, this pure and generous attachment. (p. 14)

Making the effort to cultivate intimacy will bring virtue into being. The writer's exhortation to "cultivate, with social ardour, this pure and generous attachment" announces a cultural will-to-friendship that is reflected both in contemporary literature, the writings of the Coleridge circle during the 1790s, and Coleridge's Pantisocratic project as well as in his relations with Poole, Lloyd, and Thelwall.

In celebrating mechanical attempts to generate friendship, many writers follow Abraham Skelton's lead and invest the concept with a religious formality. In his essay "On Imprudent Friendships," Caius celebrates the "lasting" friendships of the Morlacchi, a religious people who "inhabit the mountainous part of inland Dalmatia":

> Friendship is lasting among the Morlacchi. They have even made it a kind of religious point, and tie the sacred bond at the foot of the altar. The Sclavonian ritual contains a particular benediction, for the solemn union of two male or two female friends, in the presence of the congregation. The abbé says, that he was present at the union of two young women, who were made *Posestre* [half-sisters] in the church of Perussich. The satisfaction that sparkled in their eyes, when the ceremony was performed, gave a convincing proof, that delicacy of sentiments can lodge in minds not formed, or rather not corrupted by society, which we call civilized.[16]

The Morlacchi sanctify friendship by securing it within their culture's religious institutions. Friendship is a spiritual contract that binds the participants together in virtue. Within religious culture, this mechanical means of producing friendship is extremely successful, as marked by the permanence of the Morlacchi's attachments. Caius claims, "if discord happens to arise between two friends, among the Morlacchi, it is talked of over all the country as a scandalous novelty" (p. 329). The Morlacchi offer living proof that a virtuous idea can find terrestrial embodiment, and Caius implicitly identifies Dalmatia as realizing aspects of an idea of Eden. However, the Morlacchi's innocent space is exclusive and fragile. Noting the increase of failed friendships amongst the tribe, Caius blames the Morlacchi's increased contact with Italians and their "wine and strong liquors," concluding: "When these simple people become more men of the world, the romantic part of their friendships will degenerate into that motley, unintelligible thing, which many people call friendship" (p. 329). For this writer, friendship's sacred form can exist only among such primitivist societies, its continuance relying upon these societies remaining ignorant of sophisticated, worldly cultures. Such visions, however, provide the conceptual hinterland from which Coleridge's own ideas of virtuous friendship emerge. During this period, the virgin soil of America and Nether Stowey in turn offer Coleridge secluded locations that could provide settings in which to realize a Pantisocratic, sacred community of friends, untainted by the selfish passions of the old world.

Within secular English society, childhood provides another innocent space in which friendship can become sanctified. Nostalgically recalling his school days, Leigh Hunt reveals in "Remembered Friendship" (1801) how he and his friend would ramble through the "cloister'd walks of Christ's Hospital:"

> o'er our youthful heads
> The gloomy arch, that favour'd converse sweet
> Of whisper'd vowes of friendship, heav'd on high
> It's massy vault, along whose time-worn roof
> Soft murmurs ran of breathing constancy.
> While on my shoulder hung thy easy hand,
> Beyond thy bosom, not a single thought
> That flutter'd from my breast, unheeding stray'd:
> Fix'd, and for ever, was my soul in thee![17]

The almost monastic surroundings afford an appropriately sacred setting for the two friends' spiritual contract. As with the Morlacchi, formal vows provide a religious language through which friends can deny that their affections are temporal. In this cloistered space, Hunt perceives the living, "breathing" presence of old vows, a sign that "constancy" in friendship can indeed exist. Transcending earthly mutability, sacred friendship offers a sublime stasis in which a friend's soul might be "Fix'd, and for ever" in another. In Coleridge's life, his friendship with Poole illustrates his own desire to construct friendship as a similarly permanent spiritual contract. (See chapter 2.)

Coleridge also shared Hunt's nostalgic locating of friendship in their Christ's Hospital childhood. As he declares in "To a Young Lady" (the first version of which he sent to Southey in 1794):

> Much on my youth I love to dwell,
> Ere yet I bade that friendly dome farewell,
> Where first, beneath the echoing cloisters pale,
> I heard of guilt and wonder'd at the tale!
>
> (lines 1–4)[18]

Coleridge also implies, however, that beyond the enclosed innocent world of childhood, virtuous friendship cannot be so easily found. Particularly in his relations with Southey after 1799, Coleridge comes to explore the effect of organic mutability on relationships once they have progressed beyond the "friendly dome" of youth. (See chapter 8.)

Coleridge's contemporaries concurred that in adult society the meeting of spiritual aspiration within a secular context could only be uneasy, as George Bruce's encounter with one Valentine Wince exemplifies. Having heard George discourse on several "notions of friendship" (3:52) at a dinner party, Valentine decides that he must befriend him personally:

> I had hoped to cultivate those sublime ideas of true amity which you so nobly implant in every body's mind, provided the soil is at all rich and will admit of such culture. Believe me, excellent young man, believe me one of those real and sincere partizans of your doctrine, that I want nothing but opportunity to exhibit the character, which is so much above all others, *a true friend*. (3:53)

Valentine could be one of the Guardian Angel's readers. His enthusiasm for friendship does not express his liking for George as an individual but rather his desire to enact a theoretical "doctrine" of mutual benevolence. In fact, the two men create their "friendship" here entirely through speaking about their desire for it: "Instead of cards, the time was passed in mutual professions of amity between Wince and his new guest" (3:66). Intimacy is produced merely through talking about intimacy, friendship through declaring the desire to become friends.

The Amicable Quixote uses these avowals to highlight in comic form how difficult the transfer is of spiritual idea into embodied action. Valentine declares:

> "How is it, my dear new friend, how does it happen, that friendships are often so fractured after a few years continuance? Are the sons of men so weak in their resolutions, or so faithless in their performances, that they cannot adhere to the sacred pledges of interchanged oaths? No tie is so sacred as the tie of friendship: your resolutions, I know, are inviolably solemn and your actions invariably permanent."—He was re-echoed by Bruce, and a bumper was filled to the *dignity of virtue and the charms of friendship.* (3:66–67)

Despite recognizing the failure of the moderns to realize the solemnity of friendship's "sacred" vows, Valentine insists that the mechanical act of will, embodied in vows and maintained by "resolution," should guarantee permanently virtuous behavior. But the two men's vows do not usher in an attachment reminiscent of the Morlacchi: their "*indissoluble* friendship" cannot negotiate an argument "on the subject of a mite in cheese" (3:71–72). George must learn from this episode that avowals of friendship do not guarantee the transmutation of Idea into action: "Bruce was severely mortified, . . . to have been duped by a frivolous enthusiast, who had all his own romantic extravagance, without the generosity and constancy which elevated the character of Bruce" (3:72). Failing to embody itself in beneficence, "enthusiasm" becomes reduced to a "frivolous" language whose elevated diction refers to nothing beyond itself.

It becomes clear that Valentine wishes only to create an instant illusion of intimacy. In comic form, he represents a key aspect of the enthusiastic sensibility. The enthusiast's communication with the transcendent Idea makes him anticipate a rapid embodiment of the friend. Poole gives a striking expression of friendly enthusiasm in a 1799 letter to Coleridge:

> Remember me I pray you to your worthy friend . . . I doubt not but if I met him in Germany, or he me at Stowey—things which may possible happen, we should know one another as well as if we had been acquainted all our lives—when on each side every faculty of the soul is prepared to sympathize, how speedily do they blend into one.[19]

Physiognomy becomes a crucial means of discerning an individual's potential for amity. The Guardian Angel, for instance, advises his readers to pay particular attention to physical appearances:

> If you see a person of either sex, gay, vivacious, alive to every thing around, and catching pleasure from every object; . . . and see another, with care-contracted brow, and down-cast, or side-long-stealing eye, full of perturbation, timid and joyless, . . . which do you conclude to be the close and selfish, which the generous, communicative man? Which is the friend, the confident, the social being; and which the sordid wretch, who lives for himself alone? (p. 15)

The Angel confirms John Mullan's reading of the sentimental body as capable of expressing "conditions of feeling which can connote exceptional virtue or allow for intensified forms of communication."[20] The friend in particular communicates virtue through a public display of anatomical signs. The Angel provides directions on how to spot a friend and how to shape one's physical gestures in order to attract another's friendly advances. The reader is invited to have faith in the bodily appearances of sociability and to trust that they signify the embodiment of the virtuous idea.

This desire for instant friendship runs counter to the traditional Ciceronian emphasis on experience and duration as necessary criteria for the establishment of Roman *amicitia*. Cicero's *De Amicitia* represents the *locus classicus*.[21] Aware that "affection is apt to take the lead of judgment," Cicero advises that "it is the part of prudence, therefore, to restrain a predilection from carrying us precipitately into the arms of a new friend, before we have, in some degree at least, put his moral qualifications to the test." Only in this way can one judge whether a man has the "steadiness and constancy of temper" (2:94–95) requisite for friendship. In warning the overdramatizing Boswell not to make too much of any one moment, Johnson exemplifies this classical tradition:

> Think of happiness, of learning, of friendship. We cannot tell the precise moment when friendship is formed. As in filling a vessel drop by drop, there is at last a drop which makes it run over; so in a series of kindnesses there is at last one which makes the heart run over. We must not divide objects of our attention into minute parts, and think separately of each part.[22]

For Johnson, friendship points to the cumulative effect of empirical acts of kindness carried out over a lengthy period. The culture of sensibility in the 1780s and 90s, however, invests great energy in

1: TRANSCENDENCE AND ITS LIMITS: FRIENDSHIP IN THE 1780S

the speedy generation of relationship, placing a high value on those dramatic moments that summon intimacy into being.

One such moment is recorded by Coleridge as he journeys to Germany by boat in 1798. In a letter home to Poole, he relates how he so impressed a group of Danes with his conversation that "in a short time [I] became their Idol." One man in particular immediately became attached to the Englishman:

> "Vat imagination! vat language! vat fast science! vat eyes!—vat a milk vite forehead!—O my Heafen! You are a God!—Oh me! if you should tink I flatters you—no, no, no—I hafe ten tousand a year—yes— . . . vell, vat's that? a mere trifle!—I 'ouldn't give my sincere heart for ten times the money.—Yes! you are a God! . . ." (Dane squeezing my hand most vehemently) "My *dear* Friend! vat an affection & *fidelity* we hafe for each other!["]23

The Dane's desire for friendship immediately follows his physiognomical deduction of Coleridge's transcendent virtue. Moreover, the Dane declares that the affection he feels is similarly exalted, as the value of his "sincere heart" cannot be quantified. Coleridge, however, burlesques the Dane's belief that friendship can be generated through emphatic physical gestures and magical professions. Although being called "My dear Friend" a further fourteen times during this conversation, Coleridge wryly remarks that the Dane's elevated opinion of him was suddenly lowered on hearing of his Christianity: "I sunk 50 fathoms immediately in his Graces" (1:425). Like Valentine Wince, the Dane disappears from view and is not heard of again.

Coleridge's letter is reminiscent of Jane Austen's early fiction, which both satirizes and draws further attention to an English enthusiasm for embodying the Idea of friendship. In *Love and Freindship* (1790), Laura sees instantaneously that Sophia is a "real freind:"

> Imagine my transports at beholding one, most truly worthy of the Name. Sophia was rather above the middle size; most elegantly formed. A soft languor spread over her lovely features, but increased their Beauty—. It was the Charectaristic of her Mind—. She was all Sensibility and Feeling. We flew into each others arms and after having exchanged vows of mutual Freindship for the rest of our Lives, instantly unfolded to each other the most inward secrets of our Hearts.24

Again, friendship is discovered "at first sight," the body providing a surface on which the "Name" is inscribed. Sophia's physical "features" testify to the superlative character of her mind. Attachment immediately follows these swift convictions of each other's goodness and compatibility, and is cemented in "vows of mutual Freindship." As in *The Amicable Quixote*, Austen finds these religious trappings empty of meaning, and emphasizes that producing friendship on demand can signify a selfish appetite. Having eloped with Edward, Laura relates how she is welcomed at the house of Augustus and Sophia:

> In the society of my Edward and this Amiable Pair, I passed the happiest moments of my Life; Our time was most delightfully spent, in mutual Protestations of Freindship, and in vows of unalterable Love, in which we were secure from being interrupted, by intruding and disagreable Visitors, as Augustus and Sophia had . . . taken due care to inform the surrounding Families, that as their Happiness centered wholly in themselves, they wished for no other society. (6:87)

Exchanging vows of friendship is an end in itself, not demonstrating an altruistic commitment but only a linguistic means of creating instant pleasures for those whose happiness is "centered wholly in themselves."

Despite his burlesque of the overaffectionate Dane, Coleridge is heavily implicated in the cultural enthusiasm for friendship. Writing to him in February 1804, Southey expresses an Austen-like suspicion of Coleridge's precipitate displays of affection, accusing him of insincerity:

> It does vex me to see you so lavish of the outward and visible signs of friendship, and to know that a set of fellows whom you do not care for and ought not to care for, boast every where of your intimacy . . . You have accustomed yourself to talk affectionately, and write affectionately, to your friends, till the expressions of affection flow by habit in your conversation, and in your letters, and pass for more than they are worth; the worst of all this is, . . . you will be convicted of a double dealing, which, though you do not design, you certainly do practise.[25]

Like Austen's characters, Coleridge's rapid affection can easily be perceived as hypocritical. Although Southey understands Coleridge's habitual effusiveness to be merely customary, he suspects it indicates his friend's duplicity rather than his virtue:

> You say in yours to Sara, that you love and honour me; upon my soul I believe you: but if I did not thoroughly believe it before, your saying so is the thing of all things that would make me open my eyes and look about me to see if I were not deceived. (2:266)

In defence, Coleridge declared that his enthusiasm was not morally bereft, asserting that an examination of "the circumstances of each particular Case . . . would prove on the whole honorable to me rather than otherwise." Nevertheless, he conceded he had indeed

> suffered a great deal from a cowardice in not daring to repel unassimilating acquaintances who press forward upon my friendship; . . . But I have had enough—& done enough. Hereafter, I shall shew a different Face; & calmly inform those who press upon me, that my Health, Spirits, and Occupation alike make it necessary for me to confine myself to the society [of] those, with whom I have the nearest & highest connection. So help me God! I will hereafter be quite sure that I do really & in the whole of my heart esteem & like a man before I permit him to call me friend.[26]

In showing a "different Face," Coleridge suggests that he had previously embodied the Guardian Angel's advice that young men should present an amicable physiognomy in order to attract friends. Coleridge suggests that this advice has in practice often caused more harm than good.

In his letter, Southey had put forward a further objection to profuse expressions of affection. "My moral stomach loathes anything like froth," he remarked; "There is a something outlandish in saying them, more akin to a French embrace than an English shake by the hand" (2:267). Southey's comparison makes points about manliness and class. For him, Coleridge's "French" protestations represent a flowery etiquette associated with the upper orders. Southey contrasts these exhibitionist gestures with the socially egalitarian "shake by the hand." This classless, "English" mode of affection is more manly but also less friendly. In commenting on these styles of affection, Southey implicitly offers a conservative response to a question that had received vigorous attention during the previous decade: could class interests be transcended by bodying forth an idea of virtuous friendship?

The *Encyclopædia Britannica* for 1792 focuses on the extent to which conflicting class interests might be effaced within friendship. Its article on "Friendship" provides a definitive statement of the empiricist argument against generating cross-rank friendships, claiming that affection cannot exist where there is either financial or social inequality:

> *Equality of rank and fortune* is also favourable to friendship. Seldom will a man of fortune be able to gain the sincere friendship of any of his dependants. Though he treat them with the most obliging condescen-

sion, and load them with favours; yet still, either the sense of dependence, or resentment for imaginary injuries, or impatience of the debt of gratitude, . . . will be likely to prevent them from regarding him with cordial affection. (7:468)

According to this writer, friendship between ranks cannot re-create the "free easy intercourse" (7:468) enjoyed by men of equal status. The emotional economy in a cross-rank connection is imagined to be a burdensome financial transaction in which the parties feel obliged to give an equal return for what they receive. The richer man's generosity cannot be experienced as a gift but only as imposing a "debt of gratitude" upon the poorer party.

Throughout his own life, Coleridge accepted the charitable generosity of friends and patrons. A passage in Charles Lloyd's novel *Edmund Oliver* (1798) suggests that Coleridge was well aware of the *Britannica*'s conservative argument. In this scene, the philanthropical Charles Maurice offers to share his wealth with Edmund (whom Lloyd had partly modeled on Coleridge):

He evidently struggled with himself—he measured the room in long strides—he was much agitated—however in a few minutes he turned towards me and with an inexpressible look exclaimed—"I yield—I yield—I could call myself thy debtor, but I will not."[27]

As Rosemary Ashton has pointed out, the passage probably marks a "sly dig at Coleridge's way of accepting financial help."[28] Lloyd's Coleridge has difficulty in taking on a "debt of gratitude" and realizes such indebtedness could hamper the equality upon which friendship so often depended.

Coleridge's realization that material inequalities could be anathema to friendship helps drive forward his Pantisocratic project. By creating a community founded on the equality of labor and the abolition of property, Coleridge hopes to create the conditions in which cross-class friendships could flourish. (See chapter 3.) In this, Coleridge is one of many contemporary idealists who seek ways of eradicating the barriers to friendship created by inequalities of rank and fortune. For George Bruce, the restrictions articulated by the *Britannica* and *The Universal Magazine* are superficial and work to inhibit the innate virtue that every man possesses. By disguising himself as a member of a lower rank (a footman), George believes he will be able to befriend men of all social positions:

These friends too, whom I gain in an humble station, will be of the noblest kind. They will be faithful and disinterested; I shall have the best opportunity of trying their zeal and of proving their steadiness. Thus forming intimacies, as no man ever did before, I shall not be indebted to sordid views for *their* attachment to me. The world will now learn, that there still exists, in its full vigor, and in its most splendid colours, the lofty sentiment of generous regard. (1:70–71)

In referring to "sordid views," George accepts that an inequality of rank destroys affection by introducing base motives into a relationship. However, he conceives of an innately benevolent self existing beyond the confines of class identity, one that would allow his Platonic Idea of virtuous friendship to find further embodiment.

Indeed, George happily spends an evening with his fellow footmen, who reveal themselves as generous—collecting "a large sum for the widow of their late companion" (1:121)—and cultivated: as footman John remarks, "there are five or six of us who are dabs at scholarship—all these read you every play and poem as they come out—but we begin to think of leaving it off, for it grows damned vulgar" (1:118). The narrator opines that footmen are in general

> cruelly and unjustly despised, because they are dependent upon the wealth, the caprice, and the insolence of their masters, to whom they frequently find themselves superior in intellect, good sense, and knowledge of the world: among such noble dispositions, the enthusiasm of Bruce laid him to anticipate faithful friends, and perhaps his romance was seldom more excusable, for their profusion was the effect of generosity, and their civility was the language of nature. (1:121–22)

In claiming "civility" to be an attribute of "nature" rather than rank, the narrator denies that a "noble" disposition implies high birth. Here friendship offers a politically radical challenge to social hierarchies by creating cross-rank ties grounded in mankind's equal capacity for virtue. The idealism voiced in *The Amicable Quixote* continues to be expressed through the 1790s. As Coleridge celebrated cross-class attachments in *The Watchman* (1796), so in 1797 the mock-periodical *The Philanthrope* published an epistle from the Countess of Fairdale entitled "Possibility of Friendship between Persons of Unequal Ranks."[29] The aristocratic correspondent celebrates the friendship she enjoys with Miss Elder (merely a "gentleman's daughter") declaring: "Those who observe human nature must assuredly know, that friendship may subsist between persons of different ranks; but who are not different in correctness of manners, good principles, and liberal sentiments" (pp. 229–30). Again, a generalized "human nature" is evoked to justify the pervasiveness of virtue, and thus friendship, throughout society.

However, these texts celebrating friendship's potential to find embodiment across all social ranks are met by a conservative backlash. The Countess complains that the "indiscretion and rashness" of the periodical press "may have occasioned a good deal of mischief" (p. 227) through its desire "to vilify that sort of friendship" (p. 230). After reading one such article, Miss Elder abruptly quit the house, thus depriving the Countess of the "comfort I enjoyed in the society of my worthy friend" (p. 232). Perhaps Miss Elder had been devastated by Caius's article, "On Imprudent Friendships" (1793), in which "nature" is re-deployed as part of an empiricist argument denying the universality of innate virtue:

> There is a wide difference between the ignorance of a man, in whom the natural feelings have not been adulterated by vice, nor civilized and refined by education, and that of an illiterate mechanic who, while he can scarcely spell his name, or comprehend a rational argument, can yet take pride in grasping more money than he who is capable of instructing a nation.—It is one of the few good advices which lord Chesterfield gives, never to keep company with those who are at once "low in birth, low in mind, and low in manners." (p. 328)

For Caius, only the middle-ranking man possesses "natural feelings": the low-born man is morally contaminated by his mechanical profession. Excluded from the "natural," the Yahoo-like mechanic is governed by self-interest, his emotional life tainted by desire for gain. In denying the laborer meaningful bonds of community, Caius attempts to defuse the political power that might lurk in such men grouping together as "friends." By the end of the decade, following the collapse of Pantisocracy and his disillusionment with radical politics, Coleridge's own views would show the influence of this conservative line of thought.

Ann Yearsley confirms Caius and Coleridge's later view, arguing more explicitly that lower ranks cannot embody the "Idea all divine" of friendship. In "Remonstrance," Yearsley enjoys momentary insight into a Platonic realm, which gives her knowledge of friendship's perfect Form. Elsewhere she encounters a terrestrial instance of transcendent amity—among the upper echelons of educated society. In "To Stella; on a Visit to Mrs. Montagu," celebrating Hannah More's friendship with Elizabeth Montagu, Yearsley shamefacedly declares of herself:

> Unequal, lost to the aspiring claim,
> I neither ask, nor own th'immortal name
> Of Friend; ah, no! its ardors are too great,
> My soul too narrow, and too low my state.[30]

1: TRANSCENDENCE AND ITS LIMITS: FRIENDSHIP IN THE 1780S

The material conditions of Yearsley's position as a milkmaid exclude her from participating in the divine Idea. For her, to be socially circumscribed is inevitably to lack the expansiveness of soul necessary for friendship. By contrast, the intimacy of the two bluestocking women sublimates their respective selves into a higher state of union, with each other and with "deity":

> When glowing raptures rise,
> And each, aspiring, seeks her native skies;
> When Fancy wakes the soul to extacy,
> And the rapt mind is touch'd with Deity,
> Quick let me from the hallow'd spot retire,
> Where sacred Genius lights his awful fire.
>
> (p. 66)

Conversation between educated, high-ranking women brings into being the overwhelming forces of "deity" and "Genius." As such, Yearsley conflates signs of divinity with signs of class. As for herself, Yearsley is terrified by More and Montagu's alien, awe-inspiring intercourse. The "friendship of the wise" produces a power of "Genius" that "blasts pretending Wits," and their "pointed thought in polish'd diction drest, / With every grace assaults the yielding breast" (p. 67). Yearsley's yielding to the power of "polish'd diction" acknowledges both her intellectual inferiority and her lowly rank. Retreating from the sublime manifestation of friendship, she asks Stella to spare her only thoughts, "slight, trivial, neither worth a smile or tear" (p. 66).

Yearsley accepts in this poem that friendship is the exclusive property of the leisured upper orders. Nonetheless, other writers' celebrations of cross-rank friendship suggest that the relation was in practice testing conventional social hierarchies. Mary Wollstonecraft's confidence in her rationality and virtue (although she is only a governess) was witnessed by Godwin, who recalled how Mary "made many friends in Ireland, among the persons who visited lord Kingsborough's house, for she always appeared there with the air of an equal, and not of a dependent."[31] Wollstonecraft reveals how this democratization of the idea of virtuous friendship could upset established social divisions: on one occasion she aroused "the utter mortification and dismay" of a "woman of quality" who discovered that she had been happily conversing with "Miss King's governess." Similarly, Mary's "friendship" with Kingsborough's "eldest daughter" causes lady Kingsborough "uneasiness . . . lest the children should love their governess better than their mother" (pp. 56–58).

In social terms, friendship in the 1790s may find objects of affection that transgress boundaries between ranks. On a personal level, enthusiastic attachments could encourage a closeness between friends in excess of social norms of decorum. As Susie Tucker argues, for many during the eighteenth century *enthusiasm* "meant something 'excessive' by definition" (p. 4). Yearsley herself exemplifies this position in a passage from "On Being Presented with a Silver Pen":

> But, ah! what wild emotions fill the breast,
> When we behold a valu'd friend distrest!
> Rule, from the ardent soul is quickly thrown,
> She rushes on, makes every woe her own;
> Strangles the images of grief which lie
> At his sad heart—by Friendship's hand they die.
>
> (p. 86)

Unheedful of arbitrary social "rules" of behavior, friendship's "ardent soul" releases a primordial energy in the friends' affection for each other. These "wild emotions" are potentially murderous, strangling as they do any "images of grief."

Human friendship that transcends everyday self-interest is associated with a passionate sensibility. In "To a Sensible but Passionate Friend" (1787), Yearsley celebrates the capacity of a friend to abandon his self-interest by involving himself in another's being. Again, such friendship ignores propriety:

> Trivial circumstances rising
> Strike thy soul with lightning's haste;
> Quick *sensations*, *Rule* despising,
> Give thee strongest, keenest taste.
>
> Exquisite thy mental pleasure,
> Common transports are not *thine*;
> Far surpassing vulgar measure,
> All *thy* joys are near divine.[32]

While she celebrates passionate friendship as helping to achieve sublime heights of feeling, Yearsley also fears that excessive emotion might overwhelm the self and disrupt its internal order:

> such souls as *thine* must languish,
> Like majestic *ruin* lie;
> None but equals share thine anguish,
> Fools deride thy deepest sigh.

1: TRANSCENDENCE AND ITS LIMITS: FRIENDSHIP IN THE 1780S   71

> Yet Philosophy despairing,
> Mourns thy richest feelings lost;
> When from self-denial veering,
> Thou'rt on storms of passion tost.
>
> (pp. 12–13)

Overactive sympathy precipitates a calamitous lack of care for the self. Such friends are tragic figures doomed to "ruin" in being overcome by "storms of passion." Although she excludes herself from such experience, Yearsley expresses a disturbing idea of friendship. Overwhelmed by a desire for mutual benevolence, a virtuous union entails the radical undermining of individual autonomy, and the transgressing of social "rules" of propriety. On Coleridge's part, his relations with Poole, Southey, Thelwall and Wordsworth all emphasize the role of passion in friendship, and the kindling of feelings that strain conventional notions of decorum.

In becoming associated with such intensity of feeling, friendship promised to become a relation as or more significant than familial attachment. Coleridge consistently tests the boundaries between friendship and family and seeks, both in Pantisocracy and later in the friendly groupings he creates at Nether Stowey and in the Lake District, to transform his friends into kin. Such impulses were part of wider social aspirations. The *Encyclopædia Britannica* (1792) recognizes this possibility even in its privileging of fraternity over friendship. "Fraternal affection" is defined as "an hearty benevolence, an ardent concern for each other's welfare, a readiness to serve and promote it":

> This relation is formed by nature, not by choice; and though it has many things in common with, yet it is prior to, the obligations of friendship: consequently nature and reason dictate that there should be a peculiar affection between brethren. We are not obliged, however, to make a brother or sister an intimate or bosom friend in preference to one who is not akin. Diversity of temper, and want of suitable qualifications, may render it unsafe and improper. But where friendship and fraternity meet in the same persons, such a conjunction adds a lustre to the relation.[33]

Although the "natural" bond of fraternity "ordinarily" makes the familial tie the "strongest" (7:451), the encyclopedist admits friendship's more "intimate" and confidential qualities are also intrinsic to true fraternal affection. Writing in 1799, Godwin laments that his relationship with his brother is unlikely to transform itself into the more "eminent" bond of sympathetic friendship:

having long given up the hope of that sympathy & congeniality of mind between us with which I once flattered myself, I . . . have always been inclined to cultivate a kind & brotherly intercourse. If you have the same inclination, it is best for us to be contented with things as they are, & not make ourselves uneasy for the want of that eminent & exquisite sympathy, which cannot exist between minds so differently constituted.[34]

Godwin's "brotherly intercourse" compares unfavorably with the Yearsleyan, intuitive understanding that Godwin elsewhere claims is characteristic of friendship. He represents part of a growing body of opinion that elected bonds of friendship might become of greater emotional importance than kinship and marital bonds. The elopement of Lady Eleanor Butler and Sarah Ponsonby in 1779 to a cottage in Llangollen Vale had become a cause célèbre, demonstrating how women might discover in "romantic friendship" an alternative to conventional marriage.[35] For Elizabeth Mavor, what was widely perceived as a "new and hitherto unsuspected form of female friendship" (p. 79) was comprised of qualities "we would now associate solely with a sexual relationship; tenderness, sensibility, shared tastes, coquetry" (p. 81).

If Lady Eleanor and Sarah's marital friendship challenged conventional domestic institutions, across Europe a religious enthusiasm for friendship tested traditional allegiance to the Christian church. Klaus Lankheit has argued that the decline of political and social institutions in Germany during the eighteenth century weakened Germans' faith in the church, to the extent that surrogates were sought for lost religious belief:

The enthusiasm with which friendship is proclaimed is understandable only if one realizes its function as a substitute religion. . . . Countless are the affirmations of the holiness of friendship in letters and poetry from Klopstock to Jean Paul, whose novels praise *"the heaven of friendship"* and the *"new idol of a friend."*[36]

In 1804, Coleridge himself writes that "Our Friend's Reputation should be a Religion to us,"[37] and later commands his reader to "<Reverence the Individuality of your friend!> It is the religion of a delicate Soul."[38] In Britain, religious writers openly worry that friendly enthusiasts might not be loyal to the Church. The opening tract of *Sublime Friendship Delineated* (1789), a compilation of texts by John Donovan expounding the philosophy of "The Friendly Brothers of St. Patrick," defines a concept of friendship compatible with Freemasonry.[39] In "An Enquiry into the Nature and Object of

Friendship," the author criticizes those who would make a substitute religion of friendship itself:

> There are but too many people who think they make themselves estimable friends, when they advance the rights of Friendship beyond all other rights; one believes that he is the better friend, in proportion as he boasts, that he is ready to offer up to Friendship the dearest victims. (pp. 37–38)

This writer is fearful of that same excessive feeling that Yearsley celebrates, an intensity that both writers understand as contemplating violent action for the sake of a friend. The vehemence of feeling between friends is here an idolatry, one by which friendship becomes a transcendent value for which anything may be sacrificed. The writer reflects more widespread perceptions in the 1790s. In his editorial remarks upon Cicero's *De Amicitia*, William Melmoth traces the modern enthusiasm for friendship to the Earl of Shaftesbury, who,

> animated with a warm sensibility of the moral charms of this generous affection, and not being able, it seems, to discover that it is either *enjoined*, or *encouraged*, by the Christian institution, imputes this pretended omission as a capital *defect* in the code of evangelical ethics. (2:329–30)

Shaftesbury's "depreciation" of Christianity in this regard had opened up a space in which friendship might become an object of religious devotion. In particular, Melmoth views the philosopher as sanctifying an intense expression of sensibility between friends.

For Coleridge, too, friendship is often associated with passion, enthusiasm, and a Shaftesburian sensibility. However, he gives such intense personal attachments a religious justification. To Southey in 1794, Coleridge announces his Pantisocratic manifesto:

> Warmth of particular Friendship does not imply absorption. The nearer you approach the Sun, the more intense are his Rays—yet what distant corner of the System do they not cheer and vivify? The ardour of private Attachments makes Philanthropy a necessary habit of the Soul.[40]

Intense feelings of affection between friends are the means of generating a wider social benevolence. Given the religious symbolism of Coleridge's suns in general, Coleridge is arguing here that divine love is manifested through such energetic friendships. Furthermore, while lecturing in Bristol during May 1795 Coleridge identifies private friendship as Jesus Christ's key virtue:

> Jesus was a Friend, and he wept at the Tomb of Lazarus. Jesus was the friend of the whole human Race, yet he disguised not the national feelings, when he foresaw the particular distresses of his Countrymen.[41]

Jesus's example demonstrates to Coleridge how intense private affections are the basis for patriotism and a more extensive friendship for humanity.

Coleridge's lecture situated him within a lively public debate. As Melmoth points out, several Christian apologists were attempting "to prove, that '[friendship] is totally incompatible with the *genius* and *spirit* of the gospel'" (2:330). Amongst this number is the Rev. Joseph Fawcett, whose sermon, "Christianity Vindicated in not Particularly Inculcating Friendship and Patriotism," was published in *The Universal Magazine* in 1796, and may represent a response to Coleridge's Bristol lecture.[42] In justifying "our Saviour's silence" (p. 118) on the subject of friendship, Fawcett rejects the equation of intense feeling with virtuous attachment:

> An affection of this kind, to whatever transport and enthusiasm it may rise; however uniform and inflexible the fidelity that may attend it; however zealous the services it may inspire; [. . .] Such a flame, with whatever brightness it may burn, cannot be said to possess any virtuous splendor. It is lighted up only by fancy, not by reason, or religion. It burns upon the floor of mortality; it is not elevated to the altar of virtue. (p. 119)

A moral relation cannot be achieved through mere intensity of feeling, and Fawcett stresses how often ardent friends behave immorally, being as "implacable" in their "resentment" as their "friendship [is] inextinguishable" (p. 119). Whereas for Coleridge friendship is the seat of holiness, for Fawcett Christianity's virtue lies precisely in its regulation of friendship's free-flowing sensibility. Fawcett argues that in advocating universal benevolence rather than private affections,

> Christ has given us . . . the only corrective of their intemperance and lawless access. No observer of human life can want to be told, how frequently friendship, in its blind zeal to serve its object, has lost sight of the public principle. To serve a friend, how many are there, who will make no scruple of swearing deceitfully before the tribunal of their country; of espousing his cause, when his quarrel is not just; . . . It was

wise in the Author of our religion, to lay all the emphasis upon love to all men; instead of particularly recommending the preference of a few. (pp. 120–21)

Agape polices the intensity of a person's emotional life by asserting the individual's duty to the social whole. During these years, fears that friendship might exceed social sanction are common, even in those who celebrate it as a moral idea. Donovan's compilation, although declaring friendship to be the "purest of all unions" (p. 21), firmly subordinates it within a hierarchy of relationships, each of which demands an individual's duty:

> These duties have their ranks fixed, and are in such a subordination, that they cannot be displaced without being destroyed; in this settled order, the obligations of Friendship come last, as we are born creatures, we belong to the Creator; as subjects to the state; born in the bosom of a family our relation to it is inseperable; in a word, we are born men, subjects, a kin to one another, and afterwards we became friends. (pp. 31–32)

Friendship must be lived in accordance with social rules, and one must recognize that it is not a value that transcends all others. The Edinburgh artist, John Kay, illustrates the danger of friendship undermining public institutions in his engraving "Friendship. *A principal* Beard" (1793), a satire on the election of Mr. Baird ("Beard") as principal of Edinburgh University when only thirty-two: Baird married the daughter of Thomas Elder, lord provost of Edinburgh, depicted in this print as helping Baird in his election. Friendship's supposedly principled bond becomes in practice croneyism, which undermines the university's moral authority.[43] In his own experience, however, Coleridge would more frequently lament those friends of his, particularly the Wordsworths, whom he felt adhered to the kind of moral hierarchy Donovan celebrates.

The work of William Cowper offers a powerful attempt to ground an idea of friendship as a transcendent relationship within socially acceptable modes of intercourse. Coleridge's aperçu regarding "the divine Chit chat of Cowper" highlights the latter's method.[44] For Cowper, friendships embody themselves in colloquial converse on "low" trivial subjects. Through such quotidian intercourse, however, Cowper also discovers friendship to be a sanctified relation. In "A Poetical Epistle to Lady Austen" (1781), he ponders this paradox in a poem that juxtaposes "prosaic" and "poetic" levels of meaning.[45] Prose associates friendship with "Chit chat"—that is, with matters ordinary and everyday:

John Kay, "Friendship. *A principal Beard*" (1793). © Copyright The British Museum.

> Dear Anna—Between friend and friend,
> Prose answers every common end;
> Serves, in a plain, and homely way,
> T'express th'occurrence of the day;
> Our health, the weather, and the news;
> What walks we take, what books we chuse;
> And all the floating thoughts, we find
> Upon the surface of the mind.
>
> (lines 1–8)

Prosaic friendship represents the small-scale, surface without depth, expressing thoughts that are neither deeply felt nor worked out but which "float." Affection is articulated simply by verbalizing the conditions of immediate experience.

Writing as a "Poet" (line 9), however, Cowper is concerned to find deeper significance in friendship than "Chit chat." Lady Austen also inspires "sublime vagaries" (line 17) regarding the significance of their relationship: their intimacy offers "proof, that we, and our affairs / Are part of a Jehovah's cares" (lines 57–58). Cowper emphasizes that friendship testifies to the operation of divine providence:

> It is th'allotment of the skies,
> The Hand of the Supremely Wise,
> That guides and governs our affections,
> And plans, and orders our connexions.
>
> (lines 33–36)

Unlike Yearsley's conception of the Platonic sublime, however, Cowper's divine relation respects both boundaries between selves and the proceedings of daily life. Cowper is not an enthusiast: he does not become inspired by an idea that he then desires to be rapidly embodied. On the contrary, sacred friendship for him is the result of a lengthy, undramatic intercourse through which "God unfolds, by slow degrees, / The purport of his deep decrees" (lines 59–60). This process continues "day by day, and year by year" (line 53).

Organic metaphors express the connection between friendship's trivial and sublime aspects, demonstrating how the Creator "From mere minutiae can educe / Events of most important use" (lines 75–76). Cowper is surprised that his sacred tie with Lady Austen,

> Rose from a seed of tiny size,
> That seem'd to promise no such prize:

> A transient visit intervening,
> And made almost without a meaning,
> (Hardly the effect of inclination,
> Much less of pleasing expectation!)
> Produc'd a friendship, then begun,
> That has cemented us in one.
>
> (lines 95–102)

This surreptitious natural process, in which friendship grows independently of the participants' conscious intention, is Cowper's means of bringing a transcendent dimension into everyday life without disruption to his daily routine.

As early as 1791 Coleridge was exploring the idea of divine providence manifesting itself through friendship. To George he versifies a vision of happiness: "Ah! being blest! for Heaven shall lend / To share thy simple joys—a friend."[46] During the 1790s Cowper came to provide an important poetic model for Coleridge.[47] In part through Lamb's influence, Coleridge began using Cowper's colloquial style as a template for his own Conversation Poems. "Frost at Midnight," in particular, bears the imprint of Book IV of Cowper's *The Task* (1785). Furthermore, in this and other poems, such as "The Nightingale" and "This Lime-Tree Bower my Prison" (1797), Coleridge's treatment of friendship develops Cowper's procedure of discovering divine meanings in quotidian settings. In "This Lime-Tree Bower," Sara's spilling hot milk over Samuel's leg and his consequent incarceration in his bower provide the mundane context for a poetic meditation culminating in Coleridge's sublime vision of brotherly unity with Poole and Lamb. (See chapters 2 and 6.)

Cowper's celebration of prosaic friendship, however, was vulnerable to satirical attack. Friendship's quotidian practices could easily offer empirical evidence that the relation was devoid of moral significance. This is illustrated by an engraving of 1798, entitled "Enjoying a Friend."[48] In their gloomy tavern the two middle-aged friends, like Cowper and Lady Austen, articulate their affection through gossip. However, there is no suggestion that divinity works through such mundane encounters between "Happy dull and stupid creatures," let alone a Yearsleyan communication of soul. Friendship is a leisure activity for the idle, consisting of a ritualized exchange of trivialities:

> Now they have had their story out
> Two hours have past a great delay
> But nothing left to talk about
> They'll meet again another day.

1: TRANSCENDENCE AND ITS LIMITS: FRIENDSHIP IN THE 1780S   79

"Enjoying a Friend." Published 21 August 1798, by Laurie & Whittle, No. 53 Fleet Street, London. © Copyright The British Museum.

Whereas for Cowper friendship's diurnal routine represents the way divinity reveals itself, for this engraver to "meet again another day" promises only the repetition of the same meaningless chatter.

Cowper, however, refuses to accept that friendship's commonplace practices are bereft of exalted meanings. Cowper's accommodation of the divine in the terrestrial world can be seen in a reification of friendship that resonates with Coleridge's own experience. In "Gratitude. Addressed to Lady Hesketh" (1788), Cowper catalogues the gifts he has received through her "Benignity, friendship and truth" (line 44).[49] These include a cap, carpets, curtains, shelves, stoves, china, a table and mirror. He thus shows how friendship reveals itself not as a union of soul but through a plenitude of material objects that have become part of his Olney home. These objects express affection in precise ways. Hesketh's gift of a moveable "wheel-footed studying chair" (line 9) embodies the idea of harmonious interaction between friends in its responsiveness to the poet's every desire for movement. Furthermore, in being "Wide-elbow'd and wadded with hair" (line 11) the chair generously accommodates Cowper's physique rather than imposing its shape upon him. Likewise, the curtains keeping Cowper's room "warm / Or cool, as the season demands" (lines 37–38) demonstrate affection by adapting themselves to the poet's physical needs. In these ways, materiality does not obscure friendship's "Idea all divine," but provides the medium in which it can be most fully expressed. Regarding Coleridge, it is Poole who expresses friendship by offering the poet material gifts and, in similar fashion to Lady Hesketh, by creating a physical environment at Nether Stowey that aims to accommodate Coleridge's material needs and wishes. (See chapter 2.)

Cowper's stress on mediating emotion, however, implicitly rejects Yearsley's idealistic notion of a communication that transcends language. Likewise, he renounces the Yearsleyan urge to dissolve the boundaries of the self in a passionate union. In "On Friendship" (1781), Cowper stresses how intimacy relies on friends controlling the intensity of feeling:

> A Temper passionate and fierce
> May suddenly your joys disperse
> At one immense explosion.
>
> (lines 52–54)[50]

When feeling turns passionate, friendship combusts. Friends who discuss controversial issues emit "sparks of disputation" (line 93) that "Most unavoidably creates, / The thought of conflagration" (lines 95–96).[51] Cowper dedicates his oeuvre to preserving amity from the threatening presence of passion. As Maurice Golden notes, Cowperian friendship requires a "very delicate sense of balance" between friends "contriving to pour out their hearts to each other and at the same time to maintain the reserves of good breeding and avoid causing embarrassment."[52] In "On Friendship," Cowper emphasizes how "manners decent and polite" (line 148) must "save it from declension" (line 150). The need consciously to sustain a friendship is both a precept and a practice in his work, as revealed in a late epigram, "On a True Friend" (1799):

> Hast thou a friend? Thou hast indeed
> A rich and large supply,
> Treasure to serve your ev'ry need,
> Well-managed, 'till you die.
>
> (lines 1–4)[53]

"Manage" resonates here with meanings established in the eighteenth century regarding the handling of people: "To treat (persons) with indulgence or consideration.... To alter one's conduct from fear of giving offence," and "to bring (a person) to consent to one's wishes by artifice, flattery, or judicious suggestions of motives."[54] Discussing eighteenth-century conversation and letter-writing, Bruce Redford has observed how

> Swift, Addison, Steele, Shaftesbury, Chesterfield, Fielding, and a host of anonymous courtesy writers ... emphasized the importance of following rules designed to achieve an ideal of "Civility," an ideal finely poised between impertinent "Freedom" on the one hand and undue "Ceremony" on the other. The theme of conscious yet unobtrusive "Management" prevails. The aim of such management, in the words of one courtesy-writer, is "to gain, conserve, or encrease the esteem and friendship of those we Converse with."[55]

For Cowper, managing friendships introduces a shrewd pragmatism into the relationship in order to satisfy the self's "needs." As he admits in "On Friendship," the observation that "friends should be sincere and just" (line 140) is one that "savour[s] much of common place" (line 143) and does not express as profound a truth as the need for good management.

Management is part of an empiricist conception of friendship to which Coleridge and his culture increasingly subscribe. Taking into account that friends may well not live up to spiritual ideals in practice, empiricist ideas reflect experiential knowledge of how embodied friends actually behave. Samuel Johnson is in this respect an exemplary and influential figure. In his "Life of Pope" Johnson suggests that management is an inevitable part of friendship, defending Pope's sycophancy to his epistolary correspondents on the grounds that

> Friendship has no tendency to secure veracity, for by whom can a man so much wish to be thought better than he is as by him whose kindness he desires to gain or keep? Even in writing to the world there is less constraint: the author is not confronted with his reader, and takes his chance of approbation among the different dispositions of mankind; but a letter is addressed to a single mind of which the prejudices and partialities are known, and must therefore please, if not by favouring them, by forbearing to oppose them.[56]

For Johnson, a familiar correspondence does not reflect mutual commitment to an idealized altruism but an individual's self-interested desire to sustain his partner's good will. As such, "veracity" between friends should not be expected.

Johnson's thoughts resonate with Coleridge's experience in his friendships. But the Romantic poet is aware of the ethical compromises an astute management of a relationship can bring. In 1801 Coleridge meditates in his notebook on the difficulties in conversing with those, like the blind, who possess "certain internal senses" not available to others:

> It is unpleasant to be much in conversation with such men. There is no *reasoning*, of course, with them / nothing is possible but naked Dissent which implies a sort of contempt—or what I am afraid a kindness is very likely to fall into, a sort of acquiescence very like duplicity.[57]

In face of such unmalleable differences of character, Coleridge senses that "kindness" is possible only at the expense of integrity. Coleridge's note was directed at his relations with Southey, but his friendships with Wordsworth and Godwin also raise difficult questions regarding the ethical concessions necessary in successfully managing a relationship in practice.

Coleridge's moral anxiety reflects a broader Johnsonian attitude towards friendship that looms large at the end of the century, especially within other explicitly anti-Platonic texts. One notable example is Eliza Hayley's *The Triumph of Acquaintance over Friendship: An Essay for the Times*, published posthumously in 1796.[58] Hayley alludes to Johnson's comment in his "Life of Pope" in order to explain her own reluctance to correspond with friends:

> I moralized, as I usually do in rural scenes in winter, with Doctor Johnson, and discovered, that letters were not the language of truth and nature, that the Friend is required to assume the stile of the Lover, as the Lover is that of the Idolater, and that my imagination was become too languid to beguile, or to be beguiled, by tender sentiments in *black and white*. (sig. a2)

In their winter setting, both Hayley and Johnson cool the flames of Platonic friendship. Criticizing the transformation of a "Friend" into the "Idol" of another's worship, Hayley attacks the quasi-religious cult of affection articulated in poems like *The Temple of Friendship*. For her, Skelton's religious diction is merely "stile," a modern fashion for hyperbolic expressions of affection that bears no relation to the "truth and nature" of actual, embodied individuals. Both Johnson and Hayley understand man to be fallen, and

1: TRANSCENDENCE AND ITS LIMITS: FRIENDSHIP IN THE 1780S   83

that the idea of transcending human nature in friendship, despite its charm, can only be delusion.

Hayley's desire to cool down her contemporaries' ideas of sacred friendship is common during the 1790s. In "Friendship Defined. An Epistle" (1791), a poem by Mr. Elderton published in *The Gentleman's Magazine*, Platonism specifically results from an "overheated" mind, inflamed by bookish fantasies. Elderton criticizes the learned "bookworms," who

> Make Friendship take seraphic flights,
> And seat it, groping in the clouds,
> Like cabin-boy among the shrouds;
> There, overheated, let it sit,
> And, shiv'ring, cool itself to wit;
> Whilst virgins of respectful age,
> And batchelors by time grown sage,
> With Plato feast, in dainty dreams,
> Tormenting Nature by extremes;
> Whose waking anger, thus mistaken,
> Will sate itself on rusty bacon.[59]

The desire for Platonic friendship is an unmanly escapism, whose feasting on idealism will inevitably be superseded by a disillusioned acceptance of the "rusty bacon" of earthly life. For Elderton, true friendship is rooted in the worldly motivation of self-interest and represents little more than a convenient union of such interests:

> High as it may with truth be painted,
> Our int'rests brought us first acquainted;
> If e'er they clash, there will be danger
> That each to each becomes a stranger.
>
> (p. 262)

Self-interest undermines friendship's aspirations for permanence, making it an inherently unstable temporal relation.

Elderton's scepticism concerning the altruism of friends informs Hayley's Johnsonian argument that an individual creates in friendship an illusion of his virtuous nature in order to gain the other's approbation. She explicitly figures the relationship as a theatrical performance of the sympathetic virtues. Although she has been "rewarded" (p. 76) by a Johnsonian "attention to the *peculiar* bias" (p. 77) of her friends, Hayley finds her dramatic power diminishing: "A *tinge* of the *yellow* leaf, begins to *warn* me of repose, and insinuates, that all actors, like GARRICK, should gracefully quit the stage before they have lost the art of imposing upon their audience" (p. 77). As "imposing" artists, friends consciously put on an act one for another in order to sustain a mutual illusion of unity. Hayley does not differ from Skelton, Yearsley, or George Bruce in trying to appear in a virtuous light; but unlike them she realizes that an act is being performed. Shifting her metaphor, she likens friendship to alchemy: "'The heart of man . . . like iron and other metal, is hard and of firm resistance when cold, but warmed, it becomes maleable and ductile'. It ought therefore to be approached with caution, when the *magick* of the alchymist is *no more*" (pp. 77–78). As the "alchymist" attempts to transmute base metal into gold, so Hayley convinces her friends that they possess characters that transcend humanity's fallen state. She remains clear that, as alchemy cannot transform iron into gold, so friends cannot indefinitely hide the baseness of their human nature from each other. At this point, self-interest demands a curtailment of Hayley's friendly performances.

Hayley's nontranscendent friendship is deduced from her empirical observations of the behavior of self-confessed "friends." Testing the idea's validity through its embodiment in action reveals it as discredited. Hayley laments that the friend is subjected to even greater moral demands than the "lover" or "statesman" whom society allows to "retreat" (p. 73) from their respective obligations to lover and country:

> Is Friendship then the only merciless tyrant, who allows no superannuated indulgence to its zealous noviciates?
> On the failure of its votaries, when the "way of life is fallen into the sear," we have indeed lamentable testimony in every historian. (p. 73)

Hayley criticizes friendship as a quasi-religious idea whose injunctions are even more stringent than those of the Catholic Church (they at least grant "indulgences"). As "noviciates," friends are continually kept at a probationary stage within the order. In this way, Hayley satirically represents the moral demands of Skelton's Goddess as being in excess of human capabilities.

The empirical history of human friendships only further discredits the moral idea. The most pre-eminent of humankind (Addison and the "sublime" Milton) were "not sufficiently elevated for this *capricious* engagement," while Johnson himself was *"insufferable,"* despite possessing a mind "expanded beyond the common limits of human nature" (p. 74). If even such superlative figures cannot meet friendship's moral demands, so Hayley argues, the idea is now irrelevant:

An Essay on Friendship now appears as obsolete as a love elegy; and we marvel at what has heretofore amused us, since our enthusiasm no longer subsists upon credit, and we readily allow with Lord Bacon, that, "good thoughts, though God accept them, yet, towards men are little better than good dreams, except they be put in act." (pp. 31–32)

Hayley dismisses the "enthusiastic" sensibility for failing the empirical test of turning "good thoughts" into action. Johnson wrote of James Hammond's love poetry:

The truth is these elegies have neither passion, nature, nor manners. Where there is fiction, there is no passion; he that describes himself as a shepherd, and his Neæra or Delia as a shepherdess, and talks of goats and lambs, feels no passion. . . . Hammond has few sentiments drawn from nature, and few images from modern life.[60]

This encapsulates Hayley's view of friendship as the creature of an emaciated, pastoral fiction. Both she and Johnson regard personal development as an ongoing experiential process of disillusionment, which is carried out through the empirical testing of ideas such as love and friendship.

What is found utterly untenable for the empiricist is Yearsley's transcendent kind of sympathetic communication between friends. In his "Life of Pope" Johnson denied that a "friend lays his heart open" when he writes a familiar letter: "The truth is that such were simple friendships of the *Golden Age*, and are now the friendships only of children" (2:206–7). Johnson would view Yearsley's ideal as belonging to an unfallen state that has been irretrievably lost—at least for adults. Hayley concurs:

The simple sensations of youth are intelligible, as they are interesting to the weakest apprehension; but when "the strife of the world thickens on every side," the ruling passion, though still in unison, takes a different bias from habit, situation and genius.

To sympathise therefore at *this* season, requires the art of the Dervise, who could throw his soul into the body of another, and for want of *such* a faculty, many well-disposed persons, in trying to commiserate a situation they do not understand, very often suggest inconveniences which had happily escaped the observation of the sufferer. (pp. 66–67)

The complexity of an adult's experience renders it inconceivable that a friend can be found to whom we may "impart griefs, joys, hopes, fears, suspicions, counsels" (p. 66) and find perfect sympathetic understanding. It is the idea that we might do so that can cause untold damage. Hayley's comments especially resonate with

Coleridge, Lamb, and Lloyd's mutual friendship during 1796–1798. These friends' initial belief in their mutual simplicity of character gives rise to a moral idealism concerning their friendship. (See chapter 6.) However, Coleridge's increasingly Haylean view of simplicity helps to ensure such idealism was short-lived. These relationships trace a narrative common to writings of the 1780s and 1790s, in which a Platonic idealism such as is expressed by Yearsley and others is in tension with a contrasting narrative of disillusionment. It is against this conflicting background—in which friendship's transcendent ideals are opened up to satirical, empiricist attack—that Coleridge's friendships take shape. Thomas Poole was the first male figure in whom Coleridge attempted to embody the Platonic Idea of the Friend. The trajectory of this crucial relationship is the subject of the following chapter.

2
Idea and Substance: Coleridge, Thomas Poole, and the Genderings of Male Friendship

ON THE EVE OF HIS EMBARKATION TO GERMANY IN 1798 COLERIDGE WAS moved to reassert that in Thomas Poole he had found a man who embodied the high ideal of friendship: "Of many friends, whom I love and esteem, my head & heart have ever chosen you as the Friend—as the one being, in whom is involved the full & whole meaning of that sacred Title—God love you, my dear Poole!"[1] In Poole, friendship's "sacred Title" becomes embodied, the verb "involve" suggesting how the Idea "rolls and enwraps" itself within Poole the man.[2] How, though, does the Divine Friend manifest himself as an embodied individual? Does embodiment express the Idea in particular kinds of social behavior? Coleridge's friendship with Poole strongly suggests that once the Idea of friendship is embodied, questions of gender intrude. Within particular social interactions the "Friend" performs specific roles that define him and the other man as gendered agents. This focus enables a reexamination of the traditional thesis that "Coleridge, like a ship drifting at sea, was drawn to the solid dependability of Poole's character and life" while Poole was attracted to the "constant intellectual stimulation" offered by Coleridge.[3] Both these tendencies are here interpreted as gendering the male relationship, constructing for each party both manly and feminine gender identities, and situating the friends in a wider gendering of the idea of friendship in the 1790s.

Contemporary writings on friendship recognized that the relation might have differently gendered modes of intercourse, a fact witnessed by the *Encyclopædia Britannica*'s entry on "Friendship" (1792). The encyclopedist reveals that friendship is widely regarded as a manly mode of intercourse, a position implied by those who argue that "women are incapable of sincerity or constancy in friendship with each other" (7:470). The *Britannica* has in mind writers like William Roberts who deny that women have sufficient moral strength for friendship. The *Encyclopædia* permits women to participate in this manly intercourse, conceding that the female character is not "totally incapable of those virtues which are necessary to establish and support mutual friendship" (7:470). In fact, the writer posits an alternative mode of friendship that is characteristically female:

> They are in general possessed of more exquisite sensibility, nicer delicacy of taste, and a juster sense of propriety, than we: nor are they destitute of generosity, fidelity, and firmness. But such qualities are peculiarly favourable to friendship: they communicate a certain charm to the manners of the person who is adorned with them; they render the heart susceptible of generous disinterested attachment; and they elevate the soul above levity, insincerity, and meanness. (7:470)

If "generosity, fidelity, and firmness" identify a traditionally masculine kind of friendship, the female virtues of sensibility, taste, and propriety define a newer, more feminine mode of intimacy. The writer thus recognizes a cultural ambiguity concerning the gendered nature of the idea, one that lurks in his conclusion: "If friendship be ranked among the virtues, it is not less a female than a male virtue" (7:470).

The history of Coleridge and Poole's relationship suggests how male friends might construct their relation in accordance with these differently gendered modes. Issues of manliness present themselves from the early days of their acquaintance during which time the men were participating in the characteristically late-eighteenth-century enthusiasm for sanctifying friendship through a quasi-marital commitment. Informing Poole of his recent marriage to Sara Fricker in October 1795, Coleridge announces: "I talked of you on my wedding night—God bless you!—I hope that some ten years hence you will believe and know of my affection towards you what I will not now profess."[4] The strength of his affection is evidenced through his willingness to think of Poole on a night reserved for the exclusive intimacy between a married couple. Coleridge intimates that their male friendship is also a tacit form of marriage, whose affection is comparable to that enjoyed by a man and wife. Coleridge's contention that his affection will be as evident in ten years time effectively signifies a formal avowal of constancy to Poole. In the *Britannica*'s terms, this would exemplify the "fidelity and firmness" of manly friendship. Coleridge signs off with a quasi-marital proposal: "Believe me, dear Poole! your affectionate & mindful—*Friend*—shall I so soon dare to say?—Believe me, my *heart* prompts it" (1:161).

In reply, Poole declared: "I cannot tell you, my dear friend, for such I am sure I may call you, how much I am interested in everything which concerns you."[5] The deliberation with which Poole in turn calls Coleridge "friend" formally sets his seal on their friendly contract. As Coleridge brings Poole into his wedding night by "talking" about him, so Poole insinuates himself within the couple's enclosed nuptial space:

> I long to look into your *message*—& see the life of youthful Poets when they love—It is now my Friend past nine oClock [?Sunday] evening— and how are you employed—perhaps you and *your Sarah* are sitting alone in expressive silence, musing on your present happiness—your swimming eyes are fixed on each other—now raised to heaven—your hearts and not your lips pour forth gratitude to the supreme Giver— may these halcyon moments long continue—and may you ever be able to cry with a bursting heart—my God I thank thee, for I am happy.[6]

Ostensibly offering innocent blessing to his friend's marriage, Poole's voyeurism opens up the intimate evening moments of the honeymoon to the male friend's gaze. As a male friend, Poole resists being excluded by the heterosexual tie. A year later he makes explicit the terms of his and Coleridge's marital contract and hints at its manly character:

> MY DEAREST FRIEND—the friend held dearest by me. *I say it thinkingly*—and say it as a *full* answer to the first part of your last interesting letter. By you, Coleridge, I will always stand, in sickness and health, in prosperity and misfortune; nay, in the worst of all misfortunes, in *vice* . . . if vice should ever taint thee—but *it cannot*.[7]

Echoing the marriage service, these vows affirm that the friends are joined in a spiritual, quasi-marital union. Poole thus constructs the men's friendship as exemplifying a conventional model of "manly love," in which male affection transcends heterosexual love, tainted as that is by sexuality.

Both Coleridge and Poole maintain this sense of the superiority of the manly bond of friendship. Explaining to Poole in 1801 why he will not publish an account of his German travels, Coleridge boasts that it is "*beneath me*—I say, *beneath me* / for to whom should a young man utter the pride of his Heart if not to the man whom he loves more than all others?"[8] Only to a male friend can Coleridge reveal his highest thoughts and aspirations. But it is Poole who most clearly defines the transcendent character of the male relation. In 1803, Poole takes issue with Coleridge's gloomy claim that earthly ties will not endure beyond the grave:

> All that is sexual may, nay must be dissolved, and certainly this bears more or less, one way or another upon a great class of our feelings—but yet there is a great class and without doubt the highest class which cannot be twined with this origin—the maternal and filial feelings and all the feelings of advanced age—advanced age! . . . when the little work of human existence is done, and is waiting to be pushed forward, by a mere inspiration, to higher and nobler objects—but we *shall advance together*, knowing as we are known—can I forget the paps which gave me suck? the Beings which have risen with me—all the objects of nature, animated and inanimated which have made me what I am—can I forget what I know of my own creation?[9]

Poole subordinates the sexual tie to more spiritual feelings accruing to familial relations, old age, and friendship itself. While Coleridge's sexual bond with Sara shall "dissolve" at death, the men friends' spiritual love transcends such earthly change: resistant to organic decay it never becomes so weak as to rely on God's inspiration "to be pushed forward." On the contrary, the male bond is active and indestructible for the friends "*advance together*" through eternity.

However, Coleridge did not during the 1790s consistently imagine friendship's "sacred Title" as a self-consciously manly love. Coleridge's "Effusion 16, To an Old Man," first published in *Poems* (1796), suggests how the human mediation of divine love in social relations entailed a more complex gender politics.[10] These issues are raised in the speaker's encounter with a debilitated old man, which Coleridge represents as imitating the actions of Jesus,

> the GALILÆAN mild,
> Who met the Lazars turn'd from rich men's doors,
> And call'd them Friends, and heal'd their noisome Sores!
> (lines 12–14)

Jesus's holy love manifests itself through his attending to the needs of the outcasts. This the poet imitates by relieving the discomfort of an old man physically suffering from cold. Coleridge offers him his coat:

> My Father! throw away this tatter'd vest
> That mocks thy shiv'ring! take my garment—use
> A young man's arms! I'll melt these frozen dews

> That hang from thy white beard and numb thy breast.
> My SARA too shall tend thee, like a Child:
> And thou shalt talk, in our fire side's recess,
> Of purple Pride, that scowls on Wretchedness.
>
> (lines 5–11)

In giving the man his coat, the speaker both expresses affection and asserts his manliness by proving himself lusty enough to go without his own clothes. With this gesture the "Father" becomes the helpless child, and Coleridge and his Sara together introduce a note of parental domesticity as they join to "melt" and "tend" him. Such domestic love has a cost. Covered once by the poet's coat, the man is sheltered a second time within the couple's inglenook. Drawn into a maternal "recess," the poet subtly strips the old man of his own manliness.

The ideals of manliness Coleridge cherishes in this sonnet also helped to shape his friendship with Poole. In their relationship, however, it is Poole whom Coleridge figures as the savior-friend, with himself often taking the old man's role. Poole's providing Coleridge with a coat (literally so) in 1797 reveals something of their complex frame of reference. In reminding Poole to send the coat, his friend's gift-giving becomes a symbolic act by which a coat is transformed into a divine "Mantle:" "You shall be my Elijah—& I will most reverentially catch the Mantle, which you have cast off.— Why should not a Bard go tight & have a few neat things on his back? *Ey? —Eh!—Eh!*"[11] The prosaic coat becomes the prophetic mantle whereby Elijah conferred upon Elisha a "double portion" of the elder prophet's "spirit."[12] Wearing the mantle, Elisha was able to divide the sea and establish himself as a prophet and king. Coleridge teasingly suggests that, in the same way that "the spirit of Elijah doth rest on Elisha" (2:15), so Poole's coat will empower the young poet. Coleridge's allusion is one of several contemporary celebrations of these prophets' friendship. In *Sacred Friendship, Exemplified In the Case of Elijah and Elisha*, Rev. Daniel Turner argues that the relationship demonstrates how attention to practicalities is an aspect of divine friendship:

> sacred friendship spurns the narrow limits of time;—darts into the invisible world of spirits, and counts on eternity, as the parallel to its own duration and perfection. This lessens not its attention to temporals, or the minutest concerns of a present life: on the contrary, it heightens the assiduity, and improves the pleasure arising from the discharge of every tender office.[13]

At the same time, Coleridge betrays a certain testiness about receiving Poole's charity. His verbal jabs—"*Eh?—Eh!—Eh!*"—assume a self-assertive persona through which the bard demands the coat as of right. Coleridge seems to protest too much, and to sense an uncomfortable dependency. The poet fights against acknowledging how Poole's gift-giving may emphasize his weakness and ongoing reliance on the charity of a stronger, less needy man. Coleridge's difficulty in expressing gratitude highlights the uneasy transfer of divine Idea into embodied friend, whose charity can create an unequal relationship grounded in one party's plenitude and the other's impoverishment. One way of evading any gender positioning regarding this is to deny that a friend need feel indebted to his partner. Poole's organizing of a subscription for Coleridge from a group of "sincere Friends and ardent Admirers" in 1796 provides a notable instance.[14] As Sandford notes, Poole contrived that the letter informing Coleridge of the annuity "should be received on the very day on which the last number of the *Watchman* was issued," which Sandford views as "the tender forethought and considerateness that belongs to real affection" (1:142). In *Sacred Friendship*'s religious terms, Poole's "attention to temporals" would signify the holiness of his affection. Coleridge's reaction, however, was less straightforward:

> If it were in my power to give you any thing which I have not already given, I should be oppressed by the letter now before me—but no! I feel myself rich in being poor; and because I have nothing to bestow, I know how much I have bestowed. Perhaps I shall not make myself intelligible—but the *strong, and unmixed Affection*, which I bear to you, seems to exclude all Emotions of *Gratitude*, and renders even the principle of *Esteem* latent and inert: it's Presence is not perceptible, tho' it's absence could not be endured.[15]

Coleridgean friendship somehow transcends emotions like "gratitude." In this, he evades the emasculating sense of dependence that charity conveys, and so make it easier for him to accept the annuity—which he did.

But elsewhere, Coleridge willingly admits that the relation's exalted nature heightens his sense of being almost effeminately weak. He declares, on 24 September 1796:

> The Heart, thoroughly penetrated with the flame of virtuous Friendship, is in a state of glory; but "lest it should be exalted above measure, there is given it a Thorn in the flesh:"—I mean, that where the friendship of any person forms an essential part of a man's happiness, he will

at times be pestered by the little jealousies & solicitudes of imbecil Humanity.—Since we last parted I have been gloomily dreaming, that you did not leave me as affectionately as you were wont to do.[16]

Ideally, "virtuous Friendship" induces an ecstatic, transcendent state of "glory" in which friends become conscious of the presence of God.[17] In practice, however, Coleridge suggests that a proper awareness of friendship's spiritual value tends to unman the involved parties, making them morbidly sensitive to any possible diminution of feeling. In the *Britannica*'s terms, Coleridge begins to exhibit an "exquisite sensibility" that is characteristically feminine. He elaborates upon friendship's potential to feminize the male subject:

> Pardon this littleness of Heart—& do not think the worse of me for it. Indeed my Soul seems so mantled & wrapped round by your Love & Esteem, that even a dream of losing but the smallest fragment of it makes me shiver—as tho' some tender part of my Nature were left uncovered & in nakedness. (1:235)

Poole's affection consists of his charitable provision of an emotional cloak. This mantle warms a deprived individual unable to clothe himself through his inner resources. In his vulnerable nakedness Coleridge figures himself as an infant and Poole, by extension, as a mother figure. Again, Coleridge's childlike condition represents a feminine position, expressing itself through a heightened sensibility whereby even the "dream" of losing the "smallest fragment" of Poole's love produces a physical "shiver" of anxious feeling. Coleridge's letter provoked Poole to reinforce his quasi-marital vow that he would stand by Coleridge, "in sickness and health, in prosperity and misfortune." Poole thereby aimed to re-establish the manly quality of the relationship. Nevertheless, such outbursts of sensibility re-emerged in December as Coleridge began to suspect Poole of no longer wishing him to settle at Stowey. (See the Introduction.)

In practice, then, the "sacred" friendship Coleridge and Poole enjoy genders the friends in various conflicting ways. If the marital mode of spiritual brotherhood emphasizes the men's manly identities, then Poole's charity creates a maternal relation that empowers the giver and emasculates the receiver. In accepting the "mantling," Coleridge embraces a mode of friendship in which male friends perform the roles of a maternal parent and needy child. Coleridge's resistance marks his adherence to a male relation grounded in equality rather than dependence. Moreover, these competing modes of male intimacy can help to unlock the nature of the men's relations at Nether Stowey during 1797–1798, and also account for increasing tensions in their friendship after 1800.

Whilst he was dreaming of the kind of relationship he would enjoy with Poole in Somerset, Coleridge told his friend in November 1796 of his excitement at living in this "beautiful country," and how it was increased by the prospect of enjoying

> these blessings *near you*, to see you daily, to tell you all my thoughts in their first birth, and to hear your's, to be mingling identities with you, as it were; . . . Thou hast been *"the Cloud"* before me from the day when I left the flesh-pots of Egypt & was led thro' the way of a wilderness—the *cloud,* that hast been guiding me to a land flowing with milk & honey—the milk of Innocence, the honey of Friendship![18]

As his guiding "Cloud," Coleridge again figures Poole as a redemptive figure. As Moses led the Israelites to Canaan, so Poole is bringing Coleridge to the holy land of Nether Stowey. In this sanctified space, friendship will articulate itself by "mingling identities," a phrase that implies mutual identification, so that each man takes on the other's character. Questions of gender are latent in this ideal "mingling." In telling Poole his thoughts "in their first birth," Coleridge suggests he will assume a childlike identity so that the friends' *mingling* might encompass a maternal bond. In *The Winter's Tale*, however, the jealous Leontes uses "mingling" to describe sexual infidelity: "To mingle friendship far is mingling bloods" (1.2.109). "Mingling identities" can thus also suggest a disturbing eroticized union, resonant of the marital bond between husband and wife.

Coleridge went on to posit a less intimate model of friendship in order to convince Poole to let him stay. Nevertheless, once ensconced at Stowey in January 1797, it was the complex idea of "mingling identities" that Coleridge and Poole attempted to put into practice. Coleridge's "Dedication. To the Reverend George Coleridge, of Ottery St. Mary, Devon" (1797), composed six months after his arrival at Nether Stowey, reveals how both maternal and marital modes of "mingling friendship" might be operating between the two friends.[19] Coleridge explains how he actively seeks in friendship to re-create original, familial bonds:

> Me from the spot where first I sprang to light,
> Too soon transplanted, ere my soul had fix'd
> Its first domestic loves; and hence through life
> Chacing chance-started Friendships.
>
> (lines 17–20)

The most important of these "first domestic loves" is the maternal bond, which Coleridge represents in the image of the bower:

> A brief while
> Some have preserv'd me from life's pelting ills;
> But, like a Tree with leaves of feeble stem,
> If the clouds lasted, or a sudden breeze
> Ruffled the boughs, they on my head at once
> Dropt the collected shower: and some most false,
> False and fair-foliag'd as the Manchineel,
> Have tempted me to slumber in their shade
> E'en mid the storm; then breathing subtlest damps,
> Mix'd their own venom with the rain from heaven,
> That I woke poison'd!
>
> (lines 20–30)

Coleridge's reference to the beautiful and seductive Manchineel tree reveals his attraction towards protective, embowering figures with feminine characteristics. The maternal friend shelters Coleridge from a hostile, stormy world in which he would otherwise struggle to survive, and he casts himself as an infant passively reliant on the nurturing care of a mother figure. He asserts that divine providence has at last introduced into his life a true friend. Coleridge gives

> all praise to Him
> Who gives us all things, more have yielded me
> Permanent shelter: and beside one Friend,
> Beneath th'impervious covert of one Oak,
> I've rais'd a lowly shed, and know the names
> Of Husband and of Father.
>
> (lines 30–35)

Through his metaphor of embowerment Coleridge describes Poole's mode of interaction and the quality of Stowey's geography. Together the "one Oak" and the "one Friend" tower over the poet, providing the protection that a mother ideally affords her child.

However, this passage also reveals the bower to be a marital as well as maternal space. Ostensibly, the oak is a synecdoche for Coleridge and Sara's wedding bower: under the oak's branches the poet has become a "Husband" and "Father." However, Coleridge not only places himself "beneath" his "one Friend" (where the friend is figured as the "one Oak") but "beside" him as well. Spatially, the two men are themselves enclosed beneath the embowering tree. In this way, Coleridge and Poole inhabit a specifically marital space, and the verse sentence leaves ambiguous whether Coleridge has become "Husband" to Sara, Poole, or both of them. By resisting the emasculating, maternal mode and placing himself "beside" his friend within the marital bower, Coleridge suggests a more equal relationship, but a more marital one. Issues of power and gender are inescapable either way.

The possibility of a conjugal relation here complicates the idea of the men's manly friendship being a spiritual alternative to sexual ties. In depicting Stowey's sacred spot as incorporating a marital bower, Coleridge's verse invites comparison with Adam and Eve's bower in *Paradise Lost* (1667):

> Thus talking hand in hand alone they passed
> On to their blissful bower; it was a place
> Chosen by the sovreign planter, when he framed
> All things to man's delightful use; the roof
> Of thickest covert was inwoven shade
> Laurel and myrtle, and what higher grew
> Of firm and fragrant leaf; on either side
> Acanthus, and each odorous bushy shrub
> Fenced up the verdant wall.
>
> (4:689–96)[20]

For Milton, the bower offers the archetypal location in which "Innocence" and "Friendship" coexist with the free expression of sexual feeling. In "To the Reverend George," Poole himself takes on the role of "sovereign planter," providing a bower for Samuel and Sara. However, the ambiguities of Coleridge's verse suggest the two men might themselves be a marital couple for whom living together at Stowey obscurely revisits Adam and Eve's Edenic experience.

Physically inhabiting this prelapsarian space, however, inevitably raises questions of eroticism between the male friends. Both contemporaneous and more recent commentators have struggled to characterize Poole and Coleridge's mutual affection. Thomas De Quincey demurely described the Poole of 1804 as "a stout plain-looking farmer, leading a bachelor life, in a rustic old-fashioned house."[21] Poole's plain looks provide De Quincey with a plausible rationale for his "bachelor life." Modern critics speculate openly about Poole's homoerotic attachment to Coleridge: "Coleridge regarded Poole as one of his closest friends," Kathleen Jones remarks, "and expressed his affection with all the extravagance of his nature. Poole loved Coleridge with an intensity and possessiveness that lead one to suspect a more passionate attachment."[22] Poole characteristically addresses Coleridge as "MY DEARLY BELOVED,"[23] and as Elizabeth Mavor notes, the appellation "Beloved" carried in this period "about the same weight . . . as 'Darling'."[24] For Jones, Poole's homoerotic attachment reveals itself most clearly in his pain at Wordsworth's growing "ascendancy over Coleridge" from 1798 (p. 107).

But Jones underplays the sensibility of Coleridge's letters. Addressing Poole in a letter written in Germany, he exclaims: "my Friend, my best Friend, my Brother, my Beloved—the tears run down my face—God love you."[25] The intensity of Coleridge's feeling blurs the categories of friend, sibling, and marital partner. However, as Richard Holmes remarks, "the freedom with which Coleridge expressed emotion to Poole at this period . . . is disconcerting precisely because it contains no homosexual implication, or at least is utterly innocent of any such awareness."[26] Holmes's insight is crucial to understanding the kind of Miltonic marriage Coleridge and Poole enjoy. Like Adam and Eve in Eden, the men's unfallen idea of friendship allows erotic impulses to be expressed while retaining their essential innocence. In this way, the marital mode can encourage a discourse of physicality between friends that can both eroticize the relationship while not undermining the union's manly or spiritual character. A Coleridgean expression of homesickness while in Germany in 1799 exemplifies this point:

> O my God! how I long to be at home—My *whole Being* so yearns after you, that when I think of the moment of our meeting, I catch the fashion of German Joy, rush into your arms, and embrace you—methinks, my *Hand* would swell, if the whole force of my feeling were crowded there.—Now the Spring comes, the vital sap of my affections rises, as in a tree![27]

It is difficult not to interpret either the tumescence of Coleridge's swelling hand or his "rising" affections as other than overtly erotic images. Coleridge's self-distancing assertion that embracing is "the fashion of German Joy" indicates his own awareness that such Goethian sensibility tests the limits of chaste models of male friendship. However, in troping such homoeroticism as seasonal energy, Coleridge both acknowledges his impulse while leaving it innocent and unspoken. As such, Coleridge's physical embrace affirms the men's heartiness rather than their homosexuality.

Coleridge also seeks at Stowey to transform the men's friendship into a filial bond between a son and his loving mother. The history of Poole and Coleridge's relationship, however, does not reveal a simple dialectic between a self-consciously manly friendship and an infantilizing kind of maternal relation. The maternal bower that Coleridge associates with Poole's village and the man himself represents an ambivalent symbol of friendship. Although it might indeed infantilize Coleridge, it also promises to invigorate his manly identity. Rachel Crawford argues that "the bower is a literary representation of an enclosed feminized landscape occupied by a woman or female object, or instilled with some feminine principle, usually (but not always) salvational for the masculine hero/poet."[28] As an embowering figure, Poole frequently performs this feminine role of providing a "prop for the poet's emergence into subjectivity" (p. 10).

In the spring of 1803, a bed-ridden Coleridge wrote to his friend that he was in immediate danger of dying. In reply, Poole invited him to recover in his bookroom in Stowey, in which

> *you may regulate the climate as you like*—in which there is even a bed though you cant see it—I promise to get you any books you want—... I will take care that neither the cold east wind nor the damp south shall break upon you.[29]

Poole's creation of the room in 1795 emphasizes how it symbolizes Poole himself. In protecting the sick child from the elements, the Poolean friendship bower becomes a maternal space. But Poole regards this not as feminizing, but empowering. He offers Coleridge a fantasy of omnipotence whereby he will "regulate the climate" as Æolus once controlled the winds. Poole thus confirms Crawford's contention that "the bower's primary function has thus been to propagandize the exemplary status of the male subject, even when that subject is undergoing a crisis of self-confidence or poetic impotency" (p. 6). Tom Mayberry joins Poole in representing the bookroom as a dynamic space for Coleridge:

> A flight of external stairs allowed him easy access to the bookroom, and there he must often have been found when the "noise of Women & children," which made study impossible, had driven him once again from Lime Street: it is probable that most of the poems associated with the cottage were at least partly written in the bookroom.[30]

The dynamism of the bookroom-bower depends upon its adapting itself like a good mother to the contours of the poet's desire. In 1797, its quiet environment is conducive to poetic production. In 1803, Poole believes the room can revive Coleridge's health by responding sympathetically to his wish for coolness or warmth. In this, it resembles the gifts given to William Cowper by Lady Hesketh in "Gratitude."

Coleridge had long taken a dynamic view of the sympathetic parental bower. This is revealed in a note written in a volume of his 1796 *Poems* that he gave to Poole:

> My very dear Friend! I send these poems to you with better heart than I should to most others, because I know that you will read them with affection however little you may admire them. I love to shut my eyes, and bring up before my imagination that Arbour, in which I have repeated so many of these compositions to you—. Dear Arbour! an Elysium to which I have so often passed by your Cerberus, & Tartarean tan-pits![31]

Conflating his "very dear Friend" with the "Dear Arbour," Coleridge again uses the bower to signify an actual place (the lime-tree bower) and Poole's parental friendship. Crucially, the bower represents a space free from criticism, excluding all voices external to the poet's ego. Here Poole's love is unconditional—he reads his friend's poems with "affection" irrespective of their objective worth. Herein lies the dynamic potential of the friendship bower. Through the sympathy it offers, the bower can invigorate Coleridge and encourage him to re-enter the world with redoubled strength. Coleridge compares his visits to Poole's arbour with Aeneas's journey to the Elysian Fields in order to meet his father Anchises (which takes him past Cerberus and the Tartarean Pits). As Anchises motivates Aeneas to found Rome, Coleridge suggests, so the sympathy Coleridge receives from his surrogate parent will spur the poet to great literary deeds.

Writing to Poole from Shrewsbury in 1798, Coleridge reveals why sympathy should have an empowering rather than merely consolatory effect:

> I wish to be at home with you indeed, indeed—my Joy is only in the bud here—I am like that Tree, which fronts me—The Sun shines bright & warm, as if it were summer—but it is not summer & so it shines on leafless boughs. The beings who know how to sympathize with me are my foliage.[32]

As Coleridge's "foliage," the sympathetic friend acts as an organic power. In the same way that the leaves of a tree enable its growth, so Poole's sympathy is vital for stimulating the poet's natural development. Elsewhere, Coleridge extends this power of sympathy into notions of place, suggesting that Poole's friendship can transform an inert environment into a beneficial, organic space. Coming to London in 1804, Coleridge writes to Poole (also in the capital) to ask whether:

> I can have a Bed at your Lodgings—... for I have such a Dread of sleeping at an Inn or Coffee House in London, that it quite unmans me to think of it—. To love & to be beloved makes hot-house Plants of us, dear Poole.[33]

Within Poole's lodgings exists a sustaining environment that can nurture the poet's delicate organization and prevent him from becoming "unmanned."

Coleridge's imaginative connection of friendship with natural environments reflects a wider cultural preoccupation. One striking example occurs within a sentimental novel, *The Cottage of Friendship, A Legendary Pastoral*, published in 1788 under the pseudonym "Silviana Pastorella."[34] This little-known text centres on its hero Mr. Bromley's discovery of two amiable sisters (Lavinia and Miranda) in a country cottage in Berkshire. The geographical environment of friendship resonates with some Coleridgean representations of Nether Stowey. In the "front" of the Cottage of Friendship "was a field, with here and there a clump of trees," while the cottage itself "stood in a crescent of stately oaks, which stood as a relief to the paler greens that more nearly encircled this seat of rusticity" (p. 15). At the climax of "Fears in Solitude" (1798), Coleridge similarly approaches Stowey across "elmy fields" (line 215) and marks the "four huge elms / Clust'ring" (lines 219–20), behind which, "hidden from my view, / Is my own lowly cottage" (lines 221–22).[35] Both cottages are screened off from the wider world by an encirclement of trees.

In *The Cottage of Friendship*, Silviana reveals that within such embowering scenes nature has an active role in transforming human relations into those of friendship. The outer walls of the manmade dwelling are covered in plants that significantly invade the human space inside. Silviana draws attention to the "honeysuckles, and jasmines, which, as if aware of the content within, had crept thro' the window of one of the apartments to join the happy Sisters" (pp. 15–16). In entering the cottage, the woodbine implants an organic element into the human world, which has the positive impact of "joining" the sisters in friendship. This linking of a natural environment with friendship is writ large in the bower that Mr. Bromley discovers within the cottage:

> [The first room] led to the Bower; the same shrubs which graced the outside, also beautified this apartment within; and the addition of roses, and many other sweets, which lent their aid to adorn this rural spot, entwining themselves in a circumambient form entirely round the sides of the room, rendered it the most fragrant and delightful Bower Mr. Bromley had ever seen. There were a number of little birds, which hopped in or out as nature directed them, and sang and built their nests in the different branches that enriched this enchanting arbour. Here restraint and confinement were banished, and every bird, insect, or animal, found the dwelling of tenderness and benevolence. (pp. 29–30)

Mr. Bromley is delighted at how a manmade apartment has internalized nature: the honeysuckle grows "outside" the apartment and "within," while the birds "hop in and out as nature directed them." There is a direct connection here between transforming a human structure into a natural bower and the proliferation of affectionate relations.

At Nether Stowey, Coleridge and Poole attempted to recreate the kind of benevolent natural environment Silviana represents. Before he moved, Coleridge anticipated that "Nature" would be one of his "six companions" at Stowey, "looking at me with a thousand looks of Beauty, and speaking to me in a thousand melodies of love!"[36] Once there, Poole's encircling garden-bower became a focus for the communication of Nature's love. William Hazlitt's recollection is instructive:

> Thus I passed three weeks at Nether Stowey and in the neighbourhood, generally devoting the afternoons to a delightful chat in an arbour made of bark by the poet's friend Tom Poole, sitting under two fine elm-trees, and listening to the bees humming round us, while we quaffed our flip.[37]

Poole's bower is a happy combination of nature and art, consisting of "bark" but nevertheless "made" by the tanner himself. In effacing the gap between human and natural space, Poole has created an area characterized by its friendly relations. Bees coexist harmoniously with humans, whose communal quaffing reinforces their mutual affection. Through the elm-trees and humming bees Hazlitt recalls the "fronting elms" (line 35) and singing "humble-bee" (line 39) of "This Lime-Tree Bower my Prison" (1797)—which he may well have heard during his stay.[38] In doing so, he intimates connections between Coleridge's poem, a natural environment conducive of friendship, and Poole. Coleridge hinted at such a connection in his letter to Southey, c. 17 July 1797, which includes probably the first version of the poem. Coleridge tells Southey the poem was written while "sitting in the arbour of T. Poole's garden, which communicates with mine" (1:334). This literally refers to the joining of the two men's gardens by a gate Poole had built, which allowed the men to pass from one to the other. As metaphor, though, "communicates" alludes to the men's interaction itself, and Coleridge appears to invite Southey to consider this when reading the poem.

In particular, the poem ponders how the embowered space in Poole's garden, so closely identified with the man himself, might provide the poet with a nurturing environment. The image of maternal love raised by the opening scenario is stressed in the version sent to Southey:

> Well—they are gone: and here must I remain,
> Lam'd by the scathe of fire, lonely & faint,
> This lime-tree bower my prison.
>
> (lines 1–3)

Coleridge's physical disablement and emotional weakness implies his need for maternal care. However, in his lowliness of spirit, the bower appears to be an oppressive rather than a healing place. Nevertheless, the poem reveals a disjunction between the poet's initial perceptions and the bower's nature. Coleridge's melodramatic complaint that he "may never meet again" (line 4) his absent friends signals that his calling the bower a "prison" may also be a misjudgement. By the poem's end Coleridge has reached a more positive interpretation: "Nor in this bower / Want I sweet sounds or pleasing shapes" (lines 28–29).

How has he achieved this new understanding? Paul Magnuson exemplifies the critical tradition that holds that the bower becomes meaningful after it has been transformed by Coleridge's imaginative power:

> The faith in the unity of creation is prior to his appreciation of its particular beauties . . . Having established the priority of his imagination and the operation of imagination in other minds, [Coleridge] opens his eyes to see whether the physical reality of the garden will corroborate his imagination.[39]

This view focuses too narrowly on the active mind of the poet shaping his experience. It does not explain Coleridge's use of the past tense when describing his perceptions:

> I watch'd
> The sunshine of each broad transparent Leaf
> Broke by the shadows of the Leaf or Stem,
> Which hung above it: and that Wall-nut Tree
> Was richly ting'd: and a deep radiance lay
> Full on the ancient ivy . . .
>
> (lines 29–34)

Coleridge stresses how he "*watch'd* / The sunshine," how the "Wall-nut Tree / *Was* richly ting'd," and how a "deep radiance *lay* / Full on the ancient ivy." The main implication of Coleridge's use of the past tense is summarized by Michael Raiger:

> The twilight scene now described and illumined by the lights of the imagination was always there before the poet's eyes, but was not previously seen. The poet does not here create the scene: he attends to the scene, albeit with a sight recreated by the lights of the imagination, which allows the poet to see the illumined beauty of the natural world.[40]

Coleridge has been gazing on this natural scene throughout, but was not conscious earlier of what he was seeing. Rereading the poem in light of Coleridge's final consciousness suggests a more dynamic interplay between the movements within the bower and Coleridge's imaginative release from his "prison." The truth Coleridge belatedly discovers is that the bower has never been an inert prison, but a place of movement and sympathy. The leaves of the embowering trees express this dynamism. As the sunlight makes visible the shadow of the upper leaf on the lower, so Coleridge becomes aware of the ongoing relationship between the two leaves. Through the play of shadow, the lower leaf offers a surface upon which every movement of the upper leaf is sympathetically recorded.

Throughout the poem, Coleridge has imitated the responsiveness of the lower leaf. The "upper leaves" to which he responds are his absent friends' movements, which inscribe themselves upon his mind. Coleridge follows in imagination their motions as they "On springy heath, along the hill-top edge, / Wander delighted" (lines 5–6), descend into the dell and re-emerge. The resemblance between the leaves' motions and Coleridge's imaginative responsiveness to his friends suggests that the bower encourages its human occupant to imitate its own naturally occurring sympathies. One of the lessons Coleridge gleans from his experience is the bower's positive effect on his spirit:

> Henceforth I shall know
> That nature ne'er deserts the wise & pure,
> No scene so narrow, but may well employ
> Each faculty of sense, and keep the heart
> Awake to Love & Beauty.
>
> (lines 40–44)

Coleridge realizes that the bower has been a neglected but loyal friend who has never "deserted" him, despite his initial sense of isolation. Nature has acted upon the speaker, "employing" his faculties and "keeping" his heart awake to affectionate feeling. Coleridge acknowledges that nature has enabled him to reach out imaginatively to his absent friends, and that the bower has therefore been quietly fulfilling its function throughout of restoring Coleridge's spirit.

Furthermore, Coleridge comes to value the bower as a space in which divinity is most fully realized. Coleridge concentrates on the sunlight's interaction with the bower's natural objects. Coleridge's interest in the links between light and deity is well known. Before he rediscovers the bower's value, Coleridge is tempted to identify Divine Spirit purely in terms of light. He orders the "glorious Sun" (line 16) to "shine in the slant beams of the sinking orb, / Ye purple Heath-flowers! Richlier burn, ye Clouds!" (lines 17–18). Sunlight penetrates the earthly flowers, clouds, and ocean until their bodily mass is infused with light. This precipitates his sublime vision of the "One Life" in which

> all doth seem
> Less gross than bodily, a living Thing
> That acts upon the mind, and with such hues
> As cloathe the Almighty Spirit, when he makes
> Spirits perceive His presence!
>
> (lines 22–26)

In the presence of "Almighty Spirit," the world becomes disembodied; for a sublime moment, "all" natural objects become merely "hues" filtering the translucent radiance of divine light.

But Coleridge resists this mystical dissolving of physical nature and returns to the bower. Within this physical space Coleridge realizes how things "bodily" can be reconciled with divinity. He emphasizes the play of light upon object:

> that Wall-nut Tree
> Was richly ting'd: and a deep radiance lay

> Full on the ancient ivy which usurps
> Those fronting elms, and now with blackest mass
> Makes their dark foliage gleam a lighter hue
> Thro' the last twilight.
>
> (lines 32–37)

Divine light irradiates but does not dissolve the materiality of the ivy and trees. Coleridge suggests that divinity needs a physical body upon which it can demonstrate its illuminating power. The bower represents a Coleridgean symbol in that it "partakes of the Reality which it renders intelligible; and while it enunciates the whole, abides itself as a living part in that Unity, of which it is the representative."[41] Despite his physical weakness, therefore, Coleridge ultimately discovers the bower to be a place of philosophical empowerment. An analogy between the bower and Poole presents itself: as Poole embodies the Idea of "the Friend" through his maternal love, so his bower becomes a symbol of divinity, which similarly manifests itself by providing a healing balm.

Coleridge's contemporaries were less certain that the bower's feminine space was so beneficial. In August, Anna Laetitia Barbauld encountered Coleridge in Bristol, after which she composed "To Mr Coleridge," a poem that suggests Coleridge had shown her a copy of "This Lime Tree Bower." For Barbauld, Coleridge's bower is more akin to Spenser's effeminate "Bower of Bliss" than the "Garden of Adonis."[42] Barbauld denies that the bower provides a setting for sublime insight into the divinity immanent in nature. Instead, she identifies it with "Circe" (line 37), the enchantress who rendered abject those whom she lured to her cell. Barbauld's bower encourages metaphysical musings that are emasculating rather than empowering:

> Here each mind
> Of finer mould, acute and delicate,
> In its high progress to eternal truth
> Rests for a space in fairy bowers entranced,
> And loves the softened light and tender gloom,
> And pampered with most unsubstantial food,
> Looks down indignant on the grosser world
> And matter's cumbrous shapings.
>
> (lines 25–32)

Barbauld alludes to Coleridge's poem in order to highlight the bower's dangers. The "light" Coleridge celebrates is "soft" and "tender," but only helps create a landscape of feminine enchantment. Barbauld warns Coleridge that by reposing in the bower he may retreat into fantasy and inactivity:

> Nor seldom Indolence these lawns among
> Fixes her turf-built seat, and wears the garb
> Of deep philosophy, and museful sits
> In dreamy twilight of the vacant mind,
> Soothed by the whispering shade—for soothing soft
> The shades, and vistas lengthening into air
> With moonbeam rainbows tinted.
>
> (lines 19–25)

The bower's feminine, "soothing soft" shades and vistas seduce the questing poet into "Indolence." Barbauld denies that the bower can play a familial role in nurturing the poet; indeed, her final prayer is that "heaven conduct thee with a parent's love!" (line 43). Influenced by Unitarianism's stress on active social reform, Barbauld suggests that true friendship takes shape in active exertions undertaken for another in the public sphere:

> And be this Circe of the studious cell
> Enjoyed but still subservient. Active scenes
> Shall soon with healthful spirit brace thy mind,
> And fair exertion, for bright fame sustained,
> For friends, for country, chase each spleen-fed fog
> That blots the wide creation.
>
> (lines 37–42)

The figure of Poole lurks in the shadows here: both his bookroom and his garden arbor provide Coleridge with a "studious cell." For Barbauld, these Circean spaces undermine Coleridge's manly identity by encouraging him to disengage from social action.

Earlier that Summer, Coleridge had himself echoed these doubts and linked them specifically to his friendship with Poole. At the end of his verse epistle to George, he also defines Poole's bower as a contemplative rather than active space:

> We in our sweet sequester'd Orchard-plot
> Sit on the Tree crook'd earth-ward; whose old boughs,
> That hang above us in an arborous roof,
> Stirr'd by the faint gale of departing May
> Send their loose blossoms slanting o'er our heads!
>
> (lines 57–61)

Ostensibly, the falling May blossoms present Poole's bower as a benevolent feminine space. However, Coleridge's sedentary posture intimates that the men's friendship is static rather than dynamic. The previous year Poole had written: "I should think myself dishonest if I allowed you to pass a hair that would prop you."[43] Here Poole's bower acts as a more substantial "prop," providing the poet with a supportive seat as well as protective roof. Coleridge's need for such physical support quietly suggests that the friendship does not invigorate the poet but preserves him from collapse.

The verse letter ends by suggesting that Poole's sympathetic space provides consolation rather than empowerment. No longer filled with the "joy of hope" (line 63) his song now sounds "deeper notes, such as beseem / Or that sad wisdom, folly leaves behind" (lines 65–66). These notes express a private grief. He tells George that, despite all the affection of his friends,

> at times
> My soul is sad, that I have roam'd through life
> Still most a Stranger, most with naked heart
> At mine own home and birth-place
>
> (lines 39–42)

Likewise, he admits that within the bower,

> tis to me an ever-new delight,
> My eager eye glist'ning with mem'ry's tear,
> To talk of thee and thine.
>
> (lines 51–53)

Behind Coleridge's "delight" is an ongoing sense of estrangement from the Ottery Coleridges. Implicitly, the value of Poole's arbour is that it offers Coleridge consolation for such loss.

Coleridge's vision of Poole's "sweet sequestered bower" expresses desire for a retreat from public life and for a sympathetic mode of maternal friendship not primarily concerned with affirming his manly identity. For both men, this maternal mode offers an opportunity of realizing, through the signs of sensibility, a feminine self. In 1801, Coleridge recounts to Poole how he met Tom Wedgwood, "who spoke of you to me with an enthusiasm of Friendship that surprized me & brought such a gush of Tears into my eyes that I had well nigh made a fool of myself in the Street."[44] In almost making a "fool" of himself, Coleridge's sensibility compromises the reserve appropriate to manly identity. In private, both men extol friendship's generation of unrestrained feelings as part of a sympathetic converse. In an early poetic celebration of his friend, Poole commiserates Coleridge's recent alienation from Southey:

> And then I mark the starting tear that steals
> Adown thy cheek, when of a friend thou speak'st,
> Who erst, as thou dost say, was wondrous kind,
> But now, unkind, forgets—I feel and weep.[45]

Coleridge sheds tears and Poole weeps effusively. Poole's sentimental lack of restraint strives to demonstrate affection to Coleridge in a way that many, including the *Britannica*, would regard as feminine.

Sympathetic tears signify one friend's confirmation of the other's viewpoint: Coleridge's recent estrangement from Southey has been "as thou dost say"—Southey's fault. This procedure is characteristic of Poole's correspondence. Thomas McCarthy argues that, "for Coleridge and Poole, as for Romantic readers in general, to 'read with affection'" requires an immersion "in the consciousness of the author" (p. 96), such that the reader literally tries to experience the same joys and agonies as the writer. In August 1796, Poole commiserates Coleridge's failure to acquire a teaching post:

> My dear fellow, you are schooled to disappointment. I hope you bear this with steadiness. You say you do, *and never tell me what is not true*.... I write immediately, to ease my own heart, for it fears that you may be impatient to be sure that it feels as you feel, and I am in hopes also that it will reach you before you leave Darley. (1:152–53)

For Poole, displays of emotional identification are crucial to sympathetic friendship.

In a letter to Poole from central Germany, October 1798, Coleridge explicitly links friendly identification to a feminine sensibility:

> My spirit is more feminine than your's—I cannot write to you without tears / and I know that when you read my letters, and when you talk of me, *you* must often "compound with misty eyes"—. May God preserve me for your friendship, and make me worthy of it![46]

Although celebrating his more exquisite sensibility, Coleridge validates Poole as a "feminine" friend, one who is also moved to tears when reading or talking of Coleridge. The men's unity of feeling is expressed in the image of one man's tears mirroring those of the other. In Miltonic terms, such feminized friends become versions of Eve who identifies "sympathy" with her watery reflection:

> As I bent down to look, just opposite,
> A shape within the watery gleam appeared

> Bending to look on me, I started back,
> It started back, but pleased I soon returned,
> Pleased it returned as soon with answering looks
> Of sympathy and love; there I had fixed
> My eyes till now, and pined with vain desire,
> Had not a voice thus warned me, What thou seest,
> What there thou seest fair creature is thyself,
> With thee it came and goes.
>
> (4:460–69)

For Milton, seeking out a mirror-image is egotistical and dangerous. In becoming attracted to her reflection, Eve risks an emotional stultification in which, Narcissus-like, she becomes consumed by self-love. For Milton, the "shadow" (4:470) of a same-sex sympathetic union must be superseded by the substance of heterosexual love.

It is here that the maternal mode of friendship conflicts with Coleridge and Poole's marital relationship. In comparing same-sex friendships with marriage, Allan Bloom draws a pertinent distinction: "The friend is a kind of true mirror in which one can see oneself. By contrast, the friendship of a couple is founded on the imperfections or incompletenesses of each of the partners requiring complements or correctives from the others."[47] Both these modes operate in Coleridge and Poole's friendship. But Bloom underemphasizes how late-eighteenth-century culture provided male friendship with a corrective and sympathetic mode. In "On the Fidelity of Friendship," an article published in *The Universal Magazine* in 1792, "Moralis" asserts the virtue of bringing a friend's true nature into view in order to perfect it.[48] This is done through "correction and admonition." All other gestures may be "intended as the intimation of esteem or affection," but are of "little worth" in that

> however greatly they may oblige, leave us as ignorant of ourselves, as uninformed of truth, and as little acquainted with our particular propensities, failings, follies, and corruptions, as they found us; but [admonition] has an immediate, a powerful, and a natural tendency to correct and improve our hearts; and so, eminently to serve us in our best interests. (p. 266)

For "Moralis," it is the "indispensable obligation of friendship" to make an individual aware of his own character, not to obscure it within a mantle of sympathy. The instructive friend provides a truly external view of his partner that may well be at variance with that person's self-image.

To Henrietta Warwick, 6 February 1796, Poole imagines himself amending the impractical habits of "Men of Genius" such as Coleridge:

> People of genius ought imperiously to command themselves to think *without* genius of the common concerns of life. If this be impossible—happy is the genius who has a friend ever near of *good sense*, a quality distinct from genius, to fill up by his advice the vacuity of his character. Indeed I think a good book might be written entitled Advice to Men of Genius. (1:134)

Poole here is not a sympathizer but an adviser, one who displays friendship by offering a more objective view of Coleridge's nature than would be possible for a sympathizing friend. Within the advice-giving scenario, male friends assume the conventional gender roles of a conjugal pair. The advisee becomes feminized as a passive receptacle whose "vacuous" character needs a male input in order to become embodied. Coleridge himself figures Poole's influence as a solid substance at the heart of his being, declaring in 1798 that Poole is "so consolidated with myself that I seem to have no occasion to speak of him out of myself."[49]

Poole implicitly figures his friendship in the Miltonic terms of the rational Adam's relation to the fanciful Eve—who, without her husband's guidance, remains open to transgressive thoughts, as her dream of temptation at the beginning of Book 5 had demonstrated (5:30–108). In advising her, Adam identifies himself with the reason that corrects her imaginative tendencies. Without this conjugal relationship, Milton's female becomes endangered. While she sleeps, for instance,

> mimic fancy wakes
> To imitate her; but misjoining shapes,
> Wild work produces oft, and most in dreams,
> Ill matching words and deeds long past or late.
>
> (5:110–13)

Reason is needed to guarantee that the lawlessness of feminine imagination is not translated into sinful acts, and it is Adam's rational advice that provides such manly restraint.

Poole's discussion of "Men of Genius" with Henrietta replicates this Miltonic ordering. Like Eve, such men possess powers of imagination which are in similar need of restraint:

Their souls seem, at times, to start from the flesh, and to mingle with their native skies. But on their return, as if wearied by the exertion, they feel more bitterly the sad weight which surrounds them, and seem sunk even below the common standard of human nature. . . . In their career they feel like other mortals the sad burdens of mortality, and these being overlooked in their scheme of life, in the form of various passions they enter the fenceless field, making unbounded havoc. . . . What a striking instance is my beloved friend Coleridge! (1:133–34)

In the unfettered activity of his "soul," the "Man of Genius" resembles the sleeping figure of Eve. Admittedly, the genius's "abstraction" is not a delusional "misjoining" of perceptions but an exalted communication with a supersensible realm. However, Poole shares Adam's anxiety that imagination might hold his partner in thrall. Left unrestrained, both Eve and the Genius, "From her best prop so far" (9:433), may be tempted to transgress. If Eve eats the apple, the Genius causes "havoc" by disregarding social "fences." In giving advice, therefore, the firm "friend" implicitly becomes an Adamic figure of manly restraint. At times, Coleridge identified himself with Eve, telling Wordsworth in 1798, "I resemble the Dutchess of Kingston, who masqueraded in the character of 'Eve before the Fall' in flesh-coloured Silk."[50] However, Coleridge's ambiguous, feminine self-image is not a psychic aberration that generates a neurotic attraction to strong male figures like Wordsworth and Poole. George Dekker emphasizes that Poole regards Coleridge as one of the "constellation of melancholy geniuses who were associated with Chatterton at the end of the eighteenth century."[51] As Poole remarks, "Spenser, Milton, Dryden, Otway, and . . . Chatterton were the same" (1:134). For Poole, Coleridge's feminine personality represents a particular cultural type—the poet of sensibility—rather than exemplifying a unique psychopathology.[52]

However, within Coleridge and Poole's marital mode there is space for both friends to correct each other and adopt the Adamic role. In 1800, Coleridge characterizes his relationship with Poole in terms of the men's mutually corrective qualities:

> We were well suited for each other—my animal Spirits corrected his inclinations to melancholy; and there was some thing both in his understanding & in his affection so healthy & manly, that my mind freshened in his company, and my ideas & habits of thinking acquired day after day more of substance & reality.[53]

Again, Coleridge plays Eve to Poole's Adam. As Adam in *Paradise Lost* literally gave "substantial life" (4:485) to Eve, so Poole's friendship provides manly "substance & reality" to correct Coleridge's effeminate, ungrounded thoughts. Coleridge confirms his friend's belief that advice-giving confers manliness upon the feminized advisee.

But Coleridge asserts that he can also be a manly friend, his animal spirits correcting Poole's tendency towards "melancholy." Here Poole is implicitly enervated by indulging in a Werterian sensibility. In 1804, Coleridge emphasizes the need for reciprocity in advice-giving: "Different Evils beset us—you shall give me advice—& I will advise you—to look steadily at every thing & to see it as it is."[54] Coleridge did periodically perform this role. Commiserating the death of Poole's mother in 1801, Coleridge refuses to offer expressions of "tenderness & sympathy":

> In truth minds, like mine & (in it's present mood) your's too, require to be *braced* rather than *suppled*. . . . I cannot too earnestly impress upon you the solemn Duty, you owe to yourself, your fellow-men, & your maker, to exert your faculties.[55]

Here Coleridge possesses the manly substance Poole needs. His "bracing" advice provides his friend with a structure within which Poole can fix thoughts that might otherwise dissolve into an emotional miasma. Coleridge enacts his precept by exhorting Poole "to devote yourself, as soon as ever the Hurry of Grief & Mutation is over, . . . to some great work" (2:764).

Clearly, there is no reason why one man cannot be both an advising and a sympathizing friend. "Write to me all things about yourself," Coleridge declares in 1796: "where I can not advise, I can console—and communication, which doubles joy, halves Sorrow."[56] Nevertheless, in practice the men's corrective mode of friendship does not easily coexist with Coleridge's demands for maternal sympathy. In 1795, Poole displays uncertainty regarding the appropriate behavior of friends. On 10 October, he admonishes Coleridge for his belligerent political rhetoric:

> You can shock—you can charm—but the wise physician and the friend of human nature will prefer that prescription which all his patients will swallow. You see that I treat you as a friend in speaking freely. If too freely, forgive me. 'Tis the head, not the heart, which errs. (1:122–23)

As a "friend of human nature," Coleridge should sympathetically adapt his message to people's differing temperaments. But such sentimental compromise jostles uneasily with Poole's criticism of Coleridge's oratorical style Poole's protest—"I treat you as a friend"—reflects anxiety that Coleridge might in this instance not regard advice as friendship. Several of Poole's acquaintance interpreted his advice-giving as an irritating lack of tact. Southey complained that "Poole would at times come clodhopping over one's feelings," and that "he was never content to be your friend, but he must be your saviour."[57] By 1800, the men's corrective mode of friendship begins to conflict with Coleridge's demand for sympathy. Coleridge's irregularity in corresponding makes Poole fear he was "acquiring the *heart-withering* faculty of losing men's *hearts* though I retained their *heads*": "I must and will endeavour to rectify it, and when I see errors and inconsistencies in those whom I love, where I can't sympathise I will at any rate be silent."[58]

Although the advising mode aims to sustain manly identity by rectifying "errors and inconsistencies," it may in practice reinforce the advisee's sense of weakness. Under the pressure of illness during 1800–1801, Coleridge confesses to Poole how burdensome the Wedgwood annuity has become. Coleridge's failure to justify the Wedgwoods' investment highlights the gap between his ideal manly self and his actual enfeebled condition:

> When I am well & employed as I ought to be, I cannot describe to you how independent a Being I seem to myself to be. My connection with the Wedgewoods I feel to be an honor to myself, & I hope, and *almost feel*, that it will hereafter be even something like an honor to them too— but—oh Poole! you know my heart & I need not reverse the picture. Now what am I to do?[59]

Coleridge dreams of how self-reliant he would be if healthy. However, he remains ill, and asking Poole for advice only highlights his sense of debilitation. Here, basing friendship on advice seems predicated on Coleridge's inability to realize the manly empowerment he so desires.

In October 1801, Coleridge's difficulty in accepting the feminine role of advisee threatens an open quarrel. Poole's refusal to fund Coleridge's trip to the Azores triggers an acrimonious Coleridgean denigration of corrective friendship:

> In general I *detest* any thing like the giving of Advice.—I was with an acquaintance lately, & we passed by a poor Ideot boy, who exactly answered my description—he
>
> > Stood in the sun, rocking his sugar-loaf Head,
> > And staring at a bough from Morn to Sunset
> > *See-saw'd* his voice in inarticulate Noises.

I wonder, says my Companion, what that Ideot means to say.—"To give advice," I replied: "I know not what else an Ideot can do, & any Ideot can do that."[60]

As an "Ideot boy," Coleridge strips the advising friend of his manly authority and the gendered hierarchy corrective friendship encourages. Instead, he constructs friendship as a nonconfrontational mode:

> It is more accordant with my general Habits of Thinking to resign every man to himself, & the quiet influences of the great Being—& in that spirit, & with a *deep, a very deep*, affection, I *now* say—God bless you, Poole! (2:765)

In his following letter of 21 October, the conflict between advising and sympathetic modes of friendship becomes explicit:

> As to myself, advice from almost any body gives me pleasure, because it informs me of the mind & heart of the adviser—but from a very very dear Friend it has occasionally given me great pain—but, so help me Heaven, as I *believe* at least that I speak truly—on his account alone—or, *if* on my own, on my own only as a disruption of that sympathy, in which Friendship has it's Being. A thousand people might have advised all that you did, and I might have been pleased; but it [was] the *you you* part of the Business that afflicted me. (2:770)

In criticizing the "*you you* part of the Business," Coleridge attacks what "Moralis" and Poole regard as a central quality of a friend—his capacity to view another man objectively in order to improve him. Instead, Coleridge here aligns friendship with the more feminine, sympathetic mode that strives to efface the sense of "I" and "you." Coleridge's complaints against the advising friend were widely echoed throughout the 1790s. In *The Universal Magazine* (1794), "C. C." identifies the impertinent "counsels" of friends as one reason why "Friendship is to love, what an engraving is to a painting":

> Friends frequently become insupportable in adversity; they abound in counsels contrary to our inclinations, and reproach us with the faults we may have committed; they blame the principle whence they arose, although in other cases they have a thousand times admired it. When fortune is adverse, the suffering friend becomes a subject, upon which self-love, and an imperious mind are anxious to exercise an empire.[61]

Coleridge's critique of advice is as much strategic as it is principled, motivated by a desire to attack his friend's judgmentalism. However, it reveals his increasing difficulty in sustaining a conventional manly mode of male intimacy. Convalescing from illness, Coleridge attempts to reaffirm to Poole the characteristically masculine quality of their marital mode: "It mingles with the pleasures of convalescence, with the breeze that trembles on my nerves, the thought how glad you will be to hear that I am striding back to my former health with such manful paces."[62] However, Coleridge cannot sustain this discourse of masculine empowerment. Mentioning a new prospective "Work," he quickly reasserts his desire for Poole's maternal friendship:

> O my dear dear Friend! that you were with me by the fireside of my Study here, that I might talk it over with you to the Tune of this Night Wind that pipes it's thin doleful climbing sinking Notes like a child that has lost it's way and is crying aloud, half in grief and half in the hope to be heard by it's Mother. (2:669)

Coleridge identifies himself with the lost "child" and Poole with the comforting "Mother." Coleridge desires again to retreat into the embowered, fireside recess he had celebrated in the sonnet "To an Old Man." But in 1801 it is Coleridge who needs to be tended, "like a Child." The child's crying hovers between "grief" and "hope." The ambivalence suggests that Poole's maternal role also remains poised between offering Coleridge consolation and, more dynamically, hope of recovery. However, the doleful notes of the "Night Wind" ominously foreshadow "the dull sobbing Draft, that drones and rakes" (line 6) through "A Letter to —" (1802).[63] It suggests the advent of a dejection of spirit that neither Poole's maternal nor marital modes of friendship would allay.

3
Coleridge, Southey, and the Problem of Pantisocratic Friendship

IN SEPTEMBER 1794 COLERIDGE AND SOUTHEY WERE MAKING PLANS, AN "outline" of which was recorded by Poole during the young radicals' visit to Nether Stowey that month:

> Twelve gentlemen of good education and liberal principles are to embark with twelve ladies in April next. Previous to their leaving this country they are to have as much intercourse as possible, in order to ascertain each other's dispositions, and firmly to settle every regulation for the government of their future conduct.¹

The government of Coleridge and Southey's future was already known as "Pantisocracy." On the banks of the Susquehanna River the "Emigrators" would create an egalitarian community in which every man would labor for only "two or three hours in a day" (1:97), and whose members would share equally of the produce. There was much to be done before departure. Poole emphasizes the need of ascertaining through an intensive "intercourse," the emigrants' respective "dispositions," that is, their "bent of the mind. *esp.* in relation to moral or social qualities."² This chapter examines how the Pantisocratic idea encouraged Coleridge and Southey to reveal their "dispositions" regarding friendship, and how their conflicting ideas helped shape and break both the scheme and the men's relationship. Pantisocracy provides a testing-ground for friendship, a context for negotiating between the Idea and its practical realization. Once again, the trajectory of an individual Coleridge friendship helps uncover some of the detailed nuances of a concept that develops in response to the particular pressures of the relationship.

The "disposition" Coleridge discovered in Southey in July 1794 was one much inclined to William Godwin's *An Enquiry Concerning Political Justice* (1793).³ As Southey later recalled of his first reading, "I read, and all but worshipped."⁴ Southey seems to have found congenial Godwin's views on friendship, which came to have considerable impact on Southey's connection with Coleridge and Pantisocracy. In *Political Justice*, Godwin develops a rationalist, antisentimental concept of friendship, which arises from his demand that justice inform all human actions. Godwinian justice involves a disinterested benevolence and a rigid subordination of self to society. He insists that personal relationships should not to be exempt from its demands: "I ought to prefer no human being to another, because that being is my father, my wife or my son, but because, for reasons which equally appeal to all understandings, that being is entitled to preference" (2:852). To do otherwise is to be guilty of "partiality":

> All partialities strictly so called, tend to the injury of him who feels them, of mankind in general, and even of him who is their object. The spirit of partiality is well expressed in the memorable saying of Themistocles, "God forbid that I should sit upon a bench of justice, where my friends found no more favour than strangers!" In fact, . . . we sit in every action of our lives upon a bench of justice; and play in humble imitation the part of the unjust judge, whenever we indulge the smallest atom of partiality. (2:855)

Themistocles' privileging of a friend's interest is reprehensible to the degree that it puts the good of a part before the good of the whole.

In behaving partially, a man tends to be motivated by feeling rather than reason. Godwin criticizes "philanthropy, as contradistinguished to justice" for being

> rather an unreflecting feeling, than a rational principle. It leads to an absurd indulgence, which is frequently more injurious than beneficial even to the individual it proposes to favour. It leads to a blind partiality, inflicting calamity without remorse upon many perhaps, in order to promote the imagined interest of a few. (1:260–61)

Godwin scorns affections arising from "unreflecting feeling" rather than "rational principle," notoriously condemning gratitude as

> a sentiment, which would lead me to prefer one man to another, from some other consideration than that of his superior usefulness or worth: that is, which would make something true to me (for example this preferableness), which cannot be true to another man, and is not true in itself. (1:84)

A man should be judged according to an impartial moral principle and not be the recipient of sentimental favors. But if he is truly worthy, then he will be preferred by all reasonable men.

Godwin's rejection of "partial" friendships, however, does not constitute a rejection of friendship per se. On the contrary, he celebrates what he calls a "just affection" (2:855), an emotional response called into being by an act of reason. These "just affections" are grounded in the "virtuous" qualities one man discerns in another. Godwin defines "virtue" thus: "Considered as a personal quality it consists in the disposition of the mind, and may be defined a desire to promote the benefit of intelligent beings in general, the quantity of virtue being as the quantity of desire" (1:254). A virtuous man is one who acts justly, and Godwin stresses how his capacity to do so is linked to his knowledge and understanding of what is best for society. There is an almost mathematical correlation between a man's virtues and the affection that he receives. Godwin is adamant that "the virtuous man only has friends" and the means to win "esteem and affection":

> He who merits the esteem of his neighbours and fellow citizens, will at least be understood by a few. . . . There is perhaps no instance in which such men have not had a few friends of tried and zealous attachment. There is no friendship but this. No man was ever attached to an individual but for the good qualities he ascribed to him; and the degree of attachment will always bear some proportion to the eminence of the qualities. Who would ever have redeemed the life of a knave at the expence of his own? And how many instances do there occur of such heroic friendship where the character was truly illustrious? (1:370)

In defining affection as being "proportionate" to "good qualities," Godwin exposes the extreme rationalism of his position. Moreover, his analysis of the motivations for friendship shades from description ("no man was ever attached") into prescription ("attachment will always bear"). This exhortation that men befriend only the virtuous reflects the extent to which "Justice obliges us to sympathise with a man of merit more fully than with an insignificant and corrupt member of society" (2:855). Godwin is confident that these "illustrious" individuals can be found, and that virtue is sufficient to guarantee others' friendship:

> Exclusively of all groundless and obstinate attachments, it will be impossible for me to live in the world without finding one man of a worth superior to that of any other whom I have an opportunity of observing.

To this man I shall feel a kindness in exact proportion to my apprehension of his worth. (2:851)

Friendship is the inevitable concord of reasoning minds, and Godwin has faith that reasonable men will recognize those objective virtues that shine through a worthy man's conduct.

During the summer of 1794, it was something like these Godwinian ideas that helped shape Southey's conception of the Pantisocratic community he was about to establish in America. In a sonnet sent to Horace Bedford in August, he announced his allegiance to the idea of "just affection":

> If ought to Freedom friendly it convey
> To Peace or Justice, haply the Bards lay
> May not have flowd in vain.[5]

Southey's "friends" here are the abstract principles of Freedom, Peace, and Justice. Like Godwin, friendship for these principles means a concomitant hostility to sentimental, "groundless and obstinate attachments":

> To the distant shore
> Where Freedom spurns Oppressions iron reign
> I go: not vainly sorrowing to deplore
> The long-loved friends I leave to meet no more,
> But the high call of Justice to obey. (1:65)

To sorrow for those left behind merely because of the duration of the attachment would be "vain" in that the poet would unjustly place his personal affections before the public good. Southey does not deny that his "long-loved friends" are worthy of affection. However, he will remain loyal to them only if their behavior squares with the demands of Justice, embodied in the scheme of emigration.

In this first flush of Pantisocratic ardor Southey contends that his friendship is governed by the extent to which a particular individual embodies the set of virtuous principles. In response to Bedford's aristocratic disdain for one of his "republican" friends, Southey declares: "the man whose principles make you shun him—is most exemplary in his life. Those very principles have rescued him from libertinism—and made him deserving of my friendship. Those same principles make me what I am."[6] Principles represent the core of Southey's identity, and the most important aspect of his friend. Friendship inevitably results from the meeting of reasoning minds united by their intellectual commitment to a shared ideology. Ultimately, what binds these friends together is duty. In *Political Justice*, Godwin had defined "duty" as "the mode in which any being may best be employed for the general good" (1:101). A passage from *Caleb Williams* (1794) exemplifies that a man's obligation to act "for the general good" is sufficient motive to lead him into friendship. In fleeing his master's persecution, Caleb encounters Mr. Collins, whose striking virtue gives him hope that they will become friends:

> The more he excited my admiration, the more imperiously did my heart command me, whatever were the price it should cost, to extort his friendship. I was persuaded that severe duty required of him that he should reject all personal considerations, that he should proceed resolutely to the investigation of the truth, and that, if he found the result terminating in my favour, he should resign all his advantages, and, deserted as I was by the world, make a common cause, and endeavour to compensate the general injustice.[7]

As a man has a "severe duty" to behave justly at all times, so he is obliged to befriend a particular individual if he thereby furthers the general good.

Like Caleb, Southey argues that duty has a central role in binding together the Pantisocratic community and, in particular, Coleridge and himself. "It is my duty to depart," he tells Horace Bedford in August: "should the resolution of others fail, Coleridge and I will go together, and either find repose in an Indian wig-wam—or from an Indian tomahawk."[8] Southey's confidence that Coleridge will join him in duty to a greater principle reflects the extent to which he sees Coleridge as a Godwinian man of virtue. At their first encounter in June 1794, Coleridge embodied for Southey Godwin's demand that the "friend" be a man of outstanding moral and intellectual excellence. As he exclaims to Grosvenor Bedford, Coleridge "is of most uncommon merit,—of the strongest genius, the clearest judgement, the best heart. My friend he already is, and must hereafter be yours."[9] In telling Grosvenor that he too "must" become Coleridge's friend, Southey argues in Godwinian terms that friendship with the meritorious Cantab is inevitable, a happy mixture of inclination and obligation.

The extent to which Coleridge viewed his friendship with Southey in these Godwinian terms would be revealed over the coming months. His first letter to Southey, however, despite acknowledging the latter's Godwinism, marks out a very different conception of friendship. Greeting Southey with "Health & Republicanism!" he declares: "You are averse to Gratitudinarian Flourishes—else would I talk about hospitality, attentions &c &c—however as I must not thank you, I will thank my Stars."[10] What Coleridge values is "attentions"—that is, "the action of attending to the comfort and pleasure of others; ceremonious politeness, courtesy."[11] It is Southey's ability to focus on Coleridge's particular needs that signifies for him Southey's incipient affection. Coleridge therefore puts forward a philosophical response to the Godwinian view of friendship, which has recently been developed in more general terms. Lawrence Blum summarizes Iris Murdoch's view that

> morality has everything to do with our concerned responsiveness—what she also calls "loving attention"—to other particular individuals, where this responsiveness involves an element of particularity not reducible to any form of complex universality. . . . Thus loving attention to a friend or to one's child involves understanding his or her needs and caring that they are met. The moral task is not a matter of finding universalizable reasons or principles of action, but of getting oneself to attend to the reality of individual other persons.[12]

Murdoch's "loving attention" is a Coleridgean and anti-Godwinian idea. It locates the moral work of friendship in a friend's concern with needs not immediately justifiable as being beneficial for the greater social good. Coleridge's unhappy experience in the Dragoons had recently highlighted for him the importance of his friends' attentive concern. Thanking George Cornish for visiting him, Coleridge exclaims: "My heart thanks you, dear Sir! for the kindness and delicacy of your attention towards me,"[13] an action he praises to his brother George as displaying "much apparent solicitude of Friendship."[14] "Solicitude" identifies attentive friendship as entailing a scrupulous and tender caring for another's embodied needs (which characterizes Jesus's affection in "To an Old Man"). It was the absence of this particularized sympathy that Coleridge would come to lament in himself, when he remarked to Southey in 1803 that he possessed "a faulty delight in the being beloved" without having "any thing to give in return beyond general kindness & general Sympathy—both indeed unusually warm, but which, being still *general*, were not a return in kind, for that which I was unconsciously desiring to inspire."[15]

In his second letter to Southey in 1794, however, Coleridge suggests how friendly attention might work in practice, by including his first manuscript version of "Lines Written at the King's Arms,

Ross, Formerly the House of the 'Man of Ross.'"[16] Coleridge defines the "Departed Merit" (line 4) of the "man of Ross" (line 3) in Murdochian terms:

> Friend to the friendless, to the sick Man Health
> With gen'rous joy he view'd his modest wealth.
> He heard the Widow's heav'n-breath'd prayer of Praise,
> He mark'd the shelter'd Orphan's tearful gaze—
> And o'er the dowried Maiden's glowing cheek
> Bade bridal love suffuse it's blushes meek.
>
> (lines 5–10)

The "man of Ross" does not limit his affections to those who can prove themselves morally worthy. Instead, Coleridge emphasizes how the man "heard" and "mark'd" individuals' various complaints, be they a widow's lament or an orphan's unhappy tears. Through this particularized attention the man provides appropriate care, such as "Health" to the "sick Man." Like Murdoch after him, Coleridge understands such "loving attention" to be a deeply moral act. He invites travellers to

> Fill to the good man's name one grateful glass!
> To higher zest shall Memory wake the Soul,
> And Virtue mingle in the sparkling Bowl.
>
> (lines 12–14)

The "Virtue" imbibed by the reader is not an abstract principle of justice but the desire to imitate the old man's practical acts of loving kindness.

Sentiments such as these inform Coleridge's key theoretical statement on Pantisocratic friendship, which he develops earlier in this letter:

> Warmth of particular Friendship does not imply absorption. The nearer you approach the Sun, the more intense are his Rays—yet what distant corner of the System do they not cheer and vivify? The ardour of private Attachments makes Philanthropy a necessary habit of the Soul. I love my Friend—such as he is, all mankind are or might be! The deduction is evident—. Philanthropy (and indeed every other Virtue) is a thing of Concretion—Some home-born Feeling is the center of the Ball, that, rolling on thro' Life collects and assimilates every congenial Affection. (1:86)

Coleridge puts forward a theory of personal friendship and of social benevolence. Like the "man of Ross," a friend must attend to the "reality of individual other persons," loving the concrete being of his friend—"such as he is." It is from this particularized concern that friends learn "habits" of benevolence: domestic affections generate the benevolent energy needed to give impetus to a wider altruism, represented in the dynamic image of a "Ball" of beneficence rolling outwards from family and friends to society at large.

David Hartley's *Observations on Man* (1749), a well-known source of Coleridge's ideas here, draws further attention to the anti-Godwinian tenor of Coleridge's condensed argument.[17] As Leonard Deen remarks, "where Hartley differs from Godwin is in the concrete historicism of his account of human development and education. Godwin's rationalist utilitarianism tended to ignore concrete experience; Hartley's more sentimental or feeling-full utilitarianism appealed to it at every point."[18] Sentimental friendship provides for Coleridge this "concrete experience," and its elemental "home-born Feelings" are, as Kelvin Everest remarks, "an ultimate source of what Hartley called 'sociality'" (p. 80). "Sociality" is "the pleasure which we take in the mere company and conversation of others, particularly of our friends and acquaintance, and which is attended with mutual affability, complacence, and candour," and Hartley traces these pleasures back to those bestowed on children by "parents, attendants, or play-fellows" (1:472). Whereas Godwin conceives affection to be contingent on an individual's moral worth, Hartley finds sociality itself to be the source of virtue. Whether in adults or children, "good-will, or benevolence" (defined by Hartley as "that pleasing affection which engages us to promote the welfare of others to the best of our power") is

> connected with sociality, and has the same sources. It has also a high degree of honour and esteem annexed to it, procures us many advantages, and returns of kindness, both from the person obliged and others; and is most closely connected with the hope of reward in a future state. (1:473–74)

The pleasures and rewards that the child associates with domestic sociality become in later life the psychological motivation for the adult's wider beneficence.

But Coleridge adds to Hartley's account by stressing the passionate intensity of these seminal domestic attachments, arguing that these bonds are the site of a solar energy (with the potential to burn outsiders who approach too close). It is the fiery ardor of a friendship's benevolent feelings that makes a wider altruism possible. Nicola Trott notes that, "given the symbolic value of Coleridge's suns, the natural emanation of human love is implicitly an imitation of the divine."[19] Coleridge thus argues that divinity manifests itself within domestic friendship through the sunlike energy that ideally characterizes these attachments. Coleridge's remarks not only offer Southey a template for their friendship but a manifesto for the Pantisocratic community. Characterized by the strength of their affectionate bonds—which would express itself in loving attention—this Christian group would create the conditions for a dynamic Hartleian generation of benevolence, and thus become a model for a reformed society.

To maximize the affectionate energy among the prospective Pantisocrats, Coleridge desires in Autumn 1794 to transform the emigrants' mutual friendship into closer, familial bonds. Already in September, he asks Southey to "remember me to your Mother—to our Mother—am I not affiliated?"[20] In particular, Coleridge desires to create familial friendship through a series of marriages between the Oxbridge students and the various Fricker sisters. He urges Southey to "Make Edith my Sister—Surely, Southey! we shall be frendotatoi meta frendous. Most friendly where all are friends. She must therefore be more emphatically my Sister."[21] Coleridge's enthusiasm is characteristic of many contemporary celebrants of friendship who would smilarly mechanically will affectionate bonds into being. In becoming one family, Coleridge hopes to guarantee an interdependent set of passionate sibling and marital relations, grounded in "sociality" and loving attention. He develops this idea to Edith Fricker, in a letter proposing that their future friendship incorporate an unconditional familial love. Urging her to announce to him, "I will be your Sister—your favorite Sister in the Family of Soul," Coleridge declares:

> There is no attachment under heaven so pure, so endearing. The Brother, who is blest with it I have envied him! Let whatsoever discompose him, he has still a gentle Friend, in whose soft Bosom he may repose his Sorrows, and receive for every wound of affliction the Balm of a Sigh.[22]

Friendship here is sentimental, familial, and anti-Godwinian in its expression of the partial love of siblings for each other. Characterized by a sister's sympathetic attention to her brother, Coleridge founds familial friendship not on the parties' Godwinian virtue, but on their kinship.

3: PROBLEM OF PANTISOCRATIC FRIENDSHIP

Whereas Godwinian friendship depends on merit and is thus inherently elitist, Coleridge's sentimental-familial model envisions a more inclusive Pantisocratic community. As a Christian brotherhood, even animals would be embraced within the Pantisocrats' family:

> I call even my Cat Sister in the Fraternity of universal Nature. Owls I respect & Jack Asses I love: for Aldermen & Hogs . . . I have not particular partiality; they are my Cousins however, at least by courtesy. . . . May the Almighty Pantisocratizer of Souls pantisocratize the Earth.[23]

A Pantisocrat fosters affection for the whole family of God's creation. Coleridge's sentimental enthusiasm is displayed most notoriously in his "Address to a young Jack Ass & it's tethered Mother," sent to Southey in December 1794.[24] In these anti-Godwinian lines, Coleridge takes pity on a foal:

> Poor little Foal of an oppressed Race,
> I love the languid Patience of thy Face!
> And oft with friendly hand I give thee Bread,
> And clap thy ragged Coat & pat thy Head.
>
> (lines 1–4)

Coleridge's "friendly hand" does not express his admiration for the foal's superlative merit but his attentive compassionating with the animal's distress. Like the man of Ross (and Jesus himself) Coleridge's friendliness shows concern for the foal's physical condition, which he tries to comfort through his consoling touch.

To the Godwinian, friendship with animals is impossible. Mary Wollstonecraft exemplifies the rationalist's argument for limiting friendship to human beings:

> Animals have not the affections which arise from reason, nor can they do good, or acquire virtue. Every affection, and impulse . . . are like our inferior emotions, which do not depend entirely on our will, but are involuntary. If you caress and feed them, they will love you, as children do without knowing why; but . . . what principally exalts man, friendship and devotion, they seem incapable of forming the least idea of. Friendship is founded on knowledge and virtue, and these are human acquirements.[25]

Deprived of reason, the animal has no conception of "virtue" and therefore cannot discriminate between a worthy and unworthy object of affection. Coleridge, however, responds positively to the foal's affectionate gestures towards him:

> How askingly it's steps toward me bend—
> It seems to say—"And have I then one Friend?["]—
> Innocent Foal! thou poor despis'd Forlorn!—
> I hail thee Brother, spite of the Fool's Scorn!
> And fain I'd take thee with me in the Dell
> Of high-soul'd Pantisocracy to dwell.
>
> (lines 23–28)

The foal's question has such emotional appeal that Coleridge declares a passionate bond of brotherhood between himself and the animal. The Pantisocratic "Dell" marks the bucolic spot in which he might realize his sentimental ideal of familial friendship for all God's creation.

However, Coleridge and Southey had not adopted entirely contradictory notions of friendship. During 1794–1795, Coleridge seriously attempted also to embrace Southey's Godwinian mode. He initially valued Southey on his merits, praising in July Southey's "high advantages" (which include "Health, Strength of Mind, and confirmed Habits of strict Morality" [1:85]), while in September he declares himself "delighted to feel you superior to me in Genius as in Virtue."[26] In this letter, Coleridge also represents his marriage to Sara as having a higher motive than sentiment: "Yes—Southey—you are right—Even Love is the creature of strong Motive—I certainly love her" (1:103). Coleridge's "love" for Sara derives from the importance of their becoming Pantisocratic partners, and is implicitly justified by their desire to create the perfect community. George Burnett recollected in 1796 that the Pantisocratic commune would have been characterized by its Godwinian meritocracy. As he explains to Nicholas Lightfoot:

> In the present state of society, the love of di[stin]ction, the strongest motive to action, h[as] [f]or its gratification, the accumulation of [we]alth. In such a state as I am describing this passion would be diverted into a more proper channel. Here no man would gain applause or distinction from his fellow-men, unless by superiority of genius and virtue.[27]

In this scenario, affectionate applause would only be given out in recognition of merit. Burnett presents his views as the settled opinion of the Pantisocrats, which suggests Coleridge's acquiescence in this Godwinian scheme.

Coleridge's *A Moral and Theological Lecture, Delivered at Bristol* (1795) provides the clearest evidence that he imagines the Pantisocrats as combining Godwinian and familial models of friendship.

Coleridge contemplates the true character of the "friends of Freedom":[28]

> We turn with pleasure to the contemplation of that small but glorious band, whom we may truly distinguish by the name of thinking and disinterested Patriots. These are the men who have encouraged the sympathetic passions till they have become irresistable habits, and made their duty a necessary part of their self interest, by the long continued cultivation of that moral taste which derives our most exquisite pleasures from the contemplation of possible perfection, and proportionate pain from the perception of existing depravation. (p. 12)

In cultivating "sympathetic passions" until they become "habits," Coleridge reiterates Hartley's associationist model of benevolence. However, he ends with the Godwinian notion that the Patriot's "moral taste" is nurtured not through private attachments but through contemplating an abstract perfection. Furthermore, Coleridge describes how each Patriot "looks forward with gladdened heart to that glorious period when Justice shall have established the universal fraternity of Love. These soul ennobling views bestow the virtues which they anticipate" (p. 13). The Patriots combine a commitment to Godwinian "Justice" with a Christian, familial ideal of spiritual brotherhood. In fact, Coleridge argues that meditating on "Justice" directly leads the Patriots to a renewed sense of universal fraternity.

Coleridge ended by praising them as some of the "few men . . . whose intellects surpass the common stature, and who describe the green vales and pleasant prospects beyond them" (p. 19). In 1795, Pantisocracy literally represented one "green vale" that the "friends of Freedom" might inhabit. The connection Coleridge makes in his lecture between a just and a loving society is crucial to the cluster of ideas that informed Pantisocracy. In describing the scheme's conflicting Godwinian and Unitarian philosophic bases, Nicholas Roe distinguishes between the creation of a just society and a friendly one. For Coleridge, Pantisocracy's "equalitarian principles were not wholly political or economic, but religious and emotional as well: Pantisocracy was to be a 'family of Love'."[29] Several of its tenets suggest, however, that "friendship" provided the Pantisocrats with an idea that might unify their desire both for a religious community of love and a politically equitable society. Godwin and the Pantisocrats both agree that equality of labor was a necessary step in the perfectibility of man, and they link it with a spirit of friendliness. In *Political Justice*, Godwin declares:

> If superfluity were banished, the necessity for the greater part of the manual industry of mankind would be superseded; and the rest, being amicably shared among all the active and vigorous members of the community, would be burthensome to none. . . . None would be made torpid with fatigue, but all would have leisure to cultivate the kindly and philanthropical affections of the soul. (2:806)

The just division of labor testifies to a society's "amicable" nature. By giving men sufficient leisure time, this equalization would directly encourage the growth of friendly feelings within the community.

Coleridge validates such sentiments in a passage inserted into "Monody on the Death of Chatterton" for his 1796 *Poems*:

> O, CHATTERTON! that thou were yet alive!
> Sure thou would'st spread the canvass to the gale,
> And love, with us, the tinkling team to drive
> O'er peaceful Freedom's UNDIVIDED dale;
> And we, at sober eve, would round thee throng,
> Hanging, enraptur'd, on thy stately song!
> (lines 126–31)[30]

Chatterton's "love" of ploughing the fields with Coleridge suggests how Coleridge closely links his friendship to their equality of labor. This amity is mutual, for in their leisure time, the group would delight in hearing Chatterton's verse. Central to these convivial scenes is the "UNDIVIDED dale," which draws together the group's equality of labor and social unity with the scheme's central tenet: "Aspheterism," or the abolition of property.

In linking aspheterism to the creation of friendship, the Pantisocrats situate themselves within a wider contemporary debate. The *Encyclopædia Britannica* presents a more conservative position by contrasting modern relations with those of "the ancients," who "required still a closer union and a more disinterested attachment among friends than we dare venture to insist upon":

> Indeed, might we suppose all mankind absolutely faultless, . . . we need not fear . . . bad consequences from unbounded confidence in our friends. But friendship would in such a state of society be unknown; just as in the golden age of the poets there are supposed to have been no distinctions of property. (7:471–72)

Opposing such attitudes is Godwin, who writes in 1797: "I cannot ardently love a person who is continually warning me not to enter his premises, who plants a hedge about my path, and thwarts me in the impulses of my heart."[31] The logic of Godwin's metaphors suggests that friendship ideally desires to amalgamate the privacy of two individuals.

In 1794, the Pantisocrats went further than Godwin, who favored only the equalization of property. Nevertheless, aspheterism also expresses Coleridge's belief that a just organization of society will inevitably allow affection to flourish. This Coleridge elaborates in his account of the Jewish Commonwealth in his second Bristol lecture, which, for Nigel Leask, represents "a more complete theory of Pantisocracy than the fragments which have survived in letters and poems of the period."[32] Coleridge describes the positive effect of the Jews' imposition of a Jubilee, whereby private property would be relinquished every fifty years:

> The Hope of aggrandising their Family, which is so frequently the motive to Injustice, was nipped in the Bud—and where Ambition and the other selfish Influences do not powerfully counteract, the Sympathies of our Nature lead us to Benevolence. Hence such a spirit of Fraternity might be gradually produced by the expectation, as almost to supersede the actual execution of the Law. (p. 127)

By establishing an equitable social framework, Coleridge imagines that man's "naturally" sympathetic instincts will emerge. Coleridge's vision of Mosaic society is not dissimilar to Godwin's argument that "the narrow principle of selfishness would vanish" if property were equally distributed, as no man would be "obliged to guard his little store." Godwin also assumes that friendship would result: "No man would be an enemy to his neighbour, for they would have nothing for which to contend; and of consequence philanthropy would resume the empire which reason assigns her" (2:810). In 1794 Coleridge aimed to put this social theory into practice in an American vale.

Pantisocracy, then, represented a politically radical idea. Roe notes the radicalism inherent in the group's Hartleian Unitarianism. By encouraging habitual benevolence, the Pantisocrats would create "a model society, a 'center' from which the cumulative momentum of affection would proceed to the regeneration of 'all mankind'" (p. 113). At the same time, these friends would be united by a Godwinian commitment to a just society, embodied in the equitable rules governing the utopia. These rules would reinforce the friendship already enjoyed within the families by eradicating the conditions that discourage amity. Once more, the rational idea could be brought into line with the emotional reality. In general, though, critics associate Southey with the Godwinian elements in the scheme and Coleridge with the Christian and Hartleian ideals of friendship. For Roe, "the philosophic bases of Southey's and Coleridge's respective ideas of Pantisocracy were contradictory": Coleridge would have responded to Southey's Godwinism by insisting that, "love and friendship were the means to human regeneration, and in this respect Coleridge was fundamentally at odds with Godwin's disinterested rationalism in *Political Justice*" (p. 115). This oversimplifies the extent to which both men shared conflicting philosophies of Pantisocratic friendship. Nicola Trott concedes that Coleridge's attitude to Godwin was "complicated by his friendship with Southey" (p. 212) and it is this complexity I wish to explore. It becomes apparent that the friends try to reconcile sentimental-familial and rationalist-Godwinian modes in their relationship, and that these conflicting discourses helped tear apart the Pantisocratic idea and the men's friendship.

Despite the differences in their individual temperaments, both men value the energetic affection of sentimental "home-born" relations. Coleridge boasts that the warmth of his affections underpins his capacity for friendship, responding thus in September 1794 to a critical letter of Southey's: "My fire was blazing chearfully—the Tea-kettle even now boiled over on it—how sudden-sad it looks! but see—it blazes up again as cheerily as ever!—Such, dear Southey! was the effect of your this morning's letter on my heart."[33] The energy burning in Coleridge's heart is so intense that it brings his affections to boiling point. He sets his friendly warmth against Southey's more judgmental mode, claiming that he has written "in the severity of offended Friendship" (1:105). Southey becomes the Godwinian friend who regards any moral lapse as necessitating a proportionate diminution of affection. However, Coleridge's demonstrative—"but see"—invites Southey to envy Coleridge's self-renewing "blaze" of cheeriness, unaffected by the chill water of criticism. The pointedness of Coleridge's remark depends upon his understanding that Southey also conceives a friend to be a man capable of strong affectionate feeling, whose source is not his head but his heart.

Southey's "Sonnet XI. To the Fire," published in his and Robert Lovell's *Poems* (1794), confirms Coleridge's insight.[34] Southey represents friendly qualities in terms of a domestic fire, identifying emotional warmth rather than rational worth as a friend's chief characteristic:

3: PROBLEM OF PANTISOCRATIC FRIENDSHIP 131

> My friendly fire, thou blazest clear and bright,
>   Nor smoke nor ashes soil thy grateful flame;
> Thy temperate splendour cheers the gloom of night,
>   Thy genial heat enlivens the chill'd frame.
>
> (p. 67)

The fire's "clear" flame is a conventional image of friendship's moral purity. This goodness, however, is closely linked to the enlivening energy of the "blaze." The "friendly fire" becomes an image of the person Southey would like to be:

> I love to pause in meditation's sway;
> And whilst each object gives reflection birth,
>   Mark thy brisk rise, and see thy slow decay:
> And I would wish, like thee, to shine serene,
>   Like thee, within mine influence, all to cheer.
>
> (p. 67)

Southey desires to be a friend whose emotional warmth is given out quickly (a "brisk rise") and who thus has a long-term beneficial effect on "all" his acquaintance. Commenting on Southey's relish for sitting round a fire with Edith at this time, Mark Storey notes that he "half-glimpsed that such a fire was perhaps a means of providing the warmth he himself lacked."[35]

Coleridge quickly became for Southey an embodiment of the "friendly fire." To Grosvenor, Southey enthused that the "Pantisocratic system," so closely associated with Coleridge, "has given me new life new hope new energy. All the faculties of my mind are dilated."[36] The dilation of Southey's faculties reveals the warming effect upon him of Coleridge's affection. The prospective Pantisocratic community also became a potential means of revitalizing his "homeborn" attachments. As Christopher Smith notes:

> He wanted to marry Edith Fricker, he felt a loving duty to his mother and brothers which was far from the coldly rational Godwinian stance. Southey's Pantisocracy, his perfect . . . new home seems to have emerged as a replica of the old patriarchal home which Godwin's philosophy supposedly taught him to revile.[37]

Southey could indeed "conveniently ignore" (p. 75) Godwin's antisentimental denigration of partial, domestic affections. As early as August 1794, he urges Horace Bedford to "marry early in the spring and accompany us": "Excuse my mentioning it now—or rather impute it to the warmth of a friend, unwilling to lose you for ever and wishing you to partake the same tranquillity which he promises himself."[38] Southey does not feel obliged to invite Horace because of his superlative qualities or through the pair's commitment to social justice. Instead, his friendship reflects the "warmth" of a longstanding attachment.

However, the emotional energy of these domestic attachments also raises doubts in Southey's mind concerning the affections of the Pantisocrats. In a verse-letter to Grosvenor, September 1794, Southey tests the Pantisocratic idea by comparing the prospective transatlantic community with those of his English circle who remain behind. Here he emphasizes not the emotional heat of the "home-born" affections but their organic quality. Southey uses the image of the bower to represent the joy with which he has "mark'd" his "growing friendship" with Bedford:

> And if in childhoods early year,
> Some favorite tree he wont to rear
> And see with anxious joy the sapling grow,
> Till widely bowering oer his head
> A grateful shade its broad boughs spread
> Will he not heave the sigh of woe
> As to the accustomed seat he looks adieu
> And lingering as he goes oft turn again to view?[39]

Southey emphasizes the continuous benefits of his sustained cultivation of friendship's domestic tree. With its roots in the past, the tree has grown into a flourishing bower and promises ongoing, protective "shade." As the boughs' wide spread intimates generosity, so their breadth highlights the domestic shelter's strength. These benefits are the result of a lengthy period of slow growth.

The other domestic bower that Southey imagines "Far oer the Atlantic main" (1:78) is not as strong as this organic attachment. Ostensibly, the Pantisocrats combine the Coleridgean, familial idea with the classical ideal of virtuous friendship:

> Let Fancy Bedford paint the lot
> Of calm Contentments woodbind cot.
> At summer evenings gentle gloom
> The smile that bids me welcome home
> The high-heapd hearth, the social bowl
> And every charm that soothes the soul—
> Pourtray each feeling Virtue must approve
> And see me blest with Friendship and with Love.
>
> (1:78)

Southey justifies this convivial scene in Godwinian terms as being expressive of feelings "approved" by "Virtue."

However, in using the anacreontic mode Southey links these lines to earlier eighteenth-century retirement poetry, exemplified by the "Il Penseroso" tradition revived by Thomas Warton and his brother Joseph. In celebrating solitude and contemplation, this older tradition highlights the bower's capacity to keep worldly things from breaking in upon the individual.[40] In representing the Pantisocratic retreat through this old-fashioned diction, Southey intimates that such disengagement from the wider world might be an outmoded idea. This subtext lurks in the following lines:

> There each beneath his mantling vine
> Shall quaff in peace the generous wine.
> No worldly cares shall there intrude
> In our calm of Solitude.
> But stern Ambitions hideous brood
> On Europes shores shall bathe in blood
> Where Discord rouses all her hellish train
> Where Slaughter strides oer hills of slain.
> Death triumphs in the battles roar
> And the gorged Ravens surfeit them with gore.
>
> (1:79)

Southey seemingly contrasts the stillness of the transatlantic bower favorably with the ongoing violence in Europe. These "mantling vines," however, are eerily quiet spaces reminiscent of the static orchard bower Coleridge shares with Poole in "To the Reverend George" (1797). By introducing the turbulent energies of "Ambition," "Discord," "Slaughter," and "Death" into the verse, he unwittingly hints that the Pantisocrats inhabit an artificial paradise. Unlike Bedford and Southey's organic tree, whose shade makes the world manageable, the Pantisocratic bower appears undynamic, even culpably disengaged from worldly life.

Southey's verse-letter considers how the power of an individual's originating, organic attachments could provide a counter-force against establishing fresh familial ties in America. At this time, Coleridge likewise confronts the sentimental challenge of pre-existing attachments. His first love, Mary Evans, strongly expresses her disapproval of his emigration plans in a letter that Coleridge transcribed for Southey in October 1794:

> "Is this handwriting altogether erased from your Memory? To whom am I addressing myself? For whom am I now violating the Rules of female

Delicacy? Is it for the same Coleridge, whom I once regarded as a Sister her best-beloved Brother? . . . You having doting Friends. Will you break their Hearts? . . . I often reflect on the happy hours we spent together, and regret the Loss of your Society. I cannot easily forget those whom I once loved—nor can I easily form new Friendships.["]⁴¹

For Mary, the strongest friendships are formed early on within the domestic group, and she argues that Coleridge's highest allegiance should be to these attachments of the "Heart." Coleridge feels their emotional pull, and admits the Hartleian force of habit: "To love her Habit has made unalterable: I had placed her in the sanctuary of my Heart, nor can she be torn from thence but with the Strings that grapple it to Life."⁴² His love for Mary exemplifies the power of an "intense" friendship, which creates an organic blend of identities such that Mary is literally part of Coleridge's "Life": "We formed each other's minds—our ideas were blended—Heaven bless her! I cannot forget her—every day her Memory sinks deeper into my heart."⁴³ In "blending" identities, domestic attachments exert a conservative force to the degree that they temper Coleridge's enthusiasm for the creation of new, politically radical bonds.

Precisely for this reason, however, Coleridge suspects these domestic friendships of undermining his identity as a moral agent. In response to this he voices a Godwinian concern. In *Political Justice*, Godwin contends that in order to "assert the principles of justice and truth" a man must retain his intellectual independence. Godwin thus refutes the sentimentalist's contention that

> ["]The true perfection of man is to blend and unite his own existence with that of another, and therefore a system which forbids him all partialities and attachments, tends to degeneracy and not to improvement."
>
> No doubt man is formed for society. But there is a way in which for a man to lose his own existence in that of others, that is eminently vicious and detrimental. Every man ought to rest upon his own centre, and consult his own understanding. (2:854)

Coleridge employs a similar argument in reconciling himself to the loss of Mary: "Had I been united to her, the Excess of my Affection would have effeminated my Intellect. I should have fed on her Looks as she entered into the Room—I should have gazed on her Footsteps when she went out from me" (1:145). Like Godwin, Coleridge understands the potentially "vicious and detrimental" effect of private attachments. Emotional intensity "effeminates" the intellect, a term implying that maintaining an independent judgment is vital to preserving a manly identity.

In terms of friendship, Coleridge repeatedly assumes during 1794–1795 the role of disinterested Godwinian rationalist, sharing Southey's concern that sentimental attachments be subordinated to "just affections." In doing so, he constructs his friendship with Southey as a masculine bond of unshakeable virtue. Women become a foil against which to highlight the men's virtuous attachment. In October, he asks Southey to ponder whether the women do not have

> a passion for the Novelty of the Scheme, rather than the generous enthusiasm of Benevolence? Are they saturated with the Divinity of Truth sufficiently to be always wakeful? In the present state of their minds whether it is not probable, that the Mothers will tinge the Mind of the Infants with prejudications?[44]

The "mother" represents a sinister aspect of Coleridge's idealization of familial attachments. The organic influence she enjoys over her offspring makes it likely that her prejudices will sully at the deepest level the child's moral purity. Having intimated that Southey's brothers might not be eligible to join the scheme, being "already deeply tinged with the prejudices and errors of Society" (1:119), Coleridge warns his friend not to be swayed by sentiment: "Have you forgot the word 'Justice[']?—Or have the Feelings prevailed over the Dea optima maxima? They have not:—yet, Southey! be on your Guard against them!" (1:120). Coleridge plays the Godwinian friend united with Southey in his allegiance to Justice, and whose role is to help his partner maintain his principles (and manly identity). Confessing on 3 November his horror at the prospect of Mrs. Fricker teaching "the Infants Christianity,—I mean—that mongrel whelp that goes under it's name," Coleridge becomes more Godwinian still:

> I wish, Southey! in the stern severity of Judgment, that the two Mothers were not to go and that the children stayed with them—Are you wounded by my want of feeling? No! how highly must I think of your rectitude of Soul, that I should dare to say this to so affectionate a Son! (1:123)

Again, the men's shared bond of virtue affirms itself through Coleridge's comparison with female imperfection.

However, Coleridge's allegiance to this moralistic model of friendship jostles uneasily with his more sentimental and familial mode. He ends with the announcement: "A Friend of mine hath lately departed this Life in a frenzy fever induced by Anxiety!—poor fellow—a child of frailty like me: yet he was amiable" (1:123–24). In allowing friendship to be compatible with moral imperfection, Coleridge attacks Southey's "philosophy of the heart," which was often strictly limited to "virtuous affections."[45] He concludes with some verse lines addressing his dead friend, Rev. Fulwood Smerdon, which meditate further on the link between amiability and moral frailty.[46] Coleridge relates how, "Nurs'd in thy Heart the generous Virtues grew—/ And in thy Heart they wither'd!" (lines 25–26). Despite acknowledging Smerdon's "Indolence" (line 27) and "Vanity" (line 28), Coleridge refuses to judge him harshly, directing his scorn towards those who have not committed "follies" (line 31): "Were they *more* wise, the Proud who never fell?" (line 32). Instead, Coleridge offers Smerdon compassion—"Rest, injur'd Shade!" (line 33)—in a posthumous attempt to soothe his friend's wounds. A friend does not evaluate the other's vices and diminish his affection in proportion to his demerits. Coleridge theorizes this refusal to over-moralize friendship in an 1801 notebook entry:

> The unspeakable Comfort to a good man's mind—nay, even to a criminal to be *understood*—to have some one that understands one—& who does not feel, that on earth no one does. The Hope of this—always more or less disappointed, gives the *passion* to Friendship.[47]

Friendship's passionate enthusiasm derives from the hope of receiving another's nonjudgmental sympathy. This view rejects Godwin's argument in *Political Justice* that friendship is not open to "knaves": for Coleridge, even "criminals" may have a right to be "*understood*" and loved for who they are.

In sending Southey his "Lines on a Friend," Coleridge implicitly asks for the same compassionate understanding of his own follies. He confesses how

> The daring ken of Truth, the patriot's part,
> And Pity's Sigh, that breathes the gentle heart
> Sloth-jaundic'd all! and from my graspless hand
> Drop Friendship's precious Pearls, like hour glass sand.
> I weep—yet stoop not! the faint Anguish flows,
> A dreamy Pang in Morning's fev'rish Doze!
>
> (lines 41–46)

Like Smerdon, Coleridge suffers from a disease—"sloth-jaundice"—that disqualifies him from Godwinian virtue. For Godwin, a virtuous friend is never guilty of "Indolence": "The man, who depends upon his courage, his ability, or his amiable character for recommendation, will perpetually cultivate these. His constancy will be unwearied; and, conscious of the integrity of his means, his spirit will be intrepid and erect" (1:377). It is precisely this kind of friendship that Coleridge cannot sustain. Instead, Coleridge desires of Southey the compassion he had offered Smerdon, and would later seek in Poole.

Coleridge's "indolence" was exacerbated by his increasing disillusionment with rationalist and meritocratic views of friendship. As early as 21 October, he dismissed Southey's Godwinian notion that "love is a creature of strong Motive," concluding that Sara was a woman whom "I do not love—but whom by every tie of Reason and Honor I ought to love. I am resolved—but wretched!" (1:113). By "every tie of Reason" Coleridge suggests that Sara should command an affection in proportion to her merits. To his dismay, however, he discovers that reasons for loving are not sufficient to create love: "I am not conscious of having injured her otherwise, than by having mistaken the ebullience of schematism for affection . . . —However it still remains for me to be externally Just though my Heart is withered within me."[48] The principle of Justice to which Coleridge dutifully swears allegiance is now opposed to the desires of the "Heart," wherein lies the true source of affection.

Throughout 1795, in his relations with Southey Coleridge struggles to reconcile a rational bond of virtue with a less moralized familial relationship in which he would be loved for himself, failings included. In his letter of 29 December, although again lamenting his engagement to Sara, a woman "I do *not* love," Coleridge nonetheless exclaims: "Mark you, Southey!—*I will do my Duty*" (1:145). Proceeding with the marriage allows him to demonstrate to Southey the virtue that unites the two male friends. In January 1795, Coleridge becomes more outspoken in asserting that he and Southey are bound together by duty to the scheme of Pantisocracy. He reacts to Southey's frustration at his having lingered in London instead of returning to his Pantisocratic responsibilities in Bristol:

> I will not say you treat me coolly or mysteriously—yet assuredly you seem to look upon me as a man whom vanity or some other inexplicable Cause have alienated from the System— . . . Wherein when roused to the recollection of my Duty have I shrunk from the performance of it?—I hold my Life & my feebler feelings as ready sacrifices to Justice— καυχάω ὑπορᾶς [ὑφορᾶς?] γάρ [I boast because you suspect me]. I dismiss a subject so painful to me as self-vindication—painful to me only

as addressing it to you on whose esteem and affection I have rested with the whole weight of my Soul.⁴⁹

Under pressure, Coleridge reaffirms his moral rectitude that readily sacrifices "feelings" to "Justice." In doing so, he emphasizes the Godwinian basis to his male friendship, explicitly citing his moral excellence as the motive for Southey's "affection." For this reason, Southey's accusations pain Coleridge by implying that Southey is re-evaluating his worthiness as a "friend." In fact, Coleridge argues that Southey's new idea of trying out the scheme in Wales damages the men's friendship by reneging on their rhetoric of selfless duty: "Why, my dear very dear Southey! . . . do you say, I—I—I—will do so and so—instead of saying as you were wont to do—It is all our Duty to do so and so—for such & such Reasons" (1:150). To abandon this rhetoric is to act in a self-centred and thus unfriendly way.

But Coleridge cannot sustain this moralized discourse, confessing to serious moral failings of his own. Nevertheless, he will not allow Southey to judge him:

> Southey! I must tell you, that you appear to me to write as a man who is aweary of a world, because it accords not with his ideas of perfection—your sentiments look like the sickly offspring of disgusted Pride. Love is an active and humble Principle—It flies not away from the Couches of Imperfection, because the Patients are fretful or loathsome. (1:150)

Coleridge's sentiments are confused: he is now reiterating the familial mode of friendship as an unconditional kind of loving attention not proportional to another's moral worth. Lawrence Blum has remarked that "one does not need to regard someone as a virtuous person in order to care for him as a friend; nor, in caring for him for his own sake need one focus primarily on whatever morally virtuous qualities he has."⁵⁰ For Coleridge, too, a friend should confront even a friend's "loathsome" characteristics in the hope of curing him. By 1798, Coleridge was arguing that friendship inevitably brings out unhealthy aspects of friends' characters, a view he expresses in some cancelled lines of "The Triumph of Loyalty" (1798). Sandoval reconciles his affection for Earl Henry with his knowledge of his friend's faults:

> Earl Henry thou art dear to me—perchance
> For these follies; since the Health of Reason,

> Our would-be Sages teach, engenders not
> The Whelks and Tumours of particular Friendship.[51]

Sandoval objects to rationalist "would-be Sages" like Godwin who argue that, as friendship is a meeting of virtuous minds, it should express itself in healthy, virtuous deeds. For Sandoval, friendship inevitably reveals "Whelks and Tumours": he ironically concludes that personal affection must mark an irrational attraction to "follies" rather than a rational attachment to another man's virtue.

Returning to Coleridge's letter, his stress on nursing rather than judging a sick friend is part of the unconditional familial affection he hoped to realize among the Pantisocrats. He thus suggests that Southey's moral rigidity does not accord with the Pantisocratic community of love. Coleridge's frustration with his friend helps to harden during 1795 his anti-Godwinian view that virtue can only be nurtured in familial relations and not through an impersonal commitment to a moral principle. As he states in his third Theological Lecture, delivered in May:

> [Godwinism] builds without a foundation, proposes an end without establishing the means, and discovers a total ignorance of that obvious Fact in human nature that in virtue and in knowledge we must be infants and be nourished with milk in order that we may be men and eat strong meat.[52]

Moral values develop within familial relations in the same way that a baby's physical life is sustained by its mother's milk. Only through this parental infusion of beneficence can the individual develop into a responsible social agent. Focusing on this passage, Nigel Leask argues that "although Pantisocracy appears to have passed through an early phase of Godwinism, particularly in the hands of the non-Unitarian Southey, it soon emerged, in Coleridge's lecturing and journalism of 1795–96, as a radical alternative to the tenets of *Political Justice* (1793)."[53]

This view convincingly reflects Coleridge's public statements. Nevertheless, in his private correspondence with Southey there was no smooth progression from Godwinism to a radicalized Unitarian belief in private affections as a source of morality. Until the break-up of the relationship in November 1795, Coleridge continues to suggest that it represents a rational bond of virtue, expressive of both men's duty to the principle of justice. In the event, it was Southey who struggled most to sustain a friendship grounded in principle. Having finally brought Coleridge back to Bristol in February 1795, he remained excited at the prospect of realizing the Pantisocratic idea in Wales. "You ought to rejoice," he told Grosvenor, "that your friend acts up to his principles, though you think them wrong."⁵⁴ By May, however, he was beginning to eschew this classical ethos. Confessing his misanthropic mood to Bedford, Southey relates how Coleridge was attempting to sustain his friend's principles:

> [Coleridge] is applying the medicine of argument to my misanthropical system of indifference.—It will not do, a strange dreariness of mind has seized me. I am indifferent to society, yet I feel my private attachments growing more and more powerful, and weep like a child when I think of an absent friend.⁵⁵

The moral and philosophical guidance Coleridge offers "will not do." Instead, Southey declares the growing influence over him of his sentimental, domestic attachments. This move represents part of Southey's growing disillusionment with *Political Justice*, to which he confessed in October: "I have . . . seen [Godwin's] fundamental error—that he theorises for another state, not for the rule of conduct in the present."⁵⁶

For Roe, "it appears to have been Coleridge's own critique of Godwin that prompted Southey's recognition of the shortcomings of *Political Justice*; this in turn qualified his enthusiasm for Pantisocracy."⁵⁷ At the same time, Southey's unenthusiasm was owing to his disillusionment with Coleridge's alternative vision of establishing a new familial community of love. The philanthropic potential of "home-born Feeling" no longer enthuses him with desire to emigrate. The "rule of conduct" that he recognizes is that the stronger his affections grow the more restricted they become. In this letter, he relates a recent encounter with a widower:

> I—I rejoiced at his loss, because it was not my friend!—yet, without this selfishness, man would be an animal below the orang outang. It is mortifying to analise our noblest affections, and find them all bottomed on selfishness. I hear of thousands killed in battle—I read of the young, the virtuous, dying, and think of them no more—when if my very dog died I should weep for him; if I lost you, I should feel a lasting affliction; if Edith were to die, I should follow her. (1:239)

Southey no longer finds virtue a sufficient condition for affection—he is indifferent to the death of "virtuous" soldiers. The "mortifying" paradox he discovers is that a man's "noblest affections" are proportionate to that "selfishness" that enables him to feel more intensely for private attachments than for mankind. Leask contends that Coleridge's celebration of private affections "should not be confused with Burke's polemic. Burke eulogized domesticity as an *alternative* to the meddling in affairs of state by those not qualified by privileged birth or property to fulfil a representative function" (p. 46). Southey, however, demonstrates how easily the powerful emotions accruing to private friendships could encourage an individual to embrace domesticity as a conservative alternative to political action. For him, the sentimental, familial affection posited by Coleridge as central to Pantisocracy's success provides motivation for abandoning the idea of emigration. Southey's acceptance of his uncle's annuity and decision to study law in Summer 1795 constitute the practical results of his reorientation of feeling towards his domestic world. His doing so effectively represented the end of the scheme.

Coleridge, however, did not sympathize with Southey's decision. On 13 November 1795 his friend received a five-thousand-word letter lambasting his lack of principle. Coleridge rejects the sentimental compromise for which he himself had been pleading in earlier letters. Instead, he condemns Southey for failing to adhere to a classical ideal of virtue. In *De Amicitia*, Cicero had maintained that "true amity being founded on an opinion of virtue in the object of our affection; it is scarcely possible that those sentiments should remain, after an avowed and open violation of the principles which originally produced them."[58] This tenet becomes Coleridge's justification for ending their friendship: "You are lost to me, because you are lost to Virtue."[59] Coleridge emphasizes that the Pantisocrats' bonds contrast with the sentimental attachments that he himself had "abandoned." He rhetorically asks if it was Southey's "Plan" for which

> I abandoned my friends, and every prospect & every certainty, and the Woman whom I loved to an excess which you in your warmest dream of fancy could never shadow out?—When I returned from London, when you deemed Pantisocracy a DUTY—a duty unaltered by numbers—when you said, that if others left it, you and George Burnett and your Brother would stand firm to the post of Virtue. (1:170)

Coleridge declares his superiority as a "friend," whether this implies a passionate tie of feeling or an ideological bond. On the one hand, he is capable of emotional attachments that Southey even in his "warmest dream of fancy" cannot comprehend. Coleridge's mastering of his passion, however, in order to honor his duty-bound Pantisocratic friendships, identifies him all the more strongly as the classical friend of virtue. Coleridge emphasizes that the relation involved both men sustaining each other's principles. Faced with Southey's desire to accept a position in the Church, he recollects that he "performed the Office of still-struggling Friendship by writing you my free Sentiments concerning the enormous Guilt of that which your Uncle's doughty Sophistry recommended" (1:166). Southey too had once performed friendship's "Office" of sustaining Coleridge's principles: "I did not only venerate you for your own Virtues, I prized you as the Sheet Anchor of mine!" (1:173). Southey's moral failure, however, means that he can no longer perform this role, and is thus disqualified from being Coleridge's friend.

Coleridge is forced to acknowledge his own faults. However, he does so only to highlight Southey's failure to adhere to principle: "My INDOLENCE you assigned to Lovell as the Reason for your quitting Pantisocracy. Supposing it true, it might indeed be a Reason for rejecting me from the System? But how does this affect Pantisocracy, that you should reject it?" (1:171). This sentiment is Godwinian in its rigid subordination of personal attachment to an individual's duty to justice. Coleridge declares that, faced with his friend's "sloth-jaundice," Southey should have "reasoned" thus: "Much as I love Him, I love Pantisocracy more: and if in a certain time I do not see this disqualifying propensity subdued, I must and will reject him" (1:172). Implicit here is the Godwinian notion that Southey should have privileged his "just affection" for those still committed to Pantisocracy above an unworthy attachment to an incurably indolent man. Although he had opened his correspondence with Southey by stressing the paramount importance in friendship of loving attention, in his final letter Coleridge represents the relationship as founded primarily on "Virtue." Coleridge's denial of the complexity of their friendship at this point, however, is strategic, reflecting his emotional desire to attack Southey. His love for Mary Evans and dissatisfaction with his "principled" attachment to Sara had demonstrated how "home-born Feeling" undermined his own enthusiasm for Pantisocracy's radical idea. But with Southey's exit, Coleridge could deny these doubts and continue to conceive of their friendship in Godwinian terms, whereby the men were united in duty to the principle of justice embodied in Pantisocracy.

Two letters from Southey to Grosvenor Bedford in 1796 respond to Coleridge's vitriolic epistle, and reveal further how Coleridge's familial ideal could easily be used to justify a retreat from political engagement. In February Southey announces that you and I shall not talk politics. I am weary of them, and little love politicians; for me, I shall think of domestic life, and confine my wishes within the little circle of friendship. The rays become more intense, in proportion as they are drawn to a point. Heighho![60]

Friendship is an apolitical, nondisruptive intercourse. But Southey describes this retreat into domesticity through the Coleridgean discourse of "intense" private affections. In 1794–1795, Coleridge had hoped that the benevolent energy of domestic friendship would radiate outwards to "cheer & vivify" every corner of the universe. In 1796, however, Southey highlights the potential flaws in Coleridge's metaphor, arguing that benevolent rays merely dissipate in their centrifugal movement from core relationships. By May Southey is less certain about the affectionate energy inherent even in these private affections:

How does time mellow down our opinions! Little of that ardent enthusiasm which so lately fevered my whole character remains. I have contracted my sphere of action within the little circle of my own friends, and even my wishes seldom stray beyond it. A little candle will give light enough to a moderate-sized room; place it in a church, it will only "teach light to counterfeit a gloom;" and, in the street, the first wind extinguishes it.[61]

Whereas Coleridge imagined friendship to be a sun, Southey thinks of it now as a candle. In stressing the candle's inability to illuminate a church or street, Southey rejects Coleridge's Hartleian notion that energetic domestic affections create newly benevolent social agents who could mediate divine love to society. Southey invited Bedford to consult "Quarle's Emblems" (1:276) if he did not understand his metaphor. He may have in mind Francis Quarles's illustration of 1 Isaiah 50:11, in which Quarles juxtaposes a candle with the sun. In this way, Quarles illustrates the futility of fanning the flame of human love in an attempt to rival the divine sun. As an inferior power, Southey now finds friendship useful only within his private "room."[62]

In November 1795, however, Coleridge had revealed a greater belief in the dynamic, socially regenerative potential of domestic affections and, in private at least, a greater commitment to embodying a Godwinian kind of virtuous friendship based upon shared principles of social justice. In his public lectures and journalism, though, Coleridge was becoming increasingly adamant that private attachments were the primary means of nursing an individual into habits of virtuous feeling. In doing so, he lays increasing stress on

**Francis Quarles, *Emblems* (1645, repr. 1736): "*You that walk in the light of your own fire; and in the sparks that ye have kindled, ye shall lie down in sorrow*" (1 Isaiah 50:11).

the role of sentiment in radical politics. The following chapter situates Coleridge in a more general politicization of sensibility in the 1790s, and traces the extent to which Coleridge's politics reflected his sentimental friendship not only for family or for a tethered donkey but for a Platonic idea of humanity.

4

Friends of Humanity: Coleridge, Southey, and *The Anti-Jacobin*

FOR THOMAS PAINE, THE APOSTLE OF RADICALISM WHO SET THE LIBERAL agenda in the 1790s, the progress of the French Revolution in 1792 offered intimations of friendship:

> We already see an alteration in the national disposition of England and France towards each other, which, when we look back to only a few years, is itself a revolution. Who could have foreseen, or who would have believed, that a French National Assembly would ever have been a popular toast in England, or that a friendly alliance of the two nations should become the wish of either. It shews that man, were he not corrupted by governments, is naturally the friend of man.[1]

Governed by natural rather than artificial, social laws, friendship transcends class and culture. It represents an ideal for a new kind of democratic relationship, one that presupposes a fundamental equality between men based upon their common political rights. Provide man with a just political system, Paine suggests, and he will converse once more in friendship's language of sympathy and inclusion. However, if Paine makes new friends, he also discovers some new enemies. The adversary is the system of nonrepresentational government that estranges men from each other, and Paine implicitly invites his reader to fight it as the opponent of friendship itself.

Questions are raised here concerning friendship's role in the political discourse of the 1790s. To what extent does the term represent a transcendent Idea that may unite men universally in sympathetic affection? Is this Idea capable of becoming embodied, or does it create new divisions whereby friends recognize each other as friends only by identifying a common enemy? In any case, how far was friendship itself a radically egalitarian concept? Was there an alternative, conservative friendship available that could bolster the established social structure? This chapter situates Coleridge within a broader spectrum of political texts that reveals how "friendship" was appropriated by radical and counter-revolutionary forces alike. It should thus be possible to contextualize further Coleridge and Southey's Pantisocratic scheme, as well as chart the course of Coleridge's sentimental idealism in the political climate of the 1790s.

Paine's contention that man is "naturally the friend of man" creates a space in which friendship might discover politically radical meanings through the discourses of intuitive feeling, known collectively as Sensibility. The third earl of Shaftesbury provides the philosophical basis for the radicalization of the term in the 1790s. In *Sensus Communis* (1709), Shaftesbury puts forward a fully developed concept of the "Natural" faculty that binds the individual to his community, which he defines as "Common Sense."[2] Referring to "the social feelings or *Sense of Partnership* with Human Kind," "Common Sense" includes "Natural Affection, Humanity, Obligingness, or that sort of *Civility* which rises from a just *Sense* of the *common Rights* of Mankind, and the *natural Equality* there is amongst those of the same Species" (p. 61). For Shaftesbury, "Natural Affection" extends beyond embodied objects to embrace an idea of "Human Kind." This warm feeling presupposes equality amongst men and, as a consequence, universal political "*Rights*." "Common Sense" becomes a prerequisite for those who would govern society:

> A publick Spirit can come only from a social Feeling or *Sense of Partnership* with Human Kind. Now there are none so far from being *Partners* in this *Sense*, or Sharers in this *common Affection*, as they who scarcely know *an Equal*, nor consider themselves as subject to any Law of *Fellowship* or *Community*. And thus Morality and good Government go together. (p. 63)

"Natural Affection" for human kind rather than a capacity for reason becomes the ultimate criterion for a man's right to participate in matters of state. As Chris Jones remarks, although Shaftesbury was arguing merely "for the equality and naturalness of his cultured milieu . . . his formulations were taken out of this context to become the basis of a radical, even revolutionary, ideology."[3] Gary Kelly confirms that, by the 1790s, the literature of sensibility characteristically invoked:

> a rhetoric of authenticity that privileges the personal, spontaneous, improvised, and "natural" over the impersonal, learned, stylized, and

"polished" and implicitly associating the latter with a courtly, aristocratic, authoritative, and even autocratic culture and the former with a dialogical, egalitarian, "liberal," and feminized culture created by the professional middle class.[4]

Kelly directs his comments in particular to Helen Maria Williams's *Letters Written in France* (1790), a text that exemplifies how the liberal politics associated with sensibility led in turn to the radicalization of the idea of friendship. Caught up amongst the joyous scenes in Paris on the first anniversary of the fall of the Bastille, Williams finds herself instinctively sympathizing with the progress of the Revolution:

> It was the triumph of human kind; it was man asserting the noblest privileges of his nature; and it required but the common feelings of humanity to become in that moment a citizen of the world. For myself, I acknowledge that my heart caught with enthusiasm the general sympathy; my eyes were filled with tears.[5]

In realizing the ideals of Liberty and Equality, France has created the conditions in which all its citizens become aware of their "Common Sense," and sympathetic affection for each other: Williams links her intuitive sense of fellowship to "common feelings of humanity," and thus to a sensibility that everyone possesses. Within this logic, all sentient beings necessarily support a radical agenda, and Williams admits, "it is very difficult, with common sensibility, to avoid sympathizing in general happiness. My love of the French revolution, is the natural result of this sympathy, and therefore my political creed is entirely an affair of the heart" (p. 66).

For Williams, the politicization of sensibility leads to a concomitant radicalization of the idea of a friend. She argues that only those who compassionate with the victims of the ancien régime will possess the sensibility required in private attachments:

> Those who have contemplated the dungeons of the Bastille, without rejoicing in the French revolution, may, for aught I know, be very respectable persons, and very agreeable companions in the hours of prosperity; but, if my heart were sinking with anguish, I should not fly to those persons for consolation. (p. 24)

Conversely, it is inconceivable that friends be sentimentally responsive to an individual and not possess sympathies for mankind as a whole. Williams implicitly applies to friendship Lawrence Sterne's idea that "a man is incapable of loving one woman as he ought, who has not a sort of an affection for the whole sex; and as little should I [Williams] look for particular sympathy from those who have no feelings of general philanthropy" (pp. 24–25). Any personal friend will also be a general "Friend of Humanity," and thus a supporter of the Revolution: seen in these terms, the "Natural Affection" friends express is not ideologically neutral but indicative of a potentially radical sensibility.

For Williams, like Paine, the only impediment to natural affection is a rigid, hierarchical society that imposes artificial barriers between differing ranks. Many liberal writers suggest that, in a less restrictive social environment, cross-rank friendships would be possible. The continuance of these aspirations throughout the 1790s is witnessed by John Thelwall's novel, *The Daughter of Adoption; A Tale of Modern Times* (1801), which portrays the sympathetic relations between a servant, Edmunds, and his master, Henry Montfort.[6] Henry first realizes that his "sentimentalist" (3:260) servant could be a friend while walking with him on the Caribbean island of St Domingo. Separated from English society and its prejudicial mores, Henry's "Natural Affection" flourishes through conversation with this lower-ranking man of sensibility:

> "Edmunds! Edmunds!" said Henry, after a pause, seizing his hand, with the most hearty familiarity, "thou art my servant no longer! Thine is *no serving mind!* Henceforward be my confident, and my friend.
>
> "In other situations, perhaps, I might have been insensible to your worth. The proud distinction of master and servant might have deprived me of the instructive pleasure of your conversation. But here the want of equals in my own rank of society, has enabled me to discover one in the class beneath me. And, though I feel that I am by no means destitute of the pride of family and fortune, I shall endeavour not to be so much a slave to the opinions of society, as to rebel against the more sacred order of nature.["] (1:287–88)

Henry discovers that friendship can transcend the stifling "opinions of society," which keep men apart through a hierarchical system. Like Shaftesbury and Paine, Henry conceives that affectionate feeling is founded upon the "sacred order of nature," which does not restrict moral sensibility or intellectual capacity to a particular rank.

Henry's discovery is Thelwall's injunction in the 1790s. As he writes in *The Tribune* (1795):

> To mix with all ranks of men is the duty of every individual who has the opportunity so to do: for it is thus that we practically learn that great

lesson, so theoretically enforced, that *all mankind are of one family, and that mutual obligation connects every individual of the universe together in one chain of sympathy and reciprocal duty*.[7]

Inherent in Thelwall's idea of mankind as one family is the Shaftesburian view that "Natural Affection" presupposes equal legal and political rights. In a speech given at the General Meeting of the "Friends of Parliamentary Reform" in October 1795, Thelwall specifically urged his fellow citizens to pursue

> the happiness, welfare, and prosperity of mankind. The universal diffusion of equal rights and laws, which smooth the rugged asperities of unequal conditions, and make man, wherever he beholds the form of man, perceive a brother, a friend;—a being, in short, entitled to the same rights with himself, and to the same protection in the enjoyment and maintenance of his opinions.[8]

To perceive a "friend" here is to acknowledge a political equal, and Thelwall argues that in an enfranchised society men will sentimentally recognize each other as friends.

In this passage, "friend" is synonymous with "brother," a connection that testifies further to the burgeoning radical politicality of friendship. In the period, brotherhood and fraternity had, as Lynn Hunt notes, "a political charge that was indissolubly linked with radical revolution."[9] Amongst "brothers," the fraternal feeling indicated, in Felicity Baker's terms, the "emotionally empowering quality of moral obligation spontaneously assumed in relation to equals" (p. 276), expressing itself in a "jubilatory feeling which identifies this as a movement of the life-drive" (p. 277).[10] Nevertheless, in comparison with friendship, fraternity tends to emerge as a less sentimental idea. Ronald Sharp draws a pertinent distinction: "In many ways [*fraternité*] is much closer to our general sense of human commitment or human fellowship than to friendship itself, in the sense of a concrete, intimate, and ongoing relationship with a particular person."[11]

Coleridge's letters during the summer and autumn of 1794 confirm Sharp's distinction. During this period of Pantisocratic enthusiasm, Coleridge's letters compare and contrast "friendship" with "fraternity." In July, for instance, he sends to Lovell, via Southey, "Fraternity & civic Remembrances."[12] Coleridge's offer of "Fraternity" acknowledges his limited acquaintance with Lovell, which means they can share only a political bond. Coleridge makes a similar distinction in September when he sends: "To Lovell and Mrs Lovell my *fraternal* Love—to Miss F *more*. To all remember me—

tell Edith and Martha and Eliza that I even *now* see all their faces and that they are my very dear Sisters."[13] "Fraternal" love is less sentimental than the strong familial affection Coleridge feels for the Fricker sisters. By contrast, "friendship" adds an emotive and concrete aspect to a political bond. To Henry Martin, he signs off "with gratitude and fraternal friendship" whereby "friendship" adds an affective element to the men's ideological bond of fraternity.[14]

In his political writings of the early 1790s, Coleridge participates in the radical politicization of friendship articulated by Paine, Williams, and Thelwall. As we have seen, one of Pantisocracy's underlying tenets was that its just political system would allow Shaftesburian "Natural Affection" to flourish. After the scheme's collapse, Coleridge located the radical idea of "friend" in figures like Charles, third earl of Stanhope. This he articulates in "To Lord Stanhope on Reading his Late Protest in the House of Lords," a sonnet published in the *Morning Chronicle* of 31 January 1795 under the pseudonym, "ONE OF THE PEOPLE."[15] Hailing Stanhope with "ardent Hymn" (line 1) Coleridge exclaims that on his grave will be inscribed:

> "Here sleeps the Friend of Humankind!"
> For thou, untainted by CORRUPTION's bowl,
> Or foul AMBITION, with undaunted soul
> Hast spoke the language of a Free-born mind
> Pleading the cause of Nature!
>
> (lines 5–9)

In "Pleading the cause of Nature" Stanhope delivers his arguments in the tones of sensibility and its appeal to man's innate natural rights. As such, the "Friend of Humankind" represents a sentimental figure, free from artificial social prejudices or desires like "AMBITION" that would limit his instinctive affections.

Coleridge emphasizes this point in a second sonnet, "Effusion 10, to Earl Stanhope," published in *Poems* (1796), where the term "friend" again necessarily implies a general love of humanity:

> Not, STANHOPE! with the Patriot's doubtful name
> I mock thy worth—FRIEND OF THE HUMAN RACE!
> Since scorning Faction's low and partial aim
> Aloof thou wendest in thy stately pace,
> Thyself redeeming from that leprous stain,
> NOBILITY.
>
> (lines 1–6)[16]

Coleridge eulogizes the "Friend" above the "Patriot" as a truly democratic figure, whose identity is not founded on the artificial exclusions of "Faction" or rank. That Stanhope achieves this despite being an aristocrat and Pitt's brother-in-law strengthens Coleridge's case that all men might exhibit natural affections. One consequence is that friendship should be possible among all ranks, and Coleridge praises Stanhope for practising just this. In March 1796, he writes in *The Watchman*:

> Earl Stanhope does not *talk* only: he feels, and acts in contempt of aristocratic prejudices. Mr. Taylor, the son of an Apothecary at Seven Oaks, in Kent, had gained the affections of his daughter. The young Lady, truly noble from the advantages of her education, did not disguise the state of her feelings, but made her father her confidant. "Is he not honest and intelligent?" replied the Earl.—"Assuredly, I approve of your choice."[17]

Beyond class identity exists the essential, feeling self. In behaving in accordance with this innate moral center, Stanhope becomes a friend to humanity, sanctioning his daughter's marriage to a man of lower status. The worthiness of Stanhope's ability to "feel," though, necessitates the transfer of feeling into "acts." Only by doing so can his sentimental Idea of universal friendship embody itself in social alliances that cross divisions of rank.

Coleridge is at the same time suspicious of sensibility as a tool of radical politics. In his essay, "On the Slave Trade" (1796), he baldly states that "Sensibility is not Benevolence": "Benevolence which may be defined 'Natural Sympathy made permanent by an acquired Conviction, that the Interests of each and of all are one and the same', or in fewer words, 'Natural Sympathy made permanent by enlightened Selfishness'."[18] Benevolence includes the Shaftesburian quality of "Natural Sympathy," but transforming these affectionate impulses into moral action requires a reasoned understanding of the principles of social justice. Coleridge has less faith than Helen Maria Williams that the heart's instinctive movements guarantee socially benevolent action. He realizes that, without reason's intervention, sensibility may degenerate into selfishness. In his "Lecture on the Slave Trade," delivered in 1795 and the basis for his *Watchman* essay, Coleridge argues that sensibility may actually create a bar to a radical friendship for humanity:

> Sensibility indeed we have to spare—what novel-reading Lady does not over flow with it to the great annoyance of her Friends and Family— Her own sorrows . . . sit enthroned bulky and vast—while the miseries

of our fellow creatures dwindle . . . into pigmy forms, and are crowded, an unnumbered multitude, into some dark corner of the Heart where the eye of sensibility gleams faintly on them at long Intervals.[19]

Through its excessive privileging of feeling, sensibility encourages a selfishness incompatible with the attention the Lady owes to her "Friends and Family" as well as to the "miseries of our fellow creatures."

Nevertheless, as Chris Jones notes: "Coleridge, while distinguishing true benevolence from passive sensibility, used the language of sensibility in attacking the slave trade and the French War."[20] In doing so, he often rejects conservative voices that declare radical sensibility to be as ineffectual as the self-indulgent feelings of Coleridge's "novel-reading Lady." In *An Answer to "A Letter to Edward Long Fox, M. D."* (1795), Coleridge defends Dr. Fox, one of the "friends of peace, freedom, and human nature,"[21] against A. W.'s charge that Fox's "commiseration" with the "Citizens of Bristol" is fake.[22] A. W. accuses Fox of travelling in a "little Sulky" (p. 388)—a two-wheeled carriage accommodating a single person and which represented the English equivalent of the French "Désobligeant," the chaise used by Sterne's discontented traveller in *A Sentimental Journey* (1768). This antisentimental vehicle discourages social mingling, a consideration that "necessarily" leads A. W. "to the conclusion, that your present conduct has in it more of selfish policy than of real humanity and benevolence" (p. 388). For this conservative writer, using the Sulky signifies a culpable disjunction between the friend of humanity's sentimental discourse and his ungenerous practice. In reply to A. W., Coleridge admits that "the 'little sulky' is an unsocial vehicle," but rejects the accusation that Fox's fine feelings are not embodied in action:

> I must continue to think, that its greater convenience is a sufficient reason for the Doctor's having adopted it, unless I see the rich and great stop their more roomy carriages on the road, and take up into them the maim, the halt, or the blind; the decrepit old man whose snow-covered rags mock his shivering; or the soldier's deserted wife who tramps wearily on with her baby screaming at her back for cold. But as this is not likely to be the fashion, I cannot think you justified in your attack on the little Sulky, whatever credit I may give you for the wit and *liberality* of it. (p. 327)

Coleridge deflects attention from Fox's mode of transport to the lack of sensibility in the rich, who, despite having "more roomy carriages," conspicuously fail to respond to the impoverished citizens who walk the streets (who include the shivering figure from "To an Old Man"). English roads become scenes in which Coleridge views a daily politico-sentimental drama that highlights the lack of friendship for humanity in the upper ranks of English society.

Coleridge leaves unresolved, however, the issue of whether a gap exists between the radical's sentimental discourse and his actions. He does not counter A. W.'s criticism directly by suggesting the radicals do indeed share their living space with society's outcasts. Instead, he concentrates on bringing the plight of the "maim, the halt, or the blind" before the eyes of his reader. In this, he uses a sentimental rhetoric that differs from the self-indulgent sensibility of the "novel-reading Lady." Coleridge does not allow his "fellow creatures'" miseries to fade away in a "dark corner" of his reader's heart. On the contrary, his radical sensibility brings suffering into the clear light of imagination in order to evoke a benevolent response in his reader. Discussing "On the Slave Trade," Lockridge remarks that "what is needed is 'truth-painting imagination' that would put us in touch with the horror of the slave ship,"[23] and it is this which Coleridge provides his reader in his essay and lecture on the subject:

> Would you choose to be sold, to have the hot iron hiss upon your breast, to be thrown down into the hold of a ship ironed with so many victims so closely crammed together that the heat and stench arising from your diseased bodies should rot the very planks of the Ship?[24]

Through his "truth-painting imagination" Coleridge enables his audience to identify more fully with the slaves' suffering, and in doing so, feel motivated to act on their behalf.

Precisely in order to transform the reader into a radicalized Friend of Humanity, the sentimental lecturer or poet leaves a gap between the suffering he depicts and what he himself accomplishes for the objects of his compassion. This strategy is exemplified in "The Soldier's Wife," a collaboration by Coleridge and Southey, published in Southey's *Poems* (1797). The poem protests against the war by elaborating upon Coleridge's image of the "soldier's deserted wife" in his answer to A. W.:

DACTYLICS.

Weary way-wanderer languid and sick at heart
Travelling painfully over the rugged road,
Wild-visag'd Wanderer! ah for thy heavy chance!

Sorely thy little one drags by thee bare-footed,
Cold is the baby that hangs at thy bending back
Meagre and livid and screaming its wretchedness.

* Woe-begone mother, half anger, half agony,
As over thy shoulder thou lookest to hush the babe,
Bleakly the blinding snow beats in thy hagged face.

Thy husband will never return from the war again,
Cold is thy hopeless heart even as Charity—
Cold are thy famish'd babes—God help thee, widow'd One!

 * This stanza was supplied by S. T. COLERIDGE.[25]

The poets do not supply the friendship that will help the woman but focus unremittingly on the image of this broken family and the absence of any social support. Even nature is hostile: the woman turns her head towards her child in a gesture of concern, only for the snow to "beat" her face. In this way, the two poets effectively leave a gap for the reader's sentiment to fill. By witnessing society's abandonment of the woman, Coleridge and Southey invite their readers to become radical friends of humanity, imbued with a fresh sense of the sentimental values of pity, compassion, and charity.

 The "Dactylics" offered an example of radical sensibility sufficiently provocative to be satirized by the virulent organ of the party of church-and-king, *The Anti-Jacobin; or Weekly Examiner* (1797–1798). Edited by George Canning, the paper repeatedly offers a critique of the radical idea of friendship, and reveals the extent to which the concept was being challenged and redefined in the latter half of the 1790s. It is my purpose to examine this conservative challenge and explore, both here and in the next chapter, its effect upon Coleridge's own ideas of friendship. For two weeks running in December 1797, "The Soldier's Wife" became the focus of *The Anti-Jacobin*'s scorn. Its parodic imitation, "The Soldier's Friend," understands Coleridge and Southey's incitement of the reader as an anarchic threat. The role of the implied reader in "The Soldier's Wife" is performed by a drummer-boy, who becomes an intermediary between the Friend and the socially disempowered:

DACTYLICS.

Come, little Drummer Boy, lay down your knapsack here:
I am the Soldier's Friend—here are some Books for you;
Nice clever Books, by TOM PAINE the Philanthropist.

> Here's Half-a-crown for you—here are some Hand-bills too—
> Go to the Barracks, and give all the Soldiers some.
> Tell them the Sailors are all in a Mutiny.
> (*Exit Drummer Boy, with Hand-bills and Half-crown.
> —Manet Soldier's Friend.*)
>
> Liberty's friends thus all learn to amalgamate,
> Freedom's volcanic explosion prepares itself,
> Despots shall bow to the Fasces of Liberty,
> Reason, philosophy, "fiddledum diddledum,"
> Peace and Fraternity, higgledy, piggledy,
> Higgledy, piggledy, "fiddledum diddledum."
> *Et cætera, et cætera, et cætera*.[26]

The image of the drummer-boy carrying a radical message from the Friend to the mutinying troops passes comment on Southey's implied reader. The Anti-Jacobin poet deplores the fact that boy and reader are being manipulated into filling the space between classes with radical ideas of friendship based on Painite egalitarianism.

In particular, the poet fears that such sentimental affection amongst "Liberty's friends" will narrow the space between people through an organic process of "amalgamation." The older meaning of "amalgamation" referred to the chemical compounding of different elements. In the line "Liberty's Friends thus learn to amalgamate," friendship becomes analogous to chemistry: as the scientist compounds distinct organic materials, so friendship might provide a means of reconfiguring an individual's personal and social identity. In personal terms, *The Anti-Jacobin* seems uncannily aware of Coleridge's own enthusiasm for amalgamation, as revealed in a letter to John Thelwall dated 31 December 1796. Speaking of Southey, Coleridge declares that

> an admirable Poet might be made by *amalgamating him & me*. I *think* too much for a *Poet*; he too little for a *great* Poet. But he abjures *thinking*—& lays the whole stress of excellence—on *feeling*.—Now (as you say) they must go together.[27]

Organically recombined, Coleridge suggests that Southey and himself might unite the poetry of sensibility within a philosophical framework, thereby creating a powerful, radical voice.

As the *OED* states, *The Anti-Jacobin* also uses the term "amalgamation" here to signify the combining of heterogeneous social groups.[28] The periodical understands that the radical friend, armed with his sentimental rhetoric, might strive to integrate social classes and eliminate the space that preserved their estrangement. For conservatives, this was a culpable erasure of natural differences. Edmund Burke was among the first to condemn the social "amalgamation" of the French people effected by their newly written constitution. In *Reflections on the Revolution in France* (1790), Burke draws attention to the "metaphysical and alchemistical legislators" who, instead of attending to "the different kinds of citizens," "have attempted to confound all sorts of citizens, as well as they could, into one homogeneous mass; and then they divided this their amalgama into a number of incoherent republics."[29] Amalgamation is the monstrous result of a disreputable kind of scientific experiment, which has attempted to erase all signs of individuality from its populace. Burke contrasts this mutant social organization with the "antient republics" (p. 272), whose legislators recognized that the irreducible differences among men must be honored in the framing of laws. From the various circumstances of civil life "arose many diversities amongst men, according to their birth, their education, their professions, the periods of their lives, their residence in towns or in the country, . . . all which rendered them as it were so many different species of animals" (p. 273). In this conservative logic, such differences justify the disposing of citizens into "such classes, and to place them in such situations in the state as their peculiar habits might qualify them to fill" (p. 273).

The Anti-Jacobin realizes that an amalgamating friendship threatens the conservative Burkean order. The radical attachments of "Liberty's Friends" re-enact the new amalgam of the French people. Their unity is founded on a vague sentimentalism. As the drummer-boy departs with his radical message, the great ideals of "Peace and Fraternity" comically degenerate with every drumbeat into a nonsense rhyme of no social use whatsoever. The poem thus accuses Southey and Coleridge of failing to provide their own drummer-boy reader with a program of specific action to help the soldier's wife and those like her. To put such slogans into practice, however, guarantees civil unrest. Amalgamation does not promise sentimental integration but only social disintegration, for the Friend uses the boy to provoke the armed forces into rebellion. After the mutinies of the Channel fleet in April and May 1797, the prospect of widespread disorder had become a pressing anxiety for conservatives.

The Anti-Jacobin, then, criticizes radical friendship by highlighting the dangerous practical consequences arising from an indiscriminate extension of one's sympathies. However, it also questions whether sentimental friendship genuinely desires the eradication of social space. The magazine extends its attack in "The Friend of Humanity and the Knife-Grinder," written by George Canning, John Hookham Frere, and George Ellis, which parodied another of Southey's poems, "The Widow. Sapphics" (1796).[30] *The Anti-Jacobin*'s sapphics test the universal aspirations of radical friendship through the Friend of Humanity's encounter with a specific human specimen, the Knife-Grinder. The poem and accompanying illustration by Gillray deserve extended analysis, since together they form a crucial text for understanding the terms of the debate about radical friendship in the late 1790s. *The Anti-Jacobin*'s empiricist challenge to the radical idea of the Friend is announced in the poem's title, expressed by its dramatic form and emphasized through its action:

> FRIEND OF HUMANITY.
>
> "Needy Knife-grinder! whither are you going?
> Rough is the road, your Wheel is out of order—
> Bleak blows the blast;—your hat has got a hole in't,
>   So have your breeches!
>
> "Weary Knife-grinder! little think the proud ones,
> Who in their coaches roll along the turnpike-
> -road, what hard work 'tis crying all day "Knives and
>   "Scissars to grind O!"
>
> "Tell me, Knife-grinder, how you came to grind knives?
> Did some rich man tyrannically use you?
> Was it the 'Squire? or Parson of the Parish?
>   Or the Attorney?
>
> "Was it the 'Squire for killing of his Game? or
> Covetous Parson for his Tythes distraining?
> Or roguish Lawyer made you lose your little
>   All in a law-suit?
>
> "(Have you not read the Rights of Man, by TOM PAINE?)
> Drops of compassion tremble on my eye-lids,
> Ready to fall, as soon as you have told your
>   Pitiful story."
>
> KNIFE-GRINDER.
>
> "Story! God bless you! I have none to tell, Sir,
> Only last night a-drinking at the Chequers,
> This poor old hat and breeches, as you see, were
>   Torn in a scuffle.

"Constables came up for to take me into
Custody; they took me before the Justice;
Justice OLDMIXON put me in the Parish-
                    -Stocks for a Vagrant.

"I should be glad to drink your Honour's health in
A Pot of Beer, if you would give me Sixpence;
But for my part, I never love to meddle
                    With Politics, Sir."

FRIEND OF HUMANITY.

"*I* give thee Sixpence! I will see thee damn'd first—
Wretch! whom no sense of wrongs can rouse to vengeance—
Sordid, unfeeling, reprobate, degraded,
                    Spiritless outcast!"

(*Kicks the Knife-grinder, overturns his Wheel, and exit in a transport of republican enthusiasm and universal philanthropy.*) (p. 15)

Sentimental friendship cannot transcend class but is itself a class-bound idea. Although the Grinder is happy to share a drink with the Friend, he does not "love to meddle / With Politics, Sir." In refusing to fit into a sentimental narrative of class injustice, the Grinder declines forming a more intimate relation with the Friend, and highlights the politicization of friendship as a middle-class literary construct, which the lower orders reject. At the same time, the Friend's "pitying" attitude towards the object of his affection resonates with a Burkean view of love that is essentially hierarchical. As Burke writes in *A Philosophical Enquiry* (1757), "the objects of love are spoken of under diminutive epithets. . . . We submit to what we admire, but we love what submits to us."[31] Beautiful and amiable qualities are associated with weakness, which is why Homer gives "the Trojans, whose fate he has designed to excite our compassion, infinitely more of the amiable social virtues than he has distributed amongst his Greeks" (p. 158). Burkean friendship articulates itself through pity, an emotion that encodes an element of condescension. In *The Anti-Jacobin*'s poem, the Friend's violence toward the Grinder demonstrates in exaggerated form how close such condescension can be to contempt.

The Anti-Jacobin writers highlight a disjunction between the sentimental idea of socially inclusive friendship and its embodiment, arguing that in practice the Friend of Humanity has neither the means nor the inclination to bridge divisions of rank. In doing so, they indirectly draw attention to an issue that had arisen during the planning of the Pantisocracy scheme, and which brought different responses from Coleridge and Southey. The question arose regarding the candidature of Shadrach Weeks, who was both Southey's boyhood friend and a family servant in Bath. For Southey, affection for Shad did not efface their hierarchical relationship, a sentiment expressed in an unpublished verse-letter to Nicholas Lightfoot, dated 22 December 1793. In dramatizing his home life, Southey exclaims "so if you please / My good friend Shad Ill have my toasted cheese."[32] Shad may be a "good friend," but he remains subservient. Southey's view that friendship is compatible with a hierarchical relation manifests itself in his desire that the Pantisocrats take servants with them: "Let them dine with us and be treated with as much equality as they would wish—but perform that part of Labor for which their Education has fitted them."[33]

In response, Coleridge argued that the Pantisocrats would all be bound together in friendship, with that term implying the community's absolute social and political equality:

> *Southey* should not have written this Sentence—my Friend, my noble and high-souled Friend should have said—to his Dependents—Be my Slaves—and ye shall be my Equals—to his Wife & Sisters—Resign the *Name* of Ladyship and ye shall retain the *thing*. (1:114)

As a Pantisocratic "Friend," Southey should not contemplate maintaining divisions of rank. In becoming friends, the Pantisocrats aim to make hierarchical conceptions such as "slave" and "Ladyship" redundant.[34] However, despite his protestation that "SHAD GOES WITH US. HE IS MY BROTHER,"[35] Coleridge was elsewhere more ambivalent about the ideal social make-up of the community. During his tour of Wales in July 1794, Coleridge declared that his expounding upon Pantisocracy at Llanvillin had been almost too successful:

> I preached Pantisocracy and Aspheterism with so much success that two great huge Fellows, of Butcher like appearance, danced about the room in enthusiastic agitation—And one of them of his own accord called for a large Glass of Brandy, and drank it off to this, his own Toast—God save the King. And may he be the Last—Southey! Such men may be of use—they would *fell* the Golden Calf secundum Artem.[36]

Coleridge's amused, ironic tone reveals that he does not naturally associate Pantisocrats with men of "Butcher like appearance." In conceding that such men may be "of use," however, he intimates the need for a laboring class of "great huge Fellows" within their community, who would be better suited to the manual work that awaited the pioneers.

Coleridge's progress through the taverns of Wales revealed further uneasiness at the physical encounters generated by his preaching of Pantisocratic theory. Coleridge relates his adventure at Bala:

> At the Inn I was sore afraid, that I had caught the Itch from a Welch Democrat, who was charmed with my sentiments: he grasped my hand with flesh-bruising Ardour—and I trembled, lest some discontented Citizens of the *animalcular* Republic should have emigrated. (1:89)

The idea of Pantisocracy generates enthusiastic and affectionate responses in those Coleridge meets, but these new friendships bring him into proximity with some less desirable bodies. Coleridge finds that the physical passion of embodied friendship can literally be a "bruising" experience. Coleridge's qualms concerning such physical contact make a point about friendship and class. As we have seen, Coleridge did not value his friends for their boisterous physicality but rather for their solicitous "attentions," a term indicative of polite, middle-class culture. In "On Friendship" (1781), William Cowper regards unmediated expressions of affection as vulgar, more an expression of violence than friendship:

> The man that hails you Tom—or Jack
> And proves by thumping on your back
>   His sense of your great merit,
> Is such a friend that one had need
> Be very much his friend indeed
>   To pardon or to bear it.
>   (lines 151–56)

Overt physicality is no part of the middle-class manners that Cowper regards as essential to friendship. In this context, the "Welch Democrat" takes on the characteristics of the intimidating lower-class "men of Butcher like appearance." Direct physical contact with heterogeneous sections of society threatens to undermine the integrity of the Coleridgean self. In fearing that "Citizens of the *animalcular* Republic" may have "emigrated," Coleridge not only signals his anxiety of catching the Welch Democrat's fleas but also hints that low-life "animals" might emigrate en masse to America with the Oxbridge Pantisocrats.

As was seen in chapter 3, the Pantisocracy scheme brought into focus the difficulty examined throughout this book of moving the Idea of friendship to the stage of its practical application or physical embodiment. The problem of cancelling out differences in rank and education was not the least of these and tested the radical ideal of friendship for humanity. *The Anti-Jacobin* devotes itself to bringing to the fore exactly this kind of ambivalence within the radical community. James Gillray's plate, "The Friend of Humanity and the Knife-Grinder," which appeared separately one week after the poem, further interrogates the extent of the Friend's affections, and in doing so, exploits Coleridgean anxieties about embodiment.[37] In the context of the poem, the image of the Friend of Humanity alludes to Southey and Coleridge. At the same time, it associates these men with a particular contemporary radical, whose career provides *The Anti-Jacobin* with empirical social detail with which to test the Platonic Idea.

The slogan "Tierney and Liberty," visible on the wall across the street, closely associates the "Friend of Humanity" with George Tierney, M. P. for Southwark ("scene. The Borough"). Elected to parliament six months earlier, by December 1797 Tierney was rapidly becoming the sole voice of opposition. The plate thus tests the socially inclusive aspirations of radical friendship by interrogating the identity of a foremost radical of the time. To this end, Gillray focuses attention on the central visual ambiguity of the plate—whether the Friend's outstretched hand is a greeting or a repulse. The phrase "Tierney and Liberty" may suggest the image is a greeting, articulating the Friend's initial hope of befriending the Grinder. Tierney might in fact be promising the Grinder political enfranchisement itself, for the slogan identifies Tierney as the radical successor to John Wilkes, M. P., the people's champion of the 1770s, whose name had earlier lent itself to the rallying cry "Wilkes and Liberty." In Wilkes's case, a government minority repeatedly denied him taking up his Middlesex seat. Although Tierney was accepted by Parliament, he fought two lengthy election campaigns against a corrupt government-supported candidate.[38] Like Wilkes before him, Tierney's struggle created a groundswell of popular local sympathy. By situating Tierney within "The Borough," therefore, Gillray confirms the public perception of Tierney as a revolutionary Friend of Humanity, committed to universal suffrage.

Other aspects of Tierney's career, however, raised questions regarding the M. P.'s radicalism and the meaning of his outstretched hand. As his biographer H. K. Olphin suggests, Tierney was not only notoriously parsimonious but was primarily "a representative of the mercantile class" (p. 19); indeed, he supported the "society

4: FRIENDS OF HUMANITY 163

James Gillray, "The Friend of Humanity and the Knife-Grinder.—Scene. The Borough, in Imitation of Mr Southey's Sapphics,—Vide. *Anti-Jacobin*, p. 15." Published 4 December 1797 by H. Humphrey, 27 St. James's Street, London. © Copyright The British Museum.

of the Friends of the People," a parliamentary group opposed to the desire of the Society for Constitutional Information to obtain "for the people the Rights of the People in their full extent."[39] Such facts suggest that Tierney's friendship might not embrace "Humanity" in all its guises. The picture confirms that the Friend's hand does not fully extend to the Grinder but draws back before it crosses from stucco to brick. In this way, Gillray uses Tierney to undermine the "Friend of Humanity," demonstrating how human beings struggle in practice to fulfil the inclusivist aspirations of the sentimental Idea.

At the same time, the plate also suggests the dangerousness of harboring a sentimental affection for the poor. First, the diptych structure of Gillray's plate illustrates the impossibility of friendly intermingling between classes. Gillray celebrates the left-hand side of the street, presenting the Friend as the antithesis to the Grinder. Through their clothes, Gillray sets lower-class degeneracy against middle-class affluence. The Friend wears crisp, high-quality garments, while the vertical lines of his stockings and waistcoat draw the eye upwards, suggesting his progression towards the light. The Grinder's posture and garments, however, emphasize his downwards motion. As earthy brown as their surroundings, his torn trousers and socks resemble some organic material seeping towards the ground. Fundamentally, Gillray declares, the middle and lower orders move in opposite directions, the former aspiring to heaven, the latter little better than the base earth towards which he tends.

Such contraries draw attention, however, to the images testing the central line: the Friend's outstretched hand and the Knife-Grinder's machine, whose wheels are uncomfortably close to the Friend's foot. Together, these images warn of the grave dangers of inclusivist ideas of friendship, specifically, that the lower ranks will return the friendly arm of middle-class greeting through the wheels of revolution. The Grinder's wheel is already invading middle-class space, and the viewer knows he carries lethal weapons. The Friend's turning of his hand into a defensive gesture betrays his anxiety about the wheel's proximity, both to his foot and to the high street beyond. Gillray's message seems clear: sentimental gestures of friendship directly endanger all that the upper echelons of society hold dear. Their privileges depend upon an antipathetic attitude towards the lower orders, in order to preserve the necessary space between ranks.

For other Tory satirists, radical sensibility seemed unlikely to have such dangerous implications. In Ansell's 1798 print, "Tears of Sensibility," Tierney becomes a caricature of the man of feeling.[40] Drowning in a sea of sympathetic tears, the Whigs bewail the death in 1798 of Lord Edward Fitzgerald, leader of the United Irishmen. Despite Sheridan's sentimental plea that "The Man who can think of his own happiness, while his Friend is in distress deserves to be hunted as a Monster to Society," the tears of these liberal figures are self-centred. Fox's affection results from Fitzgerald being "the most, like myself," while Erskine is sorry only that he has lost the "job" of defending him at his trial. Although radical sensibility overspills all boundaries of decorum, the men's clasping of their hands highlights how sensibility enervates the moral agent. There is thus little danger of these Friends of Humanity even encounter-

Charles or James K. Ansell, "Tears of Sensibility—Sympathy a Poem—Let's all be Unhappy together—ie The Wig Club in Distress &c &c." Published 11 June 1798 by S. W. Fores, 50 Piccadilly, London. © Copyright The British Museum.

ing the objects of their compassion, be they Knife-Grinder or United Irishman.

The Anti-Jacobin, however, is a significant contributive force in redefining sentimental friendship as a politically conservative idea in the later 1790s. In a letter published in May 1798, "Mucius" argues that the French threat has only highlighted the amity within English society:

> It is impossible not to remark throughout all classes of the Community . . . an unrivalled attachment to the general cause—connected as that cause indisputably is . . . with every thing that can secure the enjoyment of private happiness, or perpetuate the blessings of social intercourse.—From this general zeal . . . we may look with confidence . . . that as, under the blessing of Providence, we enjoy an infinitely greater share of practical Liberty than has ever yet fallen to the lot of Nations, so we may continue to maintain the same superiority over all other People, with respect to the liberality of our private dealings, and the amiability and social virtues of our private lives.[41]

"Amiability" here is an exclusively English possession, fundamental to the country's social cohesion. In doing so, Mucius attempts to relieve conservative anxieties about social insubordination, gesturing instead to a class system at peace with itself. Mucius confirms Shearer West's contention that during the later eighteenth century, "friendship came to be seen as an essential aspect of British liberty."[42] In this conservative logic, defending the country's freedom becomes a defence of the amity characteristic of English life. Chris Jones argues that "a conservative Sensibility claimed that man's feelings were fostered by the associations of traditional society and were its principal support,"[43] and *The Anti-Jacobin* alludes to this notion two months later in the poem, "New Morality."[44] In scorning the idea of philanthropy, the poet distinguishes between its British and French versions:

> PHILANTHROPY—not She, who dries
> The Orphan's tears, and wipes the Widow's eyes;
> Not She, who, sainted Charity her guide,
> Of British Bounty pours the annual tide—
> But *French* PHILANTHROPY—whose boundless mind
> Glows with the general love of all mankind.
>
> (lines 89–94)

The only authentic friendship is the British variety, which emphasizes practical benevolence and focuses its affection within the local and domestic circle.

Contrasting this conservative model with radical friendship's Platonic, generalizing language, *The Anti-Jacobin* cannot conceal its derision for such diffuse Frenchified affection, which it implicitly associates with Coleridge:

> through the extended globe his feelings run
> As broad and general as th'unbounded Sun!
> No narrow bigot he—his reason'd view
> Thy interests, *England*, ranks with thine *Peru*—
> *France* at our doors, he sees no danger nigh,
> But heaves for *Turkey's* woes th'impartial sigh;
> A steady Patriot of the World alone,
> The Friend of every Country—but his own.
>
> (lines 107–14)

As in "The Friend of Humanity and the Knife-Grinder," the Coleridgean radical does not love actual people but only abstractions like "universal Man" and the "World." As Paul Magnuson remarks, *The Anti-Jacobin* "turns Coleridge's image of the sun for the love of humanity against him":[45] the warmth of affection that Coleridge hopes will come to "cheer and vivify" all corners of the "system"[46] is reduced to a Platonic sentimentalism so "broad and general" it becomes meaningless. The following year, the periodical explicitly represented Coleridge as "The Friend of every Country—but his own." Identifying "C——dge" as one of those "initiated in the mysteries of Theophilanthropism," the periodical interpreted his trip to Germany as indicative of his desertion of family and country: "He has [...] married, had children, and has now quitted the country, become a citizen of the world, left his little ones fatherless, and his wife destitute."⁴⁷ *The Anti-Jacobin* identifies Coleridge as a typical Friend of Humanity, whose lack of beneficence towards his domestic attachments undermines his sentimental idealism and renders him culpably unpatriotic.

In contrast to the radical's sentimental celebration of Humanity, conservative friendship "binds" itself tightly to empirical objects. In "New Morality," by mocking the Platonist's "impartial sigh," the poet links sentiment with "partiality": fondness for a person implies a bias towards him. *The Anti-Jacobin*'s conservatism should be distinguished, however, from that of Burke. In his *Reflections*, Burke employs an organic discourse of affection that accepts that a love for the particular may be compatible with a love for the greater whole:

> To be attached to the subdivision, to love the little platoon we belong to in society, is the first principle (the germ as it were) of public affections. It is the first link in the series by which we proceed towards a love to our country and to mankind. (pp. 68–69)

For Burke, patriotism grows out of domestic attachments, superseding but not altogether denying a generalized friendship for humanity. The Pantisocratic Coleridge exploits this Burkean discourse in his notion of philanthropy as a "home-born" virtue. Burke's "little platoon" of domestic affections acknowledges that friends can harden themselves into a militantly exclusive group. However, Burke softens such militaristic connotations in order to suggest friendship's organic potential to embrace a wider community. *The Anti-Jacobin*, however, differs from both Burke and Coleridge in magnifying friendship's potential for aggressively excluding outsiders. For these hard-line conservatives, local affection does not provide the "germ" for outward, organic growth, but rather enables the friend to discover his foe.⁴⁸ The periodical transforms Burke's "little platoon" into an army bent on the destruction of its enemy, and argues that the true friend speaks a language of hostility to his foe.

"New Morality" strives to dislodge friendship from a language of sentiment, and focuses its argument by scorning the "candid friend." "Candour" combined the sentimental notions of "sweetness of temper" and "kindness," with ideas of "openness" and "purity of mind."[49] For over thirty lines, the poet condemns the candid friend's sentimental language of conciliation:

> Candour, which softens Party's headlong rage.
> Candour—which spares its foes—nor e'er descends
> With bigot zeal to combat for its friends.
> Candour—which loves in see-saw strain to tell
> Of acting foolishly, but meaning well:
> Too nice to praise by wholesale, or to blame,
> Convinc'd that all men's motives are the same, . . .
> Give me th'avow'd, th'erect, the manly Foe
> Bold I can meet—perhaps may turn his blow;
> But of all plagues, good Heav'n, thy wrath can send,
> Save, save, oh! save me from the *Candid* Friend!
> (lines 192–98, 207–10)

For *The Anti-Jacobin*, true friendship is fanatically partial, entailing a militaristic defence of one's friends and a "zealous combat" against their enemies. An accommodating quality like candor is intolerable because it compromises with the opposition, befriending instead of destroying him. The candid friend's sympathetic tendencies therefore make him an unreliable ally in time of war. The *OED* reveals the modernity of *The Anti-Jacobin* by identifying this passage as the first ironic use of the phrase "candid friend."[50] This confirms the magazine's aim of wrenching friendship from an established sentimental discourse.

In terms of policy, *The Anti-Jacobin* fears that candor might encourage appeasement. In a letter from "A Calm Observer," one candid friend demonstrates how an enthusiasm for sympathy results in opposition to English war-mongering:

> Another evil, inseparable from this attitude of Menace and Hostility, consists in the impossibility of estimating the character and dispositions of the Enemy with a becoming candour and liberality: . . . If we are desirous of Peace, let us seek for it *"In the spirit of Peace;"* . . . Let our conduct present an amiable contrast with that of the Enemy. If we wish to recover their friendship, we must begin by disarming the animosity we have excited. Let us lay aside those Armaments and Expeditions which are so offensive to them, and return to tha[t] unsuspecting confidence which is the only natural cement of a social intercourse.[51]

This candid observer's naive belief in man's "natural" affection towards his kind creates a sentimental desire for friendship, which results in pacifism. In hoping to receive the affection he gives, this friend rejects all policies that risk "offending" the French. For *The Anti-Jacobin*, this sentimental idea of re-establishing friendly relations between England and France is damnable. The periodical launches its strongest attack on sensibility through the figure of "Cato," who, in his "Manners and Character of the Age," derides Mucius's sentimental celebration of "the increased amiability which every where shews itself in private life":[52]

> The Enemy has passed the Rubicon, and he will destroy us if he be not destroyed. There can be no compromise, no capitulation. . . . In such a conflict, there are but two descriptions of persons—Friends and Foes. Whoever is not for us, is against us. . . . Even lukewarmness is a high crime and misdemeanour, as it leads to the most fatal consequences. Then let us hear no more, at such a time, of amiability and gentleness—of candour, liberality, and moderation—of conciliating, mild, and generous feelings. Such qualities are now not virtues, but vices. . . . They are, in short, but other names for pusillanimity and treachery. . . . Whoever refuses to join in vigorously repelling the attack, is either a Coward or a Traitor, and, instead of having any claim to liberality or indulgence, deserves the scorn and execration of mankind. (p. 270)

Against a background of war, the ideological battle for the meaning of friendship becomes intense. For *The Anti-Jacobin*, the true friend recognizes his French foe and joins in the fight against him. The idea of friendship is crucial to the conservative agenda of bolstering national unity. However, Cato understands that friendship may undermine the nation as well as reinforce its identity, for the "friend" can also speak in sentimental tones and, in so doing, adopt a dangerous policy of appeasement. For this writer, controlling the meaning of friendship is literally a matter of national security.

Through the figure of Coleridge, it is possible to view the influence of such conservative ideas upon the radical community. Fundamentally, Coleridge trys to resist *The Anti-Jacobin*'s polarization of the political world. Four months before Cato's article, Coleridge vents his annoyance in a letter to his brother George, in which he famously snaps his "squeaking baby-trumpet of Sedition":[53]

> You think, my Brother! that there can be but two *parties* at present, for the Government & against the Government.—It may be so—I am of no party. It is true, I think the present ministry weak & perhaps unprincipled men; but I could not with a safe conscience vote for their removal; for I could point out no substitutes. (1:396)

Coleridge evades allegiance to either the Friends of Government or the Friends of Freedom. In doing so, however, he plays the "candid Friend," unable to support or condemn friend or foe wholeheartedly. Indeed, Cato's assault on "lukewarmness" reads like the church-and-king's public reply to Coleridge's private letter. Coleridge's recoil from his radical past did not place him comfortably within the Tory establishment; Cato would regard his equivocations as "treason."

As the "candid friend," Coleridge also risked estranging himself from the radical community. In his "Advice to the Friends of Freedom," an article published in *The Morning Post* of 12 December 1799, Coleridge attacks the radicals for adopting a language of hostility towards their conservative foe. He laments how the "most numerous" radical Friends are those

> who apologise for the French in direct and habitual opposition to the Minister; all who, with little extravagance and as little greatness of mind, are in the habits of personal dislike of Mr. Pitt and his party; who, fixing their feelings on men rather than measures, have made an ejection of the present Members from the Administration an object and a passion, and who will always find some excuse, even for the enemies of mankind, provided they happen at the same time to profess themselves the enemies of Mr. Pitt.[54]

Friendship has degenerated into merely personal alliances that define themselves through creating enemies. For Coleridge, this is a sorry descent from the sentimental friend's impartial adherence to a moral principle. He concludes that both sides are motivated by enmity, and are in effect indistinguishable: "Too much of extravagant hope, too much of rash intolerance, has disgraced all parties: and facts, well adapted to discipline us all, have burst forth, even to superfluity" (pp. 39–40).

George Tierney's actions during 1798 confirmed Coleridge's fears regarding the radical Friends' new language of antagonism. Determined to thwart Pitt on every occasion, Tierney opposed the Bill for the Better Manning of the Navy, despite admitting its necessity. Having been publicly accused by Pitt of disloyalty, the "Friend of Humanity" challenged the Prime Minister to a duel on Wimbledon common. Coleridge expressed his dismay at Tierney's behavior in *The Morning Post* of 30 July 1798, in his political verses, "Original Poetry. A Tale."[55] Coleridge argues that the war with France must now be supported as the "Ox" (the French Revolution) has gone "Mad." His new-found patriotism is interrupted by a "fierce

Aristocrat" (line 119) who recounts "That Tierney's wounded Mister PITT, / And his fine tongue enchanted!" (lines 125–26). Carl Woodring plausibly speculates that "Coleridge perhaps had originally designed the Mad Ox poem to defend the awakened patriotism of Sheridan and Tierney. If so, he would have found the thesis inappropriate in the confusion immediately after Tierney's opposition to Pitt became public comedy."[56] Tierney's animosity curtails Coleridge's desire to defend him.

In his patriotic defence of the war with France in 1798, Coleridge attempts to extricate himself from *The Anti-Jacobin*'s pejorative characterization of him as a "citizen of the world." The complexity of Coleridge's response to *The Anti-Jacobin*'s conservative discourse of friendship is revealed in the quarto, *Fears in Solitude*, published in the autumn of 1798.[57] Traditional commentaries read Coleridge's volume as a retraction of his former radicalism in light of France's invasion of Switzerland, and domestic pressure from the party of church-and-king. Paul Magnuson has recently revised this view, asking whether *Fears in Solitude* does not "intend to present Coleridge both as a loyal patriot, who loves his country, and as a devoutly religious man, on the one hand, and on the other, as one who continues to support the Jacobin ideals of liberty that he has always held?"[58] The presence of both radical and conservative discourses of friendship within the volume confirms Magnuson's view, as well as his contention that "Coleridge's oscillation should be re-read as the acrobatic feat of remaining in the public debates, when other radical voices had been either silenced or exiled" (p. 80). Such oscillations characterize Coleridge's idea of friendship in "Fears in Solitude," as he contemplates the imminent threat of invasion from "A green and silent spot amid the hills" (line 1). On the one hand, he continues to invoke the radicalized sensibility of the Friend of Humanity. He chastises his countrymen for swelling the "war-whoop" (line 86) against the French, an enthusiasm facilitated by their failure to depict war through an imaginative discourse of sensibility, which might bring home its true horror. Coleridge condemns:

> all our dainty terms for fratricide,
> Terms which we trundle smoothly o'er our tongues
> Like mere abstractions, empty sounds to which
> We join no feeling and attach no form,
> As if the soldier died without a wound; [. . .]
> As tho' he had no wife to pine for him,
> No God to judge him!
>
> (lines 110–14; 119–20)

Coleridge plays the sentimental Friend of Humanity who would employ a truth-painting imagination to evoke a compassionate sensibility in his reader. Nevertheless, he admits the necessity of fighting the French, whom he depicts in generalized terms as "an impious foe, / Impious and false, a light and cruel race" (lines 136–37). At this point he reiterates Mucius's conservative view of friendship as a British possession threatened by French aggression. "Themselves too sensual to be free" (line 140), these imperialists

> Poision life's amities, and cheat the heart
> Of Faith and quiet Hope, and all that soothes
> And all that lifts the spirit!
>
> (lines 141–43)

Confining friendship to Britain becomes part of Coleridge's Burkean argument that private affections justify a patriotic defence of one's homeland:

> O dear Britain! O my mother Isle!
> Needs must thou prove a name most dear and holy
> To me, a son, a brother, and a friend,
> A husband and a father! who revere
> All bonds of natural love, and find them all
> Within the limits of thy rocky shores.
>
> (lines 173–78)

Coleridge defends himself against *The Anti-Jacobin*'s argument that he is one of those who are "enemies / Ev'n of their country" (lines 171–72). In limiting his affections to England's "rocky shores" Coleridge in fact foreshadows the phrasing of "New Morality," published in July.[59] He particularly attempts to stifle suggestions that he is the "Friend of every country—but his own." As we shall see in chapter 5, Coleridge's subsequent celebration of his "lowly cottage" (line 222) in Nether Stowey likewise strives to demonstrate his sentimental integration within the landscape and affections of the English community.

However, Coleridge finally suggests that his solitary meditation in the "green and silent dell" (line 225) has reawakened his love for humanity. Walking back to Stowey, he declares himself

> grateful, that by nature's quietness
> And solitary musings all my heart
> Is soften'd, and made worthy to indulge
> Love, and the thoughts that yearn for human kind.
>
> (lines 226–29)

Magnuson notes that "an older meaning of 'yearn' is 'to sympathize with' or 'to pity'," and argues that Coleridge's "musings" sound "suspiciously like the abstract metaphysics that Burke saw as Jacobin" (p. 92). As in "This Lime-Tree Bower," nature acts upon Coleridge to reawaken a Shaftesburian "Natural Affection" for the universal family of "human kind." Becoming once more a Friend of Humanity, Coleridge ends the poem by tacitly gesturing towards the sentimental argument for making peace.

In the following poem, "France: An Ode," Coleridge appears to renege altogether on the Burkean discourse of domestic affections he had posited in "Fears in Solitude." The poem develops the connection between friendship and liberty, but no longer associates it with British freedoms threatened by French imperialism. Recalling his earlier support for Revolutionary France, Coleridge distances himself from the conservative ideology of sentimental friendship:

> Though dear her shores, and circling ocean,
> Though many friendships, many youthful loves
> Had swoln the patriot emotion
> And flung a magic light o'er all her hills and groves;
> Yet still my voice unalter'd sang defeat
> To all that brav'd the tyrant-quelling lance,
> And shame too long delay'd, and vain retreat!
> For ne'er, O Liberty! with partial aim
> I dimm'd thy light, or damp'd thy holy flame.
>
> (lines 32–40)[60]

The radical Coleridge feminizes England as a "dear" domestic environment, but one whose restrictive "circling ocean" suggests it does not embody "Liberty." Despite acknowledging that domestic friendships give rise to a sentimental "patriot emotion," he suggests this Burkean sensibility is "swoln" and excessive. In flinging a "magic light" across the country, conservative sensibility acts like a magic lantern, coloring the idea of England in a beautiful but illusory light. Distinguished from the pure light of Liberty, these partial domestic friendships cannot command Coleridge's deepest affections.

Coleridge admits he no longer harbors sympathy for France, whose invasion of Switzerland marks her ultimate failure to embody the idea of Liberty. However, he relocates Liberty not in England or any "forms of human pow'r" (line 92) but in nature:

> Yes! while I stood and gaz'd, my temples bare,
> And shot my being thro' earth, sea, and air,

> Possessing all things with intensest love,
> O Liberty, my spirit felt thee there!
>
> (lines 102–5)

Coleridge's intensest love is felt for those things that embody Liberty, but these are natural entities rather than the traditional institutions of English life. If Coleridge recants his former support for Revolutionary France, "France: An Ode" suggests even less than "Fears in Solitude" that he now embraces the conservative discourse of domestic affection. The continuance of these radical positions helps explain *The Anti-Jacobin*'s continued hostility to Coleridge during 1798–1799.

Despite resisting the politics of polarization, however, Coleridge had to acknowledge the conservative attack on the sentimental friendship for humanity of many English radicals. By 1798 he concurs with *The Anti-Jacobin* that the imperfect behavior of the "Friends of Freedom" towards each other has debased the sentimental idea. In his letter to George, Coleridge quotes from Cowper's poem *The Task* in denouncing the "loud Declaimers on the part / Of Liberty":

> For when was public Virtue to be found
> Where private was not? Can he love the whole
> Who loves no part? He be a *nation's* friend
> Who is, in truth, the friend of no man there?
> Can he be strenuous in his country's cause
> Who slights the charities, for whose dear sake
> That country, if at all, must be belov'd?
>
> (1:396)

Coleridge joins Cowper and *The Anti-Jacobin* in denouncing the radicals' lack of charity, and suggests that their friendship is merely theoretical. Like the magazine, Coleridge's authority derives from his empirical knowledge of the radicals' behavior; he "deprecate[s] the moral & intellectual habits ... of the Friends of Freedom" with a "deeper conviction" than George, "for my belief is founded on actual experience" (1:395). Once again, the radical, sentimental ideal founders on the rock of empiricism. Coleridge published these ideas in a contribution to *The Morning Post* of 19 December 1799, entitled "Principles not Titles."[61] Again, he concedes that *The Anti-Jacobin*'s attack on the private conduct of various "Friends" has damaged his faith in friendship as a political ideal:

> Every age has had some favourite general term—Friends of Religion, Friends of Freedom, or Philosophers: to these goodly phrases every

man is self-eligible; they stand as open to the Factious as to the Patriot—to the mischievous Visionary as to the sober Reasoner. Under the protection of these phrases bad men contrive to share the credit which their betters had gained. (1:41–42)

Although the conservatives' general condemnation of the "Friends of Freedom" is "plausible" rather than true, Coleridge sadly admits that the term "Friend" has become detached from its moral idea. Consequently, the idea itself has lost authority and appeal. Under pressure in this article, Coleridge attempted to redefine the "Friend" as a "good man" of "principle" (1:42). However, as this character also rejected a language of personal animosity, he too risked estranging himself from both Anti-Jacobins and Friends of Freedom. In such a polarized environment, Coleridge's "good man" might well discover his dream of friendship vanish into space, leaving him as isolated as the Ancyent Marinere, "all all alone / Alone on the wide wide Sea" (lines 232–33).

Coleridge's skepticism at the end of the decade with friendship's radical sensibility is illustrated in his increasing lack of faith in the possibility of cross-rank friendships. The extent of his disillusionment can be measured through comparison with his contemporaries, Thelwall and Poole. In Thelwall's novel, *The Daughter of Adoption* (1801), despite the initial declaration of friendship between Henry and Edmunds, the latter remains in a serving role almost until the very end of the novel, three volumes later. However, his "fidelity and attachment" (4:295) is finally rewarded by his formal release from a subservient role:

> "Friend Edmunds!" said Henry, stretching out his hand, . . . ["] The profession I made to you in the glen of Limbé is at length realised. I ought to have realised it before. You are no longer my servant. I am no more your master. Call me friend—call me patron—call me Henry Montfort: any thing your independent affection may prompt you to: for independent you are; and, some how or other, you shall have the means of supporting that independence."
>
> Edmunds was overcome by his feelings. He bowed, and was silent. (4:296–97)

This middle-class friend unambiguously stretches out his hand to meet his servant in amity. Thelwall's novel of 1801 thus sustains the possibility that the sentimental Idea may be "realised" in social practice.

If Thelwall marks a persistent, albeit quiescent, strand of idealism, Thomas Poole is pained to discover that his experience is at odds with his own idealism. Writing to Coleridge in 1799, Poole relates an incident that "mixes so much feeling with so much rational cause for regret, that it has altogether made me very unhappy":

> I have been used ill by some of my servants whom I treated best, whom I most confided in—in a word, whom I most loved. Now this is a proof of such melancholy insensibility on their part, not to say depravity, and so damps every benevolent feeling of my own mind, as far as relates to their class of society, that it is difficult to say how injurious to me, and to them, the consequences of it may be. Say nothing of this to anybody. I hope I have made them sensible of their errors, and that in future they will be better. . . . Thus, my dear Col., we must look to ourselves, and I am afraid to ourselves alone, for happiness.[62]

Poole's servants have rejected the sentimental scenario in which serving and ruling classes are bound in ties of affection to the extent that a servant can be the confidant of his master. For Poole, this betrayal of his trust and love demonstrates that "sensibility" is not universal. In looking "to ourselves alone," Poole restricts sentimental friendship to the educated middle orders, and tacitly acknowledges that the radical dream of cross-rank affection is at an end. If the impossibility of universal friendship strikes Poole as an unpalatable truth, Coleridge is surprised only at how long it has taken his friend to lose his illusions. He writes, on 8 April 1799:

> As to your servants & the people of Stowey in general—Poole, my Beloved! you have been often unwisely fretful with me when I have pressed upon you their depravity.—Without religious joys, and religious terrors nothing can be expected from the *inferior* Classes in society—whether or no any *class* is strong enough to stand firm without them, is to me doubtful.—There are favoured *Individuals*, but not *Classes*.[63]

Coleridge suggests that Poole has formerly played the idealistic Friend of Humanity, "unwisely fretful" that Coleridge might, like *The Anti-Jacobin*, doubt the possibility of cross-rank friendship. Coleridge even goes beyond the Tory magazine by suggesting there is little likelihood of finding friendship in any "*class.*" In doing so, he rejects friendship's role in either a radical discourse or that of church-and-king. Instead, as a relation restricted to a few "favoured Individuals," friendship retreats entirely from the public, political sphere back into its nondisruptive, domestic space.

5
"They answer and provoke each other's songs": Coleridge, Thelwall, and Oppositional Friendship

THE PREVIOUS CHAPTER EXAMINED HOW COLERIDGE, ESPECIALLY FROM 1798, resisted the polarization of English politics into "friends and foes," and how this refusal to align himself along party lines finally marked his disenchantment with radicals like George Tierney, who were unequivocally hostile towards the Tory establishment. By 1817, a conservative Coleridge was declaring in *Biographia Literaria*: "How opposite even then my principles were to those of jacobinism or even of democracy."[1] John Thelwall, however, remembered a very different Coleridge:

> M[r] C. was indeed far from Democracy, because he was far beyond it, I well remember—for he was a down right zealous leveller & indeed in one of the worst senses of the word he was a Jacobin, a man of blood— Does he forget the letters he wrote to me (& which I believe I yet have) acknowledging the justice of my castigation of him for the violence, and sanguinary tendency of some of his doctrines.[2]

Thelwall's Coleridge had been an unequivocal political radical, who may have expressed some sympathy with Robespierre and the violent politics that had culminated in the Terror (1792–1794).

During these years, the French Jacobins had themselves embraced the rhetoric of "friend and foe," epitomized by the revolutionary slogan "fraternity or death." As Lynn Hunt notes, in France fraternity "defined a kind of 'us' and 'them' of revolutionary politics, especially on the popular level," thus expressed in one Parisian sectional assembly in 1793: "For a free people, there should be no neutral being. There are only brothers or enemies."[3] One of Coleridge's wilder pronouncements during 1794 confirmed that he had himself once entertained "such a belligerent notion of fraternity" (p. 13). "The Cockatrice," he informed Southey, "is emblematic of Monarchy—a *monster* generated by *Ingratitude* on *Absurdity*. When Serpents *sting*, the only Remedy is—to *kill* the *Serpent*, and *besmear* the *Wound* with the *Fat*. Would you desire better *Sympathy?*"[4] The reference to *"kill* the *Serpent"* alludes to Brutus's soliloquy in *Julius Caesar*, in which he meditates on the planned murder of Caesar (2.1.32–34). For those subject to the monarchical tyranny of contemporary Caesars, Coleridge's *"sympathy"* expresses itself in the "sanguinary" terms of which Thelwall disapproved. Coleridge's acquaintance with Thelwall during 1796–1797 developed out of his entertaining such antisentimental, oppositional sentiments. The progress of their relations pressingly raised issues of Idea and embodiment, of putting comradeship to the test in hostile circumstances. However, the trajectory of the men's relations also challenged the assumption of Jacobins and Anti-Jacobins alike, that opposing groups are bound together only in enmity. The connection between Coleridge and Thelwall poses and tests another question: to what extent might opposition itself be the dynamic means of creating not hatred but friendship?

As Lewis Patton and Peter Mann remark, the collapse of Coleridge's friendship with Southey in November 1795 "produced, along with disillusionment, an unexpected result. In Coleridge's mind he, the weaker vessel, had become the stronger, the one more dedicated to principle. . . . This access of self-confidence doubtless nerved him for his strenuous public duties of late 1795 and early 1796."[5] Coleridge's fresh awareness of his political principles was heightened in November 1795 by the introduction into Parliament of the Treason and Convention Bills, passed in December and subsequently known as the "Gagging Acts." Coleridge responded to this attack on civil liberties by delivering a "Lecture on the Two Bills" in Bristol on 26 November. There he declared the necessity of establishing an oppositional community that could fight the repressive measures of Pitt and Lord Grenville:

> True political moderation . . . consists in not opposing the measures of Government, except when great and national Interests are at stake: and when that is the case, in opposing them with such a degree of warmth as is adequate to the nature of the evil. To oppose upon any other ground . . . is certainly faction; but it is likewise faction, and faction of the worst kind, either not to oppose at all, or not to oppose in earnest when the . . . Principles of Liberty are . . . being endangered.[6]

For Coleridge, defending democratic freedoms necessarily entailed defending the right to oppose. Coleridge included several passages from the lecture in his pamphlet, *The Plot Discovered*, which appeared two weeks later. There he identified John Thelwall as the symbol of the community of active opposition for which he had called in his lecture: Thelwall is "the voice of tens of thousands" who "speaks the feelings of multitudes," and the fundamental purpose of the Two Bills to ensure that "Mr. Thelwall should no longer give political lectures."[7] This was a lucid assessment; as chief orator of the London Corresponding Society since 1793, author of *The Tribune* (1795–1796), and defendant in the State Trials of 1794, Thelwall had become one of the most notorious radicals of the day.

It is not sentimentalism to understand the support Coleridge offers Thelwall in *The Plot Discovered* as an act of friendship. Throughout the decade, a widespread tendency developed among those opposed to Government policy publicly to demonstrate themselves bound in friendship with one another. Across the land, Corresponding Societies addressed each other as "friends" in order to highlight their solidarity.[8] Such protestations were not merely epistolary tropes, as is revealed in James Gillray's satirical print, "Copenhagen House." This illustrated Thelwall's speech against the Two Bills, delivered at the General Meeting of the Corresponding Society at Copenhagen Fields, on 12 November 1795.[9] Directly below Thelwall's platform stand two male, hatted figures facing the speaker, their arms symmetrically resting on each other's shoulders. The fraternal solidarity of these men is cemented by their mutual identification with Thelwall's oppositional rhetoric. As a corollary, the image suggests how physical gestures of intimacy might symbolize the sentimental unification of individuals, ranks, or nations, and as such intimate an egalitarian political agenda. The public comradely embrace ostentatiously demonstrated the physical solidarity of the oppositional movement. Such images became topics for satire, as in Ansell's print "An Irish Hug alias A Fraternal Embrace" (1798). This mocked Fox's affection for the Irish radical, O'Connor, expressed in a bear-hug.[10] More explicitly than Gillray, Ansell highlights how radicals might profess their ideological bond through the physical gestures of sentimental friendship. As O'Connor calls Fox "my dear Honey," so Fox declares the Irishman "*The Man after my own Heart* for he entertains the *same* Political sentiments as *every one* of the Opposition." Ansell satirizes the notion that political agreement might justify sentimental attachment, and invites the viewer to identify the men's effusiveness as unmanly and superficial.

Gillray had already noted Coleridge's participation in this kind of radical fraternization. As Nicholas Roe points out, "the two urchins

James Gillray, "Copenhagen House." Published 16 November by H. Humphrey, New Bond Street, London. © Copyright The British Museum.

playing democratic roulette" in the foreground of "Copenhagen House" "look like Coleridge, left, and Southey, right."[11] This pairing represents another politically motivated union, generated in the wake of Thelwall's democratic politics. In his Bristol lectures, Coleridge explicitly describes his ideological bonds with other radicals in terms of friendship, explaining thus his decision to answer the attacks on Edward Long Fox in 1795:

> I have started forward to answer them, though almost a perfect *stranger* to the Doctor—but the sentence of Horace concerning our du-

Charles or James K. Ansell, "An Irish Hug alias A Fraternal Embrace. The Dearest Friends must Part." Published 4 October 1798 by S. W. Fores, 50 Piccadilly, London. © Copyright The British Museum.

ties towards our particular friends I think equally applicable to our duties towards the friends of peace, freedom, and human nature:

> Who basely stabs a patriot's honest fame,
> Who skulks from his defence, when others blame,
> That man is base![12]

Coleridge regards his fellow "patriots" as bound together in friendship even if they are not personally acquainted. A central condition of this principled bond is that friends be prepared to "start forward" in active exertion to help each other. This idea underlines how Coleridge's public support for Thelwall implicitly declared a bond of amity between the radical lecturers, despite their being "perfect *strangers*."

The culture of radical friendship, then, directly contributed to Coleridge's initiation of a correspondence with Thelwall in April 1796. Roe has drawn attention to the symmetry between the two men's careers at this moment, pointing out how "in 1795 both were lecturing independently of the popular reform societies, while making a common cause with them in the campaign for reform and an end to the war with France" (p. 148). The immediate motivation, however, for Coleridge's entering into a correspondence was his discovery that Thelwall had misunderstood his praise of the radical leader in *The Plot Discovered*. In his letter, Coleridge not only disabused Thelwall that he had called him an "unsupported Malcontent" but strove to posit an idea of friendship existing between them:

> Pursuing the same end by the same means we ought not to be strangers to each other.—I have heard that you were offended by the manner in which I mentioned your name in the Protest against the Bills— . . . The words "unsupported Malcontent" are caught up from the well-known contemptuous pages of Aristocratic Writers & turned upon them: . . . I meant the passage—(not as complimentary: for I detest the vile traffic of literary adulation) but as a Tribute of deserved praise.—When I recited the Protest, the passage was "unsupported Malcontents" meaning myself & you—but I afterwards was seized with a fit of modesty & omitted myself.[13]

Seeking to befriend Thelwall, Coleridge identifies both men as political "Malcontents." Distinguishing his praise from the empty formalities of literary compliments, he asserts the sincerity of his affection, and gives body to this amicable feeling by presenting Thelwall with a copy of his *Poems* (1796), into which the letter was folded. The gift serves to validate Coleridge's contention that friendship may exist between men united by principle and similar radical activities.¹⁴

Coleridge further defined the nature of this bond in his poem "To John Thelwall," probably sent in his second letter (now lost):

> Some, Thelwall! to the Patriot's meed aspire,
> Who, in safe rage, without or rent or scar,
> Round pictur'd strongholds sketching mimic war
> Closet their valour—Thou mid thickest fire
> Leapst on the wall: therefore shall Freedom choose
> Ungaudy flowers that chastest odours breathe,
> And weave for thy young locks a Mural wreath.
>
> (lines 1–7)¹⁵

Unlike the "closet" radicals who fight imaginary battles but fail to embody their beliefs in action, Thelwall performs the role of heroic soldier in the midst of the fray. Coleridge's subsumed pun on "wall," suggesting both a barricade and the name "Thelwall," inscribes the location of dangerous action into Thelwall's very being. The Treason Trial of 1794 had demonstrated just how close he had come to being fatally injured in his fight for democratic rights.

Coleridge meets Thelwall's own exhortations to action in his *Poems Written in Close Confinement* (1795), written while awaiting trial, which Coleridge had already bought. In "Ode I. The Universal Duty" (1794), Thelwall chastises the man who would "Love's endearments claim" before his

> indignant Virtue had been prov'd
> In some brave effort. For the wretch, unmov'd
> By Patriot Virtue, tho' his outward frame,
> Blooming as spring, and gay as youthful steers,
> Promise Love's joyous harvest, yet, pursu'd
> By Slavery's abject terrors—aw'd—subdu'd—
> To Hymen's couch but half his manhood bears.¹⁶

As Thelwall celebrates active opposition as a rite of passage into manhood, so in "To John Thelwall" Coleridge upholds his addressee's criticism of the lover who refused the patriot's mantle:

> My ill-adventur'd youth by Cam's slow stream
> Pin'd for a woman's love in slothful ease:
> First by thy fair example [taught] to glow
> With patriot zeal; from Passion's feverish dream
> Starting I tore disdainful from my brow
> A Myrtle Crown inwove with Cyprian bough—

> Blest if to me in manhood's years belong
> Thy stern simplicity and vigorous Song.
>
> (lines 9–16)

Coleridge's love affair with Mary Evans cannot confer upon him the manliness that Thelwall exemplifies. Rejecting his inactive past, Coleridge shapes his future masculinity in Thelwall's image, aiming to assimilate both his style and his beliefs. As such, the example of Thelwall underpins Coleridge's decision in his contemporaneous poem, "Reflections on Entering into Active Life," to

> enjoin head, heart, and hand,
> Active and firm, to fight the bloodless fight
> Of Science, Freedom, and the Truth in Christ.[17]
>
> (lines 58–60)

In reply, Thelwall drew attention to Coleridge's lines, "Thou, mid thickest fire, / Leap'st on the perilous wall," as an image "as poetical as it is gratifying."[18] He thus accepted this martial self-image while encouraging Coleridge to become a heroic fighter himself. Indeed, from Coleridge's *Poems* Thelwall especially approved "the passage on the French Revolution . . . 'Freedom roused by high disdain etc.'" (p. 86), in "To a Young Lady with a Poem on The French Revolution."[19] In these lines Coleridge celebrates how, in her overthrow of the ancien régime, "FREEDOM" (line 17) "scatter'd battles from her eyes!" (line 22):

> Then EXULTATION wak'd the patriot fire
> And swept with wilder hand th'Alcæan lyre:
> Red from the Tyrants' wound I shook the lance,
> And strode in joy the reeking plains of France!
>
> (lines 23–26)

Coleridge glories in inflicting the fatal wounds upon society's "Tyrants." Thelwall's praise reveals how in their opening letters both men characterize their amicable bond as one between battling soldiers, manfully warring in defence of English political liberties.

However, both men's opposition to State oppression did not obscure their own significant differences of opinion, which had set them in opposition to each another before their correspondence begun. They particularly disagreed over the relative merits of Godwinism and Christianity as the basis for social benevolence. A staunch atheist, Thelwall followed Godwin's disinterested rationalism, supporting the subordination of private interests and affections to the public good. Although the situation was complicated by his friendship with Southey, by mid-1795 Coleridge was growing hostile to Godwinism. In March 1796, he singled out Thelwall as "Good Citizen——" in "Modern Patriotism," published in *The Watchman*. Coleridge derides Godwin's dismissing of the innate value of sentimental domestic attachments:

> You have studied Mr. Godwin's Essay on Political Justice; but to think filial affection folly, gratitude a crime, marriage injustice, and the promiscuous intercourse of the sexes right and wise, may class you among the despisers of vulgar prejudices, but cannot increase the probability that you are PATRIOT. . . . I would not entrust my wife or sister to you— Think you, I would entrust my country?[20]

Thelwall's Godwinism becomes the focus of Coleridge's opposition. This he articulates through his confrontational address, by which he enters into an ideological battle with his Godwinian opponent.

Most critics have assumed that the Coleridge-Thelwall intimacy developed in spite of these disagreements. Patton and Mann describe how the pair "entered into a friendly, though argumentative, correspondence."[21] Duncan Wu contends that "in spite of their differences, [Coleridge] wishes to find common ground with Thelwall in literary matters."[22] As will become apparent, these critics are right to stress the difficulties Coleridge and Thelwall had in reconciling friendship with disagreement. However, they underplay the degree to which both men strove to make opposition itself a sign of affection. In this, my position can be seen to develop Judith Thompson's recent view of the men's relations as founded on "poetic answer and provocation," in which Thelwall becomes for Coleridge an "influence, interlocutor, exemplar and opponent."[23]

In the figure of William Blake, contemporary discourse offered a template for such an oppositional relation. For the Blake of the 1790s, "Opposition is true Friendship," a proverb he expounds in *The Marriage of Heaven and Hell* (1790).[24] Blakean friendship is generated not through sympathetic agreement but through the engagement of contrary terms, a view famously represented in plate 3 of *The Marriage*: "Without Contraries is no progression. Attraction and Repulsion, Reason and Energy, Love and Hate, are necessary to Human existence." David Fairer elaborates:

> The opposing terms, by remaining in conflict, do not prevent unity. On the contrary, their sustained antagonism guarantees a unity that articulates the conflict itself. . . . Blake's contraries, through a language of

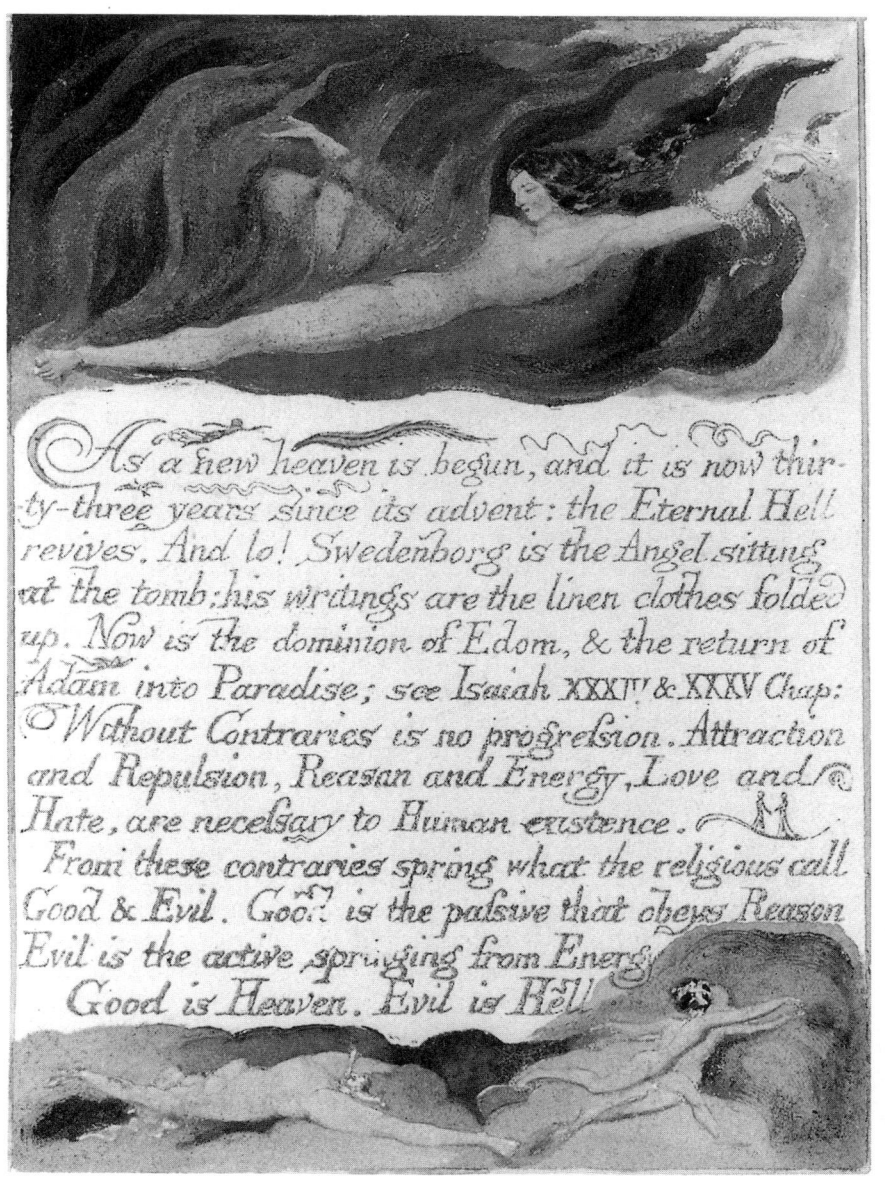

William Blake, *The Marriage of Heaven and Hell* (c 1790–1794). Plate 3. Fitzwilliam Museum, University of Cambridge.

5: "THEY ANSWER AND PROVOKE EACH OTHER'S SONGS"   187

antagonism, set up a force-field between their two terms, an energy which is mutually creative and sustaining.[25]

The two small interlinear figures on plate 3 after "Human existence" visually depict this "mutually creative and sustaining" clash of contraries. As David Erdman observes, the figures offer "a picture of companionability or neighborliness, a man and woman clasping hands on an ogee curve of beauty . . . a greeting of Heaven and Hell."[26] Opposition is the ground upon which the couple paradoxically join hands in friendship.

Blake's concept of oppositional friendship may serve as a model against which Coleridge and Thelwall's epistolary correspondence was enacted. It soon becomes apparent, however, that Blake's dictum offers an ideal that in practice was not easily sustainable. The central oppositional dynamic developed from the animated exchanges of the men's opening letters. In his first, Coleridge praises "Religious Musings" as the best of his own poems, and proceeds to goad his atheist correspondent with hopes for his conversion:

> A Necessitarian, I cannot possibly disesteem a man for his religious or anti-religious Opinions—and as an *Optimist*, I feel diminished concern.—I have studied the subject deeply and widely—I cannot say, without prejudice: for when I commenced the Examination, I was an Infidel. (1:205)

With provocative self-confidence, Coleridge suggests that Thelwall's atheism merely represents an early stage in the latter's intellectual development, one that will necessarily be superseded if he thinks as deeply as Coleridge on the subject.

Coleridge's remarks met a powerful counterforce. Thelwall's first reply is lost, but his second letter, dated 10 May 1796, rounds on Coleridge's word "Infidel," turning it against its author:

> In short, when I was yet a Christian, & a very zealous one, i.e. when I was about your age, I became thoroughly convinced that Christian poetry was very vile stuff—that religion was a subject which none but a rank infidel could handle poetically. (p. 88)

Thelwall answers Coleridge's condescension with a patronizing thrust of his own, asserting that an enthusiastic zeal for Christianity indicates youthful immaturity. Hanging over this counterattack, however, is the question of whether it expresses amity or estrangement. Thelwall acknowledges that it could be perceived to link Coleridge and himself in a Blakean intimacy of opposites. Of the religious passages of "Religious Musings," Thelwall declares: "They are the very acme of abstruse, metaphysical, mistical rant, & all ranting abstractions, metaphysic & mysticism are wider from true poetry than the equator from the poles" (p. 87). Thelwall emphasizes that there is a greater gulf between equator and the poles than between the poles themselves. He does so because he does not wish to place himself in a polar relation to his Christian correspondent on this issue. As Alan Watts states,

> To say that opposites are *polar* is to say much more than that they are far apart: it is to say that they are related and joined—that they are the terms, ends, or extremities of a single whole. Polar opposites are therefore *inseparable* opposites, like the poles of the earth or of a magnet.[27]

To indicate his hostility to religious poetry, therefore, Thelwall avoids making "poetry" and "religion" polar opposites. Instead, as "pole" and "equator" respectively, he contends that they are (to use Blake's distinction) inimical *negations*, not amicable *contraries*.

Thelwall's understanding of the intimacy of opposition was not lost upon Coleridge. In his reply of 13 May, he uses Thelwall's riposte to construct a friendship founded in the Blakean discourse of energetic contraries:

> My dear Thelwall! you have given me "the affection of a Brother:" and I repay you *in kind*. Your letters demand my friendship & deserve my esteem: the Zeal, with which you have attacked my supposed *Delusions*, proves that you are deeply interested for *me*, and interested even to agitation for what you believe to be the TRUTH.[28]

In highlighting Thelwall's "Zeal," Coleridge simultaneously attacks and befriends his correspondent. If Thelwall had associated zeal with an immature religious sensibility, then Coleridge accuses his accuser of the same vice. However, it is precisely this display of "passionate ardour," even in an oppositional "attack," which Coleridge takes to be a sign of friendship.[29] Coleridge continues to demonstrate how "I repay you *in kind*." Reiterating his accusation that Godwinian rationalism encourages promiscuity, Coleridge inquires: "Why should you not have intercourse with *the Wife* of your friend?—From the principles in your *heart*—Verily, Thelwall! I believe you—on your *heart* I should rest for my safety!" (1:213). Having faith in Thelwall's "heart" rather than his rationalist head, Coleridge aims a blow at his Godwinian disrespect for the institution of marriage. However, it is through this attack that Coleridge gives Thelwall a compliment: opposition becomes true friendship.

Fairer's exposition of Blake's doctrine of contraries indirectly bears upon Coleridge's epistolary strategies in this letter: "Polarities reaffirm through their mutual contradiction the validity of the system which sets them in opposition, just as love and hate reinforce a single shared discourse of passion in a way that love and indifference can never do" (p. 170). This "single shared discourse of passion" provides the ground for Coleridge and Thelwall's unity, despite their vehemently oppositional exchanges. Coleridge continues by praising the atheist who can express his position with passion:

> I like Holcroft a thousand times better [than Godwin], & think him a man of much greater ability. Fierce, hot, petulant, the very High priest of Atheism, he *hates* God "with all his heart, with all his mind, with all his soul, & with all his strength.". . . . But all this intolerance is founded in Benevolence. (1:215)

Although misguided, Holcroft's hatred for God is at least indicative of his passion, which makes him more likeable than the atheist Godwin, who has neither "strength of intellect" nor "powers of imagination" (1:215). Coleridge's affections are engaged by "power" and "strength," and the manliness that such qualities invoke, even in an ideological opponent.

Coleridge's interest in conflict in these years as an articulation of friendship finds poetic expression in "The Nightingale; A Conversational Poem" (1798), which in turn sheds light on the two men's relations. Coleridge represents the nightingales' "love chant" (line 48) as being brought to life in part through the birds' mock-aggressive confrontations with one other:

> and far and near
> In wood and thicket over the wide grove
> They answer and provoke each other's songs—
> With skirmish and capricious passagings,
> And murmurs musical and swift jug jug.
>
> (lines 56–60)

As a "skirmish," Coleridge understands the converse of birdsong to be an amicable fight, a contest in which provocation is the oppositional means by which nightingales generate songs of love. The birds' affectionate responsiveness is not polite. Instead, it is characterized by the unpredictable bursts of energy of creatures who capriciously interrupt the calm of evening and each other's song. Coleridge is aware that his exchanges with Thelwall embody a similar kind of verbal skirmishing. Introducing in December some criticisms of Thelwall's poetry, he declares: "And now, my dear fellow! for a little sparring about Poetry."[30] This metaphor of aggression subtly pervades the letter, which provides the field for the amicable battle. Parrying one Thelwallian criticism, Coleridge confesses himself surprised to be giving "a commentary of 35 lines in defence of a Sonnet!" However, Thelwall's next thrust—that Bowles is guilty of "Della Cruscanism"—causes Coleridge to wince: "this cuts the skin & *surface* of my Heart" (1:278). At this moment, the penetration of Coleridge's defences causes him not pleasure but pain.

Nonetheless, Coleridge celebrates how sparring may create an amicable bond through a mutual affirmation of the contestants' manly identities. To this end, he invites Thelwall in his letter of 31 December to continue their critical battling:

> In your next letter tell me what you think of the *scattered* poems, I sent you—send me any poems, and I will be minute in Criticism—for, O Thelwall! even a long-winded Abuse is more consolatory to an *Author's* feelings than a short-breathed, asthma-lunged Panegyric. (1:295)

As Coleridge probably knew, Thelwall's own lungs had been "particularly feeble and defective," especially during childhood.[31] Coleridge, though, does not aim to disparage his friend but to idealize his physical manliness: the idea of a "long-winded" yet consolatory "abuse" identifies Thelwallian opposition as the manifestation of a strong pair of lungs, and thus the expression of a manly passion. Battling correspondence, so Coleridge suggests, represents the way two virile men amicably communicate. His letter of 17 December constructed the relation in similar terms during another defence of Christianity against Thelwall's atheistic "Bigotry": "I write freely, Thelwall! for tho' *personally* unknown, I really love you, and can count but few human beings, whose hand I would welcome with a more hearty Grasp of Friendship" (1:282). Emphasizing the physicality of his "hearty Grasp," Coleridge invites Thelwall to view his amicable opposition as a specifically manly passion.

Coleridge's self-consciously physical gesture can be read as characteristic of the way contemporary radicals strove to express their solidarity. Faced with an increasingly hostile establishment, both Coleridge and Thelwall recognize that the oppositional community must heighten its concern for the welfare of its fellows. In November 1796, Coleridge enquires of his friend:

> Have you, my dear Thelwall!—no plan for your future Life? What is the state of your body? Are you sickly, or strong? Is your body so weakened by exertion & anxiety, as to make *stimulants* (such as wine & constant *animal* food) necessary to your Health? How many dear Little ones have you?—I should like to know all things *about* you—for *you*, I am confident, I know already.[32]

Comradely male friendship is intrinsically concerned with that which C. S. Lewis finds no part of the relation: "not only our physical bodies but that whole embodiment which consists of our family, job, past and connections."[33] Coleridge demands knowledge of Thelwall's physical well-being (including his sexual life), which, he imagines, might have suffered through his continuing his political work in the midst of state intimidation. Coleridge's concern was further expressed by his desire to exert himself on his friend's behalf. On hearing of his financial difficulties, Coleridge declared that "I keenly sympathize with you," suggesting a scheme through which Thelwall might sell books cheaply to the radical community. Comrades in arms, Coleridge implies, must practically support each other: "shame fall on the friends of Freedom if they will do nothing better!"[34] Moreover, in February 1797, he extols the virtues of Thelwall adopting "a country Life" (1:305), which represented a clear hint that Coleridge might help him to settle at Nether Stowey.[35]

Even in these early stages, however, the men's comradeship began to jostle uneasily with the internal oppositional dynamic of their epistolary relations. In his protestation that speaking "freely" is a sign of friendship, Coleridge betrays a lurking anxiety that Thelwall might not interpret intellectual battling as a sign of amity. Their correspondence during 1796–1797 concurrently confronts the possibility that opposition might hamper a friendship's development. On 19 November, Coleridge reassured Thelwall that arguing on points of intellectual difference was to be distinguished from personal attack: "In conversation I am impassioned, and oppose what I deem [error] with an eagerness, which is often mistaken for personal asperity—but I am ever so swallowed up in the *thing*, that I perfectly forget my *opponent*." Coleridge does not affirm here that affection is generated *by* the Blakean clash of contraries. Instead, he gestures towards the Enlightenment ideal of *containing* intellectual differences within amity.

Under pressure in the 1790s, this eighteenth-century idea is exemplified by Boswell's account of Johnson's "very curious interview" with his political enemy, John Wilkes, over dinner in May 1776.[36] "Two men more different could perhaps not be selected out of all mankind," Boswell noted, "they had even attacked one another with some asperity in their writings" (p. 764). The meeting, however, was a success and Johnson afterwards declared "how much he had been pleased with Mr. Wilkes's company" (p. 776). The Revolution debate, however, challenged the capacity of friends to accommodate increasingly bitter political divisions. Burke and Fox's quarrel in the Commons in May 1791 became a symbol of this new pressure on friendship, as demonstrated by Isaac Cruikshank's print, "The Wrangling Friends or Opposition in Disorder."[37] In condemning the Revolution, Burke disowns Fox, who bemoans the transformation of their long-standing affection into enmity: "Ah well a day my poor heart will allmost Break, 25 years Friendship & use me thus Oh—Oh—Edmund!!!" Although Sheridan (on Fox's left) expresses the sentimentalist's horror at "the man who betrays his friend," this cause célèbre dramatized how the new polarization

Isaac Cruikshank, "The Wrangling Friends or Opposition in Disorder." Published 10 May 1791 by S. W. Fores, No. 3 Piccadilly, London. © Copyright The British Museum.

of English society was undermining the established accommodation of political differences in friendship.

Despite their political unity, as the correspondence of Coleridge and Thelwall progressed, the two men's own differences of principle became increasingly apparent and, particularly in Coleridge, raised anxieties that he attempted to allay. On 13 November 1796, he reflected:

> We run on the same ground, but we drive different Horses. I am daily more and more a religionist—you, of course, more & more otherwise. I am sorry for the difference, simply because it impoverishes our sympathies: for indeed it does not lessen my esteem & friendship. (1:253)

While reassuring Thelwall that intellectual differences do not diminish affection, Coleridge hints at a sentimental discourse of "sympathies" that opposition cannot provide. These suspicions recur in his next letter: "You, & I, my dear Thelwall! hold different *creeds* in poetry as well as religion. N'importe" (1:258). Coleridge's snappy "N'importe" stifles concern that "different *creeds*" impede good feeling. Nonetheless, he needs to declare that "I *love* these two lines" of Thelwall's: "Yet sure the Verse that shews the friendly mind / To Friendship's ear not harshly flows" (1:258). The "friendly" note for which Thelwall listens is distinct from the particular opinion expressed. Coleridge concurs because he feels amity to be threatened by difference.

As early as June 1796, Coleridge had been reassuring Thelwall that amiableness was independent of holding a particular intellectual creed:

> Where the *disposition* is not amiable, an acute understanding I deem no blessing—To the last sentence in your letter I subscribe fully & with all my inmost affections—"He who thinks & *feels* will be virtuous: & he who is absorbed in self will be vicious—whatever may be his speculative opinions." (1:221)

As for Thelwall, his little surviving correspondence reveals a stronger faith than Coleridge's in friendship's powers of accommodation. In February 1797, he tells J. Wimpory that "if I had the pleasure of more frequent intercourse" with a "fraternal" acquaintance (one Howard), "I should discharge the duty of a friend by animadverting on some little eccentricities. But eccentricity is no vice of the heart; & flights of the head shake not my friendships. I am as full of maggots as a cheshire cheese myself."[38] A friend's most important characteristic is his good "heart," and Thelwall does not view unpalatable intellectual characteristics as militating against amity.

However, in the same letter of 17 December, in which Coleridge suggests that Thelwall find a country cottage near him, Coleridge nonetheless hints at a difference that might not be so comfortably accommodated:

> I doubt not, that the time will come when all our Utilities will be directed in one simple path. That Time however is not come; and imperious circumstances point out to each one his particular Road. Much good may be done in all. I am not *fit* for *public* Life; yet the Light shall stream to a far distance from the taper in my cottage window. Meantime, do *you* uplift the *torch* dreadfully, and shew to mankind the face of that Idol, which they have worshipped in Darkness! (1:277)

While Thelwall is identified with continued political engagement, the implications of Coleridge's move to his private cottage are less clear. He reaffirms that they share the same reformist aspirations, for the light from Coleridge's taper will eventually merge with Thelwall's brighter torch. However, the younger man's unfitness for "public life" signals a new distance between himself and his soldier-friend, and implies a difference of lifestyle that might impede the practical realization of their epistolary friendship. This suspicion is strengthened by a disturbing Coleridgean self-portrait of 19 November, which he evidently contrasts with Thelwall's information concerning his own physical condition:

> My face, unless when animated by immediate eloquence, expresses great Sloth, & great, indeed almost ideotic, good nature. 'Tis a mere carcase of a face: fat, flabby, & expressive chiefly of inexpression. . . . As to my shape, 'tis a good shape enough, if measured—but my gait is awkward, & the walk, & the *Whole man* indicates *indolence capable of energies.* (1:259–60)

Although physiognomically indicative of friendly "good nature," in its "awkward" gait Coleridge's body fails to meet his martial self-image as a warrior who "strode in joy the reeking plains of France," which Thelwall had approved. Despite being "capable of energies," Coleridge indirectly signals that he is not best suited to fulfilling the role of fellow soldier in the heat of battle.

In the event, Thelwall's visit to Stowey in July 1797 severely tested the strength of the radicals' bond of opposition to the state, as well as the friendship's internal Blakean dynamic. Being Thelwall's comrade in this year could have especially dangerous practical implications, as he was enduring increasing violence from the party of church-and-king: in March, a mob disrupted his attempts to lecture at Derby, while at Norwich in May "meetings in several inns were broken up by the Inniskilling Dragoons."[39] Befriending Thelwall could literally entail joining him in battle. E. P. Thompson relates how at Stockport,

> the Volunteers threatened to throw Thelwall into the canal. By his own account he "planted his back against a wall, pistol in hand," and "resolved to sell his life dearly," but he was rescued by a friend, and together they "forced their way through that 'most valiant and most loyal corps'." (p. 102)

On this occasion Thelwall's "friend" must have needed qualities of physical bravery and manliness.

In the summer of 1797, finding himself unable to lecture or publish, Thelwall set out to the West Country in search of new audiences and alliances. By the time he arrived at Bristol in July, however, events such as those at Stockport had made him acutely aware of the potential gap between the radicals' profession and practice of friendship. To his wife, "Stella," Thelwall described the welcome he had received in various towns:

> I met with many friends in Bristol who were encreasing in greater & greater degree every hour I staid—i.e. in exact proportion as it became known that I was in town; & when I returned to Bath, I found it necessary to promise to return thro Bristol in my way to Wales—In short at Bristol & Bath as at Froome I have met with some ~~frie~~ enthusiasm, & some *solid* friendship.[40]

As his manuscript deletion of "frie" reveals, Thelwall remains sceptical regarding the affectionate feeling he has witnessed. In the midst of writing "friendship" he checks himself, in order to distinguish "*solid*" attachment from insubstantial "enthusiasm." Thelwall wrote this letter, however, from within the midst of another "enthusiastic group," consisting of "C. and his Sara—W. & his sister—& myself."[41] From Coleridge's point of view, the enthusiasm to which Thelwall testifies would represent an unequivocal sign that the Alfoxden group possessed an intensity and passion indicative of mutual friendship. He had shared this positive view of enthusiasm with Thelwall the previous December, when he declared that "the *Enthusiasm* of Friendship is not with S. & me. . . . We are *acquaintances*—& feel *kindliness* towards each other; but I do not *esteem*, or LOVE Southey, as I must esteem & love the man whom

I dared call by the holy name of FRIEND!" (1:294). Nevertheless, Thelwall's remark to his wife hints that the "enthusiastic group's" fervor might not be solid enough to transform professions of affection into embodied action.

Nonetheless, Thelwall ended his letter with hope that he might realize his epistolary friendship with Coleridge by settling in this "friendly retreat": "During the whole of this ramble I have had serious thou[ght] of a Cottage—Do not be surprised if my next should inform you that I have taken one."[42] Such confidence testified to the immediate success of his visit. For Coleridge, meeting Thelwall demonstrated the truth of Blake's proverb, "Opposition is true Friendship": "John Thelwall is a very warm hearted honest man—and disagreeing, as we do, on almost every point of religion, of morals, of politics, and of philosophy; we like each other uncommonly well."[43] Emphatically, friendship thrives upon disagreement, and Coleridge even suggests that the men's mutual affection has developed in proportion to the points of opposition between them.

Despite this encomium on the relationship's oppositional dynamic, Thelwall's presence at Stowey revealed a contrary the importance of which became heightened in view of his desire to lease a house nearby. This contrary centred on the alternative implications accruing to the idea of a retired community of friends. Thelwall and Coleridge's idea of their friendship at this point thus becomes linked to a debate on the meanings of "retirement" in the 1790s. In general terms, the events at Stowey during August 1797 confirm Nigel Leask's argument that in Wordsworth and Coleridge's writings: "What began as a critical stance, the adoption and application of an integrated life-style and ideology in opposition to the contemporary order, became a tacit complicity with that order, and idealization of culture severed from history and society."[44] Leask also persuasively argues that it is necessary "to suspend judgement in order to understand exactly what the posture of retirement meant to the poet's circle in the late 1790s" (p. 13). However, whereas Leask views Thelwall as embracing the idea of retirement "as an *alternative* to political engagement" (p. 13), the events of August 1797 indicate not only a more radical Thelwall than Leask allows but also a more conservative Coleridge than he celebrates, one who is already using an idea of retired friendship to sever himself "from history and society," as well as from Thelwall himself.

Coleridge and Thelwall's famous oppositional exchange while walking in the Quantocks encapsulates the rival conceptions of friendship operating at this place and time. Of the three extant versions of the conversation, Thelwall's fictional rendering in *The Daughter of Adoption* (1801) is particularly revealing. Setting the dialogue in the wilds of St Domingo, Coleridge's words are spoken by Henry Montfort, while Edmunds dramatizes Thelwall's reply:

> "What a scene, and what an hour, Edmunds," said he [Henry], bantering, "to hatch treason in!"
> "What a scene, and what an hour, sir," replied Edmunds, with the most undisturbed composure, "to make one forget that treason was ever necessary in the world!"[45]

This dialogue exemplifies the men's Blakean dynamic, which produced an affectionate response from Coleridge—"John Thelwall had something good about him"—even in 1830 when he retold the story.[46] But the opposition they enact here points to a serious ideological conflict, which undermined their friendship in 1797. The two men disagree over the meaning of retired friendship: while Henry excitedly perceives that in a rural recess friendship might lend itself to treasonable activity, Edmunds suggests that a friendly meeting in these surroundings is congenial to a nondisruptive sociability, one that takes pleasure in erasing from consciousness the ills of the wider world.

Attention to the language here helps to reveal the organic assumptions informing the radical mode of rural friendship. Montfort's notion of "hatching" treason suggests how two friends might together germinate ideas that might otherwise not emerge. As Thelwall recalls the scene, it is Coleridge who flirts with the dangerous organic potential of radical converse. A close reading of the events of these weeks, however, suggests that, on balance, it was Thelwall who emerged in practice as the more radical of the two friends. Nevertheless, if Coleridge had spoken of hatching treason, his language would have been apposite, for Thelwall was widely regarded—by himself included—as a man with an uncommon potential to bring radicalism to life. This is demonstrated, in his letter of 17 July, by his pleasure on discovering "many friends in Bristol who were encreasing in greater & greater degree . . . in exact proportion as it became known I was in town." Containing the idea of organic growth, the "encrease" of friends around Thelwall suggests that he is a catalyst for the sprouting of radicals around him, as if in accordance with some natural law.

Conservatives like T. J. Mathias concurred that Thelwall could meld isolated individuals into interconnected, radical life-forms, declaring of his 1796 lectures at Yarmouth: "Thelwall, for the season, quits the Strand / To organize revolt by sea and land."[47] For James Walsh, the Home Office agent, Thelwall's presence at Alfoxden provided similar evidence that he was organizing individuals into a radical community. On 15 August 1797, Walsh confirmed that Thelwall "had been down some time, and that there were a Nest of them at Alfoxton House who were protected by a Mr. Poole a Tanner of this Town, and that he supposed Thelwall was there (Alfoxton House) at this time."[48] Like Henry/Coleridge, Walsh imagines that the radicals are creating an organic "Nest," a domestic space within which political eggs might be fertilized, hatched, and nurtured into fully fledged subversion. Poole's cousin Charlotte was similarly "shocked to hear that Mr. Thelwall has spent some time at Stowey this week with Mr. Coleridge, and consequently with Tom Poole. Alfoxton house is taken by one of the fraternity, and Woodlands by another. To what are we coming?"[49]

These reactions confirm E. P. Thompson's argument that "Thelwall, when he set off on the pedestrian excursion which led to Stowey, was in retreat, but he had reason to be in retreat, and he was not in retreat that *much*."[50] Although Thelwall was attracted to the idea of a "friendly retreat" from politics, the prospect of forging a political grouping was never far from his mind. The ambiguous potential of a friendship group for quietism or political intrigue expresses itself in Thelwall's depiction of Coleridge, Wordsworth, and himself enjoying "a delightful ramble to day among the plantations & along a wild romantic dell," and who, as

> a literary & political triumvirate passed sentence on the productions and characters of the age—burst forth in poetical flights of enthusiasm—& philosophised our minds into a state of tranquillity which the leaders of nations might envy and the residents of Cities can never know.[51]

Despite such relaxed contemplation, in 1797 Thelwall himself cannot distinguish between a literary "triumvirate" and a politicized grouping. As Roe points out, "on 31 July he also 'attempted to assemble' a meeting of the Corresponding Society at Bristol."[52] In this context, a "political triumvirate" of friends might indeed represent a nest of active reformers. Furthermore, Thelwall's contention that city residents cannot know the "state of tranquillity" enjoyed by these friends, suggests that the group's pastoral integration might well signify an oppositional disaffection towards the Establishment.

Thelwall develops these notions in his "Lines, Written at Bridgewater, in Somersetshire, on the 27th of July, 1797; During a Long

Excursion, in Quest of a Peaceful Retreat," in which he addresses "My Samuel!" and hopes that by living "near to thine," "I might oft / Share thy sweet converse, best-belov'd of friends!"[53] Despite its pastoral vision of "sweet retirement, tranquil joys / Of friendship, and of love" (p. 127), the poem encodes a recalcitrant opposition to the Anti-Jacobin Establishment. Stowey takes on the character of an Edenic paradise in which Thelwall and "my Samuel" sit "Alternate, in each other's bower":

> or, when, bleak,
> The wintry blast had stripp'd the leafy shade,
> Around the blazing hearth, social and gay,
> To share our frugal viands, and the bowl
> Sparkling with home-brew'd beverage:—by our sides
> Thy Sara, and my Susan, . . .
> With such, my friend!—
> With such how pleasant to unbend awhile,
> Winging the idle hour with song, or tale,
> Pun, or quaint joke, or converse, such as fits
> Minds gay, but innocent.
>
> (pp. 130–31)

Friendship is ostensibly an alternative to politics, a convivial means of relaxation delighting in imagination and humor rather than engaging with the political world. Nevertheless, Thelwall's vision of Samuel and himself "sharing our frugal viands" resonates with Coleridge's radical, Pantisocratic ideal of what Leask terms "agrarian communism" (p. 34), in which produce would be equally distributed amongst a community.

As Leask remarks, Coleridge's "agrarian communism" linked the notion that "human proclivities to vice and self-interest can be tempered and ameliorated by equalizing property" (pp. 34–35) to the idea of "Christ's millenial kingdom on earth" (p. 37), in which

> The vast family of Love
> Rais'd from the common earth by common toil
> Enjoy the equal produce.
>
> (lines 362–64)[54]

Coleridge's agrarian ideal had by late 1796 indeed found a new focus in Nether Stowey, as Leask remarks: "Poole would teach Coleridge the arts of husbandry whilst he continued to preach and write from the moral fortress of his 'cottage economy.' A combination of agriculture, domesticity and radical Christianity is the keynote of the project in this period" (p. 40). Although Thelwall objected to the Christian elements, in his "Lines" he envisions Stowey as embodying some salient aspects of Coleridge's radical ideology:

> Ah! 'twould be sweet, beneath the neighb'ring thatch,
> In philosophic amity to dwell,
> Inditing moral verse, or tale, or theme,
> Gay or instructive; and it would be sweet,
> With kindly interchange of mutual aid,
> To delve our little garden plots, the while
> Sweet converse flow'd, suspending oft the arm
> And half-driven spade, while, eager, one propounds,
> And listens one, weighing each pregnant word,
> And pondering fit reply, that may untwist
> The knotty point—perchance, of import high— . . .
> Agreeing, or dissenting—sweet alike,
> When wisdom, and not victory, the end.
>
> (p. 130)

Thelwall revisits Pantisocracy's ideal of grounding friendship in communal labor. Within this egalitarian context where friends strive for "wisdom, and not victory," "dissenting" is as generative of affection as "Agreeing," and Thelwall celebrates oppositional converse as part of this agrarian life. Furthermore, in combining communal labor and metaphysical discussion, itself not divorced from "import high," Thelwall suggests that his settlement might recreate the radical lifestyle Coleridge and Southey had hoped to realize in America.

Thelwall gestures at a further politicization of retired friendship as he contemplates Coleridge's and his own children growing up together:

> And 'twould be sweet, my Samuel, ah! most sweet
> To see our little infants stretch their limbs
> In gambols unrestrain'd, and early learn
> Practical love, and, Wisdom's noblest lore,
> Fraternal kindness; while rosiest health,
> Bloom'd on their sun-burnt cheeks.
>
> (p. 130)

In enabling the children to "bloom," this natural environment encourages "fraternal" feelings, which are realized in acts of "Practical love." "Fraternal kindness" carries a radical edge, implying the children's instinctive recognition of each other's equality and rights. Thelwall's vision resonates with what David Fairer has termed an "organic radicalism" of the 1790s: "caves, sheltered nooks or bowers" frequently offer natural spaces in which radical poets discover "a new voice by articulating feelings imbued with nature."[55] "It was certainly not paranoia," Fairer argues, to think of these locations facilitating, "a radical 'cell' of disaffection fostering 'inborn virtue' through a language of secret communication, as nurturing something that owed no allegiance to outward forms and structures and could become a growing force for change" (p. 38). Thelwall hints that retirement to the village might nevertheless come to embody a radical ideal, through the poet's settlement within a quasi-Pantisocratic agrarian community.

Despite his enthusiasm for "hatching" treason, Coleridge does not unequivocally confirm Leask's contention that "between 1795 and 1801 Coleridge persistently attempted to put his dream of Pantisocracy and agrarian communism into a practical form" (p. 34), locating Stowey as a "commonwealth" (p. 37) of spirit and property. As we have seen, Coleridge also represented Stowey as a maternal bower, associated with Poole, into which he might retreat from the "tempest's swell!" (line 69). In "Fears in Solitude" (1798), Coleridge associates the village with an organic view of friendship and society, which is distinctively conservative.[56] Coleridge attempts to extricate himself from the oppositional role that Thelwall embraces, even in retreat. As was seen in chapter 4, Coleridge argues in Burkean terms that his patriotism is bound up with his social identity as a son, brother, friend, husband, and father. He then suggests that these "bonds of natural love" (line 177) function in ways similar to the operation of the British landscape upon his soul:

> How should'st thou [Britain] prove aught else but dear and holy
> To me, who from thy lakes and mountain-hills,
> Thy clouds, thy quiet dales, thy rocks, and seas,
> Have drunk in all my intellectual life,
> All sweet sensations, all ennobling thoughts,
> All adoration of the God in nature.
>
> (lines 179–85)

Infusing themselves organically within Coleridge's being, both landscape and "bonds of natural love" provide the means by which he comes to have a patriotic love for his country. Coleridge's conservatism is evidenced by the way these sentiments resonate with those of Burke, who, in his *Reflections*, uses the organic connection between countryside, domestic attachments, and patriotic identity to justify preserving Britain's unwritten constitution:

> We have given to our frame of polity the image of a relation in blood; binding up the constitution of our country with our dearest domestic ties; adapting our fundamental laws into the bosom of our family affections; keeping inseparable, and cherishing with the warmth of all their combined and mutually reflected charities, our state, our hearths, our sepulchres, and our altars. (p. 49)

Fairer notes how Burke interconnects "the national with the local, and through that with the familial, as if they are part of the same being."[57] In a similar way, in "Fears in Solitude" Coleridge claims that his authority to speak to his countrymen derives from him literally embodying his country's values, which have been organically infused into his being through the domestic affections he enjoys and the English landscape in which he lives.

At the poem's climax, Coleridge represents Stowey's geography in ways that further express his conservative integration within English society. Walking home, he pauses at the top of a hill, and admires the "burst of prospect":

> that huge amphitheatre of rich
> And elmy fields, seems like society,
> Conversing with the mind, and giving it
> A livelier impulse, and a dance of thought;
> And now, beloved STOWEY! I behold
> Thy church-tower, and (methinks) the four huge elms
> Clust'ring, which mark the mansion of my friend;
> And close behind them, hidden from my view,
> Is my own lowly cottage, where my babe
> And my babe's mother dwell in peace!
> (lines 213–23)

Coleridge characterizes his relations with the "elmy fields" as an affectionate "Conversing"—an idea reinforced by the fact that the elm tree is a traditional symbol of sociability.[58] This friendly landscape embraces those whom Coleridge holds dear: the "four huge elms / Clust'ring" (which also represent Poole) companionably embower Coleridge's family hidden behind them. By emphasizing the unity of species of these trees and the outlying elms, Coleridge suggests that his private friendships do not oppose the Establishment but demonstrate his integration within country and community.

Although not composed until April 1798, "Fears in Solitude"

may illuminate Coleridge's decision not to encourage Thelwall to settle at Stowey in August 1797. The poem offers a conservative model of friendship into which Thelwall cannot easily fit. Coleridge's continuing identification of Thelwall with a contrary discourse of organic radicalism is evident in his letter to the Bridgwater magistrate, John Chubb, inquiring whether Chubb could find Thelwall a cottage. Coleridge admits that his friend has become "particularly unpopular, thro' every part of the kingdom" through his "particular exertions in the propagation of those principles, which *we* hold sacred & of the highest importance."[59] An older meaning of "propagation" refers to "the act of producing as offspring; . . . procreation, generation, reproduction."[60] Coleridge thus subtly reminds Chubb that Thelwall possesses a dangerous potential to breed radicalism. The magistrate, however, left the matter for Coleridge to decide, and the following day he rejected Thelwall's request, again citing his perceived role in the organic creation of subversive friendship communities:

> If *you* too should come, I am afraid, that even riots & dangerous riots might be the consequence—/ *either* of us separately would perhaps be tolerated—but *all three* together—what can it be less than plot & damned conspiracy—a school for the propagation of demagogy & atheism?[61]

Coleridge fears that a group of friends will be seen as particularly conducive to "propagation," whereby their intercourse will be the generative means of producing radical offspring. This kind of disaffected community conflicted with Coleridge's nascent desire for a Burkean integration into the established English social landscape, which he would celebrate eight months later in "Fears in Solitude."

Coleridge's inability to reconcile the contraries of radical and conservative modes is seen in a draft letter from Poole to the owner of Alfoxden, Mrs. St. Albyn, which Roe claims was "evidently written in collaboration with Coleridge and Wordsworth."[62] Allaying Mrs. St. Albyn's anxieties concerning the "company" Wordsworth kept, Poole distances Wordsworth and Coleridge from Thelwall and from the development of any subversive community:

> By accident Mr. Thelwall, as he was travelling through the neighbourhood, called at Stowey. . . . No person at Stowey nor Mr. Wordsworth knew of his coming. Mr. Wordsworth had never spoken to him before, nor, indeed, had any one of Stowey. Surely the common duties of hospitality were not to be refused to any man . . . , however they may disap-

prove of his sentiments or conduct? . . . Let me beg you, madam, to hearken to no calumnies, no party spirit, nor to join with any in disturbing one who only wishes to live in tranquillity.[63]

To acknowledge a closer bond than "common hospitality" between these men would lead to suspicion that their relation was socially disruptive, and it is from this dangerous kind of intimacy that Poole distances Coleridge. Roe highlights the "deliberate falsehoods" (p. 75) Poole perpetrates here, in order to redefine Coleridge and Wordsworth as benign, depoliticized individuals, summarizing thus the effect of this letter:

> Coleridge and Poole had sacrificed Thelwall's residence in the neighbourhood for the company of Wordsworth and Dorothy, whom they wished to distance as far as possible from Thelwall. . . . At a time when Thelwall was in greatest need—a plight that Coleridge and Wordsworth recognised—he had been let down. (p. 76)

Coleridge had presented himself and Wordsworth in terms of a conservative, nondisruptive bond, while implicitly associating Thelwall with a radical, subversive relation. Coleridge posits an opposition between himself and Thelwall that does not generate intimacy but aims to destroy the practical realization of their friendship. His comradeship—grounded in opposition to the state—could no longer be incorporated into his increasingly conservative, organic view of society. As Roe convincingly concludes, Poole's draft letter marks "a formative stage in the process towards apostasy, which would eventuall[y] lead Coleridge to deny the reality of his political opinions in *Biographia* and consign Thelwall's place in his early life to silence" (p. 76).

There is evidence that Thelwall himself understood his rejection from Stowey as a failure of friendship. In doing so, he tacitly confirms Ansell's satirical view that, despite their sentimental embraces, the affection between radicals was often merely superficial. Summarizing the conclusion of his political career in his "Prefatory Memoir" (1801), Thelwall reflects that "Friendship (the last stay of the human heart)—even Friendship, itself . . . wearied and intimidated with the hostilities to which it was exposed, has shrunk from its own convictions, and left him [Thelwall] in comparative insulation" (p. xxxiv). Thelwall hints at the failure under fire of Coleridge's esprit de corps during 1796–1797, whose "shrinking" also involved a lack of manly steadfastness. His poem "To the Infant Hampden—Written During a Sleepless Night. Derby. Oct.

1797," dated October 1797, reveals a stronger sense of betrayal.[64] In August, Coleridge had questioned whether Thelwall's country should "be made a wilderness of waters to him?" (1:342); in Thelwall's poem, this possibility has become his reality, with the world now comprising of

> a wilderness of wrongs—
> A waste of troubled waters: whelming floods
> Of tyrannous injustice, canopy'd
> With clouds dark louring; whence the pelting storms
> Of cold unkindness the rough torrents swell,
> On every side resistless. There my Ark—
> The scanty remnant of my delug'd joys!
> Floats anchorless.
>
> (p. 141)

The image of "clouds dark louring" over "whelming floods" signifies the desolate conditions inhabited by him who is deprived of a friendly bower. As such, Thelwall points to his rejection from Stowey as one reason for his descent into a world devoid of affection. Alluding to the potent image of the houseless Lear in the "pelting" and "pitiless storm" (3.4.29), he hints that Coleridge (the younger man) has imitated the unnatural actions of Lear's daughters: as Goneril and Regan shut their doors to their father, so Thelwall indirectly accuses Coleridge of "cold unkindness" and a betrayal of his paternal kin.

Nevertheless, Coleridge proved to be correct in assuming that Thelwall's friendships would inevitably be considered subversive. Eventually settling at Llyswen, Thelwall had hoped to discover in this remote Brecknockshire village a friendly bower in which he could unequivocally remove himself from public affairs: "Peaceful shades of Llyswen! shelter me beneath your luxuriant foliage: lull me to forgetfulness, ye murmuring waters of the Wye. Let me be part farmer and fisherman. But no more politics—no more politics in this bad world."[65] Nevertheless, in May 1798 Thelwall was still excusing himself to the Welsh bard Iolo Morganwg for his inability to visit, on the grounds that "the state of affairs . . . & the prejudices with which I know myself to be watched have made me deem it prudent to lay this intention aside, lest picturesque curiosity, & visits of friendship should be construed into High Treason."[66] Thelwall again discovers that for him there is no innocent mode of "friendship," and can only lament that the instability of friendship's political meanings continues to thwart its realization.

For both men, the crisis of the previous summer precipitated a sceptical questioning of friendship in the life of a political radical at this time. Despite his settlement at Nether Stowey, Coleridge does not entirely uphold the vision he presents in "Fears in Solitude," that of an amicable integration within the English socio-geographical landscape. In "Frost at Midnight," composed during February 1798, he betrays a sense of alienation from the English community that resonates with Thelwall's own experience.[67] The primary influence of Cowper's *The Task* on the poem has long been established. However, a few recent commentaries have suggested that the poem is also influenced by "To the Infant Hampden," in which Thelwall similarly addresses his sleeping child during the night.[68] Judith Thompson has argued that:

> By adopting the same narrative situation and symbolism as Thelwall . . . Coleridge is in effect answering him, sympathizing with the situation of the beleaguered reformer, and comparing it with his own, acknowledging and countering Thelwall's implied criticisms of him, and offering consolation by developing his own religious answer to the materialist philosophy which Thelwall develops. (pp. 435–36)

Attention to the theme of friendship in "Frost at Midnight," however, ultimately reveals a less optimistic comment than Thompson allows on the fate of the radical community in the late 1790s, suggesting that Coleridge now regarded his relationship with Thelwall as untenable outside the imagination.

Thelwall laments that "in his native land" he "Wanders an exile; and, of all that land, / Can find no spot his home" (p. 141). Even within his own home, Coleridge similarly presents himself as estranged from his community and surrounding landscape. Nature does not initially appear as a friend but as a collection of ominous entities, either hidden from the poet or intruding upon him:

> The Frost performs it's secret ministry,
> Unhelp'd by any wind. The owlet's cry
> Came loud—and hark, again! loud as before.
>
> (lines 1–3)

As Thompson has pointed out, the phrase "secret ministry" disturbingly connotes with the presence during Thelwall's visit, "of a spy shadowing . . . and reporting their doings to the government" (p. 438). In this light, natural process becomes associated with the powerful machinations of an oppressive establishment. The night's stillness increases Coleridge's unease:

> 'Tis calm indeed! so calm, that it disturbs
> And vexes meditation with it's strange
> And extreme silentness. Sea, hill, and wood,
> This populous village! Sea, and hill, and wood,
> With all the numberless goings on of life,
> Inaudible as dreams!
>
> (lines 8–13)

This echoes Thelwall's poem "On Leaving the Bottoms of Glocestershire; Where the Author had been Entertained by Several Families with Great Hospitality. Aug. 12, 1797," in which he regrets how "I must leave ye, pleasant haunts! brakes, bourns, / And populous hill, and dale, and pendant woods."[69] Although Coleridge is not doomed to wander far from this amicable landscape, in his cottage he nevertheless feels fundamentally estranged from the natural sociability going on around him.

Further allusions to Thelwall's poetry appear as Coleridge stares into his "low-burnt fire" that "quivers not" (line 14):

> Only that film, which flutter'd on the grate,
> Still flutters there, the sole unquiet thing,
> Methinks, it's motion in this hush of nature
> Gives it dim sympathies with me, who live,
> Making it a companionable form,
> With which I can hold commune. Idle thought!
>
> (lines 15–20)

Coleridge's fluttering film resonates with Thelwall's representation of himself in the final lines of "To the Infant Hampden," as he despairs of finding one spot of land to call his home:

>   thro' the dreary round,
> Fluttering on anxious pinion, the tired foot
> Of persecuted Virtue cannot find
> One spray on which to rest; or scarce one leaf
> To cheer with promise of subsiding woe.
>
> (p. 141)

Like Coleridge's film, Thelwall flutters like a bird. Both move restlessly, contrasting with the settled sociability of the "populous" country surrounding them. By identifying himself with the film, Coleridge expresses his own "dim sympathies" with Thelwall's isolated situation at this time. However, if the film and poet's estranged condition suggests grounds for union, upon reflection Coleridge admits that any "commune" is merely the imaginative projection of a desiring mind. Coleridge's note expresses this skepticism: "In all parts of the kingdom these films are called *strangers*, and supposed to portend the arrival of some absent friend" (p. 20). The phrase "*supposed* to portend" reveals Coleridge's doubt that the renewal of friendship, even between himself and Thelwall, is anything more than an attractive piece of folklore.

Coleridge goes on to suggest that friendship is an idea whose rhetorical and imaginative power derives from its absence from embodied life. The grate of his fire becomes associated with his schooldays, "pent mid cloisters dim" (line 57), when belief in the realization of friendship was untainted with skepticism:

> the door half-open'd, and I snatch'd
> A hasty glance, and still my heart leapt up,
> For still I hop'd to see the *stranger's* face,
> Townsman, or aunt, or sister more belov'd,
> My play-mate when we both were cloth'd alike!
> (lines 44–48)

Despite Coleridge's visions of the friends that *might* step through the door, the transformation of stranger into friend does not materialize within the poet's past or present. Coleridge depicts an endless longing for an affection that never appears other than in imagination, and conversely, a present characterized by repressive institutions and a natural landscape that is ominous and stifling.

In the poem's final section, Coleridge attempts to break this circle by leaping from his own experience to a vision of Hartley's happier future, enjoying a Wordsworthian existence amid sublime scenery. For Hartley, Nature will be a Divine system of affectionate, reciprocal relations whereby "lakes and sandy shores" as well as "crags / Of ancient mountain" (lines 60–61) are reflected in the clouds, "Which image in their bulk both lakes and shores / And mountain and crags" (lines 62–63). Thompson reads Coleridge's exclamation—"Great universal Teacher! he shall mould / Thy spirit, and by giving make it ask" (lines 68–69)—as a direct answer to Thelwall, and she highlights the oppositional stance inherent in this "explicitly Christian lesson" of divine love (p. 447). Coleridge's "counter" to Thelwall's atheism becomes a positive gesture to his friend: "Coleridge's vision of nature and humanity consecrated and unified by divine love" enables him to move "outwards and forwards, . . . towards a promise of renewed activism based on Thelwall's image of the child, awake now and full of energy and hope" (p. 448).

Thompson underplays, however, Coleridge's meditation on the realization of friendship. Hartley's place in the divinely ordained natural community has a cost: as a wandering "breeze," he becomes an eerily disembodied figure whose spiritual education necessitates a disengagement from human community. This is implicit even in the apparently joyful final lines in which the icicles make the child "stretch and flutter from thy mother's arms / As thou would'st fly for very eagerness" (lines 83–85). Thelwall's estranged, "fluttering" condition cannot be entirely erased: Hartley's eager flight into nature masks another separation—this time from his family. Despite the ending's ostensible optimism Coleridge cannot embed his son, even within imagination, within a loving and specifically human society. If Coleridge's Christian vision creates an amicable contrary to Thelwall's atheism, at this moment the Blakean dynamic is undermined by the poet's tacit denial of the two men's realizing their friendship.

Coleridge's skeptical reduction of friendship in the poem to an imaginary construct resonated strongly with Thelwall's views after his rejection from Stowey. In "The Woodbine. Dovedale, Oct. 1797," Thelwall contemplates a woodbine overhanging a stream.[70] Like Coleridge's film, this Miltonic emblem of friendship stimulates Thelwall to meditate upon his domestic attachments. Reflecting on his love for his wife, he imagines his children in turn discovering "soul-awakening passion" in some Edenic "fragrant bower":

> Gentle flower!
> The thought, perchance, is wild—the hope is vain—
> (For, ah! what blighting mildews wait the hours
> Of life's frail spring tide!) yet 'tis cheering sweet—
> And my heart hails it, gentle flower!—well pleas'd
> If o'er the sterrile scene of real life
> Imagination sometimes shed around
> Her transient blooms:—for blissful thoughts are bliss.
>
> (p. 140)

However much the imagination covers the earth with "transient blooms," the affection it promises is an illusion dissipated by empirical contact with "real life." Friendship cannot in practice be retrieved from a disembodied realm of "blissful thoughts." Read alongside "The Woodbine," Coleridge's skepticism in "Frost at Midnight" regarding the realization of human friendship both in Hartley's and his own life, suggests that his poem articulates the estranged condition of reformists like himself and Thelwall during a period of political reaction and intimidation.

The surviving Coleridge-Thelwall correspondence confirms both men's growing sense that their intimacy existed, if at all, more in imagination than as an embodied practice. It remained vital for Thelwall, isolated on his Welsh farm, that his friends demonstrate their affection through correspondence. As he wrote to Thomas Hardy in January 1798: "The names you mentioned in yours gave me pleasure—They are borne by beings I love—but they might shew their remembrance under their own hands when you send another packet."[71] The suggestion that Thelwall identifies Coleridge as an inactive friend is supported by Coleridge's opening comments in a letter dated 30 January:

> Two days after I received your letter—that to which you allude in your last—I returned you an answer. . . . And I did not hear from you—and it appears, that you did not receive my letter; for which I am sorry—but I have lately had a letter from me to Mr Wedgewood intercepted, and I suspect the *country* post masters grievously.[72]

Aware that Thelwall has noticed his silence, Coleridge protests that the same forces of reaction that had hindered his settlement at Stowey are now thwarting the men's correspondence. By March, however, Thelwall fights his sense that Coleridge had permanently ended the relation, informing Crompton that "he promised to answer write to me again in a few days; but tho' I ans.rd his letter directly, I have not heard from him ~~again~~ since."[73] In altering "again" to "since" Thelwall leaves open the possibility that his friend may yet reply, although his initial impulse is to suspect he will not.

The dispersal of Coleridge's affection in part resulted from his disillusionment with the Blakean notion that "Opposition is true Friendship." By 1801, the men's intellectual differences were not a spur but an obstacle to friendly intercourse. In January 1801, he alludes to a letter of Thelwall's that "entirely misunderstood me as to religious matters." However, Coleridge now eschews opposing his correspondent's atheism:

> your notions about the historical credibility or non-credibility of a sacred Book, your assent to or dissent from the existence of a supramundane Deity, or personal God, are absolutely indifferent to me / mere figures of a magic Lanthern. I hold my faith—you keep your's.[74]

Coleridge's final "indifference" to Thelwall's continued provocation on the subject of religion marks the demise of their friendship;

for indifference denies that which had once united them—a shared discourse of passion whether expressed in agreement or dissension. In April, Coleridge refuses Thelwall's request for a critical judgement of his *Poems, Chiefly Written in Retirement*, on the grounds that their many points of opposition effectively debar them from practical acts of friendship, such as advice-giving:

> As it is, I see no use in it—especially in a letter, in which it is at all times difficult to make your full meaning understood, & very easy to occasion yourself to be misunderstood.—Besides, we are so utterly unlike each other in our habits of thinking, and we have adopted such irreconcileably different opinions in Politics, Religion, & Metaphysics, (& probably in Taste too) that, I fear—I fear—I do not know how to express myself—but such, I fear, is the chasm between us, that so far from being able to shake hands across it, we cannot even make our Words intelligible to each other.[75]

In 1796, after calling Thelwall's atheism "bigotry," Coleridge could write that he counted "but few human beings, whose hand I would welcome with a more hearty Grasp of Friendship." Five years later, however, there is no possibility of even "shaking hands" across the chasm of their difference.

Coleridge's letter may be compared with a passage from Thelwall's contemporaneous novel, *The Daughter of Adoption* (1801), in which he represents the relation between Seraphina and her servant as also characterized by their opposing tastes and opinions. Seraphina elaborates:

> ["]Perhaps one of the most inexplicable mysteries of the labyrinth of the human heart, is the circumstance of your devoted attachment. There is between us, no single sympathy either of sentiment or of morals. Our tastes are as wide as the opposite winds of heaven—our pursuits are in diametrical hostility, and our conceptions of almost all possible things and situations are as adverse as our propensities.
>
> "And yet you have loved without any assignable reason, and I have loved because I was conscious of being beloved.
>
> "Did this dissimilarity merely produce a difference of opinion, did it merely prevent the participation of pleasures, and the reciprocations of that social communion for which my heart is formed, I should lament, indeed, our infelicity in this respect, but it should never be a cause of our separation." (3:193–94)

For Thelwall, tastes "as wide as the opposite winds of heaven" do not necessarily render amicable relations unsustainable. He may here provide a poignant insight into his view of his relationship with Coleridge.

For Coleridge, however, rejecting opposition as a basis for amity effectively reduces his principled affection to a mere attitude of mind. In his April 1801 letter, he declares that

> Moral Esteem, frequent & kind wishes, & a lively Interest in your Welfare as a good Man & man of Talents make up in my mind for the too great want of similitude in our intellectual Habits & modes of Faith; (and, I presume, the same holds good in your feelings towards me). (2:723)

Friendship no longer expresses itself in action, but only through "kind wishes." Coleridge confirms this sentiment in 1803 to Mrs Thelwall: "Believe me, I have never ceased to think with tenderness—& have often thought with an *anxious* tenderness—of him, & his—& sincerely do I rejoice in his Well-doing & Well-being."[76] Coleridge betrays his sense that a relation comprising of friendly thoughts might easily be viewed as no friendship at all.

Coleridge and Thelwall met for probably the last time in Keswick in November 1803. In arranging the visit, Coleridge made a virtue out of his failures of action, arguing that the highest friendship need not involve physical bodies. Responding to the news that a friend of Mrs Thelwall had an affection for him, Coleridge declares that this

> attachment to one unknown or at least unseen, affected & pleased me—not for myself—Heaven knows! . . . but because such feelings of Esteem & Affection for persons, who are known to us only in spirit, are the exclusive property of minds at once fervent & pure & formative:—minds untamed by "the dreary Intercourse" of common Life, & inspired by their own natures to believe, & have a Joy in the goodness of others.[77]

Coleridge dismisses the practicalities of friendship as a "dreary Intercourse" far beneath the divine "Joy" felt in contemplating the Idea of a friend. But yet again for Coleridge, there is a disconcerting gap between the Idea and its embodiment. To Stella four days earlier, Coleridge confessed his anxiety that friendship required mediation: he is "vexed at the delay" in receiving a letter from Thelwall, for, as the latter was already in the Lake District, he "would naturally think my silence a proof of neglect & forgetfulness of past kindness" (2:1017–18). Coleridge's anxiety was well-founded. In Thelwall's letter to his wife, written on 29 November from Penrith after he had visited Keswick, he explains that he spent one day longer with Coleridge than intended; Thelwall had, however, been able to inform Stella of his movements through the help of one Guy Braithwaite. "Coleridge had also promised to write," notes Thelwall in the resigned tones of experience, "but, upon him I should not have relied."[78]

6
"It is a usual concomitant of persons of his character to explain a human sympathy by a divine impulse:" Coleridge, Charles Lamb, and Charles Lloyd, 1794–98

RETURNING TO LONDON IN SEPTEMBER 1794 FROM HIS PANTISOCRATIC exploits in Bristol, Coleridge found himself drinking: "Every night since my arrival I have spent at an Ale-house by courtesy called 'a Coffee House'—The 'Salutation & Cat', in Newgate Street—We have a comfortable Room to ourselves—& drink Porter & *Punch* round a good Fire."[1] In particular, Coleridge was socializing with Charles Lamb, a friend since their school days at Christ's Hospital. Looking back in 1796, Lamb could conceive of "no higher ideas of heaven" than listening to Coleridge "repeating one of Bowles's sweetest sonnets in your sweet manner, while we two were indulging sympathy by the fireside at the Salutation."[2] A month later, these convivial occasions make Lamb exclaim: "O noctes cœnœque deum [O nights and feasts of the gods]: Anglice, Welch rabbits, punch, & poesy."[3] By June 1797 it had become "a sort of sacrilege" to let "such ideas slip out of my mind."[4] "Heaven," "sacrilege," godlike feasts: is it stretching belief to think that Coleridge's sparkling company transformed for Lamb a humble London tavern into an Olympian paradise, in which two friends felt themselves embody the Classical gods, and discover in the earthly delights of food, drink, and sentimental converse a glimpse of Heaven itself?

This chapter takes seriously the religious language that persistently gathers around Coleridge, Lamb, and Lloyd's discussions of their friendships. I want to argue that these men did indeed briefly construct their mutual friendship in religious terms, as a relation through which they might mediate a divine love and improve their spiritual nature. Such religious idealism, however, clashed with their practical experience of the friendships, which they increasingly felt to be informed by worldly, commercial models of relationship. In various ways, then, these youthful intimacies were also structured by particular late-eighteenth-century ideas regarding friendship. By tracing the trajectory of their relationships, we witness a conflict between spiritual and worldly conceptions of friendship, a clash that contributed to the group's collapse in 1798.

Despite Lamb's suggestion of Greek ecstasies, all three men's notions of friendship were more deeply informed by the Unitarianism Coleridge was preaching at this time. Unitarianism highlights difficulties traced throughout this book of moving from an Idea to its practical embodiment, for it focuses on the possibility of mediating divine love through human relations. Central to Unitarianism is a denial of the Trinity, and an affirmation of "the absolute Impersonality of the [D]eity."[5] For Unitarians, Christ was not the Son of God but the mortal son of Joseph and Mary. However, his life and resurrection exemplified a spiritual perfection that all human beings might attain. Writing in 1793, William Frend encapsulates the Unitarian view of the relationship between Christ and God: "Is he an infidel who declares his Saviour to be the great Mediator between God and man?"[6]

In 1795, Coleridge expresses his sense of Christ as "the great Mediator," declaring in his third Theological lecture that Christ's life proves "that the God of Love was in him, that the Spirit of the Most High dwelt upon him."[7] For Coleridge, Jesus perfected his human nature through his beneficence, which was nurtured and made permanent through his attachments to family, countrymen and friends:

> If we love not our friends and Parents whom we have seen—how can we love our universal Friend and Almighty Parent whom we have not seen. . . . Jesus was a Friend, and he wept at the Tomb of Lazarus. Jesus was the friend of the whole human Race, yet he disguised not the national feelings, when he foresaw the particular distresses of his Countrymen. (pp. 162–63)

J. Robert Barth has noted that Coleridge sees in the person of Christ "the perfect image of God's love—and at the same time the epitome of all human love."[8] I think we can push this further and say that Coleridge encourages his listeners to cultivate friendship as a means of mediating God's love and reconstituting society into a divine ordering.

Such ideals of friendship had been codified for eighteenth-century Unitarians by David Hartley in his *Observations on Man*

(1749). Hartley imagines how "The Pleasures of Sympathy . . . unite with those of Theopathy, and the moral Sense":

> Their union and entire coincidence with those of theopathy are evident, inasmuch as we are led by the love of good men to that of God, and back again by the love of God to that of all his creatures in and through him; also as it must be the will of an infinitely benevolent being, that we should cultivate universal unlimited benevolence. (2:283)

Love of God is both the foundation and culmination of human sympathies. Through the interconnection of sympathy and theopathy, Hartley theorizes how men's personal relationships could come to mediate divine love more fully: as the love of God induces benevolence, so "acts of benevolence, proceeding from A to B" have a tendency "to excite correspondent ones reciprocally from B to A, and so on indefinitely" (2:285). Hartley envisions an ideal social situation in which a man, "A,"

> considered every man as his friend . . . and loved him as himself; . . . Thus A, B, C, D, &c. would all become, as it were, new sets of senses, and perceptive powers, to each other, so as to increase each other's happiness without limits; they would all become *members of the mystical body of Christ*; all have an equal care for each other; all increase in love, and come to their *full stature*. (2:287)

In entering "the mystical body of Christ" an individual perfects his humanity and imitates Christ's mediation of divine love to all men.

In this way, Hartley understands friendship as contributing to "the annihilation of that *self*, carnal or spiritual, gross or refined, which is an insuperable bar to our happiness in the pure love of God, and of his works" (2:287). In "Religious Musings" (1794–1797), Coleridge versified Hartley's doctrines, and also suggested ways in which love may annihilate selfhood and so reveal divinity more fully.[9] For Coleridge, the crucifixion becomes the ultimate symbol of self-annihilation, and of love's sublime potential to transfigure the human soul:

> Lovely was the Death
> Of Him, whose Life was Love! Holy with power
> He on the thought-benighted Sceptic beam'd
> Manifest Godhead.
>
> (lines 37–40)

At this ultimately self-annihilating moment, Christ "beam'd" as a sun, radiating God's love with new power. Christ's sublimation teaches mankind to transcend the "Savage" (line 171) condition of "Feeling himself, his own low Self the whole" (line 172), and demonstrates how, by imitating the example of Christ's life, all men may become "Attracted" to and "absorbed" (line 50) in "perfect LOVE" (line 49),

> and center'd there
> GOD only to behold, and know, and feel,
> Till by exclusive Consciousness of GOD
> All self-annihilated it shall make
> GOD it's Identity: God all in all!
> We and our Father ONE!
>
> (lines 50–55)

Acknowledging that God is "all in all" is, for Coleridge, the culmination of man's humanity—which manifests itself in brotherly friendship:

> 'Tis the sublime of man,
> Our noontide Majesty, to know ourselves
> Parts and proportions of one wond'rous whole:
> This fraternizes man, this constitutes
> Our charities and bearings. But 'tis God
> Diffus'd thro' all, that doth make all one whole.
>
> (lines 141–46)

In becoming conscious of God's omnipresence in his creation, men are spurred to cultivate those amicable relations that constitute "Our charities and bearings."

In a poem "To C. Lamb," sent in a letter to Southey in December 1794, Coleridge reveals how the Hartleian theory of self-annihilation was influencing his understanding of his friendship with Charles Lamb.[10] Here, friendship provides an arena for annihilating egotism through the realization that God is "all in all." Struggling to complete "Religious Musings," Coleridge acknowledges that the original impulse informing his communication with Lamb was self-interest:

> Thus far my sterile Brain hath fram'd the Song
> Elaborate & swelling—but the Heart
> Not owns it. From thy spirit-breathing powers
> I ask not now, my Friend! the aiding Verse

> Tedious to thee, and from thy anxious thought
> Of dissonant Mood.
>
> (lines 1–6)

Coleridge requires Lamb's help in order to complete his poem. However, Coleridge subdues this selfish impulse as he calls to mind his friend's preoccupation with his bedridden sister. Through sympathetic imagination, friendship becomes a way of forgoing self-centring concerns, and Coleridge tenderly envisions how "Thou creepest round a dear-lov'd Sister's Bed" (line 7). Having lost his own sister, Coleridge understands his friend's anxiety regarding Mary's illness, and he develops the sympathetic bond by recalling his own bereavement: "O! I have woke at midnight, and have wept / Because she was not!" (lines 19–20). At this point, however, Coleridge is still aware that such familial relations militate against uniting with his friend. He could more easily confess to his sister "hidden Maladies / That shrink asham'd from even Friendship's Eye" (lines 17–18). The poem concludes, however, with the joining of Coleridge and Lamb in a religious bond that incorporates notions of both friendship and family. At the deepest level, Coleridge's sympathy for Lamb is a manifestation of God's omnific love:

> He knows (the Spirit who in secret sees,
> Of whose omniscient & all-spreading Love
> Aught to implore were Impotence of Mind)
> That my mute Thoughts are sad before his Throne,
> Prepar'd, when he his healing Ray vouchsafes,
> To pour forth Thanksgiving with lifted heart
> And praise him gracious with a Brother's Joy!
>
> (lines 27–33)

Thanking God with a "Brother's Joy," Coleridge acknowledges that God's "all-spreading Love" transforms mankind into one family. Coleridge thus understands that he is brother not only of his own sister but of Charles and Mary Lamb too. This spiritual bond is not nebulous, but means that Coleridge experiences the same joy in the recovery of Lamb's sister as he would for his own. The more Coleridge annihilates self by making God the focus of his thoughts, the more profoundly he feels united with his friend. When Coleridge spent time with Lamb during December 1794 and the New Year, both men cemented their friendship by practically focusing their thoughts on God. Southey testified to this when he came to London in January 1795 to find Coleridge. Having looked in the Salutation and Cat, Southey discovered that his friend on a Sunday "was gone with Lamb to the Unitarian chapel."[11]

For Lamb, desire for a religious friendship became heightened in the aftermath of the tragic death of his mother in autumn 1796. Informing Coleridge, Lamb asked him to write "as religious a letter as possible,"[12] and in reply Coleridge declared that he was "not a man who would attempt to insult the greatness of your anguish by any other consolation."[13] As well as urging Lamb to have faith in "the God of mercies, and father of all comfort," Coleridge represented his own friendship as a potentially healing bower: "I wish above measure to have you for a little while here; no visitants shall blow on the nakedness of your feelings; you shall be quiet, and your spirit may be healed" (1:239). (This sentiment and the fact that Lamb preserved this of all Coleridge's letters from the period tend to confirm Ronald Sharp's contention that friends have increasingly become "primary sources" of spiritual consolation, appropriating roles previously confined to the church.)

In his immediate reply, however, Lamb introduced a note of caution into Coleridge's Unitarianism. Lamb feels uncomfortable with Coleridge's suggestion, made in his letter of condolence, that all men possess "a portion as it were of His Omnipresence":

> Now, high as the human intellect comparatively will soar, and wide as its influence, malign or salutary, can extend, is there not, Coleridge, a distance between the Divine Mind and it, which makes such language blasphemy? Again, in your first fine consolatory epistle you say, "you are a temporary sharer in human misery, that you may be an eternal partaker of the Divine Nature." What more than this do those men say, who are for exalting the man Christ Jesus into the second person of an unknown Trinity,—men, whom you or I scruple not to call idolaters?[14]

For Lamb, Coleridge's desire to mediate the "Divine Mind" may become an arrogant belief that man might embody the "Divine Nature." Lamb goes on to suggest that men should not expect human friendships fully to mediate divine love:

> God, in the New Testament (*our best guide*), is represented to us in the kind, condescending, amiable, familiar light of a *parent:* and in my poor mind 'tis best for us so to consider of Him, as our *heavenly* Father, and our *best Friend*, without indulging too bold conceptions of His nature. Let us learn to think humbly of ourselves, and rejoice in the appellation of "dear children," "brethren," and "co-heirs with Christ of the promises," seeking to know no further. (1:54)

Lamb concurs that God is the basis of the social bond between "brethren." But if God is a man's "best friend," then human beings should not expect perfect friendship in embodied relationships. Lamb was developing a response to "Religious Musings" and establishing the parameters of a debate concerning the realization of a religious idea of friendship. During the next eighteen months, this debate would grow in urgency thanks to the progress of their own relationship and that between Coleridge and Charles Lloyd.

Nevertheless, while nursing Mary and laboring as a clerk at East India House, Lamb increasingly sought the twin supports of friendship and religion, both of which he found embodied in Coleridge. Despite the stress he lays on man's imperfections in his letter of October 1796, Lamb comes to consider Coleridge's letters "sacred things with me," celebrating the possibility that Coleridge might console and perfect his spiritual being.[15] Informing Lamb's aspirations is the idea of a spiritual "elect," a group to which Coleridge draws increasing attention in his revisions to "Religious Musings" during 1796–1797. In 1796 he declares:

> And blest are they,
> Who in this fleshly World, the elect of Heaven,
> Their strong eye darting thro' the deeds of Men
> Adore with stedfast unpresuming gaze
> Him, Nature's Essence, Mind, and Energy!
> And gazing, trembling, patiently ascend
> Treading beneath their feet all visible things
> As steps, that upward to their Father's Throne
> Lead gradual—else nor glorified nor lov'd.
>
> (lines 56–64)

The "elect of Heaven"—including Milton, Newton, Hartley, and Priestley—are those poets, philosophers, and scientists committed to revealing the ways in which God manifests Himself in nature and society.[16] In the 1797 version, Coleridge makes clear that the unifying factor to the elect's work is its mediation of God's love towards mankind: "With conscious zeal," each of these figures had "urg'd Love's wondrous plan / Coadjutors of God" (lines 369–70). Coleridge emphasizes that the elect's achievements are expressive of their capacity for selflessness:

> from th'Elect, regenerate thro' faith,
> Pass the dark Passions and what thirsty Cares
> Drink up the spirit and the dim regards
> Self-center.
>
> (1796, lines 102–5; 1797, lines 90–93)

Through faith and intellectual endeavor, the elect are closest to an ideal self-annihilation, and are thus also the most capable of loving their fellow men.

During 1796–1797, Lamb believed that friendship with a member of the elect could provide him with spiritual improvement. A key document is his letter to Coleridge, 7–10 January 1797, in which he praises Priestley's *A Free Discussion of the Doctrines of Materialism* (1778). Lamb says:

> **Priestly** . . . speaks of "such a choice of company, as tends to keep up that right bent, & firmness of mind, which a nec[e]ssary intercourse with the world would otherwise warp & relax. Such fellowship is the ba[lsam] of life, it[s] cement is infinitely more durable than that of the friendships of the world, & it looks for its proper fruit, & complete gratification, to the life beyond the Grave."[17]

Immediately before this passage quoted by Lamb, Priestley celebrates the "peculiar pleasure" of the theological "speculations" in which he and Dr. Richard Price have been engaging:

> from the relation they bear to the greatest of all objects, they have a dignity and sublimity in them, and eminently contribute to inspire a *serenity* and *elevation of mind*, which both improves and enlarges it, and thereby enables us to look down upon the trifling but tormenting pursuits of a bustling world.[18]

Priestley's discussion offers Lamb a tantalizing vision of friendship, which he sets before Coleridge. He continues:

> Is there a possible chance for such an one as me to realize in this world, such friendships? Where am I to look for 'em? what testimonials shall I bring of my being worthy of such friendship? Alas! the great & good go together in separate **Herds,** & leave such as me to lag far far behind in all intellectual, & far more grievous to say, in all moral accomplishments. (1:88)

To a limited extent through his reading, he posits Priestley himself as an elect friend with whom he can enjoy an elevating discussion:

> I rejoyce, & feel my privilege with gratitude, when I have been reading some wise book, such as I have just been reading, **Priestly** on Philosophical necessity, in the thought that I enjoy a kind of Communion, a kind of friendship even, with the great & good. (1:89)

Lamb's comments, however, also direct themselves at Coleridge, whom he regards as offering his best hope of experiencing this highest ideal of friendship. Lamb pleads:

> Do, do write to me, & do some good to my mind, already how much **"warped & relaxed"** by the world!— . . . I rejoyce in being, speculatively, a necessarian.—Would to God, I were habitually a practical one. Confirm me in the faith of that great & glorious doctrine, & keep me steady in the contemplation of it. (1:89)

Coleridge's friendship will mediate God's love insofar as his intellectual converse enlightens and strengthens Lamb's faith.

Furthermore, Lamb places himself in a subordinate role to his "elect" tutor, and he celebrates this hierarchy as intrinsic to a spiritually improving friendship. Explaining how Coleridge may satisfy his "occasional earnest aspiration after perfection," Lamb declares: "I gain nothing by being with such as myself—we encourage one another in mediocrity—I am always longing to be with men more excellent than myself" (1:89). Coleridge's friendship can improve Lamb's spiritual being by providing what Lamb calls a "strong religious habit" (1:79), and he suggests this relationship between teacher and pupil has a spiritual value lacking in more egalitarian friendships.

Lamb was not alone in seeking out Coleridge as a tutor in order to realize an exalted friendship. Since August 1796, this had become the dream of Charles Lloyd, son of a Quaker banker, who had met Coleridge while the latter was preaching in Birmingham. An attachment quickly formed, and a plan emerged for Lloyd to pay Coleridge £80 a year in return for private tutoring, board, and lodging. In an unpublished sonnet, probably composed at the end of their first meeting, Lloyd also portrays Coleridge as an "elect" figure. More explicitly than Lamb, Lloyd emphasizes Coleridge's capacity to mediate a divine love towards him. The poem is titled simply "To Coleridge":

> Coleridge, my soul is very sad to think
> We seperate so soon, for tho unfit
> To mould the prompt phrase with impetuous wit,
> I love thee still, & my poor heart will sink
> Musing on the departed, nor the less
> Still it regret, because it never knew
> T'expose its feelings to the careless view
> Its simple store of wayward wretchedness.
> But I did fancy as mine eye met thine

> That there than erst e'er seen the social glow
> Intenslier dwelt—(I've wept in agony
> To think that glow the human face divine
> So scantily should radiate) if t'were so—
> If t'were a ray of soul remember me![20]

In radiating a "social glow," Coleridge embodies for Lloyd the "human face divine": in this he becomes a sunlike figure, comparable to the elect man of "Religious Musings" (1796), whose soul is so saturated with love's "holy name" (line 120) that

> From HIMSELF he flies,
> Stands in the Sun, and with no partial gaze
> Views all creation, and he loves it all.
>
> (lines 124–26)

Pleading with Coleridge to "remember me," Lloyd hopes he will be warmed by Coleridge's holy rays of love, and so come to "dwell with the most High!" (line 128).

Like Lamb, Lloyd founded this exalted ideal of friendship upon a hierarchical relation. In his poem, "To ******. Written in Worcestershire, July 1797," he identifies Coleridge as "elect of Heaven," that is, a person "fitted for an immediate entrance into the paradisiacal state."[20] For proof, Lloyd points to Coleridge's "godlike scheme" (p. 11) of Pantisocracy. Two "noble souls" (p. 9), Coleridge and Southey,

> counted still beyond the Atlantic deep
> To find those virtues, of whose sweets bereft
> The unearthly soul calleth its sojourn here
> A most impure enthralment! Oh my best friend,
> That I had liv'd in high-soul'd fellowship
> With such as fancy pictures these might be,
> Tried spirits, and unspotted from the world!
>
> (p. 10)

Lloyd's "high-soul'd fellowship" involves what he would later call "sympathies of holiest love" (p. 13). In this poem, Lloyd may be using "fellowship" in a technical sense, with Coleridge acting as the Messiah to the Christian brotherhood. As Jesus reveals God to his disciples, so Coleridge provides the Pantisocrats with a similarly sanctified existence through his creation of a perfect social system. During their enthusiasm for Pantisocracy, both Coleridge and Southey referred to the other participants as "disciple[s]."[21] Lloyd strengthens his identification of Coleridge and Jesus by contending that his "godlike scheme" shall "rise again" (p. 11) to redeem mankind. In Autumn 1796, Lloyd was hoping he might himself become a disciple, bound to Coleridge in "high-soul'd fellowship" in a quasi-Pantisocratic community now located at Clevedon.

For his part, Coleridge was also optimistic that this village could offer a space "unspotted from the world" in which they might realize an exalted friendship. For him also, fellowship was connected with being a teacher to his young disciple. This became evident in his own poem "To C. Lloyd, on his Proposing to Domesticate with the Author" (1796), in which he envisions the two friends climbing a "hill of knowledge" (line 50) in an allegorical landscape evocative of the West Country hills:[22]

> How heavenly sweet, if some dear Friend should bless
> Th'advent'rous toil, and up the path sublime
> Now lead, now follow; the glad landscape round,
> Wide and more wide, increasing without bound!
>
> (lines 16–19)

In studying together, the men will sanctify their friendship. But unlike the Coleridge-Lamb hierarchy, this tutorial friendship will be an egalitarian quest for knowledge. Like Priestley, Coleridge imagines their philosophic amity to be spiritually elevating, as he envisions Lloyd and himself reaching the top of the "hill of knowledge":

> Ah! dearest LLOYD! it were a lot divine
> To cheat our noons in moralizing mood,
> While west-winds fann'd our temples toil-bedew'd:
> Then downwards slope, oft pausing, from the mount,
> To some low mansion in some woody dale,
> Where smiling with blue eye DOMESTIC BLISS
> Gives *this* the husband's, *that* the brother's kiss!
>
> (lines 39–48)

Coleridge and Lloyd achieve a level of familial intimacy in which Lloyd gives Sara a "brother's kiss!"

Central to the student-friends' "lot divine" is their new geographical and moral unworldliness, which allows the divine founts of benevolence to flow freely through their being:

> O meek retiring Spirit! we will climb,
> Cheering and cheer'd, this lovely hill sublime;
> And from the stirring world uplifted high . . .

> There, while the prospect thro' the gazing eye
> Pours all its healthful greenness on the soul,
> We'll laugh at wealth, and learn to laugh at fame,
> Our hopes, our knowledge, and our joys the same,
> As neighb'ring fountains image, each the whole.
>
> (lines 61–63; 67–71)

The "fountain" is, of course, a primary Coleridgean symbol for divine love, which receives famous expression in "The Ancyent Marinere" (1797–1798). As the Marinere's "kind saint" (line 278) generates in him a "spring of love" (line 276), so Coleridge imagines that friendship will similarly undercover in both friends a divine gushing of selfless affection.

Crucial, however, to this exalted friendship is a denial that the men's studies were bound together by a commercial contract. Motivating Coleridge's omission is a widespread cultural consciousness that financial considerations damage friendship's benevolent ideal. This may be illustrated by Ansell's print, "Mutual Confidence in the Year 1799," which satirizes the inquisitorial means used to obtain income tax.[23] One "Old Friend's" suspicion that his fellow might be spying for the Treasury destroys all openness between them. The scowling citizen literally cannot afford to assume that his friend's inquiries are disinterested, especially when a predatory look plays around his jovial features. In his personal relations, Coleridge frequently perceives that money degrades friendship, declaring in February 1796 to Cottle: "I love you as a friend—Indeed so much that I regret, seriously regret that *you* have been my Copyholder."[24] Lloyd vigorously concurred with such views, denouncing Mammon in 1797 as a "self-centring fiend!" that

> numb'st
> The nerve that throbb'd so finely to the grasp
> Of generous friendship.[25]

In his "Lines Addressed to S. T. Coleridge," also composed during autumn 1796, Lloyd responds to Coleridge's poem and agrees that friendship can save him from the world's corruptions:[26]

> My COLERIDGE! oft I muse upon the cot
> To which our footsteps bend; I envy not
> The enrobed son of wealth, the heir of fame,
> Or the more happy youth whose ardent flame
> The yielding maid returns, when I can dwell
> On the pure pleasures of our simple cell!
>
> (p. 179)

Charles or James K. Ansell, "Mutual Confidence in the Year 1799." Published 1 April 1799 by S. W. Fores, London. © Copyright The British Museum.

Friendship's "pure pleasures" offer Lloyd salvation not only from his desire for wealth but also from the "ardent flame" of sexual desire:

> My COLERIDGE! take the wanderer to thy breast,
> The youth who loves thee, and who faint would rest

> (Oft rack'd by hopes that frensy and expire)
> In the long sabbath of subdued desire!
>
> (p. 181)

In subduing desire, friendship becomes sanctified as a "sabbath." By domesticating with the Jesus-like figure of Coleridge, Lloyd hopes to enter friendship's sacred space and time, and find redemption from worldly influences and his own unruly passions.

During the following months of 1796, Coleridge, Lloyd, and Lamb attempted to embody these exalted ideals. Coleridge ended "To C. Lloyd" with the wish, "Now may Heaven realize this vision bright!" (line 76), and writing to Lloyd's father in October, he remains confident that God will operate through the men's friendship to their mutual improvement: "Your son and I are happy in our connection—our opinions and feelings are as nearly alike as we can expect: and I rely upon the goodness of the All-good that we shall proceed to make each other better and wiser."[27] Lloyd celebrated the "tranquillity of my present situation, & may I add the almost unblemish'd sanctity of manners which I find in Coleridge."[28] By December, such reports provoked Lamb enviously to exclaim, "you two seem to be about **realizing** an Elysium upon earth."[29]

For all three men, the idea of selfless friendship became realized through a series of collaborative literary endeavors, which resulted in the insertion of Coleridge and Lamb's poems in Lloyd's *Poems on the Death of Priscilla Farmer* (1796), and Lamb and Lloyd's work in the second edition of Coleridge's *Poems* (1797). Lamb and Coleridge had long been intimately involved in correcting one another's poems, responding to criticisms, and offering advice on literary and philosophical points. Such collaboration became a kind of aspheterism. In "To C. Lamb," composed in the heat of Pantisocracy, ownership becomes a concept that embraces rather than excludes another's contributions: without Lamb's "spirit-breathing powers" and "aiding Verse," Coleridge's "Heart / not owns" "Religious Musings." In his poet-making role, Lamb entertains Coleridge's communal view of intellectual property, writing in June 1796: "I am not quite satisfied now with the Chatterton, and with your leave will try my hand at it again. A master joiner, you know, may leave a cabinet to be finished by his journeyman when his own hands are full."[30] As Alison Hickey notes, while acknowledging Coleridge's supremacy, Lamb writes "as if Coleridge's 'Monody on the Death of Chatterton' were his own."[31]

Elsewhere, Lamb draws attention to the collaborators' selfless ideals at moments when he fears he is failing to meet these exacting standards. In 1797, Lamb feels his disinterestedness tested by Coleridge's decision to print Lloyd's poems before his own in the forthcoming *Poems*:

> If any one is welcome to pre-eminence from me, it is Lloyd, for he would be the last to desire it. So pray, let his name *uniformly* precede mine, for it would be treating me like a child to suppose it could give me pain. Yet, alas! I am not insusceptible of the bad passions. Thank God, I have the ingenuousness to be ashamed of them. I am dearly fond of Charles Lloyd; he is all goodness, and I have too much of the world in my composition to feel myself thoroughly deserving of his friendship.[32]

For Lamb, Lloyd embodies the moral idea of friendship as he is the "last" person to elevate himself above his collaborators. For his part, Coleridge invented an appropriate Latin epigraph to his volume, which, translated, reads: "We have a double bond: that of friendship and of our linked and kindred Muses: may neither death nor length of time dissolve it!"[33] The epigraph was credited to a group of obscure medieval scholars, "Groscollius, Utenhovius, and Tastaeus." With this ingenious touch Coleridge suggests his elevated friendships with Lamb and Lloyd are similarly grounded in the collaborative occupations of scholarship and poetry.

Not everyone, however, was impressed. In "New Morality" (1798), *The Anti-Jacobin* pilloried the group's theophilanthropic alliances in some famous lines: "C—DGE and SOUTHEY, Loyd and L—BE and Co. / Tune all your mystic harps to praise LEPAUX!" (lines 376–77). For Alison Hickey: "The 'and Co.', evoking mercantile capitalism, . . . hints at an ironic discrepancy between . . . the poets' . . . idealizing claims about brotherhood and common property in juxtaposition with their participation in the literary marketplace" (p. 763). *The Anti-Jacobin* highlighted the possibility of entering into friendship for self-interested, commercial reasons. In this, it astutely focused a connection between friendship and commercial discourse that was to undermine Coleridge's relations with both Lloyd and Lamb.

A powerful source for this is Thomas Hobbes. For Hobbes, men do not "by nature seek Society for its own sake, but that we may receive some Honour or Profit from it."[34] Friendship is a self-interested practice whose utilitarian goal is to acquire goods, be they material or symbolic:

> All free congress ariseth either from mutual poverty, or from vain glory, whence the parties met, endeavour to carry with them either some ben-

efit, or to leave behind them that same . . . esteem and honour with those, with whom they have been conversant. . . . All Society therefore is either for Gain, or for Glory, (*i.e.*) not so much for love of our Fellowes, as for love of our Selves. (pp. 5–6)

Ultimately, self-interest militates against the stability of any friendship, for "the benefits of this life" are better gained through "Dominion" than "the society of others" (p. 6).

In concrete ways, Hobbesian assumptions can be said to have informed Coleridge's collaboration with Lloyd. Part of his motive for including Lloyd's poems in his 1797 volume was profit. "Now for the saleability," he remarked to Cottle, "Charles Lloyd's connections will take off a great many more than a hundred, I doubt not."[35] Also, to Tom Poole in September 1796, Coleridge revealed a difference in the men's respective understandings of their friendship:

[Lloyd's] Joy, & gratitude to Heaven for the circumstance of his domestication with me, I can scarcely describe to you—& I believe, that his fixed plans are of being always with me.—His Father told me, that if he saw that his Son had formed Habits of severe Economy, he should not insist upon his adopting any Profession—as then his fair Share of his (the Father's) Wealth would be sufficient for him.[36]

For Lloyd, domestication with Coleridge is a gift from God. But Coleridge sees Lloyd's desire for a permanent friendship in Hobbesian terms: if Lloyd's father decides not to insist on his son adopting a profession, then Charles's desire of "being always" with his tutor might contain a lasting financial benefit.[37]

Lloyd himself had a more complex understanding of the friendship with Coleridge, which is revealed in "Sonnet 13," another unpublished poem, entitled "To the Same." It was probably composed shortly after "To Coleridge" in September 1796, as Lloyd waited to be taken to Clevedon:

> Coleridge my friend wherefore this long delay?
> Others have wrong'd me but methought thine eye
> Told me of friendship & of sympathy!
> And I have dreamt the lingering summers day
> Of all its lavish promises—then sure
> Me thou wilt not forget nor coldly leave,
> My heart in cruel vacancy to grieve,
> Snatching his scanty pittance from the poor!
> Me the world tempteth not! its glittering toys
> Unanxious I behold! but oh thy heart

> Generous & pure, enthusiastic bard!
> How would I cherish! its mysterious joys
> Could I obtain them ne'er would I desert!
> But live the pensioner of meek regard![39]

The poem negotiates between spiritual and economic discourses of relationship. Coleridge's "lavish promises" resonate with his vision of fountain-like generosity in "To C. Lloyd." But Lloyd understands this exalted friendship cannot evade economic realities. As a "pensioner of meek regard," he is literally prepared to pay for these spiritual goods. As such, friendship here hovers uneasily between a mystical union of souls and a worldly business arrangement, grounded firmly in Coleridge's financial self-interest.

In the event, the commercial basis quickly brought to earth the friendship's transcendent aspirations. In mid-November Lloyd collapsed, causing Coleridge to reassess their connection: "I can neither be his tutor or fellow-student, nor in any way impart a regular system of knowledge," he tells Lloyd's father.[39] In this letter, Coleridge is reluctance to continue with Lloyd's domestication without a commercial tie to bind them. He accepts that an affectionate relation might coexist with a commercial contract, for if Lloyd continues to "occupy a room in my cottage, he will be there merely as a Lodger and Friend" (1:263). However, he had "dissuaded" Lloyd from staying, and claims that "I never dreamt that he would have desired to continue with me" after the "literary engagement" had become "impracticable" (1:264). These comments reveal how Coleridge in *practice* linked friendship to a commercial relation, and to a much greater extent than Lloyd. Although the arrangement continued, the domestication had effectively ended: two weeks after rejoining Coleridge in Stowey at the end of February, Lloyd began a series of alarming fits that left Coleridge exhausted with nursing him. At the end of March Lloyd moved out, and, except for a visit in September, did not again reside with the poet.

If Coleridge's bond with Lloyd was undermined by its practical and commercial aspect, then so was his friendship with Lamb. However, whereas with Lloyd commercial issues intruded in a literal way, in the Lamb-Coleridge friendship they operated at a metaphorical level. Lamb is acutely aware how friendship can be entered into for Hobbesian motives. In his January 1797 letter, he admits the importance of intercourse with an elect like Coleridge, since "I gain nothing by being with such as myself." A month earlier, however, Lamb had expressed anxiety about this symbolic "gain," offering Coleridge the results of his calculation in suggestive terms:

> Continue to remember us, and to show us you do remember us: we will take as lively an interest in what concerns you and yours. All I can add to your happiness, will be sympathy. You can add to mine *more;* you can teach me wisdom. I am indeed an unreasonable correspondent; . . . I do not expect or wish you to write, till you are moved; and of course shall not, till you announce to me that event, think of writing myself. (1:79)

Whereas Lamb gains "wisdom," Coleridge receives only "sympathy." For Lamb, both concepts are commodities that "add" a quantifiable happiness to the recipient. Within these Hobbesian terms, Lamb senses their friendship might be exploiting Coleridge who receives less than he gives. Lamb worries that he is binding his friend to a quasi-commercial contract, obligating him to trade wisdom for sympathy. He subdues this possibility by denying that friendship is so narrowly contractual. Instead, Coleridge should offer his wisdom as a gift and write only when "moved" to do so.

Nevertheless, in suggesting friendship involves a contractual trade-off, Lamb entertains what was a contemporary utilitarian attitude to friendship, grounded in Hobbesian assumptions. This is illustrated in Caius's article for *The Universal Magazine*, "On Imprudent Friendship" (1793).[40] Caius laments the "error" into which many young people fall: "carrying into the world those sentiments of exalted friendship, which they have found in the writings of authors of poetical fancy," these innocents imagine that "merit will make many friends, and that friendship is a permanent and unchangeable principle." From such high expectations, however, "disappointment and chagrin are sure to follow" (pp. 126–27). For Caius, a truly beneficent relationship cannot be embodied, but exists only as a direct communication with God:

> The Creator seems to reserve, as his own great prerogative, the *perfection of friendship*. In us he has tempered it so, that we can be but partial assistants to each other; and for this wise purpose, that when the help of man fails, we should look up to Him, who is the giver of every good and every *perfect* gift. (p. 126)

Caius distinguishes such divine gift-giving from the friendships "of this world":

> The friendship of this world, where even it appears to most advantage, is a sort of mutual contract between the parties. The poor may be befriended by the rich, but the favour is not altogether gratuitous. Return must be made in some way or other; and, at least, it is expected that

> the benefit received shall not be abused. . . . There must be, in some degree, a reciprocation of kindnesses, an exchange of mutual esteem, and a certain portion of respect and gratitude from the party most obliged. (p. 127)

There is no "gratuitous" gift-giving in earthly relations. Instead, friendship represents a transaction in which, for every benefit received, a "Return" of approximately equal value must be made.

This utilitarian view of social relations becomes a topic for satire, as in George Bruce's encounter in *The Amicable Quixote* (1788) with Samuel Barter, whose name suggests his character. Samuel informs him that:

> my principles of prudence have procured me a great number [of friends], and I make them all useful. [. . . Squire Squat] has not an idea beyond horses and hounds; but he is very useful, for he supplies my table with a variety of game all the season: I therefore am always proud to shew myself his truly devoted. (3:91)

Wanting to please, George embraces Samuel's model of utilitarian friendship:

> Well, I shall often visit you; [. . . this] commerce of friendship [. . .] is a kind of trade, to which I am so little used, that I hardly know even the technical terms of mercantile intimacy: I shall, however, learn in time the tare and tret of friendship; I shall be able to truck amiably, to know the staple commodities of every acquaintance and the mart of every service: . . . I shall be able to transact my business, calculate all the 7–8ths of esteem, trace the consolidated annuities of attention. (3:102–3)

In this scenario, all friends possess a quantifiable economic value that is used in friendship's "trade."

Such commodification of the "friend" testifies to what Andrea Henderson has called "the conceptual alignment of commodities and persons" at the end of the eighteenth century.[41] This commercial subjectivity challenged the traditional "depth model" (p. 2) of identity, which emphasizes an integral, stable self. Henderson argues that: "On the one hand we have identity as it 'should' be: a matter of personality and intrinsic individual virtue. On the other hand we have a relational, changeable identity associated with the superficiality, contingency, and indeterminacy of market values" (p. 49). In commercial subjectivity, an individual has no essential worth, but only a "mercurial exchange value" (p. 7) conferred by the market, so that the commodified self might find its value changing under different conditions.

The competition Henderson traces between models of subjectivity is articulated in terms of friendship in a letter from Coleridge to Poole, dated 22 August 1796. Responding to Poole's offer of a subscription, he explains how:

> In preaching on Faith yesterday—I said that Faith was infinitely better than Good Works—as the Cause is greater than the effect—as a fruitful Tree is better than it's Fruits & as a friendly Heart is of far higher value than the Kindnesses which it naturally and *necessarily* prompts.—It is for that *friendly Heart* that I now have thanked you: and which I so eagerly accept of.[42]

Coleridge rejects the commercial mode in which a friend is valued according to the goods or "Kindnesses" he brings to a relationship. Instead, he asserts a "depth model" of subjectivity: the "friendly Heart." What Coleridge values is the essential nature of a friend's inner being rather than any outward acts he might perform.

Lamb, however, to a large extent regards himself as a commodity and his value altered by friendship with an elect. At times, Coleridge raises Lamb's sense of his economic worth, making him "think less meanly of myself" (1:89). Increasingly, however, Coleridge's spiritual treasures reinforce Lamb's feeling of impoverishment. Lloyd's visit in January 1797 brought such thoughts to Lamb's mind, which he expressed in the lines, "**To Charles Lloyd /** an unexpected visitor":

> **Alone**, obscure, without a friend,
>   A cheerless, solitary thing,
> Why seeks my Lloyd the Stranger out?
>   What offring can the Stranger bring
>
> of social scenes, home bred delights,
>   That him in aught compensate may
> For Stowey's pleasant winter nights,
>   For loves & friendships far away?[45]

Lamb is painfully aware that the goods Lloyd receives at Stowey outweigh anything he can offer. In comparison to Coleridge, Lamb feels he is a worthless commodity.

Lamb's commercial discourse is brought into relief by another of Charles Lloyd's unpublished sonnets, "To C. Lamb," composed during or immediately after this visit. For Lloyd, Lamb's character has intrinsic merit:

> Charles, I do love the day when first thy name
> Thrill'd my awaken'd heart! my God, I praise
> That I have *seen thee*—oft in after days
> Thy semblance I shall cherish to inflame
> The feeble & dishearten'd to the aim
> Of patient worth so prompted—nor forsake
> Thine arduous path e'en tho' thy bosom ake
> With sad misgivings; for thou yet mayst claim
> Solace from him who promised to bless
> The sufferers of the earth—then if fainted
> [?]Your palsied form, & She the stricken maid
> Mourners no more, shall learn with thankfulness
> That heaven in pity all your wrongs beheld,
> E'en when ye look'd & there was none to aid.
> Jan. 97[44]

Lloyd dismisses Lamb's view that his straightened circumstances devalue him in others' eyes; on the contrary, Lamb's struggle with adversity has made him a moral exemplar from whom Lloyd can take strength: "my God, I praise / That I have *seen thee*."[45]

Nevertheless, Lamb increasingly experiences a tension between his religious ideals of friendship and its mercantile practice. This is well expressed in a letter of June 1797, in which Lamb has misgivings about visiting Coleridge:

> What is such a letter to you? and if I come to Stowey, what conversation can I furnish to compensate my friend for those stores of knowledge and of fancy, those delightful treasures of wisdom, which I know he will open to me? But it is better to give than to receive; and I was a very patient hearer and docile scholar in our winter evening meetings at Mr. May's; was I not, Col.? What I have owed to thee, my heart can ne'er forget.[46]

Friendship heightens Lamb's sense of his contingent identity. Coleridge's value is extremely high, for he possesses "*treasures* of wisdom" and "*stores* of knowledge and of fancy." By comparison, Lamb feels worthless. Successful friendships here implicitly resemble business deals in which goods of equal value are exchanged. As such, Lamb fears the pedagogic relation will render friendship impossible, for the pupil cannot "compensate" his tutor for what he has received. In reasserting the friendship's spiritual basis, Lamb reminds Coleridge that it is "better to give than to receive," alluding to Paul's elaboration in Acts (20:33–35) of a key characteristic of a religious brother.

Nevertheless, the men's hierarchical relation becomes Janus-faced. Informed by a religious discourse of election, Coleridge's intellectual stature provides Lamb with an opportunity to ameliorate his spiritual being. In practice, however, the mentor's superiority heightens Lamb's sense of himself as a valueless commodity. During 1796–1797, such tensions come to the fore. Faced by a break in Coleridge's correspondence at the beginning of 1797, Lamb feels the friendship is declining into a less generous relation. He reminds Coleridge that

> Friendship, and acts of friendship, should be reciprocal, and free as the air; a friend should never be reduced to beg an alms of his fellow. Yet I will beg an alms; I entreat you to write, and tell me all about poor Lloyd, and all of you.[47]

Ideally, friendship should transcend any taint of commerce, characterized by a *free* exchange of gifts. This, Lamb feels, has broken down, and Coleridge's withholding of his treasures makes him acutely aware of Coleridge's plenitude and his own impoverishment. At other times, Lamb senses a Hobbesian desire in Coleridge to profit from their friendship. In June 1796 he perceives this in Coleridge's habit of emending his confessional poetry: "I say unto you again Col. spare my **Ewe lambs**."[48] Lamb's allusion is to the parable in 2 Samuel (2: 1–4) in which the rich man takes the sole possession—a ewe lamb—from his poor neighbor. Lamb suggests Coleridge is similarly robbing him of his most precious property: his own language.

The ambiguous character of the Lamb-Coleridge intimacy during 1797 is exposed in "This Lime-Tree Bower my Prison," written during Lamb's visit to Stowey in July. Lamb's reaction to the poem's publication 1800 is instructive.[49] As in the 1797 version, the 1800 text celebrates at its climax the men's religious bond:

> My gentle-hearted CHARLES! when the last Rook
> Beat its straight path along the dusky air
> Homewards, I blest it! deeming its black wing
> (Now a dim speck, now vanishing in the light)
> Had cross'd the mighty orb's dilated glory
> While thou stood'st gazing; or, when all was still
> Flew *creeking* o'er thy head, and had a charm
> For thee, my gentle-hearted CHARLES! to whom
> No sound is dissonant, which tells of Life.
>
> (lines 68–76)

In its flight across the sun, the black rook makes the sign of the cross. As this bird is associated with Lamb, Coleridge intimates his sublime sense of the men's religious brotherhood. Famously, however, Lamb was outraged: "For God's sake (I never was more serious), don't make me ridiculous any more by terming me gentle-hearted in print, . . . the meaning of gentle is equivocal at best, and almost always means poor-spirited."[50] Coleridge's sympathy rests upon a rhetorical impoverishment of his friend's spirit. Lamb accuses Coleridge of deliberately gaining a spiritual wealth (his capacity to bless) through an aggressive devaluing of his "gentle-hearted" friend: Lamb becomes "convinced it was all done in Malice, heaped, sack-upon-sack, congregated, studied Malice. You Dog!" (1:224).

Coleridge's aggression towards his pupils clearly manifested itself in November 1797 in his Nehemiah Higginbottom sonnets, published in *The Monthly Magazine*. To Cottle, Coleridge revealed that these poems were informed by his pedagogic relation with his friends:

> I sent three mock Sonnets in ridicule of my own & Charles Lloyd's, and Lamb's, &c &c—exposing that affectation of unaffectedness, . . . puny pathos &c &c—the instances are almost all taken from mine & Lloyd's poems—I signed them Nehemiah Higginbottom. I think they may do good to our young Bards.[51]

Coleridge's patronizing thrust at Lamb and Lloyd's youth and naïveté, his infantilization of their "puny pathos," as well as his desire to "ridicule" them, rather than serving a discourse of spiritual improvement, becomes a vehicle for belittling his neophytic subordinates.

In his second sonnet, "To Simplicity," Coleridge's ridicule was aimed specifically at Lamb and Lloyd's aspirations for a morally pure friendship. For these men, simplicity was friendship's lingua franca. In October 1796, Lloyd had celebrated his mentor's "child-like simplicity & purity of heart."[52] In November, Lamb urged Coleridge to, "Cultivate simplicity, for simplicity springs spontaneous from the heart, and carries into daylight its own modest buds and genuine, sweet, and clear flowers of expression."[53] Simplicity gives natural and unselfconscious utterance to innermost thoughts and feelings. Lamb thinks this quality necessary for friendship, praising Coleridge for "those little pictures of your feelings which you lately sent me. . . . I love them as I love the Confessions of Rousseau, and for the same reason: the same frankness, the same openness of heart, the same disclosure of all the most hidden and delicate affections of the mind" (1:59).

The danger in such confessional self-revelation, however, lies in the vulnerability of the friend, who becomes transparent to another's gaze. In his sonnet, Coleridge mocks Lamb and Lloyd's indulgence in such naked expressions of need and affection:

> O! I do love thee, meek *Simplicity*!
> For of thy lays the lulling simpleness
> Goes to my heart, and soothes each small distress,
> Distress tho' small, yet haply great to me!
> 'Tis true on Lady Fortune's gentlest pad
> I amble on; yet, tho' I know not why,
> *So* sad I am!—but should a friend and I
> Grow cool and *miff*, O! I am *very* sad!
> And then with sonnets and with sympathy
> My dreamy bosom's mystic woes I pall;
> Now of my false friend plaining plaintively,
> Now raving at mankind in general;
> But, whether sad or fierce, 'tis simple all,
> All very simple, meek SIMPLICITY!
>
> (lines 1–14)[54]

Coleridge scorns the "delicate affections" Lamb and Lloyd celebrate. But in often identifying Lamb as the poem's target, critics have overlooked how this sonnet parodies Lloyd's sonnets to Coleridge. Lloyd's "My soul is very sad" becomes Nehemiah's "I am *very* sad." Nehemiah's complaint that a friendship has cooled echoes Lloyd's fear that Coleridge will "coldly leave" him. Coleridge's scorn for the simple friend's "mystic woes" attacks Lloyd's desire to experience the philosopher's "mysterious joys." Simple language is Lloyd and Lamb's means of articulating feelings that are authentic and pure. Coleridge, however, follows Dr. Johnson in dismissing simplicity as the immature language of children. As he reassured Southey, "To Simplicity" attacked an "infantine" sensibility, characteristic only of "lady-like Friendships."

From this point, the transcendent aspirations of the three scholar-poet-friends began to unravel: Lloyd asked that his contributions to *Poems* (1797) be omitted from future editions. Coleridge admitted that his invented epigraph to *Poems* (1797) had been "a foolish & presumptuous start of affectionateness."[55] By April 1798, Lloyd was sure Coleridge was "dissociating himself from us."[56] Lloyd contributed to the group's dissociation by continuing with *Edmund Oliver* (1798), a fictional distillation of his recent experiences. With few exceptions, modern commentators have condemned the novel for its supposedly malicious representation of Coleridge. The novel certainly makes an important comment on the Coleridge relationship. However, it resists being read in conventionally reductive biographical terms, for its main characters Edmund Oliver and Charles Maurice represent a composite of characteristics shared by both Lloyd and Coleridge. What Lloyd effectively demonstrates is a "doubleness" in Coleridge at odds with the purity he had formerly thought his tutor possessed.

As Jonathan Wordsworth observes, Edmund "stands in the same relation to Charles Maurice as Lloyd himself stood to Coleridge."[57] Charles's conversion of Edmund to Priestleyan Unitarianism alludes to Coleridge's conversion of Lloyd; as Lloyd hoped to find in Coleridge "the long sabbath of subdued desire," so Edmund wishes that Charles "had taught me to subdue my wishes" (1:72–73). In time, he believes Charles's friendship would accomplish this: "could I ever be with thee" (Edmund exclaims) "my character would rise beyond the power of calculation" (1:73). Echoing his own earlier idealism, Lloyd represents Charles as mediating God's love towards Edmund: having been rescued from the army, Edmund declares, "you, Charles, were a second time destined to be my saviour" (2:48). Charles concurs, explaining that "the relations to certain individuals implies a power vested in our hands by Deity, and . . . it seems to me unjustifiable not to avail ourselves of this power, in order to work upon their minds" (1:127–28). Lloyd thus aligns his tutor with a religious mode of salvific friendship, whereby one man becomes spiritual mentor to another.

At the time of writing, Lloyd was himself keen to perform the Coleridgean role of moral guide. In a letter to Southey, written in April 1798 while *Edmund Oliver* was in proof, Lloyd explains why he was remaining in London instead of returning to Bath:

> At Bath, it seems to me, I can only giving [sic] at best a general pleasure—that pleasure which a loose & independent association necessary circumscribes—I am sure that I have have [sic] here created a sort of settled dependance upon myself for the happiness of one or two individuals—there are no beings in Bath so forlorn as Lamb—nor none to whom I can be of so much moral service as White—I cannot myself perceive that I am too susceptible of attachment—I wish to love wherever I go—& if that love never dupe me into vice surely it is no blameable feeling![58]

Confronting Southey's criticism of his speedy acquisition of friends, Lloyd celebrates his desire to "love wherever I go" as a moral quest. Through "giving" and "moral service" Lloyd can benefit the spiritual well-being of those to whom he is attached.

These comments draw attention to Edmund's failure to embody such moral ideals. If Coleridge is Charles Maurice, he is also Edmund Oliver. As Coleridge immediately realized, "Edmund Oliver's love-fit, debaucheries, leaving college & going into the army" closely identified Edmund with himself.[59] Central to Edmund's character is a dreamy self-absorption that severs him from his private attachments. Lloyd's criticism of Coleridge is sharpest in highlighting Edmund's indulgence in drink and opiates, through which he disengages from friends and family. Conscious of neglecting both his sister and friend, he exclaims: "I have some laudanum in my pocket. I will quell these mortal upbraidings!—I cannot endure them! . . . I wish to forget the existence of any other being besides myself["] (1:210). Edmund's escapism is clearly a culpable act of egotism. Lloyd's representation of his mentor is thus neither wholly satire nor eulogy. What Lloyd draws attention to is a doubleness in Coleridge's friendship: as Charles Maurice, Coleridge offers Lloyd a salvific kind of moral relation; as Edmund Oliver, he is unable to maintain his private attachments. Nevertheless, the novel ends on an idealistic note, envisioning the reconciliation of Charles and Edmund in a Pantisocratic utopia, taking "lands which lie contiguous to each other" and banishing "the words *mine* and *thine*" (2:292). The novel thus finally enacts the ideal of selfless fellowship among "high soul'd" men, which Lloyd had dreamt of realizing with Coleridge at Clevedon.

Coleridge, however, focused upon the negative (Edmund) aspects of the representation, publicly accusing Lloyd of malicious tale-telling in "To One who Published in Print what had been Entrusted to Him by my Fireside" (1802):

> Two things hast thou made known to half the nation,
> My secrets and my want of penetration:
> For O! far more than all which thou hast penn'd
> It shames me to have call'd a wretch, like thee, my friend![60]

For all three men, in fact, the protracted quarrel precipitated a reappraisal of the group's former aspirations. Writing to Lamb in May 1798, Coleridge declared:

> Both you & Lloyd became acquainted with me at a season when your minds were far from being in a composed or natural state & you clothed my image with a suit of notions & feelings which could belong to noth-

ing human. *You* are restored to comparative saneness, & are merely wondering what is become of the Coleridge with whom you were so passionately in love. (1:405)

Dismissing any suggestion of his spiritual election, Coleridge criticizes Lamb for a less than sane deification of him. The notion that he could elevate Lamb's spiritual being is implicitly dismissed as delusion. But Coleridge's distancing of himself from an overmoralized discourse is a strategy for deflecting his friends' accusations that he had failed to embody friendship's moral ideal.

From his pupils' perspective, Coleridge had indeed failed them. The hierarchical relation had become marked not by beneficence but by Coleridge's patronizing condescension. One jibe—"poor Lamb . . . if he wants any *knowledge* he may apply to me" —provoked Lamb's "Theses quædam Theologicæ," sent to Coleridge at the end of May 1798.[61] Of greater venom than *Edmund Oliver*, these sardonic mock-theological propositions highlight the gulf between an exalted ideal of friendship and its embodied practice. In the copy sent to Southey, Lamb asks:

4.
Whether the Seraphim ardentes do not manifest their goodness by the way of vision & theory? & whether **practice** be not a sub-celestial & merely human virtue?

5.
Whether the higher order of Seraphim Illuminati ever *sneer*?

6.
Whether pure Intelligencies can *love;* or whether they can love anything besides pure Intellect?[62]

Coleridge's Unitarian valuing of the "friendly Heart" above the "friendly Deed" has resulted only in a failure to put "goodness" into "practice." Lamb also attacks the connection Coleridge makes in "Religious Musings" between the elect and their capacity for love. Lamb now thinks that the intellectual is least likely to be capable of friendship, for he expresses his superiority through a contemptuous "*sneer.*"

Relations with Coleridge were terminated until 1800. Moreover, the "Theses" mark the end of Lamb's hope of realizing an exalted relation through a human friend. His disillusionment revealed itself in a letter to Lloyd's brother, Robert, in August 1798. Lamb declares that "there is always, without very unusual care there must always be, something of **self** in friendship."[63] Egotism undermines the religious goal of friendly self-annihilation by introducing into an attachment an element of commercial self-interest. He tells Robert that:

> The only true cement of a valuable friendship, the only thing that even makes it not sinful, is when two friends propose to become mutually of benefit to each other in a moral or religious way—but even this friendship is perpetually liable to the mixture of something not pure—we love our friend, because he is *ours*—so we do our money, our wit, our knowledge, our virtue, and whereever this sense of **appropriation and property enters,** so much is to be subtracted from the value of that friendship or that virtue. (1:135)

Closely following Hartley, Lamb argues that men value friends as commodities acquired for individual self-aggrandizement.[64] Even religious friendship cannot overcome the desire for gain but can only represent another expression of it. Disturbed that Robert Lloyd may be beginning to idolize him in a manner reminiscent of his previous exaltation of Coleridge, Lamb declares that "the having a friend is not indispensibly necessary to virtue or happiness":

> You complain of the impossibility of improving yourself, but be assurd that the opportunity of improvement lies more in the mind than the situation— . . . praise God for all, & see his hand in all things, & he will in time raise you up *many friends*—or be himself in stead an unchanging friend—. God bless you. (1:134–35)

If Robert desires the selfless love of a true friend, he can find it in God's permanent presence in his life.

By June 1798, Lloyd shared much of Lamb's disillusionment. But unlike Lamb, Lloyd's writings keep in play a conflicting pull towards and away from embodied relationships. Like Lamb, he now aligns Coleridge with a more "worldly" model of friendship. This is revealed in a letter to Cottle, written while Lamb was composing his "Theses." Thanking Cottle "many times" for his "pleasing information" about Coleridge, Lloyd adds:

> I cannot think that I have acted *with* or *from* passion towards him— even my solitary night-thoughts have been easy & calm when they have dwelt on him—but who am I, or what is any man, that he should make a scale of merit & demerit, & proudly refuse to lend the sanction of his friendship, till a certain degree is obtain'd in this fancied, & *self-referring* scale—. I love Coleridge—& I can forget all that has happen'd.[65]

What Lloyd seems to be saying is that men such as Coleridge calibrate moral value like a commodity in order to calculate whether an individual is worthy of another man "lending" him friendship. Lloyd contrasts Coleridge's worldly discourse with his own higher affection, which loves his friend's essential being and can "forget all that has happen'd."

Coleridge did not forget, and no reconciliation took place. But Lloyd captures here Coleridge's mercantile language at this time. Describing Lloyd's "Lies, Treachery, & Rascality" in 1800, Coleridge declared "he is not worth to the World, that I should embroil & embrangle myself in his Interests!"[66] Coleridge wrote to Southey on 15 October 1799 more explicitly:

> I have great affection for Lamb / but I have likewise a perfect Lloyd-and-Lambophobia!—Independent of the irritation attending an epistolary Controversy with them, their *Prose* comes so damn'd dear!—Lloyd especially writes with a woman's fluency in a large rambling hand—most dull tho' profuse of Feeling—/ I received from them in the last Quarter Letters so many, that with the Postage I might have bought Birch's Milton.[67]

Coleridge concedes the lack of simplicity in his feelings towards Lamb and Lloyd, whom he both loves and hates, and whom he cynically regards as having a market value.

Despite his magnanimity in his letter to Cottle, Lloyd's poetry betrays bitterness with Coleridge as it struggles to maintain faith in a spiritual mode of human relations. In "Written at Burton in Hampshire, August 1797," Lloyd laments how, in a fallen world, the idea of virtuous friendship is corrupted by "Hollow friends."[68] He invokes "Ye worldly ones,"

> Who in the free convivial scene will ape,
> With most deceitful seeming, the full soul
> Of holiest virtue; and will sigh, or smile,
> As they her delicate vicissitudes
> Had keenly witness'd: but the ready mimic
> Plant in his *proper station*, and the *thing*
> (Though late so exquisitely organiz'd)
> Will stand the *statue of obduracy*,
> And scatter back, with strange inaptitude,
> Love's unadmissible radiance.
>
> (pp. 14–15)

"Love's unadmissible radiance" may allude specifically to Coleridge, whom Lloyd in his sonnet had identified as radiating divine love from within his being. Now, however, virtuous friendship is revealed as theater; the sighs and smiles of sensibility, which Coleridge had offered, provide a set of gestures that are easily performed, but are empty of meaning. Instead of a divine sun, Lloyd intimates that Coleridge's heart is unaccountably made of stone:

> Oh my God!
> Why is the fleshly heart so petrified?
> Why all its avenues clos'd, and the high swell
> Of infinite perfection disciplin'd
> To base manœuverings, to the unnatural guilt
> Of intellectual murder?
>
> (p. 15)

Lloyd cannot understand how the apparent spiritual election of intellectuals such as Coleridge can result in a "petrified" heart, expressing itself not through love but through destructive impulses and strategic "manœuverings."

In "London. A Poem" (1798), Lloyd achieves a provisional solution by declaring his attraction to a less idealized kind of friendship. Explaining his move to the city, Lloyd declares himself

> sick of hopes that stand aloof
> From common sympathy; for I am sick
> Of pampering delicate exclusive loves,
> And silly dreams of rapture, that would pull
> The shrinking hand from every honest grasp,
> The shrinking heart from every honest pledge,
> Not trickt in gracefulness poetical![69]

Lloyd dismisses friendship's sentimental union as a "silly dream," which has hampered him from forming more manly relationships. He alludes to "Reflections on Entering into Active Life" (1796), in which Coleridge concludes that his Eden at Clevedon consists of "rose-leaf beds, pamp'ring the coward heart / With feelings all too delicate for use" (lines 45–46). But whereas Coleridge associates this feminizing bower with a marital space, Lloyd alludes to these lines to disparage the "dreams of rapture" he had there associated with Coleridge.

Only with difficulty, however, can Lloyd give up the dream of experiencing a divine love. He briefly turns away from urban society to praise the man who retires

> To some majestic solitude; his mind
> Rais'd by those visions of eternal love,
> The rock, the vale, the forest, and the lake,
> The sky, the sea, and everlasting hills.
> He best performs the purposes of life,
> And fills the measure of his destiny,
> Who holds high converse with the present God
> (Not mystically meant), and feels him ever
> Made manifest to his transfigur'd soul.
>
> (p. 61)

In this Berkeleyan vision, "converse" with God is possible through the direct experience of nature. However, Lloyd does not find the solitary communion of an "elect" satisfactory:

> But few there are who know to prize such bliss.
> And he who thus would raise his mortal being
> Must shake weak nature off, and be content
> To live a lonely uncompanion'd thing,
> Exil'd from human loves and sympathies.
> Therefore the city must detain *my* feet;
> For I would sometimes gaze upon a face
> That smiles on me, and speaks intelligibly
> Of one that answers all my hopes and fears.
>
> (pp. 61–62)

Distinguishing "human loves" from the heavenly but "uncompanion'd" converse of the Coleridgean elect, Lloyd seeks out a human "face / That smiles on me," even if such intercourse lacks a divine aspect. He celebrates relationships that accommodate more mundane feelings of quotidian existence, and that can respond "intelligibly" to his "hopes and fears."

By 1800, Lamb shares Lloyd's acceptance of a worldly, less spiritual friendship. Such acceptance was necessary in renewing contact with Coleridge and sustaining intimacy with Lloyd, whose inconsistencies had become increasingly apparent. As Lamb remarked to Thomas Manning:

> I cannot but smile at Lloyd's beginning to find out, that Col. can tell lyes. He brings a serious charg[e] against him, that he told Caldwell, he had no engagements with the Newspapers! As long as Lloyd or I have known Col. so long have we known him in the daily & hourly habit of quizzing the world by lyes most unaccountable & most disinterested **fictions**.—. With a correct knowledge of these inaccuracies on both sides, I am still desirous of keeping on kind terms with Lloyd, and I am

to sup with Coleridge to night— . . . To sum up my inferences from the above facts, I am determined to live a merry Life in the midst of Sinners. I try to consider all men as such, and to pitch my expectations from human nature as low as possible.[70]

Lamb welcomes Lloyd's new insight into Coleridge's worldly nature, capable as their friend is of "hourly" lies. But Lamb is also skeptical about believing Lloyd's charges. Friendly relations with both men remain possible, provided that Lamb does not expect a saintly affection of which they are not capable. On this basis he can look forward to a new round of convivial dining with "Col.," and sample not the glories of Olympus but "separate specimens of all English Turkeys" (1:183).

But while both Lamb and Lloyd were becoming skeptical of any friend's capacity to transcend everyday reality, and were taking steps to distance themselves from their former idol, Coleridge was coming to subordinate himself to his own new godlike friend: Wordsworth.

7
Coleridge and Wordsworth: Friendship and the Problem of "living with thyself / And for thyself"

IN JANUARY 1801, LAMB OFFERED WORDSWORTH AN EVALUATION OF *LYRI-cal Ballads* (1800), and declared that he could not enter into a "passion" for Wordsworthian "groves and vallies," attached as he was to the urban scenes of his youth.[1] Wordsworth was not slow in responding to this provocation, as Lamb observed:

> I received almost instantaneously a long letter of four sweating pages from my **reluctant Letterwriter,** the purport of which was, that he was sorry his 2d vol. had not given me more pleasure (Devil a hint did I give that it had *not pleased me*) and "was compelled to wish that my range of **Sensibility** was more extended, being obliged to believe that I should receive large influxes of happiness & happy Thoughts" (I suppose from the L. B.—).[2]

For Wordsworth, Lamb had culpably refused to open himself sympathetically to Wordsworth's beneficial influence. Lamb reports that he had then heard from Coleridge, who had compounded his chastisement:

> Coleridge, who had not written to me some months before, starts up from his bed of sickness, to reprove me for my hardy presumption: four long pages, equally sweaty, and more tedious, came from him: assuring me, that, when the works of a man of true Genius, such as W. undoubtedly was, do not please me at first sight, I should suspect the fault to lie "in me & not in them"—&c. &c. &c. &c. &c.—What am I to do with such people?—I certainly shall write them a very merry Letter. (1:273)

Coleridge forbids any critical detachment regarding Wordsworth's genius. Lamb presents Coleridge's comments as emanating from Wordsworth's sympathetic double, one who has entered so fully into Wordsworth's feelings that he has actually repeated the "sweaty" style and substance of his friend's letter. In comic vein, Lamb draws attention to a mode of friendship that structured Coleridge's relations with Wordsworth until the former left for Malta in 1804, and is the subject of this chapter.

Coleridge's chameleon-like capacity to imitate his friends has become an axiom of modern commentary. As Richard Matlak observes:

> Whether it be joining the Dragoons as a confused young man in imitation of his soldier brothers; or marrying or desiring the sisters of best friends, to wit, marrying Sarah Fricker, the sister of Robert Southey's wife, and later, hopelessly longing for Sarah Hutchinson, the sister of Wordsworth's wife; or whether it be brazen intellectual identification in its most notorious form of plagiarizing from Friedrich Schelling and other German philosophers in *Biographia Literaria*; . . . repetition and imitation are central to our understanding of Coleridge's biography and poetry.[3]

Interpreting Coleridge's compunction to imitate as a "notorious propensity for psychological identification," Matlak argues that "this propensity would have been quite novel to Wordsworth, however, and his reaction to the threat still needs to be considered" (p. 82). This chapter will also engage with Wordsworth's response to notions of "repetition and imitation," particularly in personal relations. However, it considers both men's views not primarily as illustrative of their respective psychologies but as suggestive of their participation in a contemporary discussion linking friendship to eighteenth-century notions of sympathy.

The Coleridgean pattern of imitative behavior had been theorized by David Hume in *A Treatise of Human Nature* (1739–1740).[4] Hume's theory of sympathy develops from his argument that personal identity is a fiction. The Humean self has no being distinct from any particular sense perception, but is merely "a bundle or collection of different perceptions, which succeed each other with an inconceivable rapidity, and are in a perpetual flux and movement" (p. 252). An individual does not possess a stable substratum of essential selfhood but only a capacity to respond to the sense perceptions or "impressions" that strike his consciousness. This capacity, however, underpins Hume's theory of sympathy. In general terms, sympathy begins for Hume in one man's observation of another's behavior—whether this be tears of grief or smiles of joy. This sight he considers an "impression" (p. 1). The impression strikes the first man's consciousness and produces an "idea" of the other's emotional state, where the idea is a "faint" (p. 1) mental image of the impression. At this point,

> the lively idea of any object always approaches its impression; and 'tis certain we may feel sickness and pain from the mere force of imagination, and make a malady real by often thinking of it. But this is most remarkable in the opinions and affections; and 'tis there principally that a lively idea is converted into an impression. . . . This is the nature and cause of sympathy; and 'tis after this manner we enter so deep into the opinions and affections of others, whenever we discover them. (p. 319)

The sympathetic imagination converts an idea into an impression, and in doing so a man comes to feel the same joy or grief as the man with whom he is sympathizing. As John Mullan remarks, "sympathy facilitates something more than vague fellow-feeling. It involves the direct and immediate reproduction of another's 'sentiments.'"[5] This capacity for reproduction implicitly denies that there is much in a man's inner life that can be said to be intrinsically his. Moreover, in rejecting the notion of a unique self, Hume finds little internal individual resistance that would prevent him from entering into another's experience:

> The minds of all men are similar in their feelings and operations, nor can any one be actuated by any affection, of which all others are not, in some degree, susceptible. As in strings equally wound up, the motion of one communicates itself to the rest; so all the affections readily pass from one person to another, and beget correspondent movements in every human creature. When I see the *effects* of passion in the voice and gesture of any person, my mind immediately passes from these effects to their causes, and forms such a lively idea of the passion, as is presently converted into the passion itself. (pp. 575–76)

Although the capacity to experience the same emotions is not limited to those bound by friendship, Hume stresses that personal "*acquaintance*" automatically "gives rise" to the sympathetic virtues of "love and kindness" (p. 352). Hume thus makes the transfer of emotional states between friends central to the experience of friendship.

Humean sympathy becomes a central aspect of later eighteenth-century representations of friendship, and finds satirical expression in *The Amicable Quixote*. Again, it is the novel's hero, George

Bruce, who expresses the Humean idea of a sympathetic friend's capacity to assume another's identity:

> Like a friend, it is my whole study to do every thing; I never enter the house of any man but with that design: if I only dine with him, Sir, I eat like a friend; if I drink too much, I intoxicate myself like a friend; if I sleep at his abode, I am careful to nap in a friendly way: I always set my watch by his; and in every action of his life, I strive to imitate my friend: at one man's house I don't eat fish, at another I dislike fowl, at a third meat does not agree with me, at a fourth I detest cheese. . . . I once dined for a week on bread and milk; then I went on a visit to another friend, who lived very high, and I was obliged to let my regard swim through rivers of red Port, till it landed at the house of an acquaintance, who had been forbid wine for three months; consequently, while I lived with him, I had as strong an aversion for it as if I had been a mussalman. Thus, Sir, you see friendship is my compass: I live but for my acquaintance. (3:83–85)

George is not hampered by any inner core that might militate against his sympathizing with whomever he meets. His friendship is grounded in Humean sympathy, whereby the friend instinctively "strives to imitate" another's characteristics. For George, this produces his benevolent wish to live "for my acquaintance." The reader, however, understands such sympathetic identification as compromising an ethical self; George confesses to being a social chameleon, liable to change his sentiments from one man's house to the next. Indeed, the novel's plot is driven by the question whether George can reconcile his enthusiasm for friendship with fidelity to his fiancée.

Despite his own criticisms of Hume, in a range of relationships throughout the 1790s Coleridge often concurred with the Humean view of friendship expressed by George Bruce. As he declares to Humphry Davy in 1801:

> You know how long, how ardently I have wished to initiate myself in Chemical science—both for it's own sake, and in no small degree likewise, my beloved friend!—that I may be able to sympathize with *all*, that you do and think.—Sympathize blindly with it all I do even *now*, God knows! from the very middle of my heart's heart—; but I would fain sympathize with you in the Light of Knowledge.[6]

For Coleridge, sympathizing with his new friend will not be complete until he has in some measure become a chemist like Davy. This desire to imitate helps explain Anthony Harding's comment on the "remarkable" frequency with which "a new friendship could be the beginning of an addition to Coleridge's immense range of interests."[7] However, Coleridge's sympathetic capacity might also explain the characteristic pattern of his relations in the 1790s, whereby Southey, Thelwall, Lloyd, and Lamb were in turn embraced and neglected as Coleridge began sympathizing with a new acquaintance.

Nevertheless, Coleridge was aware that by molding his identity to that of his friends, he might compromise his true opinions. Writing to Sir George and Lady Beaumont in 1803, a more conservative Coleridge explained that his radicalism had resulted from his personal friendship for democrats during the 1790s:

> Who then remained to listen to me? to be kind to me? to be my friends—to look at me with kindness, shake my hand with kindness, to open the door, & spread the hospitable board, & to let me feel that I was a man well-loved—me, who from my childhood have had no avarice, no ambition—whose very vanity in my vainest moments was 9/10ths of it the desire, & delight, & necessity of loving & of being beloved?— These offices of Love the Democrats only performed to me; . . . What wonder then, if in the heat of grateful affection & the unguarded Desire of sympathizing with these who so kindly sympathized with me, I too often deviated from my own Principles?[8]

In securing the loving attention for which he craves, Coleridge admits his preoccupation with performing the role of sympathetic friend. He acknowledges that in entering into his friend's opinions he is likely to deviate from his true principles. Kelvin Everest has observed how even in his radical years "Coleridge changes with the background against which he writes."[9] Comparing Coleridge's celebration of his early radicalism in "France: An Ode" with his "informed but detached" attitude towards the Revolution in a 1793 letter, Everest declares that the latter comment to Mary Evans "is probably conditioned in sentiment and tone by Coleridge's sense of what she wanted to hear, and as such is not reliable evidence of Coleridge's real attitude in February 1793" (pp. 14–15). In this light, even Coleridge's comments to the Beaumonts in 1803 can be understood partly in terms of his desire to sympathize with the politically conservative opinions of his newer friends.

Coleridge's contemporaries were certain that he possessed principles, but recognized that these were often endangered by his Humean capacity for sympathy. In 1800, Poole pleaded with Coleridge not to be influenced by those who "talk boldly of Atheism, etc":

> I implore you, my dear Col., not by any *levity* for a moment to countenance such principles and sentiments; not to share the withering curse

which God now scatters upon men—a curse which causes men of *no* feeling to give up all to *feeling*, contrary to the conviction which intellect must award if allowed to act. You often, from good nature, or from a certain perverseness of disposition, or from vanity, give countenance to men and principles at which in the moments of *true* self-possession you would spurn and tremble.[10]

Coleridge's willingness to adapt himself to the views of others, no matter how antithetical to his own, threatens his "self-possession," entailing a hazardous sacrificing of his religious belief. Poole situates himself within a broader contemporary desire to limit sympathetic identification, a view that found authoritative expression in the *Encyclopædia Britannica*'s entry on "Friendship" (1792).[11] The encyclopedist warns his reader to

remember, that even the amiable principle of benevolence must be subject to the directions of prudence: if incapable of taking care of ourselves, we cannot be expected to contribute to the good of others: society would not be favourable to the happiness of the human race, if every individual studied the general interest so far as to neglect his own. (7:473)

The necessity of "taking care of ourselves" and maintaining in friendship a degree of prudential self-interest, restricts the potential for two friends to unify their concerns. As no two individuals can be expected to "possess precisely the same degree of knowledge, to entertain exactly the same sentiments, or to stand in circumstances precisely similar," so "the interests of two can never be precisely the same" (7:472).

In legislating the extent to which a *"union of interests"* (7:472) is admissible in friendship, the *Britannica* follows writers like John Donovan in distinguishing between familial ties and friendship:

Where other ties besides those of friendship concur to unite two individuals, their interests will be more closely conjoined than if they were connected by the ties of friendship alone. The order of nature seems here to be,—the husband and wife—the parent and child—brothers and sisters, the offspring of the same parents—friends, connected by the ties of friendship alone. (7:472)

The absolute union of interest celebrated by characters like George Bruce is here restricted to the marital couple: "The husband and wife are more than friends; they are *one bone and one flesh*" (7:470). But the writer emphasizes that even in the most intimate relationship an immutable core of individuality in each party remains. "Scarce in any" relationship

> does it appear that the interests of two can become entirely one. Still less can that be expected to happen, where the ties of friendship act not in concert with those of nature. We give up, therefore, all those romantic notions, which some have so earnestly insisted on, of requiring the friend to consider his friend as himself. (7:472)

This view attacks the "romantic" kind of sympathetic idealism George Bruce propounds and to which Coleridge is attracted. However, the *Britannica* represents a contemporary discourse of relationship that is much closer to the views of Wordsworth. As we shall see, the early friendship between Coleridge and Wordsworth witnesses an increasingly difficult meeting between two rival contemporary views of affective relationship.

Remembering Coleridge's arrival at Racedown Lodge in 1795, Wordsworth provides an image that hints at Coleridge's inattention to the social boundaries that the *Britannica* tried to police: "he did not keep to the high road, but leapt over a gate and bounded down the pathless field, by which he cut off an angle."[12] High road and gate represent established wayfaring institutions, one of whose functions is to keep travellers from intruding upon private property. Coleridge's ebullient disregard for these topographical boundaries strikes Wordsworth as a sign of his friendly nature. This determined entrance into the Wordsworths' property may symbolize Coleridge's later determination to use his friendship with William to break into the Wordsworth family. The collapsing of the boundary between subjectivities represents a central function of Humean sympathy, and in regard to Wordsworth, Coleridge's pattern of sympathetic identification had already begun by the time he arrived at Racedown. In "Written at Shurton Bars,"[13] published in *Poems* (1796), Coleridge briefly alludes to Wordsworth's *An Evening Walk* (1793):

> I mark the glow-worm, as I pass,
> Move with "green radiance" thro' the grass
> An EMERALD of Light.
>
> (lines 4–6)

Coleridge included a note of acknowledgement that, as Lucy Newlyn points out, amounted to a "public declaration of friendship: a construction of literary myth":[14] "The expression 'green Radiance' is borrowed from Mr. WORDSWORTH, a Poet . . . whom I deem unrivalled among the writers of the present day in manly sentiment, novel imagery, and vivid colouring" (pp. 185–86). Coleridge draws attention to his self-identification with his fellow poet (by using his idiom), and publicly declares a friendship that is articulated through sympathetic imitation.

The year spent discussing, walking, and scheming with Wordsworth at Alfoxden during 1797–1798 reinforced what Thomas McFarland has called the "symbiotic" intertwinement of the two men's personalities.[15] A Coleridgean assessment of Wordsworth in May 1798 illustrates the extent to which both men strove to maximize the sense of their similarity at this time:

> On one subject we are habitually silent—we found our data dissimilar, & never renewed the subject / . . . He loves & venerates Christ & Christianity—I wish, he did more—but it were wrong indeed, if an incoincidence with one of our wishes altered our respect & affection to a man, whom we are as it were instructed by our great master to say that not being against us he is for us.[16]

Both friends ignore points of potential dyspathy in an effort to preserve their sentimental unity. If this is difficult, as in Coleridge's unhappiness at Wordsworth's relative unenthusiasm for Christianity, he commands himself not to let this become a significant division.

However, Coleridge's early responses to Wordsworth also acknowledge an implacable uniqueness, which could throw into relief differences between them. As his note in *Poems* reveals, as early as 1796 Coleridge had defined Wordsworth as the "unrivalled" poet of his age. To Cottle, Coleridge wrote:

> I speak with heart-felt sincerity & (I think) unblinded judgement, when I tell you, that I feel myself a *little man by his* side; & yet do not think myself the less man, than I formerly thought myself.—His Drama is absolutely wonderful. You know, I do not commonly speak in such abrupt & unmingled phrases—& therefore will the more readily believe me. . . . T. Poole's opinion of Wordsworth is—that he is the greatest Man, he ever knew—I coincide.[17]

In relation to his new friend, Coleridge becomes aware of his inferiority not only in terms of intellect but also of masculinity—his declaration that he does not think himself "the less man" highlighting an insecurity he attempts to allay. These sentiments confirm Berkeley Blatz's view of Coleridgean friendship as a "rhetoric of subordination,"[18] which finds unequivocal expression in a letter to

Southey: "Wordsworth is a very great man—the only man, to whom *at all times* & in *all modes of excellence* I feel myself inferior."[19] By May 1798, his perception of Wordsworth's sublime superiority had grown only more marked: "I have now known him a year & some months" Coleridge informed Estlin, "and my admiration, I might say, my awe of his intellectual powers has increased even to this hour" (1:410).

As early as his letter to Cottle, however, Wordsworth's superiority seems to be in some way at odds with a friendly persona. Coleridge admits that in describing Wordsworth he must use "abrupt & unmingled phrases." As has been seen, during the 1790s the notion of "mingling identities" is central to Coleridge's discourse of sympathetic friendship. The uncompromising nature of Wordsworth's excellence is, however, in some way at odds with this sociable quality. The following March Coleridge explicitly defends Wordsworth's amiability:

> The Giant Wordsworth—God love him!—even when I speak in the terms of admiration due to his intellect, I fear lest tho[se] terms should keep out of sight the amiableness of his manners—he has written near 1200 lines of a blank verse, superior, I hesitate not to aver, to any thing in our language which any way resembles it.[20]

In this way, these extracts begin to reveal the parameters of a debate between the two men concerning the potential for sympathetic identification in friendship that would develop during the following years.

Despite latent tensions, during 1797–1798 the two friends both entertained ideas of sociability close to the Humean model. They produced poetry in which the notion of the "One Life" could be used to promote receptivity and imitation as characteristic of "friends." Coleridge had begun to explore the personal aspects of the "One Life" in "Religious Musings." Coleridge laments that the "smooth Savage" (line 171) felt

> his own low Self the whole,
> When he by sacred sympathy might make
> The whole ONE SELF! SELF, that no alien knows!
> SELF, far diffus'd as Fancy's wing can travel!
> SELF, spreading still! Oblivious of it's own,
> Yet all of all possessing!
>
> (lines 172–77)

"Sacred sympathy" represents an individual's self-identification with another's divine aspect, a process that annihilates self-interest and forms a sublime union of spirit between disparate individuals, to create "ONE SELF!" Fundamental to this process is the opening of an individual's heart and mind to receive and acknowledge the reality of God's presence in His creation.

In "The Nightingale" (1798), Coleridge applies these ideas to the natural world and his relations with William and Dorothy. In doing so, he presents an idealized vision of their intimacy. The friends' bond is characterized by their receptive capacity to open themselves to the joy immanent in nature. Coleridge invites the Wordsworths to "rest on this old mossy Bridge" (line 4) and let their thoughts be governed by Coleridge, a man open to nature's positive influences:

> let us think upon the vernal showers
> That gladden the green earth, and we shall find
> A pleasure in the dimness of the stars.
> (lines 9–11)

Coleridge's friends are passive participants in the scene, tacitly consenting to the poet's vision of a joyous nature. Such "wise passiveness" (line 24)[21] to nature's influences becomes the basis for the group's mutual sympathy. Dismissing the conventional notion of the "melancholy" (line 13) nightingale, Coleridge presents William, Dorothy, and himself as the nucleus of an alternative community of perception, deriving its opinions from nature rather than from "ball-rooms and hot theatres" (line 37):

> My Friend, and my Friend's Sister! we have learnt
> A different lore: we may not thus profane
> Nature's sweet voices always full of love
> And joyance!
> (lines 40–43)

The friends' ability passively to let the omnipresent divine principle of joy pervade their respective beings makes them equally aware of the "One Life" in which they all participate, and this implicitly creates the grounds for their sympathetic friendship.

Coleridge highlights this by emphasizing that the merry nightingales' sociability is also predicated on their reception of nature's joyous influences. The moon

> Emerging, hath awaken'd earth and sky
> With one sensation, and those wakeful Birds
> Have all burst forth in choral minstrelsy,

> As if one quick and sudden Gale had swept
> An hundred airy harps!
>
> (lines 78–82)

The nightingales are passive recipients of the "sudden Gale" (line 81) that intoxicates all life-forms with "tipsy Joy" (line 87). As they swing harmoniously to the "motion" (lines 84–85) of the joy-giving breeze, the birds become sociable. What the nightingales and friends have in common is a sympathetic capacity to receive into themselves the "One Life" carried on the breeze. This forms the basis of the "sacred sympathy" uniting all these life-forms, so that the poet can consider the birds his "friends": "Farewell, O Warbler! till to-morrow eve, / And you, my friends! farewell, a short farewell!" (lines 87–88), and later, "Once more, farewell, / Sweet Nightingale! once more, my friends! Farewell" (lines 109–10).

Wordsworth highlighted the personal bonds implicit in the "One Life" doctrine in, "Lines Written at a Small Distance from my House, and Sent by my Little Boy to the Person to Whom they are Addressed" (1798):[22]

> There is a blessing in the air,
> Which seems a sense of joy to yield
> To the bare trees, and mountains bare,
> And grass in the green field. . . .
> Love, now an universal birth,
> From heart to heart is stealing,
> From earth to man, from man to earth,
> —It is the hour of feeling.
>
> (lines 5–8; 21–24)

Wordsworth affirms the "One Life" as a divine power infusing itself within all living entities and generating feelings of "universal" love. In revitalizing his friendships in the spring, the poet responds to a seasonal cycle that affects all men equally. The "One Life," then, is used by both Wordsworth and Coleridge as a religious theorizing of a Humean identity. They assert that all men may respond in the same way to the same sense impressions. For them, natural phenomena strike the senses and precipitate the joyous feeling of love, itself an expression of the "One Life." This acknowledgment of their common identity instinctively draws men into sympathetic relations with each other.

Wordsworth's assumption that Dorothy would identify with his joyous feelings would have been particularly well grounded, for in practice it was she who, of the three friends, most thoroughly embodied the Humean mode of sympathetic friendship. Thomas De Quincey linked Dorothy's companionable nature to that

> exceeding sympathy, always ready and always profound, by which she made all that one could tell her, all that one could describe, all that one could quote from a foreign author, reverberate as it were, *à plusieurs reprises*, to one's own feelings, by the manifest impression it made upon her. The pulses of light are not more quick or more inevitable in their flow and undulation, than were the answering and echoing movements of her sympathizing attention.²³

What impressed De Quincey was the extent to which Dorothy could enter into another's experience without any particle of self intruding.

Samuel and William's relations, however, did not match Dorothy's sympathetic capacity. Their collaboration on "The Wanderings of Cain" (1798) revealed Wordsworth's difficulty in entering into Coleridge's particular poetic vision. In 1828, Coleridge remembers Wordsworth's "look of humourous despondency fixed on his almost blank sheet of paper, and then its silent mock-piteous admission of failure struggling with the sense of the exceeding ridiculousness of the whole scheme—which broke up in a laugh." Coleridge cannot reflect "without something more than a smile" on his ever thinking that "a mind so eminently original [could] compose another man's thoughts and fancies."²⁴ Coleridge testifies to the possibility that they might be sufficiently sympathetically identified so as to enter into each other's imagination, but also records the difficulty of realizing this idea in practice. The men's next collaboration, "The Rime of the Ancyent Marinere," was marked by Wordsworth's early withdrawal.

To both friends, these failed attempts at formal collaboration were indications of the limits of sympathy and of the differences in their poetic styles. The final poem of *Lyrical Ballads* (1798) revealed the extent to which Wordsworth had incorporated Coleridge's poetic voice, but also the former's agreement with the *Encyclopædia Britannica*'s contention that a greater *"union of interest"* would be found in familial bonds than in friendship. In "Lines Written a Few Miles above Tintern Abbey, on Revisiting the Banks of the Wye during a Tour, July 13, 1798," Wordsworth's perceptions are colored by his friend's "One Life" ideology:

> I have felt
> A presence that disturbs me with the joy
> Of elevated thoughts; a sense sublime

> Of something far more deeply interfused,
> Whose dwelling is the light of setting suns, . . .
> A motion and a spirit, that impels
> All thinking things, all objects of all thought,
> And rolls through all things.
> (lines 94–98, 101–3)[25]

The rhetorical similarity between this passage and Coleridge's climactic lines in "This Lime-Tree Bower" indicates how far Wordsworth, in his perceptions of nature, had identified with his friend's religious vision.

At the time of publication, however, Coleridge's poem remained in manuscript. More immediately apparent for the readership of "Lines" would have been Wordsworth's climactic address to his sister, in a passage aligning him with the *Britannica*'s entry on "Friendship." As both friend and blood relation, Dorothy provides an alternative creative source to Coleridge's visionary poetry:

> Nor, perchance,
> If I were not thus taught, should I the more
> Suffer my genial spirits to decay:
> For thou art with me, here, upon the banks
> Of this fair river; now, my dearest Friend,
> My dear, dear Friend, and in thy voice I catch
> The language of my former heart, and read
> My former pleasures in the shooting lights
> Of thy wild eyes. Oh! Yet a little while
> May I behold in thee what I was once,
> My dear, dear Sister!
> (lines 112–22)

In identifying the "Friend" with his "Sister," Wordsworth restricts the language of sympathetic identification to familial friendship. As the ideal sympathetic friend, Dorothy becomes a repository for all his previous pleasures and opinions, which offer themselves for reclamation whenever William gazes into her eyes. Dorothy offers William what Coleridge cannot: a sense of the temporal continuity of his identity. In binding the most profound friendship to a familial relation, Wordsworth moves away from that inclusiveness of affection that his "Lines Written at a Short Distance" had seemed to promise, and in doing so, away from Coleridge.

Coleridge's awareness that his relation with Wordsworth might have to compete with his friend's familial bond became heightened during the group's trip to Germany, after the Wordsworths had traveled on alone to Goslar. In early December 1798, Coleridge sent them some "Hexameters" that set up a complex of friendly exclusions between himself and the familial pair:

> William, my head and my heart! dear Poet that feelest and thinkest!
> Dorothy, eager of soul, my most affectionate sister!
> Many a mile, O! many a wearisome mile are ye distant.[26]

Coleridge desires to amalgamate his being with his friend's, and thus incorporate himself into the Wordsworth family: as William is Coleridge's "head" and "heart," so Coleridge would make Dorothy his "sister!" However, the third line laments Coleridge's exclusion from the actuality; his "ye" identifies not Wordsworth and himself, but William and Dorothy as the intrinsic unit. The friend ends with an acute sense of his exclusion from the familial bond:

> The last line which I wrote I remember, and write it for the truth of the sentiment, scarcely less true in company than in pain and solitude:
>
> > William my head and my heart! dear William and dear Dorothea!
> > You have all in each other; but I am lonely, and want you!
>
> (lines 35–36)

To have "all" in one relationship necessarily diminishes the need for others, and Coleridge painfully feels what is lacking from his intimacy with William.

The previous month Coleridge had intimated that the Wordsworths' exclusive attachment might threaten an ideology of sympathetic friendship. Perhaps in response to their complaining about a lack of company, Coleridge tells William:

> You have two things against you: your not loving smoke; and your sister. If the manners at Goslar resemble those at Ratzeburg, it is almost necessary to be able to bear smoke. Can Dorothy endure smoke? Here, when my friends come to see me, the candle nearly goes out, the air is so thick.[27]

In "not loving smoke," Coleridge hints that Wordsworth's fraternal attachment is part of a greater reluctance to open himself to new influences. In a room filled with tobacco, friends inhale that which others have breathed out; in loving smoke, therefore, Coleridge enjoys symbolically incorporating aspects of his German friends, and suggests this is intrinsic to friendly relations. Wordsworth lacks this capacity for social mingling. Indeed, one of the Wordsworths' responses to Coleridge's socializing embodies the *Britannica*'s "directions of prudence" not to forget self-interest in the name of friendship. Dorothy relates how

> Coleridge is in a very different world from what we stir in, he is all in high life, among Barons counts and countesses. He could not be better placed than he is at Ratzeburg for attaining the object of his journey; but his expences are much more than ours conjointly.... It would have been impossible for us to have lived as he does; we should have been ruined.[28]

Dorothy highlights the dangers inherent in a Coleridgean adaptation to the lifestyle of others. In this case, mixing with "high life" might make Coleridge oblivious to his financial well-being. The Wordsworths, however, understand that looking after their immediate familial unit must override the possible pleasures of such social mingling.

Ensconced with his sister at Goslar, Wordsworth was engaged in composing a poem that would mark a new stage in his displacement of Coleridge's influence. As Paul Magnuson observes, in the 1799 *Prelude* "Wordsworth began to construct his myth of being a self-generated poet."[29] In doing so, he reverses the pattern of "Tintern Abbey" in which insight into the "One Life" was predicated on his identifiying with Coleridge's formulations. Instead, he tends to associate those "spots of time" (1.288) which contain "A fructifying virtue!" (1.290) with solitude rather than society. Wordsworth recalls a horse-riding expedition undertaken with "honest James!" (1.302), William's "encourager and guide" (1.303): "We had not travelled long ere some mischance / Disjoined me from my comrade" (1.304–5). During this separation, Wordsworth experiences a sight of "visionary dreariness" (1.322): a woman on "the lonely eminence," her garments "vexed and tossed / By the strong wind" (1.325–26). The experience's revelatory nature affirms his subsequent contention that his sudden solitariness was not a "mischance" but the means by which "power" was "Implanted in my mind" (1.329–30).

While Wordsworth was discovering the source of his poetic power in his solitary childhood encounters with nature, Coleridge continued to feel that his identity as a poet and thinker was contingent upon the good regard of friends like William. In October 1799, Coleridge expressed his excitement at the prospect of Wordsworth addressing him as a friend in "The Recluse":

> To be addressed, as a beloved man, by a thinker, at the close of such a poem as "The Recluse," a poem *non unius populi*, is the only event, I

believe, capable of inciting in me an hour's vanity—vanity, nay, it is too good a feeling to be so called; it would indeed be a self-elevation produced *ab extra*.[30]

Wordsworth's acknowledgement of Coleridge as a "beloved man" has the power to raise not just Coleridge's opinion of himself but his objective value.

For Wordsworth in the *Prelude*, however, friendship becomes less crucial. He informs Coleridge that he is making his inquiry "to understand myself" (1.456), and for his friend to know "With better knowledge how the heart was framed / Of him thou lovest" (1.459–60). The irony here is that Wordsworth will give Coleridge "knowledge" that his friend's seminal experiences do not include him. Instead, they are events characterized by their peculiarity to Wordsworth's childhood. Wordsworth explains how the landscape of his childhood has helped to foster his own self-sufficiency:

> And to my Friend who knows me I may add,
> Unapprehensive of reproof, that hence
> Ensued a diffidence and modesty,
> And I was taught to feel, perhaps too much,
> The self-sufficing power of solitude.
>
> (2.73–77)

For Berkeley Blatz, these lines represent "the essence of Wordsworthian friendship rhetoric":

> The solitude for which the poet claims exemption is at odds with the personal relationship upon which the rhetoric is based. Friendship offsets the solitude it is called upon to exonerate, and sublime selfhood loses its rhetorical edge within the context of forgiving friendship. One senses an incompatibility between theme and the rhetorical framework within which that theme struggles for expression. (p. 20)

In face of these conflicting messages, Wordsworth cannot but be expressing anxiety that Coleridge will regard his confession as a kind of betrayal.

Wordsworth's final address to Coleridge again betrays these anxieties, affirming and yet qualifying the bond between them:

> Thou, my friend, wast reared
> In the great city 'mid far other scenes,
> But we, by different roads, at length have gained
> The self-same bourne. And from this cause to thee

> I speak unapprehensive of contempt,
> The insinuated scoff of coward tongues,
> And all that silent language which so oft
> In conversation betwixt man and man
> Blots from the human countenance all trace
> Of beauty and of love. For thou hast sought
> The truth in solitude, and thou art one,
> The most intense of Nature's worshippers,
> In many things my brother, chiefly here
> In this my deep devotion.
>
> (2.496–509)

Wordsworth reasserts the men's fraternal bond as being all the more remarkable given Coleridge's very different childhood. Nevertheless, his protestation that he is "unapprehensive of contempt" testifies to his fear that a "silent language" might indeed rise up between them. Part of the reason for this may lie in the way Wordsworth qualifies his brotherhood with Coleridge, restricting its focus to their common devotion to "Nature."

In this context, Wordsworth re-emphasizes that Coleridge's affection articulates itself through a self-effacing responsiveness. Defending the inclusion of his childhood recollections, Wordsworth sets the "Friend" against other antagonistic voices:

> Nor will it seem to thee, my Friend, so prompt
> In sympathy, that I have lengthened out
> With fond and feeble tongue a tedious tale.
>
> (2.447–49)

Through his sympathetic understanding of Wordsworth's nature, the "Friend" clears him of self-involvement. Coleridge's role becomes restricted to justifying Wordsworth's self-presentation.

Identifying Coleridge with this rhetoric of sympathy is strategic for Wordsworth. Sheila Kearns points out that he "counts on Coleridge's sympathy to induce him to listen rather than take the narrative as an occasion to read into it the philosophical design of *The Recluse* project."[31] In other words, Wordsworth uses the discourse of sympathy at exactly the moment he dangerously asserts his independence. Kearns continues: "this desire for a sympathetically induced silence has an added aspect in which sympathy becomes the means by which Wordsworth can try to master Coleridge's necessary but nonetheless threatening presence" (p. 83). In doing so, Wordsworth illustrates what Stephen Bygrave has described as the "disabling" aspect of egotistic discourse, in that the egotist does not allow his friend to remain distinctly other.³² Wordsworth had revealed this tendency in "Tintern Abbey," where Dorothy appears not as an autonomous individual but as a blank space upon which Wordsworth can inscribe his thoughts. The *Prelude* repeats this pattern, whereby Wordsworth takes advantage of Coleridge's self-effacing rhetoric of sympathy in order to establish him as an ideal friendly reader, whose tacit agreement will justify Wordsworth's autobiographical project.

By the time the men returned to England in 1799, Coleridge was becoming aware that Wordsworth's limited capacity to adapt his identity had practical implications. Despite Coleridge's preference for Somerset, Wordsworth refused to settle outside the Lake District. To Poole, Coleridge admitted that irreducible personal differences could well hamper a friendship's development:

> I would to God, I could get Wordsworth to re-take Alfoxden—and the Society of so great a Being is of priceless Value—but he will never quit the North of England—his habits are more assimilated with the Inhabitants there—there he & his Sister are exceedingly beloved, enthusiastically. Such difference do small Sympathies make—such as Voice, Pronunciation, &c.—for from what other Cause can I account for it.³³

Wordsworth's attachment to the customs of his native home would potentially override any friendship if that entailed settling elsewhere. Despite his puzzlement, Coleridge concedes that even factors as slight as "Voice, Pronunciation, &c" produce an obstinate set of "differences" such as friendship cannot overcome but only accommodate. In practical terms, accommodating Wordsworth's unmalleable individuality meant sacrificing Poole's company and following Wordsworth north in the summer of 1800.

By contrast, Coleridge continued to delight in character traits that were common to all men. Two months earlier he exclaimed to Godwin:

> How many Thousand Letter-writers will in the first fortnight of this month write a 7 first, & then transmogrify it into an 8—in the dates of their Letters! I like to catch myself doing that which involves any identity of the human Race. Hence I like to talk of the Weather—& in the Fall never omit observing—How short the Days grow!³⁴

The friends' differences in attitude towards the ideal of mingling identities was already resulting in conflict. As he informs Poole in May 1799:

I still think that Wordsworth will be disappointed in his expectations of relief from reading, without Society—& I think it highly probable, that where I live, there he will live, unless he should find in the North any person or persons, who can feel & understand him, can reciprocate & react on him.—My many weaknesses are of some advantage to me; they unite me more with the great mass of my fellow-beings—but dear Wordsworth appears to me to have hurtfully segregated & isolated his Being / Doubtless, his delights are more deep and sublime; / but he has likewise more hours, that prey on his flesh & blood.[35]

With the term "hurtfully" Coleridge suggests that preserving sympathetic identification with others is a vital part of an individual's physical and moral health: solitude is for him a kind of predatory animal that "preys" on a man's "flesh & blood" and damages his moral being.

The two men's differing views of friendship became apparent in the new poems Wordsworth included in the 1800 *Lyrical Ballads*. "A narrow girdle of rough stones and crags" registered a fundamental unease with the Coleridgean rhetoric of sympathy and its philosophical correlative, the "One Life."[36] Wordsworth begins by scrutinizing the connection between friendship and self-enclosure. He describes how Coleridge, Dorothy, and himself enjoyed a walk along Grasmere's eastern shore, a place "safe in its own privacy" (line 5), but troped not as a bower but as a "narrow girdle" of rocks. Wordsworth's "girdle" links a primary symbol of embowered friendship with a feminized environment in which masculine rocks have been constricted to the shape of a woman's corseted waist. Furthermore, the friends' musings here expose the bower as a space where thought is restricted; only when the three move on do they discover their "RASH-JUDGMENT" (line 86).

Within this ambiguously confined environment Coleridge's rhetoric of natural sociability takes shape. Describing the movements of a "dandelion seed" (line 18), Wordsworth associates his perceptions with the Coleridgean rhetoric of "Frost at Midnight" (1798).[37] The floating seed

> Skimm'd along
> Close to the surface of the lake that lay
> Asleep in a dead calm, ran closely on
> Along the dead calm lake, now here, now there,
> In all its sportive wanderings all the while
> Making report of an invisible breeze
> That was its wings, its chariot, and its horse,
> Its very playmate, and its moving soul.
>
> (lines 20–27)

Wordsworth's animated seed echoes Coleridge's "film, which flutter'd on the grate" (line 15). Coleridge's "idle thought" found "dim sympathies" (line 18) with the film, and made it a "companionable form" (line 19). In their "vacant mood" (line 16), Wordsworth's trio imagine a similar communion to be in play between the dandelion and the "invisible breeze."

Wordsworth's allusions to "Frost at Midnight," however, are part of an attack on Coleridge. Expecting humans to be similarly sociable, the group misjudges the "idle" (line 57) fisherman who "stood alone," "Angling beside the margin of the lake" (lines 51–52), and did not join the "busy mirth" of the reapers nearby. Only when they leave their shared retreat do they see the harsher truth of his emaciated body:

> The man was using his best skill to gain
> A pittance from the dead unfeeling lake
> That knew not of his wants.
>
> (lines 70–72)

This old man does not know a companionable nature but one that is "dead" and "unfeeling." His solitariness comes to signify not a culpable lack of sociability but a heroic struggle against a hostile environment. As Frederick Garber observes, "the sight of the real man reeks of brutality in what it tells of him and of all men and in what it does to the observers. Suddenly each of them stands alone, forced into himself—'my single self'—by what he sees."[38] Wordsworth realizes that we need to "temper all our thoughts with charity" (line 79). But such new-found benevolence supersedes a Coleridgean natural sociability, evolving from a recognition that there is no naturally benevolent order. To think otherwise is a delusion produced through the unrepresentative experience of personal friendship.

Garber argues that Wordsworth's "poetry of encounter" is motivated by "his concern with the kind and quality of those objects which were not like himself." Wordsworth understands that "he could share very little at all" with most things: "Such points of continuity as there were tended, frequently, to be overshadowed by that fact" (pp. 118–19). However, in other poems in *Lyrical Ballads* (1800) Wordsworth tests the extent to which differences might be accommodated or erased in friendship. "The Fountain, A Conversation" is an instructive meditation on the expression and limitation of sympathetic impulses.[39] The converse between a youthful narrator and the aged Matthew recalls Coleridge and Wordsworth's ongoing debate regarding friendship. The Coleridgean narrator opens with a declaration of amicable union:

> We talk'd with open heart, and tongue
> Affectionate and true,
> A pair of Friends, though I was young,
> And Matthew seventy-two.
>
> (lines 1–4)

For this Coleridgean figure, an open-hearted friendship, in which friends generously communicate their inner thoughts and feelings, erases any differences of age and temperament. Matthew's responses, however, question such easy assumptions about the men's identity of feeling. He obstructs the narrator's wish to harmonize their converse with the pleasant natural landscape: the old man cannot adjust his song to suit the "summer's noon" (line 12) or the fountain's "pleasant tune" (line 10). Neither can he escape the reflections that experience enjoins upon him, and his eyes fill with "childish tears" (line 29) as he contemplates the difference between his decayed state and a similarly "delightful day" (line 25) when he was a younger, more "vigorous Man" (line 27). Such contrasts bring to Matthew's mind a sense of loss, not only of his youthful power but of "His kindred laid in earth" (line 50). These responses reveal the unassimilable differences in perspective that age brings.

The narrator, however, denies that warm feeling need be curtailed by another's temperament or experience. He claims that his friendship with Matthew can provide a substitute for the bonds the old man has lost:

> ["]And, Matthew, for thy Children dead
> I'll be a son to thee!"
> At this he grasp'd his hands, and said,
> "Alas! that cannot be."
>
> (lines 61–64)

For the old man, the narrator's desire is touching but unrealistic. In grasping his hands, Matthew signals his gratitude while remaining adamant that friendship cannot replace his familial ties. Wordsworthian friendship recognizes the limitations of sympathetic identification: affection cannot wholly bridge the differences of history and culture that divide people. In one way "The Fountain" confirms Brian Cosgrove's view that "even where relationship is foregrounded as community between men, Wordsworth may still strive to maintain the ideal of solitude-in-relationship."[40] However, Wordsworth's consciousness of friendship's limitations can intensify an expression of intimacy when it is offered. Coleridge relates one such example in a letter to William Sotheby, declaring that "among the last things, which [Wordsworth] said to me, was—'Do not forget to remember [me] to Mr [So]theby with whatever affectionate terms, so slight an Intercourse may permit—and how glad we shall all be to see him again.'"[41] Propriety dictates that a slight acquaintance should restrict a man's expression of affection for another. However, Wordsworth's desire to strain these limits with Sotheby intensifies his expression of affection.

After 1800, Coleridge's ideals of relationship continued to aspire to unity. Against the background of an unhappy marriage, he more insistently attempts to enter the Wordsworth family at Grasmere, particularly through his attachment to William's sister-in-law, Sara Hutchinson. The boundary between being a friend to Wordsworth and a member of his family became increasingly fraught. On occasion, Dorothy could think of Coleridge as being at the very heart of the Wordsworthian family—witness the sheet of blotting paper inserted in her journal entry of 15 May 1802, upon which she has written the names of her immediate family in the form of a family tree with Coleridge's name at the center.[42] As a corollary, Coleridge exclaimed in 1804:

> O dear dear Friends! I love you, even to anguish love you: & I know no difference, I feel no difference, between my Love of little Sara, & dear little John. Being equally with me, I could not but love them equally: how could I—the child of the man, for whom I must find another name than Friend, if I call any others but him by the name of Friend.[43]

Coleridge's need to make such an assertion, however, reveals his anxiety that friendship could never be coterminous with familial love.

The ambiguous relation between these categories became focused in Coleridge's forlorn pursuit of Sara Hutchinson. His ideals are apparent in "A Day-Dream," a poem possibly written as early as 1801.[44] Coleridge attempts to combine friendship and family, Platonic and sexual love:

> My eyes make pictures, when they are shut:
>   I see a fountain, large and fair,
> A willow and a ruined hut,
>   And thee, and me and Mary there.

> O Mary! make thy gentle lap our pillow!
> Bend o'er us, like a bower, my beautiful green willow!
>
> > A wild-rose roofs the ruined shed,
> > And that and summer well agree:
> > And lo! where Mary leans her head,
> > Two dear names carved upon the tree!
> > And Mary's tears, they are not tears of sorrow:
> > Our sister and our friend will both be here to-morrow.
>
> (lines 1–12)

Friendship here contains both familial and sexual connotations; as a bower, Mary becomes a maternal friend, offering her lap as a pillow for the poet's head. The positive effect of such embowerment is immediately witnessed in the second stanza whereby "A wild-rose roofs the ruined shed." This image suggests how maternal love imparts an organic component into Coleridge's dilapidated structure of self and somehow makes him whole. The benefit seems predicated upon his becoming part of Wordsworth's family through this friendship with Mary. At the same time, her bower provides the space for the poet's furtive contact with Sara, so that Coleridge's friendship encompasses erotic feelings. In addition, Wordsworth is represented as a friend and brother. Coleridge imagines a situation in which friendship could include all these various familial and sexual ties.

Coleridge's poem was written against a background of personal depression, which eventually found its outlet in "A Letter to —," part of which he recited to the Wordsworths at Dove Cottage on 21 April 1802.[45] There he registered the impossibility of realizing his idealized fantasies of affection. His unhappy marital situation creates one intractable obstacle to his integration within the Wordsworthian family:

> My own peculiar Lot, my household Life
> It is, and will remain Indifference or Strife—
> While ye are well and happy, 'twould but wrong you,
> If I should fondly yearn to be among you—
> Wherefore, O! wherefore, should I wish to be
> A wither'd Branch upon a blossoming Tree?
>
> (lines 163–68)

The organic unity of the Wordsworth family only emphasizes Coleridge's inability to join their "blossoming Tree."

If Coleridge's desire to amalgamate with the Wordsworths cut across the conservative ideology of friendship to which Wordsworth subscribed, then so did Coleridge's central discussion in the poem regarding the importance for an individual in giving and receiving love. Coleridge links the failure of his creative genius to his inability to realize friendly or "genial Spirits" (line 44) within himself. As Robert Barth remarks, Coleridge's loss of love represents the crucial aspect of Coleridge's dejection: "Without love there can be no poetry. Without love, no joy; without joy, no working of that shaping power, imagination."[46] Coleridge's philosophical formulations at the climax of the poem tend to confirm Barth's reading. Only the affectionate man is blessed with the creative power to discover positive meanings in the natural world around him:

> O Sara! we receive but what we give
> And in *our* Life alone does Nature live—
> Our's is her Wedding-garment, our's her Shroud!
> And would we aught behold of higher worth
> Than that inanimate cold World allow'd
> To the poor loveless, ever-anxious Crowd,
> Ah!, from the Soul itself must issue forth
> A Light, a Glory, and a luminous Cloud
>   Envelloping the Earth!
>
>   (lines 295–303)

Coleridge's vision of nature contrasts with that presented in "This Lime-Tree Bower" (1797). There, Coleridge had realized that nature could act as a friend even when he could not perceive its benevolence. In "A Letter to —," however, he re-evaluates this idea as an affective fallacy by which the mind creates the nature it perceives. Nevertheless, as a "Wedding-garment" Coleridge sustains a faith that he may perceive his relation to nature as a mutual love between a bridegroom and bride. But this consummation depends on his radiating affection from within. Only an affectionate giving produces joy whose divinely transformative power "gives in dower / A new Earth and new Heaven" (lines 316–17).

In reply to "A Letter to —," Wordsworth took issue with Coleridge's emphasis on radiating love. Wordsworth again situates himself within the broader antisentimental discourse of friendship in the 1790s, illustrated by Caius's articles in *The Universal Magazine*. In "On Imprudent Friendship" (1793), Caius is concerned with limiting the abuses of friendship that result from overdependency:

> No man has a right to expect friendship from others, who is not a *friend to himself*. This is the first great duty of mankind, to be friends to them-

selves; and there are thousands who are not only hostile to themselves, but who thwart the best intentions of others to serve them, and yet they are the persons from whom may be heard the loudest complaints, "that there is no such thing as a *friend* in the *world*."[47]

The friendship of others will be wasted if an individual does not behave benevolently towards himself. Caius puts forward the correlative view that:

> No man can be a friend to others, who is not a friend to himself, and it will not be disputed, that according to this maxim, the virtuous only have the will and the power to be *friends*. It is obviously necessary, therefore, to avoid connexions with men whose characters are deficient in the amiable qualities of the heart. (p. 127)

An individual's attitude towards himself will be reflected in his actions towards others. Only he who treats himself in a virtuous way can be a "friend to others," for only he possesses the "will and the power" to sustain a moral relation over time. This view is anti-Humean in that the "friend to himself" has an integrity not undermined by his encountering unworthy objects, which might influence the unstable Humean self. In another essay, "C." develops this line as a corrective to friends' tendency to support each other irrespective of propriety:

> To oppose this growing corruption, an opposite virtue appears now and then, and is, at least the *professed* admiration of mankind: it is called *Independence* . . . , a word used to express the character of a man who allows no earthly consideration to interpose between him and his duty, in all possible cases. . . . That it *is* a virtue which confers the highest honour on him who acts agreeably to it, is acknowledged by that esteem which the worst of men dare not refuse for such a character.[48]

In allowing "no earthly consideration to interpose between him and his duty," the independent man does not undermine his integrity, and thus acts as a "friend to himself."

By 1799, Coleridge and Wordsworth have diverging attitudes regarding Caius's ideas. Coleridge's ambivalence is evidenced by his copying into a notebook in May 1799 an epigram by Friedrichs von Logau, entitled "Wahl eines Freundes":

> Der sey dir nicht erkiest,
> Wer Freund ihm selbst nicht ist:
> Wer Freund ihm selbst nur ist,
> Der sey dir nicht erkiest!

> [Let not him be chosen for your friend
> Who to himself is not a friend:
> Who to himself alone is friend
> Let him not be chosen for your friend!][49]

Coleridge agrees that the man who is a friend to others should behave in a morally responsible way towards himself. However, he is aware that being a "friend to himself" may harden into selfishness, and a concomitant failure to behave benevolently to others.

Wordsworth, however, celebrates with greater enthusiasm the "friend to himself," first in the 1799 *Prelude* and then in "Resolution and Independence" (1802). At the end of the *Prelude*, Wordsworth hopes that Coleridge will follow Caius's advice and become the object of his own affections:

> Health and the quiet of a healthful mind
> Attend thee! seeking oft the haunts of men
> But yet more often living with thyself
> And for thyself, so haply shall thy days
> Be many and a blessing to mankind.
>
> (2.510–14)

In echoing Caius, Wordsworth implicitly refutes Coleridge's depiction of him as having "hurtfully segregated and isolated his being"—he claims such self-sufficiency would give Coleridge an inner strength that would enable him to become a "blessing to mankind." Living "for thyself" is not a sign of selfishness but a means by which Coleridge can develop virtues that will qualify him as a moral guide.

Wordsworth develops this line in "Resolution and Independence" as an answer to Coleridge's "A Letter to —."[50] Meditating on his own experience of dejection, Wordsworth rejects Coleridge's stress on generating "genial spirits":

> My whole life I have liv'd in pleasant thought
> As if life's business were a summer mood,
> And they who liv'd in genial faith found nought
> That grew more willingly than genial good
> But how can he expect that others should
> Build for him, sow for him, and at his call
> Love him who for himself will take no heed at all.
>
> (lines 36–42)

Wordsworth rejects the Coleridgean equation that giving out "genial faith" entails a reciprocal "genial good," whether this be personal friendship or a perception of the "genial spirits" in nature. Instead, the individual must nurture himself if he is to find love or friendship; only then, Wordsworth argues, will there be an independent, virtuous selfhood worthy of another's emotional investment.

Wordsworth discovers his new-found wisdom after his encounter with the leech gatherer, who gives the dejected poet "human strength, & strong admonishment" (line 126). The leech gatherer is one whom economic necessity has forced to become a "friend to himself," and focus his remaining energies on grinding out a subsistence in a harsh environment. Wordsworth admires the stoical independence of this man who "stood alone" (line 60). His perseverance in life's struggle confirms the necessity of not expecting happiness through giving and receiving affection, but on enduring hostile conditions with fortitude. However, the leech gatherer's firmness of mind is also a sign of his separation from the human community. Wordsworth describes the man's speech as "beyond the reach / Of ordinary men" (lines 109–10). The gatherer displays an almost supernatural disconnection from human society—a contrast with Coleridge's desire to speak in tones emphasizing human commonalty. Wordsworth imagines the old man pacing "About the weary Moors continually, / Wandering about alone and silently" (lines 144–45). As Paul Magnuson remarks, "the leech gatherer is comforted neither by a community nor by nature, which presents him only with trials. He is free from all dependence and influence." He represents the cost of Wordsworth's attempt to support "the myth that increasingly in his later years he fosters: that myth of himself as a self-generated poet."[51]

In response, Coleridge published (in *The Morning Post* of 4 October 1802) "Dejection: An Ode, Written April 4, 1802," "as a sort of gift for Wordsworth, whose wedding-day it was."[52] Among his revisions, Coleridge presents Wordsworth as an idealized figure of independence, secure in his moral authority, one whose inner well-being enables him to be a friend to others:

> To thee do all things live from pole to pole,
> Their life the eddying of thy living soul!
> O simple spirit, guided from above,
> O lofty Poet, full of light and love,
> Brother and friend of my devoutest choice,
> Thus may'st thou ever evermore rejoice!
>
> (lines 134–39)

Wordsworth's virtue derives from his direct communication with the divine authority. The guidance received explains Wordsworth's self-sufficiency and his capacity for love. Coleridge, by contrast, cannot internalize the Wordsworthian values of independence and inner strength. Part of the stanza's pathos derives from Coleridge's admiration of those who can be friends to themselves, together with his admission that he has no similar inner resources on which to draw. Instead, he again desires to imitate his more powerful, self-assured friend, and to this end offers William a prayer:

> With light heart may he rise,
> Gay fancy, cheerful eyes,
> And sing his lofty song, and teach me to rejoice!
> (lines 126–28)

Coleridge's capacity for joy and love is dependent on imitating his friend, rather than discovering within the "fountains" of "passion and the life" (line 47).

An 1805 *Notebook* entry epitomizes Coleridge's belief that he might energize himself through a sympathetic mingling with Wordsworth's more powerful being: "To W.—in the progression of Spirit / . . . O that my Spirit purged by Death of its Weaknesses, which are alas! my *identity* might flow into *thine*, & live and act in thee, & be Thou."[53] Sympathetic identification becomes self-humiliation whereby Coleridge, in order to "progress," must abase his being before his all-powerful friend. Practicing this ideology of friendship had ominous implications, both for Coleridge's sense of self as well as for his identity as a poet. As early as 1798, Coleridge and others had intimated unease at the possible practical implications of transforming his soul "into a conformity with the object loved."[54] Poole was delighted to receive Coleridge's news from Germany that he had separated from the Wordsworths:

> The Wordsworths have left you—so there is an end of our fears about amalgamation, etc. I think you both did perfectly right. It was right for them to find a cheaper situation; and it was right for you to avoid the expense of travelling, provided you are where *pure German* is spoken.[55]

Poole's anxiety about "amalgamation" intimates how easily Coleridge might allow external influences to enter his being and undermine his independence of mind. In immediately practical terms, Poole fears the daily proximity of Coleridge to Wordsworth would hamper his attempts to learn German. The dangers of amalgamation, though, could not be removed by the friends' physical separation. Reflecting two months later on the Wordsworths' plans for settling him in the Lake District, Coleridge declared to William: "I am sure I need not say how you are incorporated into the better part of my being; how, whenever I spring forward into the future with noble affections, I always alight by your side."[56] Being "incorporated" suggests that Wordsworth has physically taken over the space that is "the better part" of Coleridge's being. This image of Coleridge "always alighting" by Wordsworth's side suggests he continually finds himself arriving where Wordsworth already *is*, as if his friend were a gothic doppleganger from whom there might be no escape.

After 1800 the conformity between the men's souls was marked by Coleridge's accommodation to the contours of Wordsworth's identity rather than vice versa. Raimonda Modiano concludes that Coleridge's increasing interest in nature poetry represents his acceptance of a Wordsworthian invitation to "surrender his sovereign territory [supernatural poetry] and join in a truly communal enterprise":

> But by giving in to the pressure of becoming a naturalistic poet, Coleridge was forced into an impossible competition on his rival's home ground. In this context, his inability to complete his topographic poems . . . become[s] increasingly comprehensible.[57]

Friendly self-effacement hampers Coleridge's development of his particular poetic genius. This was Coleridge's criticism when he complained in 1818 that the Wordsworths had thwarted every effort of his to "roll onward in a distinct current of my own."[58] The practical result for Coleridge of his forcing himself into an "impossible competition" with Wordsworth was a self-destructive perception of his comparative inferiority, which precipitated his decision to abandon poetry altogether. As he told Godwin in 1801:

> If I die, and the Booksellers will give you any thing for my Life, be sure to say—"Wordsworth descended on him, like the Γνῶθι σεαυτόν from Heaven; by shewing to him what true Poetry was, he made him know, that he himself was no Poet."[59]

However, Coleridge's ideology of sympathetic friendship had more positive consequences. If Wordsworth discouraged Coleridge's poetic ambitions, in his subsequent role as Wordsworth's critic, Coleridge uses friendship to justify his privileged understanding of his friend's work. He first develops this opinion in a letter to Godwin in June 1801:

I must add too . . . that there are few better reasons than the accidental circumstance of private Friend[ship] why, as a *touchstone* by which to come at a decision in my own mind concerning a Man's Taste & Judgment, the works of a contemporary writer hitherto without fame or rank ought "to take the lead of Milton, Shakespear, & Burke."[60]

Coleridge's thinking resonates with contemporary German theorists of sympathy who contend that the perfect textual exegesis depends on a friendship between author and critic. For E. S. Shaffer, Coleridge concurred with Friedrich Schleiermacher that

it is when in intimate conversation with a friend that one is closest to knowing the mind with which one is engaged, and thus, as Schleiermacher said, hermeneutic rules can begin to be formulated with greater confidence and at a deeper level of understanding.[61]

In Shaffer's view, Coleridge practices this theory in his evaluation of Wordsworth in *Biographia Literaria* (1818), thereby demonstrating Schleiermacher's principle that "the 'friend' is privileged in that he may 'become aware of many things of which the author himself may have been unconscious'" (p. 214). Wordsworth and Coleridge's sympathetic friendship provides Samuel with a unique knowledge of the nature of his friend's genius, which authorizes his position as critic and, implicitly, his claim to genius.

If Coleridge's ideology of sympathetic identification had mixed results, then so too did the Wordsworthian dictum of living for oneself. In his public writings, Coleridge came to espouse the importance of being a friend to oneself, as evidenced by his comments in the third issue of *The Friend* (1809). Justifying his decision to "address my countrymen as a Friend," Coleridge argues that "Ingratitude, sensuality, and hardness of heart" only arise when men fail

to contemplate the Past in the Present, and so to produce by a virtuous and thoughtful sensibility that continuity in their self-consciousness, which Nature has made the law of their animal Life. . . . Men are ungrateful to others only when they have ceased to look back on their former selves with joy and tenderness. They exist in fragments.[62]

An individual must act as a loving friend towards his "former selves" if he is to possess that integrity necessary for virtuous relations with others. Coleridge acknowledges this idea as Wordsworthian, declaring that a "contemporary poet has exprest and illustrated this sentiment" in the lines, "My heart leaps up when I behold / A rain-bow in the sky!" (1802). Coleridge emphasizes Wordsworth's conclusion:

> *The Child is Father of the Man,*
> *And I would wish my days to be*
> *Bound each to each by natural piety.*
>
> (2:41)

Wordsworth is a friend to himself to the extent that he treats his past being with "natural piety," and this reverential self-acceptance guarantees his ongoing capacity to take joy in the natural world. Coleridge justifies his "assumption" of the "sacred title" of "Friend" by referring to his own "open-heartedness" (2:41), a quality he would interpret as proof of his embodying this Wordsworthian ideology.

Coleridge's praising of Wordsworth reflects how the latter's integrity of character continued to demand Coleridge's admiration and affection, a sentiment he expresses to Richard Sharp in 1804. Coleridge explains why Wordsworth "both deserves to be, and *is*, a happy man":

> Not . . . by an accidental confluence of amiable and happy-making Friends and Relatives, for every one near to his heart has been placed there by Choice and after Knowlege and Deliberation—but he is a happy man, because . . . he feels, and with a *practical* Faith, the Truth . . . that we can do but one thing well, & that therefore we must make a choice—he has made that choice from his early youth, has pursued & is pursuing it—and certainly no small part of his happiness is owing to this Unity of Interest, & that Homogeneity of character which is the natural consequence of it—& which [. . . is] the characteristic of Wordsworth. Wordsworth . . . no more resembles Shakespere than Shakespere resembles Milton—he is himself.[63]

In stating "he is himself," Coleridge implies that Wordsworth rejects the Coleridgean (and Humean) ideal of "mingling identities" in which an individual infuses other characteristics within himself. Wordsworth's laudable "Homogeneity of character" has been formed by insulating himself from such external influences. Friendship is not a necessity of his being: although he enjoys an "accidental confluence" of friends, such acquaintances are not primarily responsible for his happiness, and the lack of suitable people to befriend would not destroy his "genial spirits." By 1829 Coleridge could suggest that the presence of others might be detrimental to his friend's well-being, commenting, "Of all the men I ever knew, Wordsworth has the least femineity in his mind. He is *all* man. He is a man of whom it might have been said,—'It is good for him to be alone.'"⁶⁴

But Wordsworth's masculine self-sufficiency could easily be interpreted as creating the conditions for an abandonment of the feminine virtue of friendship. Certainly, the Wordsworths increasingly failed to give Coleridge the sympathetic encouragement he needed in order to sustain his poetic powers. Wordsworth's omission of the "Ancyent Marinere" from *Lyrical Ballads* (1802) and his refusal to publish "Christabel" represented two important expressions of lack of sympathy. In broader terms, Coleridge increasingly lamented the egotism of the Wordsworthian family and its vigorous policing of the boundary between family and friends. As De Quincey remarked in 1816, Wordsworth was "incapable of friendship out of his own family."⁶⁵ As early as 1803, however, Coleridge was voicing similar criticisms, as in his complaint to Poole that "I now see very little of Wordsworth," blaming this on his friend's "Indolence, &c" which "keeps him at home."⁶⁶ Coleridge laments Wordsworth's failure to visit him on his sick-bed for two months—"me, who had ever paid such unremitting attentions to him":

> The concern, which I have felt in this instance, and one or two other more *crying* instances, of Self-involution in Wordsworth, has been almost wholly a Feeling of friendly Regret, & disinterested Apprehension—I saw him more & more benetted in hypochondriacal Fancies, living wholly among *Devotees*—having every the minutest Thing, almost his very Eating & Drinking, done for him by his Sister, or Wife—& I trembled, lest a Film should rise, and thicken on his moral Eye. (2:1013)

"Self-involution" presents Wordsworth's friendship for himself as disturbing. As has been seen, "involve" is part of Coleridge's vocabulary of sympathetic affection, suggesting a metaphorical wrapping of one friend around his partner's being. Self-involution, however, suggests that Wordsworth is himself the object of his twining affection, resulting in a parody of Coleridge's ideal of "mingling identities." Restricting himself to his first outer circle of self, his family, Wordsworth's self-directed love has hampered him from carrying out his duties to his friend. Rather than forming a solid central core from which his affections can expand, it represents a moral cataract, which threatens to blind him to his friends' needs. A few weeks after writing the letter, Coleridge embarked for Malta in an attempt to try out Wordsworth's advice of living "for thyself."

8
Managing Friendship: Coleridge, Godwin, and Southey, 1799–1804

FINDING HIMSELF IMPRISONED IN A FOREIGN LAND, ST. LEON LOST NO time in trying to enlist the help of his jailer:

> Would you be my friend?
> I do not know what you mean, sir. I have been used to call the man I love, my friend. If you mean that, you know I cannot choose whether I will be a man's friend; it comes of itself.
> Can I not make you my friend?
> That is, make me love you? . . . I do not know, sir, continued he. If I see that you are a good man, I believe I shall love you. But if it happened that you were good and generous to me, I am sure I should love you very much.[1]

This exchange questions the extent to which friendship can be willed into being by the reasoning mind. Leon thinks this is possible, if only for the prospect of mutual gain. Eventually, the jailer also contends that friendship is a function of reason, in that he feels affection for qualities that are objectively "good." His initial response, however, posits another more disturbing possibility, that friendship might not be amenable to any human contrivance but rather "comes of itself," subject only to its own inscrutable laws. The dialogue thus raises crucial issues of friendship that informed Coleridge's relations with Godwin and Southey during 1799–1804.

This chapter examines how Coleridge, Godwin, and Southey pose questions at a theoretical level as to whether friendship can be controlled, while providing answers to these questions within their ongoing epistolary intercourse. I begin by developing the issue of social management, which lays emphasis on controlling personal relations through politeness and etiquette, in order to regulate potential disagreements. This ideology acknowledges that sincerity must be compromised in order to preserve good feeling. In this respect, Coleridge's relations with Godwin become particularly instructive, for Godwin was an ideological opponent of etiquette in the 1790s, and a proponent of candor in social relations. While Godwin poses a practical challenge to Coleridge's managerial skills, the ideologies of management and sincerity both presume that friendship can be secured by reason and volition. In this, they are challenged by a variety of contemporary speculations, derived from natural science, which explain friendship by reference to physical laws of, for example, propulsion and animal magnetism. Although Godwin and Coleridge suggest that the operation of attractive, repulsive, and other forces need not subvert reason's control of friendship, both men face the possibility that friendship might resist rational management, subject only to the ebb and flow of forces operating beneath consciousness. For Coleridge, Godwin, and in particular Southey, such anxieties are deepened by their idea of friendship as an organic phenomenon obeying independent laws of growth and decay. In restoring the friendship that had collapsed in November 1795, from 1799 onwards Coleridge and Southey confront this dark possibility, but increasingly set the human will against nature in an effort to restore amity. They thus participate in a contemporary cultural desire to guarantee friendship's permanence by reconstituting the friend as a Platonic Idea, which could remain inviolate into eternity. Coleridge and Southey's renewal of friendship reaffirms the importance of Platonic idealism in controlling a relation increasingly viewed as subject to a process of disintegration.

In March 1798, under pressure for his outspoken political views, and desiring to reintegrate himself into English society, Coleridge informed his brother George that he had laid down "maxims" governing how he would now conduct his social relations:

> With regard to others, I never controvert opinions except after some intimacy & when alone with the person, and at the happy time when we both seem awake to our own fallibility—and then I rather state *my* reasons than argue against his.—In general conversation & general company I endeavor to find out the opinions common to us—or at least the subjects on which difference of opinion creates no uneasiness—such as novels, poetry, natural scenery, local anecdotes & (in a serious mood and with serious men) the general evidences of our Religion.[2]

Coleridge's modification of his views to suit his company does not merely reflect his desire for sympathetic identification. Not broaching certain subjects and attending to the way he voices criticism signals a pragmatic awareness that social behavior must be controlled. The key term for Coleridge is "regulation": "I am in the habit of regulating myself" by this maxim, he declares, as it is "a most important rule for the regulation of the intellect & the affections—as the only means of preventing the passions from turning the Reason into an hired Advocate" (1:398). Coleridge situates himself in a Cowperian tradition of social management whereby polite friends abide by rules of conduct, designed to minimize the "Danger of conflagration" (line 96) in social relations.[3]

The rationale behind such rules had been recently expounded by the posthumous publication of Eliza Hayley's *The Triumph of Acquaintance over Friendship* (1796). Hayley identifies "etiquette" as the "infallible regulator" (p. 50) of personal relations, and an attribute intrinsic to "the great art of life, / To manage well the restless mind" (p. 49):

> "Etiquette restores the *mind* to its proper tone, reanimates nature without the least violence; quickens the circulation of discourse; absorbs the acid and acrimonious particles, and," I will add, "restores the whole system to its natural functions"; as I never can believe, what many would persuade me, that sincerity and politeness are incompatible, and that human nature is naturally a state of hostility. (p. 50)

Here sincerity is potentially at odds with etiquette, and must be tempered with "politeness" if friendship is not to descend into a "state of hostility." Sincerity becomes especially problematic in the giving of "good advice," which, "when you request it on one subject, it is generally presented you on an hundred," until it becomes a veritable "persecution" (p. 59). To counter the hostility that advice-giving may provoke in the advisee, etiquette demands that an individual demonstrate "reserve" and refrain from criticizing a friend directly:

> When the nerves and spirits relax, we grow inconstant to our darling weaknesses, and do not chuse to have them called into view. It is therefore safer to sport with the foibles of absent friends and acquaintance, who, if my scheme of reserve is adopted, will never be conscious of the injury. (p. 52)

If a friend does criticize, he should imitate an "acquaintance" and offer no more than some "benevolent *hints*" (p. 60). Hayley laments, however, that in the modern day "few persons are sufficiently well bred for the familiar intercourse of friendship" (p. 55), concluding that if the Augustan values of social management are no longer being practiced in friendship, then she must "insist on being spoken to as an acquaintance" (p. 54).

An incident involving Southey, Godwin, and Coleridge in 1804 may introduce how Hayleian values operated in Coleridge's social milieu. Southey relates that, in reviewing Godwin's "most despicable" *Life of Chaucer*,

> I, with a sort of unconscientious conscience about abusing a man whom it is my lot to meet sometimes in company and to speak to in the streets, did spare the lash when it ought to have been more, yea most heavily laid on. Godwin however it seems had somewhat less management about me. One night at Lambs lately, he took it into his fools head to say something very disrespectful of me to Coleridge of all men living.[4]

Southey displays his Hayleian capacity for "management" in withholding his true opinions for the sake of cordiality. In the event, Godwin's disparaging criticisms of Southey confirmed Hayley and Cowper's warning that without management friendly relations can end in passionate explosion: Coleridge, unable to regulate his emotions in the face of Godwin's continued provocation, "in the presence of all the company anatomized him alive" (1:355).

This incident exemplifies how Godwin posed a challenge to the pragmatic, Hayleian stress upon exercising self-control in social situations. Throughout the decade, Godwin declared an ideological hostility to the managerial qualities that Coleridge was coming to value. Instead, he expounded the virtue of sincerity, arguing in *Political Justice* (1793) that an individual's duty was solely to follow the dictates of justice and truth:

> It is evident . . . that a strict adherence to truth will have the best effect upon our minds in the ordinary commerce of life. This is the virtue which has commonly been known by the denomination of sincerity; and, whatever certain accommodating moralists may teach us, the value of sincerity will be in the highest degree obscured, when it is not complete. (1:238–39)

Godwinian "sincerity" entails telling any man exactly what one believes to be the truth about him or anyone else. Godwin rhapsodizes on the beneficial effect that would be produced,

> if every man were sure of meeting in his neighbour the ingenuous censor, who would tell to himself, and publish to the world, his virtues, his good deeds, his meannesses and his follies. . . . One such man, with

genius, information and energy, might redeem a nation from vice. (1:240)

There is no room here for management, concerned as it is with tempering the ways friends converse, and what they know of each other. In a 1797 letter, Godwin scorns this eighteenth-century tradition:

> It is, I believe, a part of the English character, to feel that sort of mauvai[s]e honte, which prevents men from giving utterance to their sentiments of each other; & two friends here will sometimes hold commerce for years, [?abound] talking upon [?general] subjects, & neither assur'd of the [?sentiments] [?either] with the other. I conceive this to be very vicious. I regard it to be my duty, & . . . pleasure, to tell every man what I think of him, more especially when I find cause for approbation. We all of us, I believe, stand in need of this encouragement. I love these overflowings of the heart, & cannot endure to be always treating, & being treated by my friends, as if they were so many books.[5]

Friendship cannot be exempted from a man's moral duty sincerely to express his thoughts and feelings, be they sentimental "overflowings of the heart" or more judgmental remarks. Putting sincerity into practice, however, opens up for Godwin the possibility of achieving in friendship a profound fusion of identities. As he argues in *The Enquirer* (1797), "Friendship requires that the hearts of the persons should, as it were, be amalgamated into one substance, that their thoughts should be transparent to each other, and their communications entire."[6] Two years later, he was even more strident, not only regarding friendship's potential for intimacy but also its fragility. "Friendship is an object of a peculiar sort," he remarked in *St. Leon*,

> the smallest reserve is deadly to it. I may indeed feel the emotions of a friend towards a man who in part conceals from me the thoughts of his heart; but then I must be unconscious of this concealment. The instant I feel this limitation of confidence, he drops into the class of ordinary men. A divorce is effected between us. Our hearts which grew together, suffer amputation; the arteries are closed; the blood is no longer mutually transfused and confounded. (2:81–82)

Despite his own enthusiastic sensibility, Coleridge was critical of Godwinian sincerity, as becomes apparent in a 1796 letter to Thelwall:

> Gerald & Dr Darwin are polite & good natured men & willing to arrive at good by attainable roads—they deem Insincerity a necessary virtue

in the present imperfect state of our Nature. Godwin, whose very heart is cankered by the love of singularity & who feels no disinclination to wound by abrupt harshness, pleads for absolute Sincerity, because such a system gives him a frequent opportunity of indulging his misanthropy.—Poor Williams, the Welch Bard—(a very meek man) brought the tear into my Eye by a simple narration of the manner in which Godwin insulted him, under the pretence of Reproof.[7]

Like Hayley, Coleridge argues that in practice "absolute Sincerity" does more harm than good. Despite such criticisms, while in London during the winter of 1799–1800 Coleridge began to see "a good deal of Godwin,"[8] and he stayed at The Polygon for three days in March. In pressing ways, the friendship that developed revealed a tension between Coleridge's characteristic impulse to embrace aspects of a friend's sensibility as his own, and his awareness that management is required to maintain intimacy.

Coleridge's sympathetic embodying of Godwinian sincerity revealed itself in the rumbustious evenings the men evidently shared, discussing Christianity, poetry, and science. An extreme unreservedness reveals itself in a letter from March 1800, in which Coleridge asks Godwin to excuse as "Tipsiness" his talking "very extravagantly" the previous night: "as when sober, I talk extravagantly enough for any *common* Tipsiness, it becomes a matter of nicety in discrimination to know when I am or am not affected."[9] Despite such anxiety that unregulated talk might cause offence, Coleridge nevertheless celebrates his habitual openness, asserting in May that there should be no gap between a feeling and its expression. On failing to write to Godwin from Greta Hall earlier, he declares:

> I ought to have written to you first; & as I am not behind you in affectionate esteem, so I would not be thought to lag in those outward & visible signs, that both shew & vivify the inward & spiritual grace.— Believe me, you recur to my thoughts frequently, & never without pleasure, never without my making out of the past a little day dream for the future.[10]

Producing "outward & visible signs" of affection is intrinsic to bringing friendship fully to life. This was calculated to appeal to Godwin who, in a draft letter to Coleridge, expressed similar ideas in discussing the character of John Curran, with whom he had been staying in Dublin during September 1800:

> He has the reputation of insincerity, for which he is indebted, not to his heart, but to the mistaken, cherished calculations of his practical

prudence. He maintains in argument that you ought never to inform a man, directly or indirectly, of the high esteem in which you hold him.[11]

Godwin rejects a "prudential" concern about the possible risks involved in openly declaring affection, and implicitly encourages Coleridge to do so too.

Despite actively encouraging sincerity in their friendship, around this time Coleridge began intimating his reluctance to meet Godwin's desire for candor, and to express in subtle ways a degree of reserve, through which he aims to regulate the passion in their relationship. This becomes evident in an exchange initiated by Godwin in his next letter. He bemoans not receiving Coleridge's invitation to visit him directly from Dublin and proceeds to embody his ideology of sincerity, confessing the extent of his affectionate feeling for Coleridge, and his hopes for an organic fusion of the two men's identities:

> There is nothing on earth of which I am more desirous, than spending some time under the same roof with you. There are many circumstances, which it might perhaps cost me some trouble fully to define, that render your conversation singularly adapted to amuse, to instruct & to interest me. This is partly because we have thought a good deal of the same subjects; but not less because we have pursued dissimilar objects, & contemplated the same objects in a dissimilar spirit. I longed for the opportunity of engrafting your quince upon my apple-tree, & melting & combining several of your modes of feeling & deciding, into the substance of my mind. Perhaps too I mention something better than this, when I say, that I feel myself a purer, a simpler, a more unreserved and natural being in your company than in that of almost any human creature.[12]

Godwin expresses feelings that Curran would find imprudent, by making the writer vulnerable to rejection. He predicates his openness on Coleridge's "unreserved" behavior, which has encouraged Godwin to believe that his high ideals of friendship could be realized. In his enthusiasm, he thus proposes that Coleridge and himself amalgamate their beings, to the extent that Coleridge will allow Godwin access into his "modes of feeling & deciding," and so become a living part of Godwin's self.

Coleridge was not, however, encouraged to confess the extent of his feeling for his friend. Instead, he retreats into a more reserved mode and strives to re-establish a greater degree of distance in the relation:

You are kind enough to say, that you feel yourself more natural and unreserved with me, than with others. I suppose, that this arises in great measure from my own ebullient Unreservedness—something too, I will hope, may be attributed to the circumstance, that my affections are interested deeply in my opinions—. But here you will meet too with Wordsworth "the latch of whose Shoe I am unworthy to unloose"—and four miles from Wordsworth Charles Lloyd has taken a house.[13]

Coleridge does not reciprocate Godwin's affectionate effusions, but instead analyzes why he makes Godwin feel "natural and unreserved." He does not connect his answer ("my own ebullient Unreservedness") to Godwin's specific presence, but indicates that it is merely characteristic of the Coleridge personality. Whereas Godwin proposes blending the two men into one organism, Coleridge emphasizes that Godwin will meet several other men at Keswick—one of whom, Wordsworth, would be a much worthier choice. Coleridge thus tactfully rejects Godwin's desire for amalgamation and maintains a degree of reserve towards him.

If Coleridge limits the degree of intimacy between the two men, equally important is his managerial capacity to reject Godwin's proposal without offense. Subsequent events, however, provided sterner tests of his ability to reconcile the ideological tension between sincerity and reserve. Of particular importance in this regard was Godwin's decision in May 1801 to send Coleridge a draft of his new play, *Abbas, an Historical Tragedy*, for critical comment. Sensing Godwin's sensitivity to criticism, Coleridge's initial managerial response was to deprecate his own talent, and then to prevaricate. When two months later he finally returned the manuscript, he revealed deep uncertainty concerning the appropriate style of his criticisms. He conceded he was unable to send some other comments and, having just received a letter of Godwin's, declared himself "glad, that I was prevented":

> My Criticisms &c were written in a style & with a boyish freedom of censure & ridicule, that would have given pain & perhaps, offence. I will rewrite them, abridge them, or rather extract from them their absolute meaning, & send them in the way of [a] Letter.[14]

Despite Godwin's desire for sincerity, Coleridge perceives that critical candor might cause "offence." At the same time, his annotations of *Abbas* displayed little attempt to lessen the blow of his sincere disapproval. He had devised four symbols referring to different faults, and, as William St. Clair remarks,

There is scarcely a page of manuscript which is not liberally spattered. One passage of five lines is condemned on all four counts. . . . The marks are sometimes reinforced by comments—"Execrable metre," "a solecism in manners," "Too bad," "a foul line," "Whoo!!" . . . In only [three] places is there a word of commendation "well written" to offset the 111 separate faults that Coleridge had noted before he began to tire somewhere in Act II.[15]

Godwin's reply indicated that Coleridge had satisfied his friend neither through his tactfulness nor through his sincerity:

> I thank you most sincerely for your circumstantial answer to my last, which was perhaps more than I was entitled to; & for your criticisms on my Abbas. I am sorry I have not yet the whole of them before me: I am sorry you did not give me the part you allude to, unrefined, unaltered. I can bear harsh words, I can bear even such as, did they flow from an unfriendly temper, would have been contumelious; I should despise myself if I could not. What I objected to in my last was not the severity of criticism, but unconcocted criticism. . . . I could wish that my friends would not present to me their crude remarks, which, during the very interval perhaps that I am meditating them in all the scepticism & humility of an ambitious, beating heart, they are preparing themselves to retract.[16]

On the one hand, Godwin's peeved tone suggests that "circumstantial," withholding letters are not what he desires from a friend, and he reaffirms his possession of an "heroic, patient temper, & an iron fortitude to endure all that friends or foes shall think fit to lay upon me" (p. 255). However, his intimation that Coleridge's criticism verges on contumely betrays Godwin's pain. Despite distinguishing between severe but honest criticism (which he welcomes) and undigested opinion (which he does not), Godwin's suggestion that Coleridge "retract" his remarks reveals his disappointment at the whole tenor of the criticisms. Despite his ideological desire for sincerity, in practice Godwin's hurt reaction suggests that such candor might prove a threat to the preservation of friendship.

Coleridge's awareness of Godwin's upset became apparent in September, in his reluctance to criticize Godwin's *Thoughts Occasioned by . . . Dr Parr's Spital Sermon* (1801):

> On the most deliberate reflection I do think the introduction clumsily worded—and . . . your retractations always imprudent, & not always just.—But it is painful to me to say this to you—I know not what effect it may have on your mind—for I have found, that I can not judge of other men by myself. I myself am dead indifferent as to censures of any

kind—... The censure or dislike of my dearest Friend, even of him, whom I think the wisest man, I know, does not give me the slightest pain / it is ten to one but I agree with him—& if I do, then I am glad. If I differ from him, the pleasure I receive in developing the SOURCES of our disagreement entirely swallows up all consideration of the disagreement itself.[17]

Coleridge's "On the most deliberate reflection" ostentatiously meets Godwin's demand that criticisms should not be "unconcocted," but he remains unconvinced that his friend will be able to cope emotionally with even digested opinions about his work. Coleridge's fear that his annotations had been interpreted as an unfriendly act induces him to renounce criticism within familiar correspondence:

> I will never therefore willingly criticize any manuscript composition, unless the author and I are together / for then I know, that say what I will, he cannot be wounded—because my voice, my look, my whole manner, must convince any good man, that all I said was accompanied with sincere good-will & genuine kindness. (1:762)

The incident over Godwin's manuscript strengthened Coleridge's conviction that friendship requires conscious tact in order to avoid acrimony, a belief he dramatized in "A Dialogue between an Author and his Friend," published in *The Morning Post* of 11 October 1802:

> *Author.* Come; your opinion of my manuscript!
> *Friend.* Dear Joe! I would almost as soon be whipt.
> *Author.* But I will have it!
> *Friend.* If it must be had—(hesitating)
> You write so ill, I scarce could read the hand—
> *Author.* A mere evasion!
> *Friend.* And you spell so bad,
> That what I read I could not understand.[18]

Despite pressure from the author, the "Friend" performs a variety of evasive tactics in order not to reveal his sincere unenthusiasm. Deliberate insincerity, hesitation, and reserve all prove necessary to the pragmatic preservation of a friendship's well-being.

Coleridge's role in Godwin's life, however, extended beyond criticizing his plays. In particular, Godwin praised him for "conversations" that led him into a theistic, "reverent and soothing contemplation of all that is beautiful, grand, or mysterious in the system of the universe."[19] Among the areas of natural mystery that Coleridge appears to have discussed with Godwin were the possible connections between friendship and the operation of invisible energies, whose power issued from mysterious unconscious sources in the self. In their more optimistic moments, both men argue that friends may remain in control of the energies brought into play by sympathetic relations, and use them for their mutual advantage. Responding in September to the news that Godwin's play, *Antonio*, was being performed in London, Coleridge reflected on what he meant when he said, "I wish you success":

> Indeed, indeed, Godwin! such a stream of hope & fear rushed in on me, when I read the sentence, as you would not permit yourself to feel. If there be any thing yet undreamt of in our philosophy; if it be, or if it be possible, that thought can impel thought out of the visual limit of a man's own skull & heart; . . . I seem to feel within myself a strength & a power of desire, that might dart a modifying, commanding impulse on a whole Theatre.[20]

In ways supposedly unknown to his rationalist friend, Coleridge feels himself physically gripped by a mysterious inner energy acting within him: "a stream of hope & fear rushed in on me."

This energetic "power of desire" is for Coleridge an expression of will, which he elsewhere distinguishes from "Volition," or "the faculty *instrumental* to the Will."[21] Laurence Lockridge defines Coleridgean volition as "the capacity of consciously choosing which motive to yield to."[22] Volition's conscious reasoning identifies it as the attribute used in the "management" of friendship. It is, however, distinct from the will, which as Lockridge argues, "is anterior to, or more suggestively beneath, reason . . . and is therefore unknowable" (p. 58). The "power of desire" experienced by Coleridge confirms Lockridge's view that "will" originates in "unconscious expressions of energy . . . more powerful than conscious deliberation" (p. 60). In relation to Godwin, Coleridge suggests that friendship can generate such inner energies of will, which can be used for the friends' mutual benefit: his will, he imagines, might in some mysterious way compel Godwin's first audience to be sympathetic to his play.

Three weeks later, Coleridge formulated these speculations and, in doing so, challenged Godwin's celebration of a rational exchange of sincerely held opinions. Lamenting his friend's tendency to be unduly influenced by criticism, Coleridge declared:

> You have too soon submitted your notions to other men's censures in conversation. A man should nurse his opinions in privacy & self-fondness for a long time—and seek for sympathy & love, not for detection

or censure—. Dismiss, my dear fellow! your theory of Collision of Ideas, & take up that of mutual Propulsions.[23]

As an agent of propulsion, Coleridge argues that one friend might act as a life-force for another: through "sympathy & love" both might generate energies of will to impel each other onward in their respective pursuits. Coleridge applies to friendship a contemporary scientific discourse of natural force. In *Geological Essays* (1799), Richard Kirwan had offered the first scientific usage of the term "propulsion," linking it to the force of water: "The materials are unceasingly carried forwards by the circulation and propulsion of water into the unfathomable regions of the sea."[24] Coleridge explicitly links friendship's energies with water's propulsive force when he meditates on the game of "duck and drake" (in which stones are skimmed across a smooth surface of water): "In the Duck and drake projecting across the stream of Error and misery, let the Friend be as the elastic force of the water, giving a new bound to the stone and preventing its touch of the stream being the submersion."[25] What Coleridge proposes to Godwin is that both friends employ this "elastic force" within their own relationship. In experiencing a "stream of hope & fear" on behalf of his friend, Coleridge thinks of his will as already bringing into being a propulsive force that could drive Godwin on to theatrical success. Likewise, it is this notion of propulsion that informs his encouragement of Godwin to persevere after the harsh reviews of *Antonio* when it was performed in December 1800:

> But cheerily, Friend! it is worth something to have learnt what will not please. . . . There is a Paint, the first coating of which, put on paper, becomes a dingy black, but the second turns to a bright *gold* Color.—So I say—Put on a second Coating, Friend![26]

Coleridge's enthusiasm strives to propel Godwin into energetic activity and ensure he does not slump into a "stream of misery."

Coleridge's pedagogic tone in these letters indicates that he regarded himself as introducing Godwin to a new way of contemplating friendly communication. Nevertheless, both Coleridge and Godwin's writings in the 1790s explore the operation of nonrational energies in friendship, and reveal the extent to which both figures participated in a widespread cultural inquiry into friendship's relation to the laws governing the physical world. As A. R. Humphreys points out, eighteenth-century "moral sense" philosophy had already made room "in the forefront of men's attention for the recognition of many subtle, instinctive, and 'unaccountable' qualities of mind and feeling."[27] The connection between sympathy and magnetism was increasingly taken up during the 1790s, and used to account for the mysterious kinds of positive energy generated in friendship. Godwin remarks in *The Enquirer* (1797):

> Society in any undertaking, lightens all its difficulties, and beguiles us of all our weariness. When my friend accompanies me in my task, and our souls mutually catch and emit animation, I can perform labours that are almost more than human with an undoubting spirit. Where sympathy is strong, imitation easily engrafts itself. Persons who are filled with kindness towards each other, understand each other without asking the aid of voice and words. There is, as it were, a magnetical virtue that fills the space between them: the communication is palpable, the means of communication too subtle and minute to be detected. (p. 124)

In catching and emitting animation, sympathizing friends generate electric sparks, the accumulation of which creates a "most powerful engine" of virtuous energy. This enables them to perform tasks impossible for the solitary individual. The "means," however, by which friends generate this magnetic force is not governed by the conscious mind. Coleridge's wider interest in the mysterious magnetic forces in nature has been explored by John Beer. Tracing his early knowledge of theorists such as Mesmer and Euler, Beer helpfully formulates one of Coleridge's primary questions regarding magnetism: "If there were indeed subtle attractions and instincts in the universe, and if human beings could be acted on by forces such as those of the hypnotist's art, might it not be possible to attune the processes of association to these underlying powers?"[28] This kind of speculation informs Coleridge's confidence in the "The Nightingale" (1798) that he will make Hartley "Nature's playmate" (line 97), a friendship already evidenced by the baby's magnetic attraction to the moon.

Both Coleridge, Godwin, and their contemporaries, however, acknowledge that other forces might operate in friendship, and this tends to undermine their confidence that these energies could be controlled and used to benefit human relations. In science, a magnetic field requires the interaction of opposite forces if it is to generate energy, and in seeking to understand friendship in terms of such a universal physical law, several theorists suggest that a successful friendship involves more than the action of attractive forces between friends. In *Metaphysics of Morals* (1797), Immanuel Kant argues that "human beings'" external relations with one another are held in creative tension through the play of opposing, yet necessary, forces:

> We consider ourselves in a moral (intelligible) world where, by analogy with the physical world, attraction and repulsion bind together rational beings (on earth). The principle of mutual love admonishes them constantly to come closer to one another; that of the respect they owe one another, to keep themselves at a distance from one another; and should one of these great moral forces fail, "then nothingness (immorality), with gaping throat, would drink up the whole kingdom of (moral) beings like a drop of water."[29]

Love and respect operate in every individual and their opposing attractive and repulsive principles serve to control the degree of closeness and distance across the spectrum of human relations. For Kant, friendship represents the "equal balance" between these opposing forces in a "Most Intimate Union of Love with Respect": "For love can be regarded as attraction and respect as repulsion, and if the principle of love bids friends to draw closer, the principle of respect requires them to stay at a proper distance from each other." To achieve this balance is to realize "an ideal of each participating and sharing sympathetically in the other's well-being through the morally good will that unites them." For this to take place, though, the two friends must keep in play the same degree of attractive and repulsive force, both within themselves and towards each other. The difficulties in achieving this leads Kant to declare that friendship "is only an idea (though a practically necessary one) and unattainable in practice" (p. 215).

The encounter between St. Leon and Bethlem Gabor in *St. Leon* (1799) may well indicate Godwin and Coleridge's shared interest during the period of their intimacy in tracing the influence of attractive and repulsive forces in friendship. In some unpublished notes, Godwin quoted Coleridge's opinion that the "prime beauty is in the encounter, not sufficiently developed, of the unsympathetic St Leon & the furiously misanthropic Bethlem Gabor,"[30] a comment Coleridge repeated in a notebook entry, probably made in January 1800: "Bethlem Gabor—sublime their friendship."[31] Central to this friendship is the play of attractive and repulsive forces operating between Leon and Bethlem. As Coleridge implies, Bethlem is a figure of the Burkean "sublime." His strength, towering presence, and ferocious manners primarily demand respect, qualities that Leon describes in Kantian terms, as "better adapted to repel than attract" (4:118). This repulsion limits Bethlem's capacity for intimacy, even with his children:

Though he had an atmosphere of repulsion beyond which no mortal ever penetrated, they came to the edge of that, and rested there; they trembled involuntarily at his aspect, but at the same time they adored and they loved him. The rest of the world viewed him from a more fearful distance; respected him, but dared not even in fancy be familiar with him. (4:121–22)

Nevertheless, Leon declares "I felt an inexplicable attachment to his person still increasing in my bosom" (4:121). This attraction, with its source in the "similarity in our fortunes that secretly endeared him to me," is a product of sympathy: "Often over our gloomy bowl we mingled groans" (4:122) and "frequently continued whole nights in the participation of these bitter joys" (4:123). Leon feels both repulsion and attraction for Bethlem, and these opposite forces lead him to believe that a friendship between them is possible: "For some time I regarded Bethlem Gabor as entirely my friend, and I consulted him in every thing, in which . . . I could consult him" (4:124).

In the event, however, Leon cannot keep these opposing forces in creative tension. Realizing that Bethlem's "regard for me, instead of increasing, suffered perceptible diminution" (4:129), Leon gestures towards a Kantian explanation, arguing that whereas his own character has a predominance of love, Gabor knows only those repellent emotions: "Our propensities were diametrically opposed to each other. He rejoiced in disorder and desolation as in his congenial element; my present pursuit was the restoration of public order and prosperity" (4:129–30). Overpowering the initial sympathetic attraction between the two men, Bethlem's repellent force directs itself at Leon, destroying their friendship when Leon is imprisoned by Bethlem in a dungeon. The subtext of opposing forces that runs through this encounter suggests Godwin's concern for, and Coleridge's fascination with, the hidden energies acting through and between people and which make the practice of friendship radically unstable.

In his contemporary work, Coleridge explored in greater depth than Godwin the disturbing possibility that friendship might be more influenced by esoteric, natural forces than by reason. In "The Rime of the Ancyent Marinere" (1797–1798), Coleridge warns that neither the presence of attractive, repulsive, or propulsive forces can be relied upon either to establish or sustain friendship. The initial hypnotic encounter between the Marinere and the Wedding Guest posits the existence of electromagnetic forces of attraction and repulsion operating between people. The wedding guest simultaneously experiences an attraction to the Marinere's "glittering eye" (line 3) and a desire to repel him: "get thee hence, thou greybeard Loon!" (line 15).[32] This scenario witnesses, however, not a balance of opposing energies but an overwhelming force of attraction. Fixing him with his eye, the Marinere compels the reluctant Wedding Guest to adhere to the other's "will" (line 20) so that he "cannot chuse but hear" (line 22) the succeeding tale. This magnetic attachment, however, is not friendship but mesmeric domination.

Coleridge then switches the focus from magnetic attraction to the positive propulsive force that one friend can generate for another. The crew's befriending of the Albatross has a dynamic effect on their ice-bound ship:

> The Marineres gave it biscuit-worms,
>   And round and round it flew:
> The Ice did split with a Thunder-fit;
>   The Helmsman steer'd us thro'.
>
> And a good south wind sprung up behind,
>   The Albatross did follow;
> And every day for food or play
>   Came to the Marinere's hollo!
>
> (lines 65–72)

The affectionate relation between Albatross and Marinere is mysteriously but intimately connected to the literally propelling force of the "good south wind" upon the ship. Immediately, however, the poem reveals that this might not be the only energy indwelling within friends:

> "God save thee, ancyent Marinere!
>   "From the fiends that plague thee thus—
> "Why look'st thou so?"—with my cross bow
>   I shot the Albatross.
>
> (lines 77–80)

Despite having every reason to continue the friendship, the Marinere inexplicably kills the creature. As Lockridge points out, the energy emanating from the Marinere is an act of will, and the shooting of the Albatross "is portrayed without hint of conscious motive perhaps because acts of will . . . originate from the abyss below consciousness."[33] The Marinere's inscrutable will indicates that the energy that one friend communicates to the other may not be positive and propulsive but precipitately destructive.

Lockridge convincingly argues that "just as the Mariner, without 'motive', kills the Albatross, so also, by means not of motive but of impulse directly aligned with the will, does he bless the water-snakes 'unaware.'" Lockridge concludes, however, that "an act of alienation must precede an act of reunion" and that "it is the Mariner's and Coleridge's fate to find human alienation more enduring than human love" (pp. 73–74). This view overlooks the Marinere's initial, albeit brief, friendship with the bird, which suggests that the amicable union preceded alienation. What the poem portrays is the sheer unpredictability of the energic will, either in its duration or moral valence. The Marinere, of course, attempts to rationalize his experience in terms of Christian doctrine:

> A spring of love gusht from my heart,
>   And I bless'd them unaware!
> Sure my kind saint took pity on me,
>   And I bless'd them unaware.
>
> (lines 276–79)

For the Marinere, the "spring of love" represents a divine impulse, a gift from God. At the poem's end, he clings to his religious explanation:

> He prayeth best who loveth best,
>   All things both great and small:
> For the dear God, who loveth us,
>   He made and loveth all.
>
> (lines 647–50)

The Marinere's attempt to sustain a loving self through religious observance is unconvincing, for it does not account for the baleful impulses of will that his narrative has revealed. If, as appears possible, loving impulses cannot be ensured, then the individual's communication with God can no longer be guaranteed. Despite the Marinere's Christian exegesis, his experience suggests that individuals may well be left isolated in a Godless universe, subject to a variety of irrational internal forces beyond conscious control, impelling them either to acts of love or of destruction.

Coleridge's interest in such forces was grounded in experience. Throughout the 1790s, he felt his contact with his internal sources of affectionate energy to be distressingly inconsistent. At times, he confessed to destructive impulses, as in "Effusion XXXIV. To an Infant" (1795), in which he revealed that, like an unreasoning babe, he could "Break Friendship's Mirror with a tetchy blow" (line 19).[34] Elsewhere, as in "Lines on a Friend who Died of a Frenzy Fever" (1794), he found his powers of "Energic Reason" (line 40) unaccountably "sloth-jaundic'd" (line 43), leaving him powerless to stop "Friendship's precious Pearls" falling from his grasp like "hour glass sand" (line 44). In September 1801, Coleridge understood his feelings towards Godwin to be suffering from a similar depletion in energy: "When once a correspondence has intermitted from whatever cause, it scarcely ever recommences without some impulse ab extra."[35] Coleridge suggests that no friend can be relied upon always to impart propulsive impulses to another, but instead may find himself lacking the energic will necessary to invigorate a flagging relationship.

Although they met again in London later that autumn, Coleridge's unenthusiasm had become apparent to his friend. Returning to the capital in January 1802, Coleridge discovered a brief Godwinian missive inviting him to a "little party," but owning that

> I am not satisfied with the comparison of your conduct towards me before & since midsummer last. I would not mention this but that I understand it has been hinted to you, and I like to speak for myself. Perhaps it is better such points should never be discussed. Circumstances & the operation of time will determine the question for us.[36]

Despite his unhappiness at Coleridge's neglect, Godwin is also uncertain that the friendship will benefit from each man's sincere expression of his feelings. By asserting that "circumstances & the operation of time" will prove the best guide to the relation's continuance, Godwin recognizes that the two men's intimacy can ultimately rely neither on sincerity nor conscious powers of management.

Although reaffirming the "bare story of the constancy of my friendship," in reply Coleridge repeated that the friendship was rendered unstable by the unaccountable absence of energic impulses working through his being.[37] Explaining why he had failed to visit, Coleridge declared:

> The same causes, that have robbed me to so great a degree of the self-impelling self-directing Principle, have deprived me too of the due powers of Resistances to Impulses from without. If I might so say, I am, as an acting man, a creature of mere Impact. "I will" & "I will not" are phrases, both of them equally, of rare occurrence in my dictionary. (2:782–83)

The passivity that allows him to be propelled by others marks Coleridge out as an extremely malleable being. However, this lack of "self-impelling" energy makes it difficult for him to sustain particular relationships. As he remarked in his previous letter:

> If you had ever asked me & fixed a day, I should most certainly have come—not, that I wanted an invitation in any other light than as a mere determinant ab extra—for in London I never go any where, nor in any degree follow my free-inclination—I am pushed / & waste my time because of all words I find it most difficult to say, No.[38]

Owing to the unpredictable nature of his will, Coleridge concedes he cannot be relied upon to sustain a friendship consisting of "mutual Propulsions." Coleridge's desire to manage the relationship through visiting also collapses in the face of an absence of inner energy to propel him and the relationship into action. Although the two men's friendly acquaintance continued, their epistolary intimacy effectively ended here.

There was, however, a discourse related to that of natural force that permeated the reflections of Coleridge's circle in the 1790s, and which posed a more radical challenge to the preservation of friendship through acts of volition. Looking back in a later note, Godwin uses an organic metaphor to describe how his acquaintance with Coleridge "was ripened in the year 1800 into a high degree of affectionate intimacy."[39] In some way, he suggests, the two men's friendship had been imbued with a principle of natural growth. The possible connection between affection and organic law had been hinted at by Coleridge in his letter of 22 September 1800. He invited Godwin to consider "whether there be reason to hold, that an action bearing all the semblance of pre-designing Consciousness may yet be simply organic, & whether a series of such actions are possible?" (1:625). Coleridge's speculation developed from his previous conjecture that a vital principle beyond "pre-designing Consciousness" might apply to feelings. Could "feelings," he wondered, "ever propagate themselves without the servile ministrations of undulating air or reflected light?" (1:624). One latent idea here, that friendship might develop and propagate itself according to organic law, had been explored by Godwin himself in the third edition of *Caleb Williams* (1797). Caleb describes his encounter with a noble Italian family:

> While our familiarity gained in duration, it equally gained in that subtlety of communication, by which it seemed to shoot forth its roots in

every direction. There are a thousand little evanescent touches in the development of a growing friendship, that are neither thought of, nor would be understood, between common acquaintances.[40]

For Caleb, friendship develops through a mysterious process of growth operating at the very edge of conscious perception. Positing an analogy between friendship and the life of plants, he argues that the "thousand little evanescent touches" of affection between friends are not insubstantial impulses, but nourish an extensive underground root system that makes the relationship grow.

Coleridge and Godwin situate themselves within a wider organic understanding of social relations that owed much to the development of botany in the eighteenth century. Alan Bewell has drawn attention to the ways in which botanists such as Carl Linnaeus had begun to "import social analogies into his descriptions of plant life":

> [Linnaeus] often personified the flower, calling it a "house," and its parts, the stamens being designated as "males" or "husbands," the pistils, as "females" or "wives." Groups of stamens were called "brotherhoods." . . . A major effect of this tendency to import social categories into the description of plants was that a wide analogical thoroughfare was built between plants and humans.[41]

It was perhaps in Coleridge and Southey's relations that the possible analogies between friendship and the life of plants were explored in greatest depth and with the most pressing urgency. For both men, their early Pantisocratic experiment and its acrimonious aftermath during 1796–1799 precipitated a variety of reflections upon the patterns of growth and decay in friendship.

Increasingly, both men began to perceive an organic principle working through their various relationships. As early as December 1794, Coleridge informed Southey of his disillusionment with his recent attachment to Sara Fricker: "I am not conscious of having injured her otherwise, than by having mistaken the ebullience of schematism for affection, which a moment's reflection might have told me, is not a plant of so mushroom a growth."[42] Coleridge laments not drawing an analogy between his speedy attachment and a rapidly growing plant. In doing so, he would have realized that instant affections develop on the same pattern as mushrooms, which spring up overnight only to die soon after. Acknowledging this organic law enables him to assert that his heart, after only a few weeks, is "withered within me." His experience provides a practical example of what Southey came to regard as an organic principle active throughout English society. In his "Metrical Letter, Written from London" (1798), Southey reassures his cousin Margaret that

> I am no sworn friend
> Of half-an-hour, as apt to leave as love;
> Mine are no mushroom feelings that spring up
> At once without a seed and take no root,
> Wiseliest distrusted. In a narrow sphere
> The little circle of domestic life
> I would be known and loved; the world beyond
> Is not for me.[43]

Instant intimacy represents a natural phenomenon by which affections "spring up" in the heart independently of human agency. For Southey, Charles Lloyd's friendships were characteristic of such speedy, unstable attachments. As he remarks of Lloyd's brief flirtation with Mary Hays, "Lloyd made one of his mushroom intimacies with her and you know how it was broken off."[44]

Furthermore, both Coleridge and Southey distinguish between the different types of principle organizing human affections. In an adaptation of an epigram by Friedrichs von Logau, "Freundschaft," which Coleridge penned while in Germany in May 1799, he declares: "To change old Friends for new / Is giving fruits for flowers."[45] Recent and long-established friends give rise to differing kinds of natural product: an old friendship entails a long ripening process, less immediately exciting than a new friend-bloom but ultimately more substantial. In "Sonnet II" (1798), published in *The Annual Anthology* (1799), Southey develops the distinction between "fruits" and "flowers," identifying the latter with short-lived attachments and the former with slower processes of growth, which result in sturdy oaks. These embowering presences represent the most enduring friendships, and are implicitly associated with an individual's earliest domestic group:

> Beware a speedy friend, the Arabian said,
>   And wisely was it he advised distrust.
>   The flower that blossoms earliest fades the first.
> Look at yon oak that lifts its stately head
> And dallies with the autumnal storm, whose rage
>   Tempests the ocean waves; slowly it rose,
> Slowly its strength increas'd thro' many an age,
>   And timidly did its light leaves unclose
> As doubtful of the spring, their palest green.
>   They to the summer cautiously expand,

> And by the warmer sun and season bland
> Matured, their foliage in the grove is seen,
> When the bare forest by the wintry blast
> Is swept, still lingering on the boughs the last.[46]

Explaining the concept of "organic law," M. H. Abrams emphasizes that "the laws of the inanimate world, that is, are fixed and given laws, and operate without consciousness or the possibility of choice."[47] This informs Southey's notion that strong oak tree–friendships appear only after a lengthy process of development, which again cannot be accelerated by conscious acts of volition.

At the time of writing, Southey continued to be estranged from Coleridge. Despite their reconciliation of 1796, during the next three years the men's quarrel had grumbled on: Southey interpreted Coleridge's sonnet "To Simplicity" as a personal slight, while Coleridge was outraged by Southey's providing Lloyd with details of his life for inclusion in *Edmund Oliver*. In this context, it seems likely that Southey in "Sonnet II" identifies his friendship with Coleridge not as a tree but a flower that quickly bloomed and died. Writing in December 1796, Coleridge had also conceived his Pantisocratic friendship as having once been a living organism. For him, the relation may have been more treelike but, in his view also, was now dead:

> We quarreled—& the quarrel lasted for a twelvemonth—We are now reconciled; but the cause of the Difference was solemn—& "the blasted oak puts not forth it's buds anew"—we are *acquaintances*—& feel *kindliness* towards each other; but I do not *esteem*, or LOVE Southey, . . . and vice versâ Southey of me.[48]

The quarrel is analogous to lightning striking a tree, and equally fatal. Coleridge is left with a "painful" (1:294) sense of the permanent decline of their relation from friendship to acquaintance.

Both Coleridge and Southey sense that the quarrel and subsequent death of their friendship-tree was governed by a mysterious principle of mutability. Coleridge's attitude reveals itself in some famous lines representing the estrangement of Sir Leoline and Sir Roland in Part II of "Christabel" (1800).[49] As George Whalley remarks, the "heart-felt cry of personal anguish" of Coleridge's verse "recalls Southey, the creative excitement of their first friendship never to be recovered, the bitterness of first disenchantment":[50]

> Alas! they had been Friends in Youth;
> But whispering Tongues can poison Truth;

> And Constancy lives in Realms above;
> And Life is thorny; and Youth is vain;
> And to be wroth with one, we love,
> Doth work, like madness in the Brain:
> And thus it chanc'd, as I divine,
> With Roland and Sir Leoline.
> Each spake words of high Disdain
> And Insult to his Heart's best Brother,
> And parted—ne'er to meet again!
>
> (lines 387–97)

Fixing constancy in "realms above," the poet suggests that the key quality of all earthly relations is mutability. In lieu of explanation, he offers a series of proverbial commonplaces that only highlight his difficulty in finding a sufficient reason why the knights' relationship disintegrated.

The destructive mutability that Coleridge perceives to be acting upon his relation with Southey was becoming for his friend a key aspect of his own organicist conception of relationship. Southey comes to argue that all affections, and friendship in particular, are subject to inexorable natural laws of change and decay beyond human control. As he confides to Grosvenor Bedford in January 1799:

> It is a favourite article of belief with me Grosvenor that friendships and affections will continue in the next world; yet there are some awkward objections to it; it is not analogous to what passes here, nothing lasts, Nature seems to delight in disorganizing to reproduce. Not only does every thing change around us but we change ourselves—the oak indeed was contained in the acorn but it is not to the human eye that the resemblance is visible.[51]

In "disorganizing to reproduce," Southey emphasizes Nature's disassembling of the affectionate bonds it has created. One reason for this is the radical instability of personal identity: in an individual's development from acorn into oak any pair of friends becomes transformed. Where identity is subjected to continual flux, the prospect of sustaining attachment becomes remote.

However, Southey goes on to argue that the bond of friendship is peculiarly subject to this irreversible process of growth and decay:

> There is a great difference between love and friendship; absence and cohabitation increase the one and slowly destroy the other. If I wishd to preserve a friend I would rather perhaps have him in the East Indies than in the house with me, but even absence weakens this kind of at-

tachment, for the apartments of friendship in the heart are never long vacant. (1:179)

Friendship differs from love in its resistance to conscious control. Attempts to manage friendship, whether through cohabitation or separation, are futile when faced with the power of organic process. In concluding that the "apartments of friendship" are "never long vacant," Southey suggests that friendship is an ever-renewing form of life. The cost, however, lies in the continual dwindling of particular relationships. Writing from Lisbon in 1801, Southey reflects on this pattern of change:

> Four years have altered Lisbon & the little world in which I moved. deaths & removals—where is one? dead! another? in England! a third? at Madrid. a fourth? God knows where. & the momentary feeling passes away like an electric shock—sudden & transitory! So we feel for our acquaintance—so others in their turn will feel for us. the place of every one is soon supplied, as one plant grows in the place of another. our very feelings change also. do you know Spensers Cantos of Mutability?[52]

Like Godwin, Southey understands that affectionate feelings may generate powerful electrical energies. But all is "transitory." The most dismal aspect of friendship's process of natural renewal, in which one plant-friend replaces another, is that lost friends are finally not mourned but merely forgotten.

In identifying friendship as an ever-renewing vital principle, Southey distinguishes his position from a central tenet of elegy. In this Classical tradition, part of the tragedy of human affections is that lost friends do not resemble other natural organisms that "Renew their Bloom, and with the Spring return," but instead remain "Fast Bound, no more to tread the Walks of Men."[53] In 1794, Southey embraced this view, adopting the pseudonym "Bion" in his *Poems* (1795), while his collaborator, Lovell, identified himself as the grieving poet-friend, "Moschus." By 1800, however, Southey's organicist conception of friendship can lead him to deny that the loss of a particular human attachment has tragic significance. In 1801, he reflects with equanimity on the inevitable decline of his friendship with Humphry Davy:

> The silent estrangement which I foresaw is growing between us. His regard for and attachment to me grew up briskly, but the thorns have choacked it. This is in the natural course of things—our habits of life and of thinking and of study grow more and more dissimilar. It is not a thing to wonder at, hardly to regret.[54]

The shadow of Coleridge lurks within many of Southey's reflections on Nature's "disorganizing to reproduce." Griggs argues that Southey's "growing resentment" towards him during 1797–1799 can be traced to the summer of 1797, when "Coleridge's acquaintance with William and Dorothy Wordsworth had ripened into a warm friendship. Wordsworth, now repository of Coleridge's inmost feelings, had supplanted Southey. This may partly explain Southey's attack on the Lyrical Ballads."[55] Griggs's organic metaphor hints that Coleridge's affection for Wordsworth is the expression of friendship's vital principle renewing itself in Coleridge's life, but only through disorganizing the Southey bond. The extent to which Southey and Coleridge themselves understood their relation between 1799 and 1804 in organic terms is one subject of the following pages. Coleridge's representation of Sir Leoline and Sir Roland in "Christabel" offers a helpful starting point, qualifying as it does Southey's view of organicism's corrosive power. Continuing to reflect upon the estrangement of the two knights, the poet declares:

> But never either found another
> To free the hollow Heart from Paining—
>
> They stood aloof, the scars remaining,
> Like Cliffs, which had been rent asunder;
> A dreary Sea now flows between,
> But neither Heat, nor Frost, nor Thunder
> Shall wholly do away, I ween,
> The Marks of That, which once hath been.
>
> (lines 398–405)

In these poignant lines, Coleridge measures that which nature irrevocably destroys against that which remains. Although "Heat," "Frost," and "Thunder" erode even the traces of the old friendship, an intrinsic element of affection somehow resists decaying into indifference. Not to "wholly do away" with the past, however, indicates the poet's ambivalence whether to emphasize the extent of loss or the residue of attachment. The two cliffs represent this tension spatially: separated by a dreary sea, they remain close enough for the distance between them to be continually felt. Nevertheless, the poem demonstrates how this immutable element of affection becomes articulated in a conscious desire to recreate lost friendship. Discovering that Geraldine is Sir Roland's daughter, Sir Leoline takes action, sending his servant Bracy to Sir Roland and ordering him to

> take the Youth, whom thou lov'st best,
> To bear thy Harp, and learn thy Song,
> And cloath you both in solemn Vest.
>
> (lines 466–68)

By presenting Roland with this symbolic pair of friends, Leoline will demonstrate his desire to renew the knights' own bond. Although Leoline's fantasy of renewal is not fulfilled, his ultimate leading forth of Geraldine, the "th'Insulted Daughter of his Friend" (line 624), bears witness to the powerful desire to restore, even vicariously, his male friendship.

"Christabel" raises issues that press directly on Coleridge and Southey's attempts to restore their friendship at the end of the 1790s. Both men strive to deny the influence of mutability upon their relationship. Like Sir Leoline, Southey and Coleridge participate in what Philippe Ariès has termed a "fantasy of continuity" originating in eighteenth-century discourse.[56] The poets' early fascination with this fantasy is witnessed by their admiration for, and editing of, Joseph Cottle's "Monody on the Death of John Henderson" (1795).[57] Although mourning the death of his friend, Cottle suggests that the two men will nevertheless meet again:

> If Friendship be a flower, whose am'ranth bloom
> Endures that heavenly clime; beyond the tomb
> I, haply I (low scenes of earth, retreat!)
> Am doom'd once more thy honor'd form to meet;
> Behold thee stand "girt in a starry zone"
> Where Wisdom wells beneath th'Omniscient's throne;
> And thou to me with outstretch'd arm shalt bring
> Nectar ebullient from that living spring.
>
> (lines 105–12)

If friendship can be conceived to be a flower that never dies (an amaranth), then Cottle can hope it transcends earthly rules of mortality. Coleridge responded with a poetic tribute of his own:

> But lo your HENDERSON awakes the Muse—
> His Spirits beckon'd from the mountain's height!
> You left the plain and soar'd 'mid richer views!
> So Nature mourn'd, when sunk the First Day's light,
> With stars, unseen before, spangling her robe of night!
>
> (lines 32–36)[58]

Coleridge echoes Cottle's hope for permanence in the life of affections. In replacing the sun with stars, Nature provides a permanent trace of the "First Day's light," suggesting that what might seem to be lost has only moved further away: the "Spirits" of the friend remain close enough to still "beckon" the living.

Terry Castle has described how in its purest form, a late-eighteenth-century "fantasy of continuity" sought to break down "the limit between life and death" and make "the dead seem to 'live' again" (p. 241). Castle summarizes Ariès's argument that from early on in the century there emerges

> a "romantic cult of the dead"—a growing subjective fascination with idealized images of the deceased. Older ideas of the afterlife . . . had not typically emphasized the possibility of meeting one's family and friends after death. . . . In the era of romantic individualism, however, the theme of sentimental reunion became paramount. . . . Much of nineteenth-century spiritualism, Ariès argues, was simply an extenuation of the notion that the familiar souls of the dead continued to dwell in a nearby invisible realm, invited communication with the living, and awaited a happy future meeting with those who had mourned them in this life. (pp. 242–43)

For Southey, ideas of this kind helped him deny the corrosive activity of time upon relationships. In 1796, he inquired of Grosvenor Bedford: "If you die before me, will you visit me? I am half a believer in apparitions, and would purchase conviction at the expense of a tolerable fright."[59] This desire to believe was one Southey was increasingly interested in rationalizing, especially after the death in 1795 of his undergraduate friend, Edmund Seward.

In an elegy, "The Dead Friend" (1799), Southey highlights his struggle to dissociate friendship from decay and to reassert Seward's presence in his life.[60] The poem opens with Southey's order, "Not to the grave, not to the grave my Soul / Descend":

> The Spirit is not there!
> It is but lifeless, perishable flesh
>   That moulders in the grave,
> Earth, air, and waters ministering particles
>   Now to the elements
>   Resolv'd, their uses done.
>
> (p. 258)

Southey fights his instinctive belief that "Spirit" is coterminous with the body, and instead articulates a "fantasy of continuity," in which death alters nothing but the friend's physical state:

> And we have often said how sweet it were
> With unseen ministry of angel power
> To watch the friends we loved.
> **!we did not err!
> Sure I have felt thy presence! thou hast given
> A birth to holy thought,
> Hast kept me from the world unstain'd and pure.
>
> (p. 259)

With new influx of "angel power," Seward has continued to develop his friend's spiritual life, by encouraging a "birth" of holy thought. Southey remains, however, a half-believer in ghosts. In the final stanza, he both acknowledges and represses his anxieties regarding his friend's disembodied presence:

> Not to the grave, not to the grave, my Soul,
> Follow thy friend beloved!
> But in the lonely hour
> But in the evening walk,
> Think that he companies thy solitude,
> Think that he holds with thee
> Mysterious intercourse,
> And tho' Remembrance wake a tear
> There will be joy in grief.
>
> (p. 260)

Southey's demand to "think" that Seward is present testifies to his fear that the "friend" may not now exist outside his desiring mind.

Nevertheless, this self-conscious desire to "think" friendship into being plays a crucial role in renewing the bond between Southey and Coleridge. Writing in July 1799 after his return from Germany, Coleridge inquired whether Southey could feel "shootings within you of an affection, which ('tho' fall'n, tho' chang'd') has played too important a part in the events of our lives & the formation of our characters, ever to be forgotten."[61] Coleridge hovers between accepting the unalterable decay of the relation and hoping that "shootings" of new growth are possible. Like Southey, however, Coleridge understands that conscious effort will be required to stimulate such growth, and he suggests a variety of reasons Southey could use to justify re-establishing amicable relations:

> Southey, we have similar Talents, Sentiments nearly similar, & kindred pursuits—we have likewise in more than one instance common objects of our esteem and love—I pray and intreat you, if we should meet at

any time, let us not withhold from each other the outward Expressions of daily Kindliness. (1:523)

Aware that these positive justifications might not be sufficient, Coleridge suggests that Southey might at least find a reason to suspend his harsh opinion:

> And if it not be no [any] longer in your power to soften your opinions, make your feelings at least more tolerant towards me—/ a debt of humility which assuredly we all of us owe to our most feeble, imperfect and self-deceiving Nature.—We are few of us good enough to know our own Hearts—and as to the Hearts of others, let us struggle to hope that they are better than we think them / & resign the rest to our common maker. (1:523-24)

For Coleridge, the religious imperative of humility should provide reason enough for Southey to "make" his feelings more tolerant, irrespective of whether he can control his opinions.

The influence of these sentiments on Coleridge's estranged friend may be seen in an unpublished letter written two weeks later, from Southey to Grosvenor Bedford. Southey urges Bedford to alter his opinion of another acquaintance, who had fallen considerably in Bedford's esteem. Southey makes explicit the idea that remains implicit in Coleridge's letter—despite disillusionment, a man can reason himself into amicable relations with a lost friend:

> You perhaps over rated his good qualities once—but do you not underrate them now? & subtracting the due deficit from them, are there not enough remaining to constitute him—if not quite a friend—yet something very near it—one to regard & from whose company much pleasure may be derivable? it is very painful—for I know it by much experience, to have your friends sink in the thermometer of your esteem. but I am afraid we are with friends like astronomers, who when they discover a spot in the sun, look at nothing else. friendship on the wane is like the sick person who loathes the favourite food of his health. by all this I only mean that tho Carlisle has some faults he has more good qualities, that tho bipennated beings are much better, a great proportion of bipeds are much worse.[62]

Southey understands that in a deteriorating friendship, a man finds it increasingly difficult to perceive any good in his friend. Nevertheless, he suggests that this natural phenomenon might be controlled through a determined effort of Godwinian rationalism, by which a friend mathematically calculates another's objective worth.[63]

Coleridge's offices succeeded to the extent that Southey could "surprise" Charles Danvers in September, by writing to him while sitting "at the same table with Coleridge."[64] Reflecting on this rapprochement, Southey revealed that the renewal of warm relations, both during 1796 and at present, owed much to his capacity for reasoning himself back into friendship:

> Probably what most influenced me was the habit of mind which induces us rather to remember the good qualities of a lost friend than his faults, & to select for remembrance chiefly what is pleasurable to recollect. With similar pursuits & similar opinions we differed in practice,— but unless you domesticate with a man his inconsistencies are not forced upon notice.[65]

Meditating on Coleridge's "good qualities" helps create a mental construct towards which he can feel affection. Southey also points here to the element of imagination involved in creating such positive mental images. By a deliberate process of "selection," Southey's memory erases the "inconsistencies" that threaten affection. He admits that this process may represent a fragile kind of self-deception, dependent on avoiding situations in which a friend's faults are "forced upon notice." Nevertheless, memory provides Southey with a way of imaginatively controlling his image of the friend, bathing it in a softer, warmer glow. Reflecting in 1800 on his time in Portugal, Southey elaborates further: "I have associations with Lisbon that give me a friendship for the place—recollected feelings and hopes, pleasures and anxieties—all now mellowed into remembrances that endear the associated scenes."[66] Southey's friendship for Lisbon develops once he has distanced himself in space and time from its people and associated events. Separation encourages friendship, for in solitude even uncongenial materials can be nostalgically refashioned through imaginative recollection, and "mellowed" into immutable images towards which Southey can feel affection.

Two years earlier Coleridge had reflected how "people in general are not sufficiently aware how often the imagination creeps in and counterfeits the memory—perhaps to a certain degree it does always blend with our supposed recollections."[67] Like Southey, Coleridge relies on this counterfeiting power of imagination to create a permanently lovable image of the friend. "The time returns upon me, Southey!" he declared in April 1800,

> when we dreamt one Dream, & that a glorious one—when we eat together, & thought each other greater & better than all the World beside, and when we were bed fellows. Those days can never be forgotten, and

till they are forgotten, we cannot, if we would, cease to love each other.[68]

Coleridge's enraptured memory conveniently edits out all reference to the tensions that had broken the Pantisocrats' friendship and their scheme for emigration. Coleridge's idealizing imagination is evident in his recollection of being bedfellows: in August 1794, Southey had demonstrably not been impressed, remarking of one particular night, "Coleridge is a vile bedfellow and I slept but ill."[69]

During the next two years, Coleridge made several invitations to Southey to come and stay. Coleridge's invitation in July 1801 demonstrates how his memory of the men's shared past now motivates his desire for renewed contact:

> Oh! how I have dreamt about you—Times, that *have* been, & never can return, have been with me on my bed of pain, and how I yearned toward you in those moments, I myself can know only by feeling it over again!—But come! "strengthen the weak hands, & confirm the feeble knees. Then shall the lame man leap as a hart, and sorrow & sighing shall flee away."[70]

Coleridge's strongest feelings of affection occur when he dwells on past moments, and on a friend who no longer exists in his exalted Pantisocratic guise. Nevertheless, Coleridge's dream of young Southey is here the basis for his current enthusiasm of friendship.

When Southey did indeed visit Keswick in September, Coleridge was struck by the difficulty in reconciling an Idea of the friend with his embodied presence. After his departure, he wrote to Southey of his determination to separate from Sara, and took the opportunity to reflect also on his current feelings for his friend:

> Southey! much as we differ in our habits, you do indeed possess my esteem & affection in a degree that makes it uncomfortable to me not to tell you what I have told you. I once said—that I missed no body—I only enjoyed the present. At that moment my heart misgave me, & had no one been present, I should have said to you—that you were the only exception—/ for my mind is full of visions, & you had been so long connected with the fairest of all fair dreams, that I feel your absence more than I enjoy your society: tho' that I do not enjoy your society so much, as I anticipated that I should do, is wholly or almost wholly owing to the nature of my domestic feelings, & the fear, or the consciousness, that you did not & could not sympathize with him [them].[71]

In declaring "I feel your absence more than I enjoy your society," Coleridge admits his emotional engagement is primarily with the disembodied idea of Southey, linked to their Pantisocratic past, and best sustained as imaginative "vision." Reconciling this idea with his friend's embodied self creates a fraught discourse in which Coleridge cannot decide whether to emphasize the permanence of his affection or the "difference in the men's habits," and his sense of Southey's practical failure to act the friend.

For Southey, it was even more difficult to sustain his "trick of thinking too well of those I love."[72] Informing Danvers of Coleridge's separation, Southey likewise reveals how his recent encounter threatened to invalidate his affectionate idea of his friend:

> Something I saw myself. Edith saw a great deal. in no one instance was Mrs Coleridge ever to blame. . . . He complains that she irritates him & makes him so ill that he can do nothing. this is a wretched excuse for idleness. ill he assuredly is & that illness has perhaps so changed his temper. he is in debt to the booksellers—to Johnson. to Longman—this preys upon him—he has not resolution enough to clear it off by exertion—letters come to him which he often will not open—still they vex him—& he can vent the vexation only upon his wife.[73]

Empirical evidence not only makes it difficult to sympathize with Coleridge's marital woes but also to believe in him as a "friend": "[Sara] told [Coleridge] once in Ediths [sic] hearing that he had been a bad son, a bad brother, a bad friend, & a bad husband. It stung him—because it was true." From this time, such uncomfortable meetings of Idea and embodiment renew Southey's sense of what has been lost in his friendship. Reflecting on Coleridge's desire to travel to the South of France in 1802, he declares, "I do not however wish that we should go abroad together. Our habits are not enough alike. I wish the similarity, or the dissimilarity were greater."[74] Like two cliffs separated by a dreary sea, the relation is now an uncomfortable mixture of intimacy and estrangement.

The disappointment of reunions testifies to the way in which organic process undermines Southey's determination to create an idea of the friend. Coleridge echoes in these years Southey's lament that "we are all changing; one wishes sometimes that God had bestowed upon us something of his immutability. Age, infirmities, blunted feelings, blunted intellect, these are but comfortless expectancies!"[75] As he remarks in December 1801, on hearing of the death of Southey's mother, "Life passes away from us in all modes & ways—in our friends, in ourselves. We all 'die daily.' "[76] Coleridge is gripped by an entropic sense of life draining away in his friendships. In January 1803 he confesses: "O Southey! I am not the Coleridge, which you knew me."[77] In May, the ill health of both men provokes him to compare the immutable dead favorably with the decay of the living: "What mouldering Temples we seem to be! . . . Old People, good dear old Ladies, are like Infants, that die at 9 months old / they gain by Death an unchangeable sort of Being in the minds of the Survivors."[78]

Ironically, however, Southey's difficulty in maintaining a positive mental image of Coleridge does not lead to the inevitable collapse of the relationship. Instead, he consistently draws attention to the way his affection has an organic life of its own. Briefly captivated by Coleridge's fancy that the men emigrate to the West Indies, Southey remarked: "I shall have with me the man, to whom, in all the ups & downs of six years, my heart has clung with most affection, despite even its own efforts."[79] Southey's metaphor of his heart, rather than mind, "clinging" to Coleridge intimates an organic principle connecting Southey to his friend, independently of his reason. Similarly, in October 1802 Southey confesses: "I never feel so little satisfied with myself as upon recollection that my inclination to like him has always got the better of a judgement—felt at first sight—and deliberately and perpetually strengthened by every experience."[80]

If Southey finds himself drawn to Coleridge by an uncontrollable inner impulse, Coleridge continues to experience friendship as undermined by subconscious drives, but salvageable through even greater efforts of the reasoning mind. These ideas were focused by Southey's visit to Coleridge in autumn 1803, in the wake of Southey's loss of his daughter, Margaret. In his immediate epistolary response, Coleridge enclosed his first draft of "Pains of Sleep." When awake, the poet's creed is simple: "To live belov'd is all I need, / And whom I love, I love indeed."[81] In his dreams, however, Coleridge is beset by destructive impulses: "Rage, sensual Passion, mad'ning Brawl, / And Shame, & Terror over all!" (1:983). Coleridge's inclusion of these lines to Southey may represent a sympathetic act: as Southey had been powerless to prevent his daughter's death, so Coleridge dramatizes his own powerlessness to control his inner drives that, in his dreams at least, menace his friendships.

Coleridge immediately returned to Keswick, where he comforted his friend, spending much time walking with him in the country. The visit provoked some intensive reflection on his relations with Southey, which centred on the power of reason in managing friendship:

> Prodigious Efficacy in preventing Quarrels and Interruptions of Friendship among Mankind in general, but especially among young warm-

hearted men, would the habitual Reflection be, that the Almighty will judge us not by what we *do*, but by what we *are*; and in forbidding us to judge each other has manifestly taught us by implication, that we cannot without hazard of grievous error & without hazard of grievous Breach of Charity deduce the latter from the Former.[82]

Coleridge goes on to "Apply this now to my former Quarrel with Southey":

On what ground, in the first place, did I form a friendship with him? . . . Not that he was Perfection; but because he was a far better man, than the vast majority of the young men, whom I knew. What had I to oppose to all this?—An alteration of any of these *Habits*? Had Southey ceased to be Southey?—No. What then?—Why, one or two *Actions*— . . . If either of us in some moment when from some accidental association a feeling of old Tenderness had revisited our Hearts, had paused—& asked our selves—Not what C. has *done*? or what has S. *done*?—but—Well! in spite of this—a bad business, to be sure—but spite of it—what is C. or S. on the whole? (1603)

Recalling that Southey was "a far better man" than others, Coleridge revisits his early Godwinian valuation of his friend's objective merit. However, Coleridge transmutes the character of this embodied, Pantisocratic Southey into an idea of his friend's true Being. He claims that the friendship could be permanently sustained if he kept in mind this disembodied, unchangeable reality and disregarded the accidental actions of Southey's mutable, embodied self.

In a contemporaneous notebook entry, Coleridge generalizes these reflections, urging himself to practice mental exercises that might help him preserve a positive image of a friend:

Deeplier than ever do I see the necessity of understanding the whole complex mixed character of our Friend— . . . intensifying our Love of the Good in it, & making up our mind to the Faulty—it would be a good Exercise to imagine & anticipate some painful Result of the faulty part of our Friend's character—fancy him acting thus & thus to you—when it would most wound you / then to see how much of the wound might not be attributed to some lingering Selfishness in one's self—and at all events to fancy yourself forgiving it, passing it over, turning the attention forcibly to the valuable Parts of the character, & connecting a feeling of Respect & love with the *Person*, the visual Form—even during the manifestation of this unpleasant part of the Character.[83]

Sustaining affection requires a "forcible" act of volition. However, whereas Southey would regard such exercises as a conscious self-deception, for Coleridge these efforts reflect a profoundly Platonic understanding of the "Friend." He distinguishes the "visual Form" of the "Person" from the present individual. In perceiving this ghostly image superimposed upon the friend's "unpleasant" bodily manifestation, Coleridge hopes to maintain contact with the friend's permanently worthy self. In the event, Coleridge's mental effort was rewarded by his feeling increasingly affectionate towards Southey. "Southey I like more & more," Coleridge exclaims to Poole, "he is a good man / & his Industry stupendous! Take him all in all, his regularity & domestic virtues, Genius, Talents, Acquirements, & Knowledge—& he stands by himself."[84] This renewal of affection was reciprocated by Southey who, in 1804, declared that "Coleridge and I are the best companions possible, in almost all moods of mind, for all kinds of wisdom, and all kinds of nonsense."[85]

Coleridge's departure for Malta in the spring of 1804 enabled both men to reaffirm their friendship once more. If presence still threatens intimacy by forcing "inconsistencies upon notice" then absence can paradoxically become the means of restoring affection. As Southey remarks to Coleridge:

> Your going abroad appeared to me so doubtful, or, indeed, so improbable an event, that the certainty comes on me like a surprise, and I feel at once what a separation the sea makes; when we get beyond the reach of mail coaches, then, indeed, distance becomes a thing perceptible. I shall often think, Coleridge, *Quanto minus est cum reliquis versari quam tui meminisse!* [*How much less pleasurable it is to dwell with those left behind than to remember you!*] God grant you a speedy passage, a speedy recovery, and a speedy return![86]

Once more, Southey uses memory to erase Coleridge's imperfections. He believes that the affectionate relation he will enjoy with the imaginary construct "Coleridge" will be preferable to any present relationships. In response, Coleridge reinvokes the "fantasy of continuity" as a means of somehow guaranteeing the continuance of the friendship: "O dear dear Southey! old days crowd in upon me—I love & honor you from my Soul.—You will go on as you have gone /—Love & Blessing to all of you!"[87] Seeing before him the immutable Pantisocratic Form of Robert Southey, Coleridge can assert the temporal continuity of his friend's identity, which will "go on as you have gone." In his final letter before disembarking, Coleridge offers himself up to the friend as a ghost: "Write instantly, franked or unfranked, S. T. Coleridge, Esqre, Mr J. C. Mottley's,

Portsmouth—just as if I was really the[re. God b]less you, DEAR Southey!"[88]

At this moment, the men's Platonic discourse is not undermined by a nagging sense of organic decay or irrational forces. Southey is particularly struck by the way he connects Coleridge with his own vitality: "Your departure hangs upon me with something the same effect that the heavy atmosphere presses upon you—an unpleasant thought, that works like yeast, and makes me feel the animal functions going on."[89] Deeper than any rational attachment, an organic bond remains between the two men, such that the vital energies of one are mysteriously dependent on attachment to the other. In 1802, Southey had declared that having "one friend within a half-hour's walk is among the necessaries of life. It is as essential almost as air and water,"[90] and this sentiment informs his poignant response to the news that Coleridge has actually set sail:

> Coleridge is gone for Malta, and his departure affects me more than I let be seen. Let what will trouble me, I bear a calm face; and if the Boiling Well could be drawn (which, however it heaves and is agitated below, presents a smooth, undisturbed surface), that should be my emblem. . . . I am perpetually pained and mortified by thinking what he ought to be, for mine is an eye of microscopic discernment to the faults of my friends; but the tidings of his death would come upon me more like a stroke of lightning than any evil I have ever yet endured; almost it would make me superstitious, for we were two ships that left port in company.[91]

Deeper than Southey's rational dissatisfaction with his friend exists a "Boiling Well" of affectionate energy, which continues regardless of other considerations. The force of this natural energy makes Southey fearful that Coleridge's death would blast his own existence.

And so Coleridge left for Malta, having managed to preserve ongoing friendly relations with both Godwin and Southey. Of the many friends that he was leaving behind, it was Wordsworth who most fully expressed at this moment many of the positive ideals that Coleridge had striven to embody during the previous years:

> Far art Thou wander'd now in search of health,
> And milder breezes, melancholy lot!
> But Thou art with us, with us in the past,
> The present, with us in the times to come:
> There is no grief, no sorrow, no despair,
> No languor, no dejection, no dismay,

> No absence scarcely can there be for those
> Who love as we do. Speed Thee well! divide
> Thy pleasure with us, thy returning strength,
> Receive it daily as a joy of ours;
> Share with us thy fresh spirits, whether gift
> Of gales Etesian, or of loving thoughts.[92]

Wordsworth does not ground friendship on the empirical evidence offered by embodied existence, marred as it is by tension in the two men's relations and by Coleridge's "melancholy" decline. Instead, he articulates many features of a transcendent Idea. Timeless, this friendship is not altered by physical separation nor organic decay. Neither can Wordsworth distinguish between love of family and love for his friend—Coleridge is "with us." With the words "Speed thee well!," the poet offers Coleridge the propulsive force he so desires from his friends (and Wordsworth especially). Imagining Coleridge's "returning strength," Wordsworth uses friendship to celebrate the other's manly identity, which will manifest itself through propulsive "gales Etesian." Offering these gales by way of "gift," Coleridge's affection transcends the worldly self-interest of commercial modes of relationship and rational management. Satisfied with Coleridge's "loving thoughts," Wordsworth asserts the value of the friendly heart above the friendly deed. Finally, he declares that Coleridge's joys are his own, and so foregrounds his friend's sympathetic ideal of participating in another's being. In imagination the idea of friendship has its greatest power.

9

Postscript: "Our excellent transatlantic friend:"Coleridge and Washington Allston, 1806–18

COLERIDGE'S DEPARTURE TO THE MEDITERRANEAN DID NOT SIGNIFY the end of the structural influence on his relationships of the ideas of friendship he had been exposed to and helped develop during the 1790s. Their continuity is evident in his friendship with the American painter, Washington Allston, whom Coleridge first encountered in Rome during 1805. In particular, the relationship illustrates how many of the foregoing notions of friendship continued to provide means by which Romantic friends could negotiate perceived mutual differences and points of union.

Of similar ages, temperaments, interests, and both exploring a foreign land, Allston and Coleridge quickly formed an attachment, becoming inseparable companions in Rome and later at Allston's retreat at Olevano. From the outset, they appear not only to have founded their intimacy on the classical doctrine of virtuous friendship, but also to have expressed their affection through a discourse of Humean sympathy. Joseph Henry Green declared that both men were profoundly attracted to the quality of each other's "moral being":

> I hold it scarcely possible that Coleridge could have felt the affection, which he undoubtedly did, toward Allston, without having had the strongest assurance of those excellent qualities of the heart, which, whatever sympathy their common tastes and pursuits might have produced, were the real ground of his attachment and undeviating friendship. It is unnecessary to say that Allston cherished similar and responsive feelings toward Coleridge.[1]

In his letters, Coleridge repeatedly praises the "religious Purity of his moral character,"[2] and in valuing Allston's virtue, Coleridge places him in a line of friends beginning with Poole and Southey, and including Thelwall and Wordsworth. For his part, Allston suggests that his own friendships are Godwinian in that he feels affection towards those he discovers to be virtuous. In 1816, for instance, Allston informs Coleridge that in James Gillman he has found a "strength of mind and manly integrity which command both my respect and esteem. You who know me know how I *must* appreciate [him]."[3] In this classical scenario, part of the friend's role is to help maintain the other's virtue. Richard Dana, Sr., Allston's brother-in-law, recollected how Coleridge practiced this idea while traveling through Italy, advising Allston on one occasion to put down an "execrable" book whose "exceeding badness" was amusing him: "You may think that it amuses you," Coleridge warned, "but you had better be doing nothing. You cannot touch pitch without being defiled."[4]

At the same time, the intimacy that developed in Italy bears many characteristics of the sympathetic friendship Coleridge had known in his relationships with other male friends. Two portraits Allston painted during this period are suggestive of the men's mutual sympathy. As several critics have observed, Allston's unfinished portrait of Coleridge in Italy (1806) resembles Allston's recent *Self-Portrait* (1805)[5] "in tonality, setting . . . , expression, and even in the placement of the figure within a canvas of almost equal dimensions."[6] Gerdts and Stebbins interpret the paintings as "pendants, a commemoration of a newly formed but already intense personal relationship."[7] Imitating his own self-portrait, Allston's *Coleridge* represents the poet as a cosmopolitan figure whose similarly meditative expression hints at the friends' mutual sympathetic identification and a mingling of their inner spirit.

Coleridge's lengthy notebook entry on Allston's *Diana and Her Nymphs in the Chase* (1805) in turn illustrates his Humean wish to participate in his friend's experience. As E. S. Shaffer argues, the poetic "power" of Coleridge's entry lies in its imaginative reanimation of "the natural scene which the painter must have experienced."[8] As if Coleridge and Allston were themselves together in the actual landscape, Coleridge exclaims on seeing Allston's "perilous bridge": "take care, for heaven sake." Then, as Coleridge views the "great Bowder Stone," he appears literally to put himself in the place of the artist gazing at the scene and to enter his imagined mental experience: "I must climb over it to get the prospect of the far valley, hidden by the Stone & the Rock, and a Tree all Foliage, growing behind the great stone."[9]

To an extent, the sympathy flowing between both men encourages them to discern Italy through each other's eyes. Describing

Washington Allston, *Portrait of Samuel Taylor Coleridge (Unfinished)* (1806). Courtesy of the Fogg Art Museum, Harvard University Art Museums, Loan from the Washington Allston Trust. © President and Fellows of Harvard University.

the geography of Olevano, Coleridge writes: "How exquisitely *picturesque* this effect is (in the strictest sense of the word) Mr Alston has proved in his Swiss Landskip [i.e., *Diana and Her Nymphs in the Chase*]."[10] Allston's picture now helps to structure Coleridge's vision. Likewise, Coleridge's conversation provides the means by

Washington Allston, *Self-Portrait* (1805). Bequest of Miss Alice Hooper, 1884. Courtesy, Museum of Fine Arts, Boston. © 2000. Museum of Fine Arts Boston. All rights reserved.

which Allston could sympathetically mold his perceptions to those of his friend. Recalling twenty-five years later the "honour" of Coleridge's continued "friendship," Allston writes:

> To no other man whom I have known, do I owe so much *of intellectually*, as to Mr. Coleridge. . . . . He used to call Rome the *silent* city; but I never could think of it as such, while with him; for, meet him when,

9: POSTSCRIPT: "OUR EXCELLENT TRANSATLANTIC FRIEND" 319

or where I would, the fountain of his mind was never dry, . . . its living stream seemed specially to flow for every classic ruin over which we wandered. And when I recall some of our walks under the pines of the Villa Borghese, I am almost tempted to dream that I had once listened to Plato, in the groves of the Academy.[11]

Coleridge's intellectual converse not only provides Allston with an ideal kind of Socratic education but also shapes his perceptions themselves, such that he now views Rome through Coleridge's words.

In 1806, fear of a Napoleonic invasion of Italy drove Coleridge first to Allston's villa outside Rome and then back to England. Once on board ship and thinking again of his English attachments, Coleridge retreats from a sympathetic converse and moves towards a more conservative, Wordsworthian discourse, which emphasizes the limits of sympathetic identification. Writing to his friend, Coleridge first distinguishes Allston and himself from those who continue the late-eighteenth-century indulgence in exaggerated protestations of friendship; Coleridge declares he had recently heard "a sad sad character of one of those, whom you call acquaintance—but who call you their dear Friend," and tries in this way subtly to dampen down Allston's enthusiam for friendship.[12]

Coleridge then situates himself within the conservative ideology of the 1790s, which highlights how an individual's previous attachments make new friendships harder to establish:

My dear Alston! somewhat from increasing age, but much more from calamity & intense pre-affections my heart is not open to more than kind good wishes in general; to you & to you alone since I have left England, I have felt more / and had I not known the Wordsworths, should have loved & esteemed you *first* and *most* / & as [it] is, next to them I love & honor you. (2:1173)

Coleridge honours Allston while reminding him of a hierarchy of intimacy, at the top of which are the Wordsworths. In Wordsworthian fashion, Coleridge suggests that the sincerity of his affection for Allston is underwritten by his acknowledgement of the limitation inherent in his friendship.

However, as Coleridge approached Grasmere in autumn 1806, thoughts of Allston brought still more late-eighteenth-century ideas of friendship into his mind. He confides to his notebook his experience of absence as transforming a sociable intercourse into friendship:

> To Alston / After the formation of a new acquaintance found by some weeks or months unintermitted Communion worthy of all our esteem, affection & perhaps admiration, an intervening Absence—whether we meet again or only write—raises it into friendship, and encourages the modesty of our nature, impelling us to assume the language and express all the feelings, of an established attachment.[13]

Coleridge draws again on the contemporary cultural drive to discover in absence an opportunity for figuring friendship as a spiritual bond with an idealized other. Absence works to erase the sense of difference Coleridge had experienced on his voyage, and it paradoxically intensifies his awareness of the men's bond. Thus Coleridge oscillates between feeling unable to mingle identities fully with Allston and experiencing the depth of their sympathetic correspondence.

If Coleridge's sojourn in Italy provoked a series of reflections on the degree to which his friendship with Allston could tend towards sympathetic unity, so these thoughts continued to develop during the renewal of the men's acquaintance on Allston's settlement in England (1811–1818). At its best, the friendship during these years illustrates how Coleridge's role could be not only that of the sympathizer but also the "advising" friend, one whose difference from Allston was as beneficial to the relationship as his capacity to participate in his friend's joys and woes.

The sympathetic aspect of Coleridge's friendship displayed itself in summer 1813, during Allston's serious illness. In hastening from London to Salt Hill to nurse his friend, Coleridge offered Allston the maternal mode of loving attention he had valued in Poole but had found wanting in Southey. Two years later, on hearing of Allston's devastated reaction to his wife's death, Coleridge reaffirms the centrality of sympathy in his friendship for the painter:

> I could have wished to have learnt more particulars from you respecting Yourself. I have, perhaps, felt too great an awe for the sacredness of Grief. But those of our Household know, with how deep and recurrent a sympathy I have followed you: and *I* know, what consolation it has been to *me*, that YOU have in every sense the consolations & the undoubting Hopes, of a Christian.[14]

Coleridge desires to hear "particulars" so as to enter more sympathetically into his friend's experience. As it is, Coleridge declares he feels his friend's loss as his own. Coleridge's desire to immerse himself in his friend's consciousness indicates the continuing importance to him of this typically Romantic mode of affection, so evident in his friendship with Poole in the mid-1790s.

Nevertheless, to the extent that advice-giving was as much a part of Coleridge's friendship with Poole as was sympathy, so advice continues to be a fundamental aspect of Coleridge's communications with Allston. Thanks in part to Allston's easy acceptance of Coleridge's advice, the friendship does not experience the tension between sympathy and advice-giving that mars other Coleridgean friendships. Coleridge's advice-giving was founded on his recognition of the men's difference, in particular their respective talents for painting and philosophy. In 1811, Coleridge informs Beaumont that Allston "means to exhibit but two or at the most three pictures, all poetical or history painting—in part, by my advice."[15] As a friend, Coleridge preserves a critical detachment in order to give advice and offer practical help. In a more personal context, on the death of Allston's wife, Coleridge delivers to his grieving friend the kind of bracing advice he had earlier offered Poole:

> Allston should say to himself, "*Nothing is me but my will*. These thoughts, therefore, that force themselves on my mind are no part of *me*, and there can be no guilt in them." If he will make a strong effort to become indifferent to their recurrence they will either cease, or cease to trouble him.[16]

According to his friend Charles Leslie, on hearing this advice Allston became less troubled by such disturbances.

However, the friends' relations during 1814 also demonstrate how they might struggle to make creative use of their different personalities. Faced with Allston's lack of communication during this period, Coleridge feels that the friendship is being undermined by cultural differences. Coleridge complains to Morgan that

> Allston has altogether forgot me: but I have not forgot him!—but I am an Englishman, & he is an American!—I was in my bitterest affliction glad to hear that his Picture had been noticed, however unworthily & by such a scurvy set of Judges. I intreated Bird to call on him and intreat him to write to me, tho' but *two* Lines—But I fear, Allston, tho' the very best & prime, is an American![17]

Americans lack the loyalty of their English counterparts, who sustain friendship even in "bitterest affliction." In defining Allston as the product of his culture, Coleridge suggests, in conservative terms reminiscent of *The Anti-Jacobin*, that their friendship will inevitably be undermined by their opposing national characteristics.

As he remarks to Morgan in June, despite his wish "to think with at least comparative respect of the New Englanders," Coleridge cannot "altogether get over, the almost uniform Experience of all who have had any concerns with any Americans."[18]

After a further meeting in July, Coleridge is astounded that "such a man with such a Heart & such Genius should be—not *an* American, but downright *American*,"[19] and in dismay Coleridge develops his argument that national allegiances create an artificial bar to friendship. At this point, however, as if turning the wheel of friendship into a new position, Coleridge voices dissatisfaction with the conservative ideology that sees inherent limitations to friendship. Instead, he invokes once more a radical cosmopolitan ideal of cross-cultural friendship grounded in religious premises. "The same game in Bristol as in London" Coleridge complains to Morgan:

> A. can visit *me*; but his own House & real Feelings belong as exclusive Property to his "Countrymen," as he called one of the Beasts last night: . . . "Countryman?" (said I) "Live the age of Methusalem, & you *may* have a right to say *that*, Allston!—At present, either the World is your Country, & England with all it's faults your *Home* [. . .] or you are *morally* not worthy of your high Gifts, which as a Painter give you a *praeternational* Privilege, even beyond the greatest Poet, by the universality of *your* Language: and you prefer the accident of Place, naked Place, unenriched by any of the associations of Law, Religion, or intellectual *Fountaincy*, to the essential grandeur of God in Man." (3:518)

Now Coleridge is echoing the Godwinian/Pantisocratic dictum that an individual's desire to retain "exclusive Property" (whether a chattel or private feelings) negates friendship's communal ideal. In these terms, Allston's perceived allegiance to his countrymen is an offence against his friendship with Coleridge. Conveniently forgetting that he, like Allston here, could periodically espouse the Wordsworthian sentiment that true confidence may be restricted to one's countrymen or even close family, Coleridge revisits the old radical idea of the "friend of humanity." He argues that painters are particularly capable of embodying this ideal, for the painter's visual language transcends the linguistic barriers that separate the mass of humanity from each other. Echoing "Religious Musings," Coleridge reaffirms the Christian underpinning to such radical notions, founding it on the omnipresent reality of "God in Man." Such a deep-seated unity of mankind represents for Coleridge a truth more profound than any insistence on cultural difference.

At the same time, Coleridge makes clear in this letter to Morgan that his vision of universal, cross-cultural friendship continues to be an idea from which women are excluded. In this he rehearses the traditional notion of friendship as a manly love, which both in his relations with Poole and during his Pantisocratic period, had expressed itself through an explicit denigration of women. As Southey's mother would corrupt the Pantisocratic children with false views of Christianity, so Coleridge represents Allston's wife as another conservative force confining friendship within a national group and spoiling the potential for transnational male brotherhood. "9 parts in 10" of Allston's "American" character is "owing" to his wife, whom Coleridge condemns in excremental terms as a "little Hydatid"—that is, a watery cyst caused by the larval stage of the tapeworm! He goes on:

> O that ... instead of being a *good* little Hydatid she had been an absolute Sarah +Mary +Edith +Eliza—*Fricker* ... with all the discontent, and miserableness of the Angel of the Race, self-nibbling Martha!— Then perhaps he might have hated her, & been a fine Fellow. (3:518)

Only by ridding himself of female company and influence could Allston realize Coleridge's ideal of male friendship.

Coleridge's unhappiness did not however break their bond. Allston's contemporary comments to another friend, Samuel Morse, suggest that he could ignore criticisms that might otherwise disturb the friendship, by utilizing a Coleridgean notion of respect for a man-in-himself. Allston reassures Morse that he remains unaffected by his friend's previous "hasty expressions":

> Be assured that they never were remembered by me a moment after; nor did they ever in the slightest degree diminish my regard or weaken my confidence in the sincerity of your friendship or the goodness of your heart. Besides, the consciousness of warmth in my own temper would have made me inexcusable had I suffered myself to dwell on an inadvertent word from another.[20]

Allston demonstrates another aspect of the conceptual framework needed to meet the various demands made on him by Coleridgean friendship. Indeed, the two men's relations show how Allston somehow managed to meet as they came along each of Coleridge's challenges to their friendship. Not only does Allston sympathize with Coleridge's various joys and sorrows, but he can happily participate in a pedagogic friendship based on Coleridge's philosophical teachings, accept his friend's advice, and allay Coleridge's periodic perception of their cultural differences.

In the following years Allston was often at Highgate for several days together, and by 1818, the two men both suggest that they have redeveloped the eighteenth-century ideal of accommodating differences with friendship. Coleridge's inclusion in *Sybilline Leaves* (1818) of Allston's poem "America to Great Britain" finds room for resolving their potentially alienating differences by bridging the personal and national.[21] While Coleridge emphasizes that the poem is "written by an American gentleman, a valued and dear friend" (p. 276), Allston's poem affirms the kinship existing between America and Great Britain.

Allston's editorial note confirms that in postulating a "moral union of the two Countries," he did not desire to end "the independence of *that* [country] which gave him birth" (p. 278). Nevertheless, as Coleridge and other radicals in the 1790s had striven to fill the space between nations and classes with amalgamating friendship, so Allston imagines England to be stretching its "mighty hand" across the Atlantic, while "conchs" on the seabed erase the nations' cultural divide by proclaiming their "kindred league" (pp. 276–77) Allston emphasizes that "the blood of England" still lives in American veins to the extent that this "voice of blood" will affirm "We are One" (pp. 277–78). Such unity is guaranteed for Allston by the influence of English "manners" and "arts" still clinging "around our hearts" (p. 278). As fraternity had provided the radicals with rhetorical grounds for transnational unities in the 1790s, so kinship continues to offer Allston a way of conceiving a deep organic bond between the two nations. Such a bond both renders superficial England and America's cultural divisions and underwrites Allston's optimistic vision of an amicable difference-in-unity between the recently warring nations.

In terms of their respective characters, Allston reflected throughout his life on the ways in which independent personalities could be joined in friendship. In *Monaldi* (1819–1822), his novel with an Italian setting, he rejects the Blakean model of opposition being true friendship.[22] In depicting the fictional relationship between the painter Monaldi and the philosopher-poet Maldura, Allston appears to draw on his encounter with Coleridge during 1805–1806. Allston represents these two friends as possessing "opposite" (p. 22) natures, which become expressed in part through their differing pursuits. In explaining how a friendship developed "so sincere that [Maldura] believed he could even lay down his life for [Monaldi]" Allston implicitly dismisses opposition as a cause for their "mutual attraction" (p. 22). Instead, he affirms Maldura's pleasure at Monaldi's praise for his extraordinary intellectual attainments.

Ultimately, in showing Maldura to be a villain, the novel demonstrates how opposite characters cannot sustain friendship.

It is in Allston's painting *The Sisters* (1818), however, that we can glimpse something of how he and Coleridge appreciated the role of difference in helping to define and strengthen their friendship.[23] As several critics have suggested, the painting's two "sisters" may represent the sister arts of painting and poetry—the figure of Poetry looking away from the viewer, Painting gazing directly at us.[24] But through this duality the painting may also reflect upon Coleridge and Allston's own friendship, an argument supported by Coleridge's naming of the painting and by Allston's special regard for the piece, which he never exhibited. (He sold it only for a high price twenty-five years later.)

As Gerald Eager observes, Coleridge viewed poetry and painting as two overlapping but distinct activities, with poetry as the "established, mature sister" (p. 301). While united by their embrace, the figures are, as Eager demonstrates, very different in appearance and attitude: "one is blonde with long flowing hair who looks at the viewer in three-quarter view; the other has dark, tightly bound hair, and she looks in lost profile towards the first figure" (p. 299). In turning her head towards the viewer, the dominant left-hand figure resists fully moving with the sister's embracing arm. Instead, she moves towards the viewer and away from her sister, thus asserting her separate identity. At the same time, the blonde figure's body willingly assents to her sister's intimate embrace. In this way, the painting suggests the deep sympathies between Allston and Coleridge while reaffirming their mutual independence. Indeed, through the metaphor of sisterhood both men emphasize that such difference-in-unity is consonant with a central ideal of Coleridge and his culture: to transform friendship into a familial bond.

Allston's departure to America in 1818 effectively marked the end of his correspondence and intimacy with Coleridge. Nevertheless, Coleridge continues to refer to Allston affectionately, and almost twenty years later Allston reaffirms the depth and unity of feeling achieved by these two friends in his sonnet "On Coleridge," which mourns the philosopher's death in 1834:

> And thou art gone, most loved, most honored friend!
> No, never more thy gentle voice shall blend
> With air of earth its pure ideal tones,
> Binding in one, as with harmonious zones,
> The heart and intellect. And I no more
> Shall with thee gaze on that unfathomed deep,

Washington Allston, *The Sisters* (c. 1816–1817). Courtesy of the Fogg Art Museum, Harvard University Art Museums, Gift of Mrs. Edward Moore. © President and Fellows of Harvard University.

> The Human Soul,—as when, pushed off the shore,
> Thy mystic bark would through the darkness sweep,
> Itself the while so bright! For oft we seemed
> As on some starless sea,—all dark above,
> All dark below,—yet, onward as we drove,
> To plough up light that ever round us streamed.
> But he who mourns is not as one bereft
> Of all he loved; thy living truths are left.[25]

Allston follows the eighteenth-century tradition of attempting to sustain the dead friend's presence in the mourner's consciousness. Allston poignantly testifies to the way in which Coleridge, as an adviser, mentor, and spiritual guide, had once lit up his friend's intellectual world. But by identifying Coleridge with his teachings, Allston strives to affirm once more the friends' intellectual unity through his assimilation of Coleridge's "living truths."

Finally, one possible truth regarding Coleridge's continuing attitude towards friendship might reveal itself in a letter to William Collins, written shortly after Allston's return to America in 1818. On the one hand, the middle-aged Coleridge can by this time easily express a general disillusionment with friendship, based on long experience. He declares that, "to feel the full force of the Christian religion, it is perhaps necessary, for many tempers, that they should first be made to feel, experimentally, the hollowness of human friendship." His final paragraph, however, immediately reaffirms the solidity of his bond with Allston: "We are all anxious to hear from, and of, our excellent transatlantic friend." Thus disillusionment for Coleridge may itself continue to give way to his deapseated passion for friendship. Indeed, with Allston's removal, Coleridge's enthusiasm for society immediately directs itself towards new objects: "I need not repeat," Coleridge flatters Collins,

> that your company, with or without our friend Leslie, will gratify
> Your sincere,
> S. T. Coleridge.[26]

Notes

INTRODUCTION

1. *The Notebooks of Samuel Taylor Coleridge*, ed. Kathleen Coburn [vol. 4 ed. with Morten Christensen], 4 double vols. (London: Routledge & Kegan Paul, 1957–), 4175 (reference to note no.). Hereafter, *Notebooks*.

2. Samuel Johnson, *A Dictionary of the English Language*, 2 vols. (London: J. Knapton and others, 1755), s.v. "Irruption," n. 1: "The act of any thing forcing an entrance." Johnson cites *Harvey*: "A full and subtle *irruption* of thick melancholick blood into the heart puts a stop to its pulsation;" and *Burnet*: "There are frequent inundations made in maritime countries by the *irruption* of the sea."

3. Geoffrey Yarlott, *Coleridge and the Abyssinian Maid* (London: Methuen, 1967), 32.

4. Molly Lefebure, *The Bondage of Love: A Life of Mrs Samuel Taylor Coleridge* (London: Victor Gollancz, 1986), 76.

5. Charles Atkinson, Jr., *The Mind's Monitor; or, A Serious Discourse on the Advantages of Self-Preservation, Society, Friendship, Love, Learning, Religion, and on Death* (Leeds: Thomas Gill, 1793), 25–27.

6. Southey to John May, [18 February 1800]; *The Letters of Robert Southey to John May, 1797 to 1838*, ed. Charles Ramos (Austin: Pemberton Press, 1976), 50–51.

7. Anthony John Harding, *Coleridge and the Idea of Love: Aspects of Relationship in Coleridge's Thought and Writing* (London: Cambridge University Press, 1974); J. Robert Barth, *Coleridge and the Power of Love* (Columbia: University of Missouri Press, 1988).

8. "Caius," "On Imprudent Friendships," *The Universal Magazine of Knowledge and Pleasure* 92 (1793):327.

9. *Dictionary*, s.v. "Friendship," n. 1.

10. *Dictionary*, s.v. "Friendship," n. 2; "Friend," n. 2, 6, 4, 5.

11. *The Complete Poetical Works of Samuel Taylor Coleridge*, ed. Ernest Hartley Coleridge, 2 vols. (Oxford: Clarendon Press, 1912), 2:1012.

12. Barth, *Coleridge and the Power of Love*, 7.

13. Lockridge, *Coleridge the Moralist* (Ithaca: Cornell University Press, 1977), 185, 111, 185–86.

14. Coleridge, *Complete Poetical Works*, 1:4.

15. Lucy Newlyn, "Coleridge and the Anxiety of Reception," *Romanticism* 1 (1995): 207.

16. E. S. Shaffer, "The Hermeneutic Community: Coleridge and Schleiermacher," in *The Coleridge Connection: Essays for Thomas McFarland*, ed. Richard Gravil and Molly Lefebure (Basingstoke: Macmillan, 1990), 200–229.

17. Coleridge, *The Friend* (1809–1810, 1818), ed. Barbara E. Rooke, 2 vols.

(London: Routledge & Kegan Paul; Princeton: Princeton University Press, 1969), 2:75.

18. Deirdre Coleman, *Coleridge and "The Friend" (1809–1810)* (Oxford: Clarendon Press, 1988), 51.

19. *Notebooks*, 904.

20. Stephen Bygrave, *Coleridge and the Self: Romantic Egotism* (Basingstoke: Macmillan, 1986), 3.

21. *Notebooks*, 1772.

22. Coleridge, *Poems on Various Subjects* (London: G. G. and J. Robinson; Bristol: J. Cottle, 1796), viii.

23. Walter Jackson Bate, *Coleridge* (London: Weidenfeld and Nicolson, 1969), 50.

24. Eugene L. Stelzig, "Coleridge in *The Prelude*: Wordsworth's Fiction of Alterity," *Wordsworth Circle* 18 (1987): 25.

25. Charles J. Rzepka, *The Self as Mind: Vision and Identity in Wordsworth, Coleridge, and Keats* (Cambridge: Harvard University Press, 1986), 101.

26. Mary Shelley, *Frankenstein: or, The Modern Prometheus* (1818) (London: Henry Colburn and Richard Bentley, corr. and rev. 1831), 16.

27. Lockridge, *The Ethics of Romanticism* (Cambridge: Cambridge University Press, 1989), 445.

28. Lockridge, *Coleridge the Moralist*, 115.

29. William Godwin, *An Enquiry Concerning Political Justice, and its Influence on General Virtue and Happiness*, 2 vols. (London: G. G. J. and J. Robinson, 1793), 2:848.

30. Coleridge to Godwin, 22 January 1802; *The Collected Letters of Samuel Taylor Coleridge*, ed. Earl Leslie Griggs, 6 vols. (Oxford: Clarendon Press, 1956–1971), 2:784. All quotations by permission of Oxford University Press.

31. Coleridge to Godwin, 22 September 1801, *Letters of Samuel Taylor Coleridge*, 2:761.

32. Beverly Fields, *Reality's Dark Dream: Dejection in Coleridge*, (Kent, Ohio: Kent State University Press, 1967), 13.

33. Kelvin Everest, *Coleridge's Secret Ministry: The Context of the Conversation Poems 1795–1798* (Hassocks: Harvester Press, 1979), 41.

34. Charles Lloyd, *Poems on Various Subjects* (Carlisle: J. Richardson, 1795), 3.

35. Coleridge to John Prior Estlin, 14 May 1798, *Letters of Samuel Taylor Coleridge*, 1:245.

36. Timothy Fulford, *Coleridge's Figurative Language* (Basingstoke: Macmillan, 1991), 4–5.

37. Ronald A. Sharp, *Friendship and Literature: Spirit and Form* (Durham, NC: Duke University Press, 1986), 113–14.

38. Coleridge, "First Draft. An Effusion at Evening Written in August, 1792," in *Complete Poetical Works*, 1:49–50.

39. Thomas McFarland, *Romanticism and the Forms of Ruin: Wordsworth, Coleridge, and Modalities of Fragmentation* (Princeton: Princeton University Press, 1981), 56–103.

40. Coleridge to Thomas Clarkson, 13 October 1806, *Letters of Samuel Taylor Coleridge*, 2:1197.

41. M. H. Abrams, *The Mirror and the Lamp: Romantic Theory and the Critical Tradition* (New York: Oxford University Press, 1953), 224.

42. William Roberts, "Female Friendship," in *The Looker-On, A Periodical*

Paper by the Rev. Simon Olive-Branch, A. M., 3rd ed., 4 vols. (London: G. G. and J. Robinson, 1795), 4:311–12.

43. John Beer, *Coleridge's Poetic Intelligence* (Basingstoke: Macmillan, 1977).

44. *Samuel Taylor Coleridge: Selected Letters*, ed. H. J. Jackson (Oxford: Clarendon Press, 1987), ix.

45. William C. Dowling, *The Epistolary Moment: The Poetics of the Eighteenth-Century Verse Epistle* (Princeton: Princeton University Press, 1991), 36.

46. Lockridge, *Coleridge the Moralist*, 34.

47. Poole to Henrietta Warwick, 6 February 1796; Mrs. Henry Sandford, *Thomas Poole and his Friends*, 2 vols. (London: Macmillan, 1888), 1:131–32.

48. Godwin to Coleridge, 5 September 1800, MS MA 1857 (10), Pierpont Morgan Library, New York.

49. Thomas J. McCarthy, *Relationships of Sympathy: The Writer and the Reader in British Romanticism* (Aldershot: Scolar Press, 1997), 87.

50. Coleridge, *Marginalia: Camden to Hutton*, ed. George Whalley (London: Routledge & Kegan Paul; Princeton: Princeton University Press, 1984), 232.

51. Griggs, "Coleridge as Revealed in his Letters," in *Coleridge's Variety: Bicentenary Studies*, ed. John Beer (London: Macmillan, 1974), 33.

52. [Anon.], *The Complete Letter-Writer, Containing Familiar Letters on the most Common Occasions in Life* (Falkirk: Patrick Mair, 1792), 38.

53. Grosvenor Charles Bedford to Southey, 20 January 1795, MS Eng. Lett. d.50, fols 3v–4r, Bodleian Library, Oxford. By permission of The Bodleian Library.

54. Coleridge to Godwin, 23 June 1801, *Letters of Samuel Taylor Coleridge*, 2:736.

55. Southey to Grosvenor Bedford, 19 August 1801, MS Eng. Lett. c.23, fol. 104r, Bodleian Library, Oxford. By permission of The Bodleian Library.

56. Grosvenor Bedford to Southey, 23 August 1801, MS Eng. Lett. d.50, fol. 15v, Bodleian Library, Oxford. By permission of The Bodleian Library.

57. Coleridge to Poole, 13 December 1796, *Letters of Samuel Taylor Coleridge*, 1:273.

58. Coleridge to Poole, 5 November [1796], *Letters of Samuel Taylor Coleridge*, 1:249.

59. Coleridge to Poole, [endorsed: 12 December 1796], *Letters of Samuel Taylor Coleridge*, 1:271.

60. In Coleridge, *Poems* (1796), 110.

61. William Christie, "The Act of Love in Coleridge's Conversation Poems," *Sydney Studies in English* 7 (1981–1982): 14.

62. Coleridge, ed., *Sonnets from Various Authors* (Bristol: the author, 1796).

63. George McLean Harper, "Coleridge's Conversation Poems," in *English Romantic Poets: Modern Essays in Criticism*, ed. M. H. Abrams, 2d ed. (London: Oxford University Press), 189.

64. Coleridge to Southey, [c. 17 July 1797], *Letters of Samuel Taylor Coleridge*, 1:334.

65. Stuart Curran, *Poetic Form and British Romanticism* (New York: Oxford University Press, 1986), 109.

66. Coleridge to Sir George and Lady Beaumont, 2 [1] February 1804, *Letters of Samuel Taylor Coleridge*, 2:1054–55.

67. Julie Ellison, *Delicate Subjects: Romanticism, Gender, and the Ethics of Understanding* (Ithaca: Cornell University Press, 1990), 31.

68. Janet Todd, *Sensibility: An Introduction* (London: Methuen, 1986), 140.

69. Coleridge to Southey, [7 December 1797], *Letters of Samuel Taylor Coleridge*, 1:359.

70. Jeffrey Richards, "'Passing the love of women': Manly Love and Victorian Society," in *Manliness and Morality: Middle-Class Masculinity in Britain and America 1800–1940*, ed. J. A. Mangan and James Walvin (Manchester: Manchester University Press, 1987), 93.

71. *Notebooks*, 1065.

72. C. S. Lewis, *The Four Loves* (London: Geoffrey Bles, 1960), 83–84.

73. Coleridge to Southey, [13] November 1795, *Letters of Samuel Taylor Coleridge*, 1:166–67.

74. In *Reality's Dark Dream*, Beverly Fields highlights the homoerotic subtext of Coleridge's letters to Southey during 1794–1795: see 16–17.

75. Wayne Koestenbaum, *Double Talk: The Erotics of Male Literary Collaboration* (New York: Routledge, 1989), 77.

76. Shearer West, "Libertinism and the Ideology of Male Friendship in the Portraits of the Society of Dilettanti," *Eighteenth-Century Life* 16 (1992): 97.

77. Mary A. Favret, *Romantic Correspondence: Women, Politics and the Fiction of Letters* (Cambridge: Cambridge University Press, 1993), 27.

78. Paul Magnuson, *Reading Public Romanticism* (Princeton: Princeton University Press, 1998), 67.

79. Karl Kroeber, "Coleridge's 'Fears': Problems in Patriotic Poetry," *Clio: An Interdisciplinary Journal of Literature, History and the Philosophy of History* 7 (1978): 368.

80. A. R. Humphreys, "'The Friend of Mankind' (1700–60)—An Aspect of Eighteenth-Century Sensibility," *RES* 24 (1948): 203.

81. David Aers, Jonathan Cook, and David Punter, "Coleridge: Individual, Community and Social Agency," in *Romanticism and Ideology: Studies in English Writing 1765–1830* (London: Routledge & Kegan Paul, 1981), 87.

82. Michel de Montaigne, *Essays* (1580), trans. and introd. J. M. Cohen (London: Penguin, 1958), 99.

83. Allan Bloom, *Love and Friendship* (New York: Simon & Schuster, 1993), 419.

84. Carl R. Woodring, *Politics in the Poetry of Coleridge* (Madison: University of Wisconsin Press, 1961), 90.

85. Coleridge, *The Plot Discovered; or An Address to the People, Against Ministerial Treason* (Bristol, 1795), in *Lectures 1795 on Politics and Religion*, ed. Lewis Patton and Peter Mann (London: Routledge & Kegan Paul; Princeton: Princeton University Press, 1970), 289. All quotations by permission of Routledge Press.

86. *Notebooks*, 4441.

87. "Friendship," in *Encyclopædia Britannica; or, A Dictionary of Arts, Sciences, and Miscellaneous Literature, on a Plan Entirely New*, 18 vols. (Dublin: J. Moore, 1790–1797), 7:467–76.

1. Transcendence and Its Limits

1. Abraham Skelton, *The Temple of Friendship* (York: W. Blanchard, 1792), 1.

2. Coleridge, "The Nightingale; A Conversational Poem, written in April, 1798," in *Lyrical Ballads* (1798), 63–69.

3. *Dictionary*, s.v. "Experience," n. 2.

4. Jean H. Hagstrum, *Samuel Johnson's Literary Criticism* (Chicago: University of Chicago Press, 1952), 7.

5. Wendell V. Harris, *The Omnipresent Debate: Empiricism and Transcen-

dentalism in Nineteenth-Century English Prose (Dekalb: Northern Illinois University Press, 1981), 8, 10.

6. Ann Yearsley, *The Rural Lyre; A Volume of Poems: Dedicated to the Right Honourable the Earl of Bristol, Lord Bishop of Derby* (London: G. G. and J. Robinson, 1796), 68.

7. Lucinda Cole and Richard G. Swartz, "'Why Should I Wish for Words?': Literacy, Articulation, and the Borders of Literary Culture," in *At the Limits of Romanticism: Essays in Cultural, Feminist, and Materialist Criticism*, ed. Mary A. Favret and Nicola J. Watson (Bloomington: Indiana University Press, 1994), 152.

8. Ann Yearsley, *Poems, on Several Occasions* (London: T. Cadell, 1785), 80.

9. The Bible (Authorized Version), Mal. 3: 2.

10. *The Poems of Samuel Johnson*, 2nd ed., ed. David Nichol Smith and Edward L. McAdam (Oxford: Clarendon Press, 1974), 38.

11. Ann Yearsley, *Poems, on Various Subjects* (London: G. G. J. and J. Robinson, 1787), 83–91.

12. Coleridge to Thelwall, 31 December 1796, *Letters of Samuel Taylor Coleridge*, 1:294.

13. [Anon.], *The Amicable Quixote; or, The Enthusiasm of Friendship*, 4 vols. (London: J. Walter, 1788).

14. Wordsworth, "Ode," in *Poems, in Two Volumes* (London: Longman and others, 1807), 2:150.

15. "The Guardian Angel," *Universal Magazine* 89 (1791): 13.

16. "Caius," "On Imprudent Friendships," *Universal Magazine* 92 (1793): 329.

17. Leigh Hunt, *Juvenilia; or, A Collection of Poems: Written between the Ages of Twelve and Sixteen*, 2nd ed. (London: J. Whiting, 1801), 31.

18. Coleridge, "To a Young Lady," *Poems* (1796), 36–39.

19. Poole to Coleridge, 24 January 1799, Add. MS 35343, fol. 201v, British Library, London. By permission of The British Library.

20. John Mullan, *Sentiment and Sociability: The Language of Feeling in the Eighteenth Century* (Oxford: Clarendon Press, corr. ed. 1990), 201.

21. Marcus Tullius Cicero, *Cato and Lælius: or, Essays on Old Age and Friendship*, ed. William Melmoth, 2 vols. (London: J. Dodsley, 1795).

22. James Boswell, *Life of Johnson*, 3rd ed., ed. R. W. Chapman, rev. J. D. Fleeman (London: Oxford University Press, 1970), 848.

23. Coleridge to Mrs. S. T. Coleridge, 3 October 1798, *Letters of Samuel Taylor Coleridge*, 1:421.

24. *The Works of Jane Austen*, ed. R. W. Chapman, 6 vols. (London: Oxford University Press,1923–1954; repr. and rev. 1959–1963), 6:85.

25. Southey to Coleridge, February 1804; *The Life and Correspondence of the Late Robert Southey*, ed. Charles Cuthbert Southey, 6 vols. (London: Longman and others, 1849–1850), 2:266.

26. Coleridge to Southey, 20 February 1804, *Letters of Samuel Taylor Coleridge*, 2:1073.

27. Lloyd, *Edmund Oliver*, 2 vols. (Bristol: Joseph Cottle), 2:57.

28. Rosemary Ashton, *The Life of Samuel Taylor Coleridge: A Critical Biography* (Oxford: Blackwell, 1996), 132.

29. [Anon.], "Possibility of Friendship between Persons of Unequal Ranks—Situation of the Countess of Fairdale," in *The Philanthrope: After the Manner of a Periodical Paper* (London: T. Cadell, Jr., and W. Davies, 1797), vii.

30. Yearsley, "To Stella," *Poems, on Several Occasions*, 65.
31. William Godwin, *Memoirs of the Author of "A Vindication of the Rights of Woman"* (London: J. Johnson, 1798), 57.
32. Yearsley, "On Being Presented with a Silver Pen," *Poems, on Various Subjects*, 11.
33. "Fraternal," in *Encyclopædia Britannica* (1792), 7:451.
34. Godwin to unnamed brother, 20 November 1799, Ab. MS Dep. b227/8(a), Bodleian Library, Oxford. By permission of Lord Abinger, conveyed through The Bodleian Library, Oxford.
35. Elizabeth Mavor, *The Ladies of Llangollen: A Study in Romantic Friendship* (London: Penguin, 1971).
36. Klaus Lankheit, *Das Freundschaftsbild der Romantik* (Heidelberg: Carl Winter, Universitätsverlag, 1952), 71–72. I am grateful to Dr. Felicity von Peter for this translation from the German.
37. Coleridge to James Webbe Tobin, 19 April 1804, *Letters of Samuel Taylor Coleridge*, 2:1131.
38. Coleridge, *Shorter Works and Fragments*, ed. H. J. Jackson and J. R. de J. Jackson, 2 vols. (London: Routledge & Kegan Paul; Princeton: Princeton University Press, 1995), 2:1337.
39. *Sublime Friendship Delineated*, comp. John Donovan (Cork: J. Cronin, 1789).
40. Coleridge to Southey, 13 July [1794], *Letters of Samuel Taylor Coleridge*, 1:86.
41. Coleridge, *Lectures 1795 on Politics and Religion*, ed. Lewis Patton and Peter Mann (London: Routledge & Kegan Paul; Princeton: Princeton University Press, 1970), 162–63.
42. Rev. Joseph Fawcett, "Christianity Vindicated in not Particularly Inculcating Friendship and Patriotism," *Universal Magazine* 98 (1796): 117–22.
43. John Kay, "Friendship," in *Catalogue of Political and Personal Satires, Preserved in the Department of Prints and Drawings in the British Museum*, ed. Frederick George Stephens and Mary Dorothy George, 11 vols. (London: By Order of the Trustees, 1870–1954), 8369. © Copyright The British Museum.
44. Coleridge to Thelwall, 17 December [1796], *Letters of Samuel Taylor Coleridge*, 1:279.
45. *The Poems of William Cowper*, ed. John D. Baird and Charles Ryskamp, 3 vols. (Oxford: Clarendon Press, 1980–1995), 1:453–56.
46. Coleridge to George Coleridge, 22 June 1791, *Letters of Samuel Taylor Coleridge*, 1:13.
47. See Ann Matheson, "The Influence of Cowper's *The Task* on Coleridge's Conversation Poems," in *New Approaches to Coleridge: Biographical and Critical Essays*, ed. Donald Sultana (London: Vision Press, 1981), 137–50.
48. [Anon.], "Enjoying a Friend," *Catalogue of Political and Personal Satires*, 7:9330. © Copyright The British Museum.
49. Cowper, "Gratitude. Addressed to Lady Hesketh," *Poems of William Cowper*, 3:21–22.
50. Cowper, "On Friendship," *Poems of William Cowper*, 1:445–53.
51. Manuscript variant, *Poems of William Cowper*, 1:447.
52. Morris Golden, *In Search of Stability: The Poetry of William Cowper* (New Haven: College and University Press, 1960), 31.
53. Cowper, "On a True Friend," *Poems of William Cowper*, 3:245.
54. *OED*, s.v. "manage," v. 6b, first recorded 1714; v. 8a, first recorded 1706–1707.

55. Bruce Redford, *The Converse of the Pen: Acts of Intimacy in the Eighteenth-Century Familiar Letter* (Chicago: University of Chicago Press, 1986), 3.

56. Samuel Johnson, *Lives of the English Poets*, ed. George Birkbeck Hill, 3 vols. (Oxford: Clarendon Press, 1905), 3:207.

57. *Notebooks*, 987.

58. [Eliza Hayley], *The Triumph of Acquaintance over Friendship: An Essay for the Times* (London: T. Cadell, Jr., and W. Davies, 1796). Hayley's "dedication" is dated 1788.

59. Elderton, "Friendship Defined. An Epistle," *The Gentleman's Magazine (and Historical Chronicle)* 61 (1791): 261–62.

60. Johnson, "Life of Hammond," in *Lives of the Poets*, 2:315.

2. Idea and Substance

1. Coleridge to Poole, [15 September 1798], *Letters of Samuel Taylor Coleridge*, 1:415. An edited version of this chapter appeared in the *Coleridge Bulletin*, 15 (2000): 41–55. It is reproduced here by permission of the editors of the *Coleridge Bulletin*.

2. *OED*, s.v. "Involve," v. 1.

3. Thomas McCarthy, *Relationships of Sympathy: The Writer and the Reader in British Romanticism* (Aldershot: Scolar Press, 1997), 98–99.

4. Coleridge to Poole, [7 October 1795], *Letters of Samuel Taylor Coleridge*, 1:160.

5. Poole to Coleridge, 10 October 1795, *Thomas Poole and his Friends*, 1:121–22.

6. Poole to Coleridge, 10 October 1795, Add. MS 35343, fol. 86r–v, British Library, London. By permission of The British Library.

7. Poole to Coleridge, 26 September 1796, *Thomas Poole and his Friends*, 1:160–61.

8. Coleridge to Poole, [16 March 1801], *Letters of Samuel Taylor Coleridge*, 2:707.

9. Poole to Coleridge, 25 May 1803, Add. MS 35343, fol. 330r–v, British Library, London. By permission of The British Library.

10. Coleridge, "Effusion 16, To an Old Man," *Poems* (1796), 61. This sonnet is better known by its later title, "Pity."

11. Coleridge to Poole, [?26] July 1797, *Letters of Samuel Taylor Coleridge*, 1:338.

12. 2 Kings 2.9.

13. Rev. Daniel Turner, *Sacred Friendship, Exemplified In the Case of Elijah and Elisha. A Sermon Preached [. . .] on the Death of Mrs. Eliza Turner* (London: G. G. J. and J. Robinson, 1786), 3–4.

14. Poole to Coleridge, 28 March 1796, *Thomas Poole and his Friends*, 1:143.

15. Coleridge to Poole, [13 May 1796], *Letters of Samuel Taylor Coleridge*, 1:210–11.

16. Coleridge to Poole, 24 September 1796, *Letters of Samuel Taylor Coleridge*, 1:235.

17. See Introduction, 28–29.

18. Coleridge to Poole, 5 November [1796], *Letters of Samuel Taylor Coleridge*, 1:249.

19. *Poems, by S. T. Coleridge, Second Edition. To which are Now Added Poems*

by Charles Lamb, and Charles Lloyd (Bristol: J. Cottle; London: Messrs Robinson, 1797), vii–xii.

20. John Milton, *Paradise Lost* (1667), ed. Alastair Fowler (London: Longman, 1971).

21. Thomas De Quincey, *Recollections of the Lakes and the Lake Poets*, ed. David Wright (Harmondsworth: Penguin, 1970), 35.

22. Kathleen Jones, *A Passionate Sisterhood: The Sisters, Wives and Daughters of the Lake Poets* (London: Virago, 1998), 107.

23. Poole to Coleridge, [January 1798], *Thomas Poole and his Friends*, 1:259.

24. Elizabeth Mavor, *The Ladies of Llangollen: A Study of Romantic Friendship*, (London: Michael Joseph, 1971).

25. Coleridge to Poole, 28 September 1798, *Letters of Samuel Taylor Coleridge*, 1:418.

26. Holmes, *Coleridge: Early Visions*, 125.

27. Coleridge to Poole, 6 May 1799, *Letters of Samuel Taylor Coleridge*, 1:490.

28. Rachel C. Crawford, "The Romantic Subject and the Poetry of the Bower: Coleridge, Wordsworth, and Keats" (unpublished doctoral thesis, University of Washington, 1989), 9.

29. Poole to Coleridge, 25 May 1803, Add. MS 35343, fol. 330v, British Library, London. By permission of The British Library.

30. Tom Mayberry, *Coleridge and Wordsworth in the West Country* (Stroud: Alan Sutton, 1992), 69.

31. Coleridge to Poole, 11 April 1796, *Letters of Samuel Taylor Coleridge*, 1:204.

32. Coleridge to Poole, [27 January 1798], *Letters of Samuel Taylor Coleridge*, 1:381.

33. Coleridge to Poole, 15 January 1804, *Letters of Samuel Taylor Coleridge*, 2:1036.

34. Silviana Pastorella, *The Cottage of Friendship, A Legendary Pastoral* (London: J. Bew and H. G. Pridden, 1788).

35. Coleridge, *Fears in Solitude, Written in 1798, During the Alarm of an Invasion. To which are Added, France, An Ode; and Frost at Midnight* (London: J. Johnson, 1798), 1–12.

36. Coleridge to Poole, [endorsed: 12 December 1796], *Letters of Samuel Taylor Coleridge*, 1:271.

37. William Hazlitt, "My First Acquaintance with Poets" (1823), in *The Complete Works of William Hazlitt*, ed. P. P. Howe, 21 vols. (London: J. M. Dent, 1930), 17:119.

38. Text from the earliest manuscript version, included in a letter to Southey, c. 17 July 1797, *Letters of Samuel Taylor Coleridge*, 1:334–36.

39. Paul Magnuson, *Coleridge's Nightmare Poetry* (Charlottesville: University Press of Virginia, 1974), 27–28.

40. Michael Raiger, "The Poetics of Liberation in Imaginative Power: Coleridge's 'This Lime Tree Bower my Prison,'" *European Romantic Review* 3 (1992): 72.

41. Coleridge, *The Statesman's Manual* (1816), in *Lay Sermons*, ed. R. J. White (London: Routledge & Kegan Paul; Princeton: Princeton University Press, 1972), 30.

42. Anna Laetitia Barbauld, "To Mr Coleridge" (1797), *Monthly Magazine* 7 (1799): 231–32.

43. Poole to Coleridge, 8 August [1796], *Thomas Poole and his Friends*, 1:153.

44. Coleridge to Poole, 14 December 1801, *Letters of Samuel Taylor Coleridge*, 2:776–77.

45. Poole, "Hail to thee Coldridge, youth of various powers!," 12 September 1795, *Thomas Poole and his Friends*, 1:126.

46. Coleridge to Poole, 26 October 1798, *Letters of Samuel Taylor Coleridge*, 1:430.

47. Allan Bloom, *Love and Friendship* (New York: Simon & Shuster, 1993), 205.

48. "Moralis," "On the Fidelity of Friendship," *Universal Magazine* 91 (1792): 266.

49. Coleridge to Cottle, [7 March 1798], *Letters of Samuel Taylor Coleridge*, 1:391.

50. Coleridge to Wordsworth, [23] January 1798, *Letters of Samuel Taylor Coleridge*, 1:379.

51. George Dekker, *Coleridge and the Literature of Sensibility* (London: Vision Press, 1978), 64.

52. Poole's gendering of advice-giving reflects a broader cultural pattern, as is revealed in texts such as John Donovan's compilation, *Sublime Friendship Delineated* (1789).

53. Coleridge to Josiah Wedgwood, 1 November 1800, *Letters of Samuel Taylor Coleridge*, 1:643–44.

54. Coleridge to Poole, 15 January 1804, *Letters of Samuel Taylor Coleridge*, 2:1036.

55. Coleridge to Poole, 5 October 1801, *Letters of Samuel Taylor Coleridge*, 2:763–64.

56. Coleridge to Poole, 5 November [1796], *Letters of Samuel Taylor Coleridge*, 1:251.

57. Quoted in Cornelia A. H. Crosse, "Thomas Poole," *Temple Bar* 87 (1889): 364.

58. Poole to Coleridge, 21 January 1800, *Thomas Poole and his Friends*, 2:3.

59. Coleridge to Poole, 7 [5] July 1801, *Letters of Samuel Taylor Coleridge*, 2:740.

60. Coleridge to Poole, 5 October 1801, *Letters of Samuel Taylor Coleridge*, 2:764–65.

61. "C. C. C.," "Gleanings," *Universal Magazine* 94 (1794): 118–19.

62. Coleridge to Poole, 1 February 1801, *Letters of Samuel Taylor Coleridge*, 2:668.

63. The Cornell Manuscript, *Coleridge's "Dejection": The Earliest Manuscript and the Earliest Printings*, ed. Stephen Maxfield Parrish (Ithaca: Cornell University Press, 1988), 106–31.

3. The Problem of Pantisocratic Friendship

1. Poole to Mr Haskins, 22 September 1794, *Tom Poole and his Friends*, 1:97.
2. *OED*, s.v. "Disposition," n. 6
3. William Godwin, *An Enquiry Concerning Political Justice, and its Influence on General Virtue and Happiness*, 2 vols. (London: G. G. J. and J. Robinson, 1793).
4. Southey to Grosvenor Bedford, 1 October 1795, *Correspondence of the Late Robert Southey*, 1:247.

5. Southey to Horace Walpole Bedford, 1 August 1794; *New Letters of Robert Southey*, ed. Kenneth Curry, 2 vols. (New York: Columbia University Press, 1965), 1:65.
6. Southey to Grosvenor Bedford, [27 September 1794], *New Letters of Robert Southey*, 1:80.
7. William Godwin, *Things as they are; or, The Adventures of Caleb Williams*, 3 vols. (London: B. Crosby, 1794), 3:261.
8. Southey to Horace Bedford, 22 August 1794, *New Letters of Robert Southey*, 1:70.
9. Southey to Grosvenor Bedford, 12 June 1794, *Correspondence of the Late Robert Southey*, 1:210.
10. Coleridge to Southey, [6 July 1794], *Letters of Samuel Taylor Coleridge*, 1:83.
11. *OED*, s.v. "Attention," n. 3, first recorded 1752.
12. Lawrence A. Blum, *Moral Perception and Particularity* (Cambridge: Cambridge University Press, 1994), 12.
13. Coleridge to George Cornish, 12 March 1794, *Letters of Samuel Taylor Coleridge*, 1:72.
14. Coleridge to George Coleridge, [14 March 1794], *Letters of Samuel Taylor Coleridge*, 1:73.
15. Coleridge to Southey, 1 August 1803, *Letters of Samuel Taylor Coleridge*, 2:959.
16. Coleridge to Southey, 13 July [1794], *Letters of Samuel Taylor Coleridge*, 1:87.
17. David Hartley, *Observations on Man, his Frame, his Duty, and his Expectations* (1749), 2 vols. (repr. London: J. Johnson, 1791).
18. Leonard W. Deen, "Coleridge and the Sources of Pantisocracy: Godwin, the Bible, and Hartley," *Boston University Studies in English* 5 (1961): 242.
19. Nicola Trott, "The Coleridge Circle and the 'Answer to Godwin,'" *RES* 41 (1990): 216.
20. Coleridge to Southey, 1 September 1794, *Letters of Samuel Taylor Coleridge*, 1:99.
21. Coleridge to Southey, 18 September [1794], *Letters of Samuel Taylor Coleridge*, 1:103.
22. Coleridge to Edith Fricker, 17 September 1794, *Letters of Samuel Taylor Coleridge*, 1:102.
23. Coleridge to Francis Wrangham, 24 October 1794, *Letters of Samuel Taylor Coleridge*, 1:121.
24. Coleridge to Southey, 17 December 1794, *Letters of Samuel Taylor Coleridge*, 1:142–43.
25. Mary Wollstonecraft, *Original Stories from Real Life; with Conversations, Calculated to Regulate the Affections, and Form the Mind to Truth and Goodness* (London: J. Johnson, 1791), 15–16.
26. Coleridge to Southey, 18 September [1794], *Letters of Samuel Taylor Coleridge*, 1:104.
27. George Burnett to Nicholas Lightfoot, 22 October 1796, MS Eng. Lett. c.453, fol. 198r, Bodleian Library, Oxford. By permission of The Bodleian Library, Oxford.
28. Coleridge, *A Moral and Theological Lecture, Delivered at Bristol* (Bristol, 1795), in *Lectures 1795*, 11.
29. Roe, *Wordsworth and Coleridge: The Radical Years*, 113.

30. Coleridge, "Monody on the Death of Chatterton," *Poems* (1796), 1–11.
31. William Godwin, *The Enquirer. Reflections on Education, Manners, and Literature* (London: G. G. and J. Robinson, 1797), 130.
32. Nigel Leask, "Pantisocracy and the Politics of the 'Preface' to *Lyrical Ballads*," in *Reflections of Revolution: Images of Romanticism*, ed. Alison Yarrington and Kelvin Everest (London: Routledge, 1993), 47.
33. Coleridge to Southey, 19 September [1794], *Letters of Samuel Taylor Coleridge*, 1:105.
34. Robert Lovell and Robert Southey, *Poems: Containing "The Retrospect," Odes, Elegies, Sonnets, &c.* (Bath: R. Cruttwell, 1794).
35. Mark Storey, *Robert Southey: A Life* (Oxford: Oxford University Press, 1997), 78.
36. Southey to Thomas Southey, 12 October 1794, *New Letters of Robert Southey*, 1:81–82.
37. Christopher J. P. Smith, *A Quest for Home: Reading Robert Southey* (Liverpool: Liverpool University Press, 1997), 75.
38. Southey to Horace Bedford, 22 August 1794, *New Letters of Robert Southey*, 1:71.
39. Southey to Grosvenor Bedford, 10 September 1794, *New Letters of Robert Southey*, 1:77.
40. In "Retirement: An Ode," Joseph Warton desires to escape the corruption of the city by retreating into the depths of the countryside. He asks the "Nymphs of the Groves" to

> Conduct me to your thickest Shade,
> Deep in the Bosom of the Vale,
> Where haunts the lonesome Nightingale;
> Where *Contemplation*, Maid divine,
> Leans against some aged Pine,
> Wrapt in stedfast Thought profound,
> Her Eyes fixt stedfast on the Ground.

(*Poems on Several Occasions. By the Reverend Mr. Thomas Warton* [London: R. Manly and H. S. Cox, 1748], 15.)

41. Coleridge to Southey, 21 October [1794], *Letters of Samuel Taylor Coleridge*, 1:112–13.
42. Coleridge to Southey, postmark: 29 December 1794, *Letters of Samuel Taylor Coleridge*, 1:145.
43. Coleridge to Southey, [3 November 1794], *Letters of Samuel Taylor Coleridge*, 1:123.
44. Coleridge to Southey, [c. 23 October 1794], *Letters of Samuel Taylor Coleridge*, 1:119.
45. Southey to Sara Fricker, [25 October 1794], *New Letters of Robert Southey*, 1:85.
46. Text from letter to Southey, [3 November 1794], *Letters of Samuel Taylor Coleridge*, 1:127–28.
47. *Notebooks*, 1082.
48. Coleridge to Southey, [9 December 1794], *Letters of Samuel Taylor Coleridge*, 1:132.
49. Coleridge to Southey, [19 January 1795], *Letters of Samuel Taylor Coleridge*, 1:149. I am grateful to Dr. Ben Tipping for this translation of Southey's Greek.

NOTES   339

50. Lawrence Blum, *Friendship, Altruism and Morality* (London: Routledge & Kegan Paul, 1980), 82.
51. Coleridge, "The Triumph of Loyalty," *Complete Poetical Works*, 2:1062–73. The cancelled lines occur before line 355.
52. Coleridge, "Lectures on Revealed Religion, its Corruptions and Political Views," in *Lectures 1795*, 164.
53. Leask, "Pantisocracy and the Politics of the 'Preface' to *Lyrical Ballads*," 46.
54. Southey to Grosvenor Bedford, 8 February 1795, *Correspondence of the Late Robert Southey*, 1:231.
55. Southey to Grosvenor Bedford, 27 May 1795, *Correspondence of the Late Robert Southey*, 1:240.
56. Southey to Grosvenor Bedford, 1 October 1795, *Correspondence of the Late Robert Southey*, 1:247.
57. Nicholas Roe, *The Politics of Nature: Wordsworth and Some Contemporaries* (Basingstoke: Macmillan, 1992), 54.
58. *Cato and Lælius: or, Essays on Old Age and Friendship*, ed. William Melmoth, 2:61–62.
59. Coleridge to Southey, [13] November 1795, *Letters of Samuel Taylor Coleridge*, 1:163.
60. Southey to Grosvenor Bedford, 24 February 1796, *Correspondence of the Late Robert Southey*, 1:271.
61. Southey to Grosvenor Bedford, 27 May 1796, *Correspondence of the Late Robert Southey*, 1:275–76.
62. Francis Quarles, *Emblems, Divine and Moral; Together with Hieroglyphicks of the Life of Man* (1645) (repr. London: D. Midwinter and others, 1736), 64–66. By permission of the Syndics of Cambridge University Library.

4. FRIENDS OF HUMANITY

1. Thomas Paine, *Rights of Man: Part the Second. Combining Principle and Practice* (London: J. S. Jordan, 1792), 76–77.
2. [Third Earl of Shaftesbury], *Sensus Communis: An Essay on the Freedom of Wit and Humour* (London: Egbert Sanger, 1709), 61.
3. Chris Jones, *Radical Sensibility: Literature and Ideas in the 1790s* (London: Routledge, 1993), 8.
4. Gary Kelly, *Women, Writing, and Revolution 1790–1827* (Oxford: Clarendon Press, 1993), 40.
5. Helen Maria Williams, *Letters Written in France, in the Summer of 1790, to a Friend in England* (London: T. Cadell, 1790), 14.
6. [John Thelwall], *The Daughter of Adoption; A Tale of Modern Times*, 4 vols. (London: R. Phillips, 1801). The novel was published under the pseudonym "John Beaufort, L. L. D."
7. *The Tribune, A Periodical Publication, Consisting Chiefly of the Political Lectures of J. Thelwall*, 3 vols. (London: the author, 1795–1796), 2:186.
8. John Thelwall, *Peaceful Discussion and not Tumultuary Violence the Means of Redressing National Grievance* (London: the author, 1795), 7.
9. Lynn Hunt, *The Family Romance of The French Revolution* (Berkeley: University of California Press, 1992), 13.

10. Felicity Baker, "Rousseau's Oath and Revolutionary Fraternity: 1789 and Today," *Romance Quarterly* 38 (1991): 276–77.
11. Sharp, *Friendship: Spirit and Form*, 116.
12. Coleridge to Southey, 6 July [1794], *Letters of Samuel Taylor Coleridge*, 1:85.
13. Coleridge to Southey, [1 September 1794], *Letters of Samuel Taylor Coleridge*, 1:99.
14. Coleridge to Henry Martin, 22 September 1794, *Letters of Samuel Taylor Coleridge*, 1:94.
15. Coleridge, "To Lord Stanhope on Reading his Late Protest in the House of Lords," *Complete Poetical Works*, 1:89.
16. Coleridge, "Effusion 10, to Earl Stanhope," *Poems* (1796), 54.
17. *The Watchman* (1796), ed. Lewis Patton (London: Routledge & Kegan Paul; Princeton: Princeton University Press, 1970), 1 March 1796, 46.
18. Coleridge, "On the Slave Trade," *Watchman*, 25 March 1796, 139, 132.
19. Coleridge, "Lecture on the Slave-Trade," in *Lectures 1795*, 249.
20. Jones, "Radical Sensibility in the 1790s," in *Reflections of Revolution*, 69–70.
21. Coleridge, *An Answer to "A Letter to Edward Long Fox, M. D."* (Bristol, 1795), in *Lectures 1795*, 330.
22. A. W., *A Letter to Edward Long Fox, M. D.* (Bristol, 1795), in *Lectures 1795*, 387.
23. Lockridge, *Coleridge the Moralist*, 208.
24. Coleridge, "Lecture on the Slave-Trade," 247–48.
25. Southey, *Poems* (Bristol: Joseph Cottle; London: G. G. and J. Robinson, 1797), 145–46.
26. *The Anti-Jacobin; or, Weekly Examiner*, 11 December 1797, 39.
27. Coleridge to Thelwall, 31 December 1796, *Letters of Samuel Taylor Coleridge*, 1:294.
28. According to the *OED*, this *Anti-Jacobin* poem marks the first time "amalgamate" is used figuratively to mean "To unite together (classes, races, societies, ideas etc.) so as to form a homogeneous or harmonious whole" (s.v. "Amalgamate," v. 4b).
29. Edmund Burke, *Reflections on the Revolution in France, and on the Proceedings in Certain Societies in London Relative to that Event* (London: J. Dodsley, 1790), 274. The *OED* suggests this passage marks the first figurative usage of "amalgam" to refer to the "complete combination of various elements" (s.v. "Amalgam," n. 3).
30. *Anti-Jacobin*, 27 November 1797, 15.
31. Edmund Burke, *A Philosophical Enquiry into the Origin of our Ideas of the Sublime and Beautiful* (1757), ed. James T. Boulton (Oxford: Basil Blackwell, rev. 1987), 113.
32. Southey to Nicholas Lightfoot, 22 December 1793, MS Eng. Lett. c.453, fol. 191v, Bodleian Library, Oxford. By permission of The Bodleian Library.
33. Coleridge to Southey, 21 October [1794], *Letters of Samuel Taylor Coleridge*, 1:114. Coleridge is quoting from a letter recently received from Southey.
34. Cf. Paine's praise of the "French constitution," which declares that "*there shall be no titles*; and of consequence, all that class of equivocal generation, which in some countries is called '*aristocracy*', and in others '*nobility*', is done away, and the *peer* is exalted into MAN" (*Rights of Man: Being an Answer to Mr. Burke's Attack on the French Revolution* [London: J. Johnson], 66). Coleridge's letter may

be seen as an informal kind of constitution in which the term "Friend" implies the abolition of titles and a concomitant exaltation of all members of the Pantisocracy.

35. Coleridge to Southey, 18 September [1794], *Letters of Samuel Taylor Coleridge*, 1:103.

36. Coleridge to Southey, 13 July [1794], *Letters of Samuel Taylor Coleridge*, 1:88.

37. James Gillray, "The Friend of Humanity and the Knife-Grinder,—Scene. The Borough, in Imitation of Mr Southey's Sapphics." *The Anti-Jacobin*'s sapphics were etched in two columns under the title, and beside them the dedication: "*To the Independent Electors of the Borough of Southwark, this Print is most respectfully dedicated—*" (*Catalogue of Personal and Political Satires*, 9045. © Copyright The British Museum). In 1798, the plate was bound into the volume of *The Anti-Jacobin*'s collected numbers, opposite its accompanying poem (15). This book reproduces the latter printing.

38. For the turbulent history of Tierney's campaign see H. K. Olphin, *George Tierney* (London: George Allen & Unwin, 1934), 26–40.

39. Quoted in Olphin, *George Tierney*, 21.

40. *Folios of Caracatures Lent out for the Evening, Catalogue of Personal and Political Satires*, 9227. © Copyright The British Museum.

41. *Anti-Jacobin*, 7 May 1798, 203.

42. Shearer West, "Libertinism and the Ideology of Male Friendship in the Portraits of the Society of Dilettanti," *Eighteenth-Century Life* 16 (1992): 97.

43. Jones, "Radical Sensibility in the 1790s," 69.

44. *Anti-Jacobin*, 9 July 1798, 282–87.

45. Paul Magnuson, *Reading Public Romanticism* (Princeton: Princeton University Press, 1998), 83.

46. Coleridge, "Lecture 3," in *Lectures 1795*, 163.

47. *The Beauties of The Anti-Jacobin; or Weekly Examiner; Containing Every Article of Permanent Utility in that Valuable and Highly Esteemed Paper, Literary and Political* (London: C. Chapple, 1799), 306.

48. Hazlitt's essay "On the Pleasure of Hating" (1826) exemplifies *The Anti-Jacobin*'s attitude when he asks sarcastically: "Does any one suppose that the love of country in an Englishman implies any friendly feeling or disposition to serve another bearing the same name? No, it means only hatred to the French, or the inhabitants of any other country which we happen to be at war with for the time" (*Complete Works of William Hazlitt*, 12:130).

49. *Dictionary*, s.v. "Candour," n.

50. *OED*, s.v. "Candid," a. 5b: "*ironically*, in phrase *candid friend*: one who claims to be a friend, and, in the name of candour, speaks unpleasant things."

51. *Anti-Jacobin*, 25 June 1798, 261.

52. *Anti-Jacobin,* 14 May 1798, 269.

53. Coleridge to George Coleridge, [c. 10 March 1798], *Letters of Samuel Taylor Coleridge*, 1:397.

54. Coleridge, *Essays on his Times in "The Morning Post" and "The Courier,"* ed. David Erdman, 3 vols. (London: Routledge & Kegan Paul; Princeton: Princeton University Press), 1:39.

55. Coleridge, "Original Poetry. A Tale," *Complete Poetical Works*, 299–303. The poem is better known by its subsequent title, "Recantation Illustrated in the Story of the Mad Ox."

56. Woodring, *Politics in the Poetry of Coleridge*, 143.

57. Coleridge, *Fears in Solitude, Written in 1798, During the Alarm of an Inva-*

sion. *To which are Added, France, An Ode; and Frost at Midnight* (London: J. Johnson, 1798).
58. Magnuson, *Reading Public Romanticism*, 78.
59. The *Anti-Jacobin* poet in satirical mode inquires of the cosmopolitan radical:

> What shall a name [England], a word, a sound, controul
> Th'aspiring thought, and cramp th'expansive soul?
> Shall one half-peopled Island's rocky round
> A love that glows for all creation, bound?
>
> (lines 101–4)

60. Coleridge, *Fears in Solitude*, 13–18.
61. Coleridge, *Essays on his Times*, 1:41–42.
62. Poole to Coleridge, 15 March 1799, *Thomas Poole and his Friends*, 1:294.
63. Coleridge to Poole, 6–8 April 1799, *Letters of Samuel Taylor Coleridge*, 1:480.

5. "They Answer and Provoke Each Other's Songs"

Quotation in chapter title is from Coleridge, "The Nightingale; A Conversational Poem" (1798), line 58.
1. Coleridge, *Biographia Literaria or Biographical Sketches of My Literary Life and Opinions* (London, 1817), ed. James Engell and W. Jackson Bate, 2 vols. (London: Routledge & Kegan Paul; Princeton: Princeton University Press, 1983), 1:184.
2. Burton R. Pollin, assisted by Redmond Burke, "John Thelwall's Marginalia in a Copy of Coleridge's *Biographia Literaria*" *Bulletin of the New York Public Library*, 74 (1970): 81.
3. Hunt, *The Family Romance of the French Revolution*, 13.
4. Coleridge to Southey, 6 July [1794], *Letters of Samuel Taylor Coleridge*, 1:84.
5. Patton and Mann, "Editors' Introduction," in *Lectures 1795*, xlii.
6. Coleridge, "Lecture on the Two Bills," in *Lectures 1795*, 261.
7. Coleridge, *The Plot Discovered*, in *Lectures 1795*, 296–97.
8. Favret, *Romantic Correspondence: Women, Politics and the Fiction of Letters*, 29.
9. James Gillray, "Copenhagen House," *Catalogue of Personal and Political Satires*, 8685. © Copyright The British Museum.
10. Charles or James K. Ansell, "An Irish Hug alias A Fraternal Embrace," in *Folios of Caracatures Lent out for the Evening, Catalogue of Personal and Political Satires*, 9249. © Copyright The British Museum.
11. Roe, *Wordsworth and Coleridge*, 151.
12. Coleridge, *An Answer to "A Letter to Edward Long Fox, M. D.,"* in *Lectures 1795*, 330.
13. Coleridge to Thelwall, [late April 1796], *Letters of Samuel Taylor Coleridge*, 1:204–5.
14. Thelwall himself engaged in this kind of symbolic activity, as revealed by a manuscript dedication to "Citizen Thomas Paine," dated 26 October 1796, in the fly leaf of the first of his three-volume collection of political lectures, *The Tribune*

(MS fly-leaf, Acton. c. 25. 418, Cambridge University Library, Cambridge. By permission of the Syndics of Cambridge University Library):

> To Citizen Thomas Paine,
> As a small tribute of respect & admiration for that most entrepid & truely enlightened of all the known advocates for human liberty & universal benevolence, this complete set of the political works of a humble fellow labourer in the vineyard of truth, is presented (through the friendly hand of Citizen De Lugo)
> by the Author

In presenting these volumes, Thelwall invites Paine to understand the "friendly hand of Citizen De Lugo" as embodying his own affection, and demonstrating the single spirit of friendship pervading this radical community.

15. Coleridge, "To John Thelwall," *Complete Poetical Works*, 2:1090.

16. Thelwall, *Poems Written in Close Confinement in the Tower and Newgate, under a Charge of High Treason* (London: the author, 1795), 14. To Thelwall, Coleridge described the Odes as "the best" of the poems (6 February 1797; *Letters of Samuel Taylor Coleridge*, 1:307).

17. Coleridge, "Reflections on Entering into Active Life," *The Monthly Magazine, and British Register* 2 (1796): 732.

18. Thelwall to Coleridge, 10 May [1796]; "An Unpublished Letter from John Thelwall to S. T. Coleridge," ed. Warren E. Gibbs, *Modern Language Review* 25 (1930): 85.

19. Coleridge, "To a Young Lady with a Poem on The French Revolution," *Poems* (1796), 36–39.

20. Coleridge, *Watchman*, 17 March 1796, 98–99.

21. Patton and Mann, *Lectures 1795*, 296.

22. Duncan Wu, "Coleridge, Thelwall, and the Politics of Poetry," *Coleridge Bulletin* 4 (1994): 28.

23. Judith Thompson, "An Autumnal Blast, a Killing Frost: Coleridge's Poetic Conversation with John Thelwall," *Studies in Romanticism* 36 (1997): 453, 428.

24. William Blake, *The Marriage of Heaven and Hell* (c. 1790–1794), Fitzwilliam Museum (copy E), plate 3. Reprinted by permission of Fitzwilliam Museum, University of Cambridge.

25. David Fairer, "Pope, Blake, Heraclitus and Oppositional Thinking," in *Pope: New Contexts*, ed. David Fairer (Hemel Hempstead: Harvester Wheatsheaf, 1990), 170–71.

26. David V. Erdman, *The Illuminated Blake: William Blake's Complete Illuminated Works with a Plate-by-Plate Commentary* (New York: Dover Publications, 1974), 100.

27. Alan Watts, *The Two Hands of God. The Myths of Polarity* (1963), quoted in Fairer, "Pope, Blake, Heraclitus, and Oppositional Thinking," 173.

28. Coleridge to Thelwall, 13 May 1796, *Letters of Samuel Taylor Coleridge*, 1:212.

29. *Dictionary*, s.v. "Zeal," n.

30. Coleridge to Thelwall, 17 December [1796], *Letters of Samuel Taylor Coleridge*, 1:277.

31. Thelwall, "Prefatory Memoir," *Poems, Chiefly Written in Retirement* (Hereford: W. H. Parker, 1801), vi.

32. Coleridge to Thelwall, 13 November 1796, *Letters of Samuel Taylor Coleridge*, 1:254.

33. Lewis, *The Four Loves*, 83.

34. Coleridge to Thelwall, 19 November [1796], *Letters of Samuel Taylor Coleridge*, 1:258.

35. Coleridge to Thelwall, 6 February 1797, *Letters of Samuel Taylor Coleridge*, 1:305.

36. Boswell, *Life of Johnson*, 776.

37. Isaac Cruikshank, "The Wrangling Friends or Opposition in Disorder," *Catalogue of Personal and Political Satires*, 7855.© Copyright The British Museum.

38. Thelwall to J. Wimpory, 15 February 1797, MS fms Eng. 947.2 (19), Houghton Library, Harvard. By permission of The Houghton Library, Harvard University.

39. Thompson, "Hunting the Jacobin Fox," *Past and Present* 142 (1994): 103.

40. Thelwall to Mrs. Thelwall, 18 July 1797, MS MA 77 (17), Pierpont Morgan Library, New York.

41. Thelwall to Mrs. Thelwall, 18 July 1797, MS MA 77 (17), Pierpont Morgan Library, New York.

42. Thelwall to Mrs. Thelwall, 18 July 1797, MS MA 77 (17), Pierpont Morgan Library, New York.

43. Coleridge to Josiah Wade, 1 August [17]97, *Letters of Samuel Taylor Coleridge*, 1:339.

44. Leask, *The Politics of Imagination*, 13.

45. Thelwall, *The Daughter of Adoption*, 1:283.

46. Coleridge, *Table Talk Recorded by Henry Nelson Coleridge (and John Taylor Coleridge)*, ed. Carl Woodring, 2 vols. (London: Routledge & Kegan Paul; Princeton: Princeton University Press, 1990), 1:180.

47. *The Pursuits of Literature* (9th ed., 1799), quoted in Thompson, "Hunting the Jacobin Fox," 99.

48. James Walsh to John King, [?]15 August 1797, quoted in Roe, *Wordsworth and Coleridge*, 258.

49. Charlotte Poole, journal entry, 23 July 1797, *Thomas Poole and his Friends*, 1:235.

50. Thompson, "Disenchantment or Default? A Lay Sermon," 160.

51. Thelwall to Mrs Thelwall, 18 July 1797, MS MA 77 (17), Pierpont Morgan Library, New York.

52. Thompson, "Coleridge and John Thelwall," 74.

53. Thelwall, *Poems* (1801), 129.

54. Coleridge, "Religious Musings," *Poems* (1796), 135–75.

55. Fairer, "Baby Language and Revolution: The Early Poetry of Charles Lloyd and Charles Lamb," *Charles Lamb Bulletin* 74 (1991): 35–36.

56. Coleridge, *Fears in Solitude*, 1–12.

57. Fairer, "Organizing Verse: Burke's *Reflections* and Eighteenth-Century Poetry," *Romanticism* 3 (1997): 8.

58. In *Sylva, or a Discourse of Forest Trees* (1664), John Evelyn represents the elm as "a sort of consort, sociable and so affecting to grow in company" (quoted in S. Hester E. Jones, "Some Literary Treatments of Friendship: Katherine Phillips to Alexander Pope" [unpublished doctoral thesis, University of Cambridge, 1993], 16).

59. Coleridge to John Chubb, [20 August 1797], *Letters of Samuel Taylor Coleridge*, 1:342.

60. *OED*, s.v. "Propagation," n. 1.

61. Coleridge to Thelwall, [21 August 1797], *Letters of Samuel Taylor Coleridge*, 1:343–44.

62. Roe, "Coleridge and John Thelwall," 76.
63. Poole to Mrs. St. Albyn, 16 September 1797, *Thomas Poole and his Friends*, 1:242–43.
64. Thelwall, *Poems* (1801), 140–41.
65. Thelwall to Thomas Hardy, 24 May 1798, quoted in Thompson, "Hunting the Jacobin Fox," 116.
66. Thelwall to [Iolo Morganwg], 10 May 1798, MS 21283 E, no. 471, National Library of Wales, Aberystwyth.
67. Coleridge, *Fears in Solitude*, 19–23.
68. See Wu, "Coleridge, Thelwall," 41; Jeffrey C. Robinson, *The Current of Romantic Passion* (Madison: University of Wisconsin Press, 1991), 69; Thompson, "An Autumnal Blast, a Killing Frost," 427–56.
69. Thelwall, *Poems* (1801), 136.
70. Thelwall, *Poems* (1801), 139–40.
71. Thelwall to Thomas Hardy, 16 January 1798; "John Thelwall in Wales: New Documentary Evidence," ed. P. J. Corfield and Chris Evans, *Bulletin of the Institute of Historical Research* 59 (1986): 234.
72. Coleridge to Thelwall, 30 January 1798, *Letters of Samuel Taylor Coleridge*, 1:382.
73. Thelwall to Crompton, 3 March 1798, MS fms Eng. 957.2 (21), Houghton Library, Harvard. By permission of The Houghton Library, Harvard University.
74. Coleridge to Thelwall, 23 January 1801, *Letters of Samuel Taylor Coleridge*, 2:667.
75. Coleridge to Thelwall, 23 April 1801, *Letters of Samuel Taylor Coleridge*, 2:723.
76. Coleridge to Mrs. Thelwall, [22 November 1803], *Letters of Samuel Taylor Coleridge*, 2:1018.
77. Coleridge to Thelwall, 26 [25] November 1803, *Letters of Samuel Taylor Coleridge*, 2:1019.
78. Thelwall to Mrs. Thelwall, 29 November 1803, MS MA 77 (18), Pierpont Morgan Library, New York.

6. Coleridge, Charles Lamb, and Charles Lloyd, 1794–98

Quotation in chapter title is from Lloyd, *Edmund Oliver*, 2 vols. (Bristol: Joseph Cottle, 1798), 2:64–65. An edited version of this chapter appeared in *Romanticism*, 6 (2000): 78–97. It is reproduced here by permission of the editors of *Romanticism*.

1. Coleridge to Southey, [1 September 1794], *Letters of Samuel Taylor Coleridge*, 1:99.
2. Lamb to Coleridge, 10 December 1796; *The Letters of Charles and Mary Anne Lamb*, ed. Edwin W. Marrs, Jr., 3 vols. (Ithaca: Cornell University Press, 1975–1978), 1:78.
3. Lamb to Coleridge, 16 January 1797, *Letters of Charles and Mary Anne Lamb*, 1:93.
4. Lamb to Coleridge, [29 June 1797], *Letters of Charles and Mary Anne Lamb*, 1:114.
5. Coleridge to Matthew Coates, 5 December 1803, *Letters of Samuel Taylor Coleridge*, 2:1022–23.
6. *Howell's State Trials*, quoted in H. W. Piper, "Coleridge and the Unitarian Consensus," in *The Coleridge Connection*, 275.

7. *Lectures 1795*, 160.
8. Barth, *Coleridge and the Power of Love*, 20.
9. Coleridge, "Religious Musings. A Desultory Poem, Written on Christmas' Eve, in the Year of our Lord, 1794," *Poems* (1796), 135–75.
10. Text from Coleridge to Southey, postmark: 29 December 1794, *Letters of Samuel Taylor Coleridge*, 1:147–48. The poem was published in *Poems* (1796) as "Effusion XXII. To a Friend Together with an Unfinished Poem."
11. Southey to Edith Fricker, [12 January 1795], *Correspondence of the late Robert Southey*, 1:91.
12. Lamb to Coleridge, [27 September 1796], *Letters of Charles and Mary Anne Lamb*, 1:44.
13. Coleridge to Lamb, [28 September 1796], *Letters of Samuel Taylor Coleridge*, 1:238.
14. Lamb to Coleridge, 24 [23] October 1796, *Letters of Charles and Mary Anne Lamb*, 1:53–54.
15. Lamb to Coleridge, 10 December 1796, *Letters of Charles and Mary Anne Lamb*, 1:78.
16. "Religious Musings," *Poems* (1797), 145.
17. Lamb to Coleridge, 7–10 January 1797, *Letters of Charles and Mary Anne Lamb*, 1:88.
18. Joseph Priestley, *A Free Discussion of the Doctrines of Materialism, and Philosophical Necessity, In a Correspondence between Dr. Price, and Dr. Priestley* (London: J. Johnson, 1778), sigs. a3v–a4r.
19. MS Ashley 1005, fol. 13r, British Library, London. By permission of The British Library. "Sonnet 12" is part of an autograph volume of published and unpublished poems written by Lloyd during 1795–1800, and annotated by Coleridge.
20. Lloyd and Lamb, *Blank Verse* (London: John and Arthur Arch, 1798), 11.
21. Coleridge to Southey, [13] November 1795, *Letters of Samuel Taylor Coleridge*, 1:163–64.
22. Coleridge, "To C. Lloyd;" *Poems* (1797), 111–15.
23. Charles or James K. Ansell, "Mutual Confidence in the Year 1799," in *A Collection of Caricatures Belonging to Mr. Anthony de Rothschild*, vi. 136, *Catalogue of Personal and Political Satires*, 9367. © Copyright The British Museum.
24. Coleridge to Cottle, 22 February 1796, *Letters of Samuel Taylor Coleridge*, 1:186.
25. Lloyd, "Address to Wealth. Written July 1797," *Blank Verse*, 53.
26. *Poems* (1797), 179–81.
27. Coleridge to Charles Lloyd, Sr., 15 October 1796, *Letters of Samuel Taylor Coleridge*, 1:240.
28. Lloyd to Mary Lloyd, 31 October 1796; Lynda Pratt, "'Perilous Acquaintance'? Lloyd, Coleridge and Southey in the 1790s: Five Unpublished Letters," *Romanticism* 6 (2000): 103.
29. Lamb to Coleridge, [9 December 1796], *Letters of Charles and Mary Anne Lamb*, 1:75.
30. Lamb to Coleridge, [13–16 June 1796], *Letters of Charles and Mary Anne Lamb*, 1:30.
31. Alison Hickey, "Double Bonds: Charles Lamb's Romantic Collaborations," *ELH*, 63 (1996): 740.
32. Lamb to Coleridge, 13 [12] June 1797, *Letters of Charles and Mary Anne Lamb*, 1:111.
33. *Poems* (1797), title page. Translation by Griggs, *Letters of Samuel Taylor Coleridge*, 1:390.

34. Thomas Hobbes, *Philosophicall Rudiments concerning Government and Society* (London: R. Royston, 1651), 3.
35. Coleridge to Cottle, [10 March 1797], *Letters of Samuel Taylor Coleridge*, 1:313.
36. Coleridge to Poole, 24 September 1796, *Letters of Samuel Taylor Coleridge*, 1:237.
37. Lloyd, on the other hand, betrays anxiety *not* to burden his tutor financially. In a letter to his brother James, 2 December 1796, inserted into a presentation copy of *Poems on The Death of Priscilla Framer*, Lloyd urges him to "see that some are circulated among your friends. I find that the printing of these comes to more than I expected—& if they are not disposed of, I shall be embarrassing Coleridge" (MS HEW 15.12.5, Houghton Library, Harvard. By permission of The Houghton Library, Harvard University).
38. MS Ashley 1005, fol. 14r, British Library, London. By permission of The British Library.
39. Coleridge to Charles Lloyd, Sr., 4 December 1796, *Letters of Samuel Taylor Coleridge*, 1:263.
40. "Caius," "On Imprudent Friendship," *Universal Magazine* 93 (1793): 125–29.
41. Andrea K. Henderson, *Romantic Identities: Varieties of Subjectivity, 1774–1830* (Cambridge: Cambridge University Press, 1996).
42. Coleridge to Poole, [22 August 1796], *Letters of Samuel Taylor Coleridge*, 1:230–31.
43. Lamb to Coleridge, 16 January 1797, *Letters of Charles and Mary Anne Lamb*, 1:92.
44. MS Ashley 1005, fol. 19r, British Library, London. By permission of The British Library.
45. Lloyd brings out his desire to imitate Lamb in a textual emendation, "emulation," written above line 6. This correction clarifies the sense: "Thy semblance I shall cherish to inflame / The feeble & dishearten'd to the aim / Of patient emulation."
46. Lamb to Coleridge, 24 June 1797, *Letters of Charles and Mary Anne Lamb*, 1:113.
47. Lamb to Coleridge, 7 April 1797, *Letters of Charles and Mary Anne Lamb*, 1:106.
48. Lamb to Coleridge, [8–10 June 1796], *Letters of Charles and Mary Anne Lamb*, 1:20–21.
49. "This Lime-Tree Bower my Prison, a Poem, Addressed to Charles Lamb, of the India-House, London," *The Annual Anthology. Volume II* [ed. Southey] (Bristol: T. N. Longman and O. Rees, 1800), 140–44.
50. Lamb to Coleridge, 6 August 1800, *Letters of Charles and Mary Anne Lamb*, 1:217–18.
51. Coleridge to Cottle, [c. 20 November 1797], *Letters of Samuel Taylor Coleridge*, 1:357–58.
52. Lloyd to Mary Lloyd, 9 October1796, "Perilous Acquaintance," 101.
53. Lamb to Coleridge, 8 November 1796, *Letters of Charles and Mary Anne Lamb*, 1:60–61.
54. Coleridge, "To Simplicity," *Monthly Magazine* 4 (1797): 374.
55. Coleridge to Cottle, [7 March 1798], *Letters of Samuel Taylor Coleridge*, 1:390.
56. Lloyd to Southey, 4 April [1798], MS MA 225 (28), Pierpont Morgan Li-

brary, New York. As Griggs notes, the letter is "misdated 4 Apr. 1797, the year certainly being 1798," *Letters of Samuel Taylor Coleridge*, 1:403. An edited text is included in *The Letters of Charles Lamb to which are Added those of his Sister Mary Lamb*, ed. E. V. Lucas, 3 vols. (London: J. M. Dent & Methuen, 1935), 1:104.

57. "Introduction," *Edmund Oliver 1798*, facsimile reprint, introd. Jonathan Wordsworth (Oxford: Woodstock Books, 1990), ii–iii.

58. Lloyd to Southey, 4 April [1798], MA 225 (28), Pierpont Morgan Library, New York. The passage "I have . . . service as White" is included in *The Letters of Charles Lamb*, 1:104.

59. Coleridge to Lamb, [early May 1798], *Letters of Samuel Taylor Coleridge*, 1:404.

60. Coleridge, "To One who Published in Print what had been Entrusted to Him by my Fireside," *Complete Poetical Works*, 2:964.

61. Lamb to Coleridge, [c. 23 May to June 6 1798], *Letters of Charles and Mary Anne Lamb*, 1:129.

62. Lamb to Southey, 28 July 1798, *Letters of Charles and Mary Anne Lamb*, 1:131.

63. Lamb to Robert Lloyd, [13 or 23 August 1798], *Letters of Charles and Mary Anne Lamb*, 1:134.

64. See Hartley; *Observations on Man*, 2:302.

65. Lloyd to Cottle, 7 June 1798, MS RP479, British Library, London. By permission of The British Library. The passage "but who am I . . . self-referring scale" is omitted from the published text, in Cottle's *Reminiscences of Samuel Taylor Coleridge and Robert Southey*, 2nd ed. (London: Houlston & Stoneman, 1847), 170–71.

66. Coleridge to Southey, 25 January 1800, *Letters of Samuel Taylor Coleridge*, 1:563.

67. Coleridge to Southey, 15 October 1799, *Letters of Samuel Taylor Coleridge*, 1:542.

68. Lloyd, *Blank Verse*, 14.

69. Lloyd, *Blank Verse*, 58–59.

70. Lamb to Manning, [8 February 1800], *Letters of Charles and Mary Anne Lamb*, 1:183.

7. COLERIDGE AND WORDSWORTH

Quotation in chapter title is from Wordsworth, *The Prelude: 1798–1799*, ed. Stephen Parrish (Ithaca: Cornell University Press, 1977), 2.512–13.

1. Lamb to Wordsworth, [30 January 1801], *Letters of Charles and Mary Lamb*, 1:267.

2. Lamb to Manning, [15 February 1801], *Letters of Charles and Mary Lamb*, 1:272.

3. Richard E. Matlak, *The Poetry of Relationship: The Wordsworths and Coleridge, 1797–1800* (Basingstoke: Macmillan, 1997), 82.

4. David Hume, *A Treatise of Human Nature* (1739–1740), ed. L. A. Selby-Bigge, 2nd ed. (Oxford: Clarendon Press, 1978), 252.

5. John Mullan, *Sentiment and Sociability: The Language of Feeling in the Eighteenth Century* (Oxford: Clarendon Press, corr. 1990), 35.

6. Coleridge to Humphry Davy, 3 February 1801, *Letters of Samuel Taylor Coleridge*, 2:671.
7. Harding, *Coleridge and the Idea of Love*, 35.
8. Coleridge to Sir George and Lady Beaumont, 1 October 1803, *Letters of Samuel Taylor Coleridge*, 2:1000.
9. Everest, *Coleridge's Secret Ministry*, 15.
10. Poole to Coleridge, 1 January 1800, *Thomas Poole and his Friends*, 2:4–5.
11. *Encyclopædia Britannica*, 7:467–76.
12. William and Mary Wordsworth to Sara Coleridge, [7 November 1845]; *The Letters of William and Dorothy Wordsworth: The Later Years*, ed. and rev. Alan G. Hill, 2nd ed., 4 vols. (Oxford: Clarendon Press, 1988), 4:719.
13. Coleridge, "Epistle I. Written at Shurton Bars, Near Bridgewater, September 1795, in Answer to a Letter from Bristol," *Poems* (1796), 111–18.
14. Newlyn, *Coleridge, Wordsworth, and the Language of Allusion* (Oxford: Clarendon Press, 1986), 18.
15. McFarland, *Romanticism and the Forms of Ruin*, 56–103.
16. Coleridge to John Prior Estlin, [18 May] 1798, *Letters of Samuel Taylor Coleridge*, 1:410.
17. Coleridge to Cottle, [8 June 1797], *Letters of Samuel Taylor Coleridge*, 1:325.
18. Berkeley Stevenson Blatz, "Romanticism and the Rhetoric of Friendship" (unpublished doctoral thesis, University of California at Long Beach, 1994), 103.
19. Coleridge to Southey, [c. 17 July 1797], *Letters of Samuel Taylor Coleridge*, 1:334.
20. Coleridge to Cottle, [7 March 1798], *Letters of Samuel Taylor Coleridge*, 1:391.
21. Wordsworth, "Expostulation and Reply," *Lyrical Ballads* (1798), 183–85.
22. Wordsworth, "Lines Written at a Small Distance from my House . . . ," *Lyrical Ballads* (1798), 95–97.
23. Thomas De Quincey, "William Wordsworth" (1839), in *Recollections of the Lakes and the Lake Poets*, ed. David Wright (Harmondsworth: Penguin, 1970), 132–33.
24. Coleridge, *Complete Poetical Works*, 1:286–87.
25. Wordsworth, "Lines Written a Few Miles above Tintern Abbey," *Lyrical Ballads* (1798), 201–10.
26. Coleridge to Wordsworth, [early December 1798], *Letters of Samuel Taylor Coleridge*, 1:451–52.
27. Coleridge to Wordsworth, [c. 17 November 1798], *Letters of Samuel Taylor Coleridge*, 1:440–41.
28. Dorothy Wordsworth to Christopher Wordsworth, 3 February 1799; *The Letters of William and Dorothy Wordsworth: The Early Years 1787–1805*, rev. Chester L. Shaver, 2nd ed. (Oxford: Clarendon Press, 1967), 1:245.
39. Paul Magnuson, *Coleridge and Wordsworth: A Lyrical Dialogue* (Princeton: Princeton University Press, 1988), 11.
30. Coleridge to Wordsworth, 12 October 1799, *Letters of Samuel Taylor Coleridge*, 1:538.
31. Sheila M. Kearns, *Coleridge, Wordsworth, and Romantic Autobiography: Reading Strategies of Self-Representation* (Madison, NJ: Fairleigh Dickinson University Press, 1995), 83.
32. Bygrave, *Coleridge and the Self*, 3.
33. Coleridge to Poole, [21 March 1800], *Letters of Samuel Taylor Coleridge*, 1:582.

34. Coleridge to Godwin, 8 January 1800, *Letters of Samuel Taylor Coleridge*, 1:560.
35. Coleridge to Poole, 6 May 1799, *Letters of Samuel Taylor Coleridge*, 1:491.
36. Wordworth, "A narrow girdle of rough stones and crags;" *Lyrical Ballads* (1800), 2: 190–94.
37. Coleridge, "Frost at Midnight," in *Fears in Solitude*.
38. Frederick Garber, *Wordsworth and the Poetry of Encounter* (Urbana: University of Illinois Press, 1971), 115.
39. Wordsworth, "The Fountain, A Conversation," *Lyrical Ballads* (1800), 2: 127–31.
40. Brian Cosgrove, *Wordsworth and the Poetry of Self-Sufficiency: A Study of the Poetic Development 1796–1814* (Salzburg: Universität Salzburg, 1982), 27–28.
41. Coleridge to William Sotheby, 13 July 1802, *Letters of Samuel Taylor Coleridge*, 2:811.
42. Dorothy Wordsworth, *The Grasmere Journals*, ed. Pamela Woof (Oxford: Oxford University Press, 1991), 100.
43. Coleridge to the Wordsworths, 4 April 1804, *Letters of Samuel Taylor Coleridge*, 2:1117–18.
44. Coleridge, "A Day-Dream," *Complete Poetical Works*, 1:385–86.
45. The Reading Text of the Cornell Manuscript, in *Coleridge's "Dejection": The Earliest Manuscripts and the Earliest Printings*, ed. Stephen Maxfield Parrish (Ithaca: Cornell University Press, 1988), 23–24.
46. Barth, "Coleridge's *Dejection*: Imagination, Joy and the Power of Love," in *Coleridge's Imagination: Essays in Memory of Pete Laver*, ed. Richard Gravil, Lucy Newlyn, and Nicholas Roe (Cambridge: Cambridge University Press, 1985), 187–88.
47. "Caius," "On Imprudent Friendship," *Universal Magazine* 93 (1793): 126.
48. "C.," "On the Errors which Arise from Friendship," *Universal Magazine* 96 (1795): 16.
49. Friedrichs von Logau, *Sinngedichte. Zwölf Bücher. Mit Anmerkungen über die Sprache des Dichters*, ed. C. W. Ramler and G. E. Lessing (Leipzig, 1759), 1:24; *Notebooks*, 432 (19), trans. Kathleen Coburn.
50. Text from Coleridge to Sir George and Lady Beaumont, [13 August 1803], *Letters of Samuel Taylor Coleridge*, 2:966–70.
51. Magnuson, *Coleridge and Wordsworth: A Lyrical Dialogue*, 316–17.
52. Wu, *Romanticism: An Anthology*, 560. Text of "Dejection: An Ode" from *Coleridge's "Dejection": The Earliest Manuscripts and the Earliest Printings*.
53. *Notebooks*, 2712.
54. *Notebooks*, 189.
55. Poole to Coleridge, 8 October 1798, *Thomas Poole and his Friends*, 1:278.
56. Coleridge to Wordsworth, [December 1798], *Letters of Samuel Taylor Coleridge*, 1:453.
57. Raimonda Modiano, *Coleridge and the Concept of Nature* (London: Macmillan, 1986), 40.
58. MS New York Public Library, quoted in *Letters of Samuel Taylor Coleridge*, 1:631.
59. Coleridge to Godwin, 25 March 1801, *Letters of Samuel Taylor Coleridge*, 2:714.
60. Coleridge to Godwin, 23 June 1801, *Letters of Samuel Taylor Coleridge*, 1:738.
61. Shaffer, "The Hermeneutic Community: Coleridge and Schleiermacher," 205.

62. *The Friend*, 10 August 1809, 2:41.
63. Coleridge to Richard Sharp, 15 January 1804, *Letters of Samuel Taylor Coleridge*, 1:1033–34.
64. *Table Talk*, c. 5 May 1829, 2:391.
65. *Henry Crabb Robinson on Books and their Writers*, ed. Edith J. Morley, 3 vols. (London: J. M Dent, 1938), 1:196.
66. Coleridge to Poole, 14 October 1803, *Letters of Samuel Taylor Coleridge*, 2:1012.

8. Managing Friendship

1. Godwin, *St. Leon: A Tale of the Sixteenth Century*, 4 vols. (London: G. G. and J. Robinson, 1799), 2:298–99.
2. Coleridge to George Coleridge, [c. 10 March 1798], *Letters of Samuel Taylor Coleridge*, 1:398.
3. Cowper, "On Friendship" (1781).
4. Southey to John King, 5 March 1804, *New Letters of Robert Southey*, 1:354.
5. Godwin to unnamed correspondent, 19 September 1797, Ab. MS Dep. b227/8(a), Bodleian Library, Oxford. By permission of Lord Abinger, conveyed through The Bodleian Library.
6. Godwin, *The Enquirer. Reflections on Education, Manners, and Literature* (London: G. G. and J. Robinson, 1797), 130.
7. Coleridge to Thelwall, 13 May 1796, *Letters of Samuel Taylor Coleridge*, 1:214.
8. Coleridge to Thomas Wedgwood, postmark: 2 January 1800, *Letters of Samuel Taylor Coleridge*, 1:559.
9. Coleridge to Godwin, [3 March 1800], *Letters of Samuel Taylor Coleridge*, 1:580.
10. Coleridge to Godwin, 21 May 1800, *Letters of Samuel Taylor Coleridge*, 1:588.
11. Godwin to Coleridge, [September 1800]; C. Kegan Paul, *William Godwin: His Friends and Contemporaries*, 2 vols. (London: Henry S. King, 1876), 2:6.
12. Godwin to Coleridge, 5 September 1800, MS MA 1857 (10), Pierpont Morgan Library, New York.
13. Coleridge to Godwin, [8 September 1800], *Letters of Samuel Taylor Coleridge*, 1:620.
14. Coleridge to Godwin, [8 July 1801], *Letters of Samuel Taylor Coleridge*, 2:742.
15. St. Clair, *The Godwins and the Shelleys*, 235.
16. Godwin to Coleridge, 13 July 1801; *The Carl H. Pforzheimer Library: Shelley and his Circle 1773–1822*, ed. Kenneth Neill Cameron (Cambridge: Harvard University Press, 1961), 255.
17. Coleridge to Godwin, 22 September 1801, *Letters of Samuel Taylor Coleridge*, 2:761–62.
18. Coleridge, "A Dialogue between an Author and his Friend," *Complete Poetical Works*, 2:967.
19. Godwin, undated note, *William Godwin: His Friends and Contemporaries*, 1:358.
20. Coleridge to Godwin, 22 September 1800, *Letters of Samuel Taylor Coleridge*, 1:624.

21. Coleridge to J. J. Morgan, 14 May [1814], *Letters of Samuel Taylor Coleridge*, 3:489.
22. Lockridge, *Coleridge the Moralist*, 60.
23. Coleridge to Godwin 13 October 1800, *Letters of Samuel Taylor Coleridge*, 1:636.
24. Richard Kirwan, *Geological Essays* (1799), 434, quoted in *OED*, s.v. "Propulsion," n. 2.
25. *Notebooks* (?), quoted in Stephen Potter, *Coleridge and S.T.C.* (London: Jonathan Cape, 1935), 160. No reference given.
26. Coleridge to Godwin, 17 December 1800, *Letters of Samuel Taylor Coleridge*, 1:656–57.
27. A. R. Humphreys, "'The Friend of Mankind', (1700–60)—An Aspect of Eighteenth-Century Sensibility," *RES* 24 (1948): 212.
28. John Beer, *Coleridge's Poetic Intelligence* (Basingstoke: Macmillan, 1977), 74.
29. Immanuel Kant, *The Metaphysics of Morals* (1797), trans. and ed. Mary Gregor (Cambridge: Cambridge University Press, 1996), 198–99.
30. Godwin, "Judgments on the Novel of St Leon, 1799," Ab. MS Dep. c.604/2, Bodleian Library, Oxford. By permission of Lord Abinger, conveyed through The Bodleian Library.
31. *Notebooks*, 254.
32. Coleridge, "The Rime of the Ancyent Marinere," *Lyrical Ballads* (1798), 5–51.
33. Lockridge, *Coleridge the Moralist*, 70.
34. Coleridge, "Effusion XXXIV. To an Infant," *Poems* (1796), 94–95.
35. Coleridge to Godwin, 22 September 1801, *Letters of Samuel Taylor Coleridge*, 2:761.
36. Godwin to Coleridge, 6 January [1802], Add. MS 35344, fol. 181r, British Library, London. By permission of The British Library.
37. Coleridge to Godwin, 22 January 1802, *Letters of Samuel Taylor Coleridge*, 2:783.
38. Coleridge to Godwin, 21 [January 1802], *Letters of Samuel Taylor Coleridge*, 2:781.
39. Godwin, undated note, *William Godwin: His Friends and Contemporaries*, 1:119.
40. William Godwin, *Things as they are; or, The Adventures of Caleb Williams* (1794), 3rd ed, 3 vols. (London: G. G. and J. Robinson, 1797), 3:248–49.
41. Alan Bewell, "'Jacobin Plants': Botany as Social Theory in the 1790s," *Wordsworth Circle* 20 (1989): 133–34.
42. Coleridge to Southey, [9 December 1794], *Letters of Samuel Taylor Coleridge*, 1:132.
43. Southey, *Poems* (Bristol: T. N. Longman and O. Rees, 1799), 86–87.
44. Southey to Coleridge, 16 January 1800, *New Letters of Robert Southey*, 1:215.
45. Adapted from Logau, *Sinngedichte*, 10:3; *Notebooks*, 432 [26].
46. *The Annual Anthology. Volume I* [ed. Southey] (Bristol: T. N. Longman and O. Rees, 1799), 132.
47. Abrams, *The Mirror and the Lamp*, 224.
48. Coleridge to Thelwall, 31 December 1796, *Letters of Samuel Taylor Coleridge*, 1:294.
49. *Christabel by Samuel Taylor Coleridge Illustrated by a Facsimile of the Manuscript*, ed. Ernest Hartley Coleridge (London: Henry Frowde, 1907).

50. George Whalley, "Coleridge and Southey in Bristol, 1795," *RES* 1 (1950): 340.

51. Southey to Grosvenor Bedford, 3 January 1799, *New Letters of Robert Southey*, 1:179.

52. Southey to Bedford, 9 May 1800, MS Eng. Lett. c.23, fol. 93v, Bodleian Library, Oxford. By permission of The Bodleian Library, Oxford.

53. "A Pastoral On the Death of Bion. From the Greek of Moschus," *Poems on Several Occasions. By the Reverend Mr. Thomas Warton* (London: R. Manly and H. S. Cox, 1748), 205–6. For the son's authorship, see Fairer, "The Poems of Thomas Warton the Elder?," 297–98.

54. Southey to Charles Danvers, 2 December 1801, *New Letters of Robert Southey*, 1:261.

55. Earl Leslie Griggs, "Robert Southey's Estimate of Samuel Taylor Coleridge: A Study in Human Relations," *Huntington Library Quarterly* 9 (1945): 65.

56. Terry Castle, "The Spectralization of the Other in *The Mysteries of Udolpho*," in *The New Eighteenth Century: Theory, Politics, English Literature*, ed. Felicity Nussbaum and Laura Brown (New York: Methuen, 1987), 243.

57. Joseph Cottle, "Monody on the Death of John Henderson, A. B. of Pembroke College, Oxford," *Poems* (Bristol: J. Cottle; London: G. G. and J. Robinson, 1795), 95–105.

58. Coleridge, "Epistle IV. To the Author of Poems Published Anonymously at Bristol in September, 1795," *Poems* (1796), 125–28.

59. Southey to Grosvenor Bedford, 17 July 1796, *Correspondence of the Late Robert Southey*, 1:284.

60. Southey, "The Dead Friend," *Annual Anthology* (1799), 258–60.

61. Coleridge to Southey, 29 July 1799, *Letters of Samuel Taylor Coleridge*, 1:523.

62. Southey to Grosvenor Bedford, 2–3 August 1799, MS Eng. Lett. c.23, fol. 70r, Bodleian Library, Oxford. By permission of The Bodleian Library.

63. In reply, however, Bedford suggested that this rationalist argument could equally be used to conclude that friendship should not be restored:

> You are certainly right—that I overrated his good qualities once and perhaps I have of late underrated them—but of what importance is that?—to be *very nearly* a friend, is not to be a friend, nor any more like one than grey is like black or white. What *pleasure* can one derive from the company of a man whom there is more than one reason to think meanly of?—I grant you there are many bipeds worse—but there are many so much better that I cannot but think it would be a pity—to *stop* half way in one's choice. (Grosvenor Bedford to Southey, 22 August 1799, MS Eng. Lett. d.50, fol. 12r, Bodleian Library, Oxford. By permission of The Bodleian Library.)

64. Southey to Danvers, 20 August 1799; *Selections from the Letters of Robert Southey*, ed. John Wood Warter, 4 vols. (London: Longman and others, 1856), 1:78.

65. Southey to May, 19 September [1799]; *The Letters of Robert Southey to John May, 1797 to 1838*, ed. Charles Ramos (Austin, TX: Pemberton Press, 1976), 47.

66. Southey to May, 18 February 1800, *Correspondence of the Late Robert Southey*, 2:50.

67. Coleridge to John Wicksteed, 9 March 1798, *Letters of Samuel Taylor Coleridge*, 1:394.

68. Coleridge to Southey, [10] April 1800, *Letters of Samuel Taylor Coleridge*, 2:586.
69. Southey to Grosvenor Bedford, 1–21 August 1794, *New Letters of Robert Southey*, 1:68.
70. Coleridge to Southey, 22 July 1801, *Letters of Samuel Taylor Coleridge*, 2:745–46.
71. Coleridge to Southey, 21 October 1801, *Letters of Samuel Taylor Coleridge*, 2:767.
72. Southey to Coleridge, 16 October 1801, *Correspondence of the Late Robert Southey*, 2:172.
73. Southey to Danvers, 9 January 1802, Add. MS 47890, fol. 167r–v, British Library, London. By permission of The British Library.
74. Southey to Danvers, [6 February 1802], *New Letters of Robert Southey*, 1:272.
75. Southey to Coleridge, 1 April 1800, *Correspondence of the Late Robert Southey*, 2:55.
76. Coleridge to Southey, 31 December 1801, *Letters of Samuel Taylor Coleridge*, 2:778.
77. Coleridge to Southey, [8] January 1803, *Letters of Samuel Taylor Coleridge*, 2:913.
78. Coleridge to Southey, 17 May [1803], *Letters of Samuel Taylor Coleridge*, 2:942–43.
79. Southey to William Taylor, 27 July 1801, quoted in Storey, *Robert Southey: A Life*, 144.
80. Southey to John Rickman, 18 October 1802, *New Letters of Robert Southey*, 1:294.
81. Coleridge to Southey, 10 [11] September 1803, *Letters of Samuel Taylor Coleridge*, 2:984.
82. *Notebooks*, 1603.
83. *Notebooks*, 1605.
84. Coleridge to Poole, 14 October 1803, *Letters of Samuel Taylor Coleridge*, 2:1015.
85. Southey to Mary Barker, 1804, *Selections from the Letters of Robert Southey*, 1:253.
86. Southey to Coleridge, 12 March 1804, *Correspondence of the Late Robert Southey*, 2:271. I am grateful to Daniel Alexander for this translation of Southey's Latin.
87. Coleridge to Southey, 20 March 1804, *Letters of Samuel Taylor Coleridge*, 2:1098.
88. Coleridge to Southey, 7 April 1804, *Letters of Samuel Taylor Coleridge*, 2:1124.
89. Southey to Coleridge, 14 March 1804, *Correspondence of the Late Robert Southey*, 2:273.
90. Southey to May, 7 June 1802, *Selections from the Letters of Robert Southey*, 1:199.
91. Southey to Barker, 3 April 1804, *Selections from the Letters of Robert Southey*, 1:270–71.
92. Wordsworth, *The Thirteen-Book Prelude* (1805–1806), ed. Mark L. Reed, 2 vols. (Ithaca: Cornell University Press, 1991), 6.249–60.

9. Postscript

Quotation in chapter title is from Coleridge to William Collins, [6] December 1818, *Letters of Samuel Taylor Coleridge*, 4:892.

1. Joseph Henry Green to Richard H. Dana, Sr, quoted in Jared Flagg, *The Life and Letters of Washington Allston* (London: Bentley, 1893), 106–7.
2. Coleridge to Sir George Beaumont, 7 December 1811, *Letters of Samuel Taylor Coleridge*, 3:352.
3. Allston to Coleridge, [5 October 1816]; *The Correspondence of Washington Allston*, ed. Nathalia Wright (Lexington: University of Kentucky Press, 1993), 352.
4. *Life and Letters of Washington Allston*, 357.
5. Washington Allston, *Portrait of Samuel Taylor Coleridge (unfinished)* (1806), 8.1955.176, Fogg Art Museum, Harvard University. Courtesy of the Fogg Art Museum, Harvard University Art Museums, Loan from The Washington Allston Trust. Photographic Services. © President and Fellows of Harvard College. Allston, *Self-Portrait* (1805), 84.301, Museum of Fine Arts, Boston. Bequest of Miss Alice Cooper, 1884. Courtesy of the Musuem of Fine Arts, Boston. Reproduced with permission. © 2000 Museum of Fine Arts, Boston. All rights reserved.
6. William H. Gerdts and Theodore E. Stebbins, Jr., *"A Man of Genius": The Art of Washington Allston (1779–1843)* (Boston: Museum of Fine Arts, 1980), 50. Morton D. Paley has recently endorsed this interpretation; see *Portraits of Coleridge* (Oxford: Clarendon Press, 1999), 43.
7. Gerdts and Stebbins, *"A Man of Genius,"* 50.
8. E. S. Shaffer, "'Infernal Dreams' and Romantic Art Criticism: Coleridge on the Campo Santo, Pisa," *Wordsworth Circle* 20 (1989): 15.
9. *Notebooks*, 2831.
10. *Notebooks*, 2796.
11. Allston to William Dunlap, [c. 18 February 1834], *Correspondence of Washington Allston*, 352.
12. Coleridge to Allston, 17 June 1806, *Letters of Samuel Taylor Coleridge*, 2:1173.
13. *Notebooks*, 2909.
14. Coleridge to Allston, 25 October 1815, *Letters of Samuel Taylor Coleridge*, 4:606–7.
15. Coleridge to Beaumont, 7 December 1811, *Letters of Samuel Taylor Coleridge*, 3:352.
16. Charles R. Leslie, *Autobiographical Reflections* (1860), quoted in John R. Welsh, "An Anglo-American Friendship: Allston and Coleridge," *Journal of American Studies* 1 (1971): 87.
17. Coleridge to J. J. Morgan, 15 May 1814, *Letters of Samuel Taylor Coleridge*, 3:492.
18. Coleridge to Morgan, 11 June 1814, *Letters of Samuel Taylor Coleridge*, 3:507.
19. Coleridge to Morgan, 7 July 1814, *Letters of Samuel Taylor Coleridge*, 3:518.
20. Allston to Samuel Finley Breese Morse, [after 16 June 1816], *Correspondence of Washington Allston*, 92–93.
21. Coleridge, *Sybilline Leaves: A Collection of Poems* (London: Rest Fenner, 1817), 276–78.

22. Allston, *Monaldi: A Tale* (Boston: Charles C. Little and James Brown, 1841).

23. Allston, *The Sisters* (c. 1816–1817), 1957.1, Fogg Art Museum, Harvard University. Courtesy of the Fogg Art Museum, Harvard University Art Museums, Gift of Mrs. Edward W. Moore. © President and Fellows of Harvard College.

24. Gerald Eager, "Washington Allston's *The Sisters*: Poetry, Painting, and Friendship," *Word and Image: A Journal of Verbal/Visual Enquiry* 6 (1990): 298–307.

25. *Life and Letters of Washington Allston*, 409.

26. Coleridge to William Collins, [6] December 1818, *Letters of Samuel Taylor Coleridge*, 4:892.

Bibliography

PRIMARY TEXTS

Manuscripts

Bodleian Library, Oxford
 MS Eng. Lett. c.23
 MS Eng. Lett. c.453
 MS Eng. Lett. d.50
Abinger-Shelley papers:
 MS Dep. b.227/8(a)
 MS Dep. b.227/2(a)
 MS Dep. c.511
 MS Dep. c.526
 MS Dep. c.604/2

British Library, London
 MS Ashley 1005
 MS RP479
 Add. MS 35343
 Add. MS 35344
 Add. MS 47890

Cambridge University Library
 Acton. c.25.418, MS fly-leaf

Houghton Library, Harvard
 fms Eng. 947.2 (19)
 fms Eng. 947.2 (21)
 MS HEW 15.12.5

National Library of Wales, Aberystwyth
 MS 21283 E, no. 471

Pierpont Morgan Library, New York
 MS MA 77 (17)
 MS MA 77 (18)
 MS MA 225 (28)
 MS MA 1857 (10)

Printed Sources

Allston, Washington. *Monaldi: A Tale*. Boston: Charles C. Little and James Brown, 1841.

———. *The Correspondence of Washington Allston*. Edited by Nathalia Wright. Lexington: University of Kentucky Press, 1993.

Anonymous. *The Amicable Quixote; or, The Enthusiasm of Friendship*. 4 vols. London: J. Walter, 1788.

———. *The Complete Letter-Writer, Containing Familiar Letters on the most Common Occasions in Life*. Falkirk: Patrick Mair, 1792.

———. *The Philanthrope: After the Manner of a Periodical Paper*. London: T. Cadell, Jr., and W. Davies, 1797.

The Anti-Jacobin; or, Weekly Examiner (1797–1798).

———. *The Beauties of The Anti-Jacobin; or Weekly Examiner; Containing Every Article of Permanent Utility in that Valuable and Highly Esteemed Paper, Literary and Political*. London: C. Chapple, 1799.

Atkinson, Charles, Jr. *The Mind's Monitor; or, A Serious Discourse on the Advantages of Self-Preservation, Society, Friendship, Love, Learning, Religion, and on Death*. Leeds: Thomas Gill, 1793.

Austen, Jane. *The Works of Jane Austen*. Edited by R. W. Chapman. 6 vols. London: Oxford University Press, 1923–1954; repr. and rev. 1959–1963.

The Bible (Authorized Version). Edited by John Stirling. London: The British & Foreign Bible Society, first impression 1954.

Blake, William. *The Marriage of Heaven and Hell* (c. 1790–1794). Fitzwilliam Museum, University of Cambridge (copy E).

———. *The Illuminated Blake: William Blake's Complete Illuminated Works with a Plate-by-Plate Commentary*. Edited by David V. Erdman. New York: Dover Publications, 1974.

Boswell, James. *Life of Johnson* (1791). Edited by R. W. Chapman. 3rd ed. Revised by J. D. Fleeman. Oxford: Oxford University Press, 1970.

Burke, Edmund. *A Philosophical Enquiry into the Origin of our Ideas of the Sublime and Beautiful* (1757). Edited by James T. Boulton. Oxford: Basil Blackwell, rev. 1987.

———. *Reflections on the Revolution in France, and on the Proceedings in Certain Societies in London Relative to that Event*. London: J. Dodsley, 1790.

Cameron, Kenneth Neill, ed. *The Carl H. Pforzheimer Library. Shelley and his Circle, 1773–1822*. Cambridge: Harvard University Press, 1961.

Cicero, Marcus Tullius. *Cato and Lælius: or, Essays on Old Age and Friendship*. Edited by William Melmoth. 2 vols. London: J. Dodsley, 1795.

Coleridge, Samuel Taylor. *The Collected Works of Samuel Taylor Coleridge*. Edited by Kathleen Coburn. Bollingen Series LXXV. London: Routledge & Kegan Paul; Princeton: Princeton University Press:

(i) 1. *Lectures 1795 on Politics and Religion*. Edited by Lewis Patton and Peter Mann (1970).

(ii) 2. *The Watchman* (1796). Edited by Lewis Patton (1970).

(iii) 3. *Essays on his Times in "The Morning Post" and "The Courier."* Edited by David Erdman. 3 vols. (1978).

(iv) 4. *The Friend* (1809–1810, 1818). Edited by Barbara E. Rooke. 2 vols. (1969).

(v) 6. *Lay Sermons*. Edited by R. J. White (1972).

(vi) 7. *Biographia Literaria or Biographical Sketches of My Literary Life and Opinions* (1817). Edited by James Engell and W. Jackson Bate. 2 vols. (1983).

(vii) 11. *Shorter Works and Fragments*. Edited by H. J. Jackson and J. R. de J. Jackson. 2 vols. (1995).

(viii) 12: II. *Marginalia: Camden to Hutton*. Edited by George Whalley (1984).

(ix) 14. *Table Talk Recorded by Henry Nelson Coleridge (and John Taylor Coleridge)*. Edited by Carl Woodring. 2 vols. (1990).

———. *The Collected Letters of Samuel Taylor Coleridge*. Edited by Earl Leslie Griggs. 6 vols. Oxford: Clarendon Press, 1956–1971.

———. *Samuel Taylor Coleridge: Selected Letters*. Edited by H. J. Jackson. Oxford: Clarendon Press, 1987.

———. *The Notebooks of Samuel Taylor Coleridge*. Edited by Kathleen Coburn. 4 double vols. London: Routledge & Kegan Paul, 1957–. Vol. 4 edited with Morten Christensen.

———, ed. *Sonnets from Various Authors*. Bristol: the author, 1796.

———. *Poems on Various Subjects*. London: G. G. and J. Robinson; Bristol: J. Cottle, 1796.

———. *Poems, by S. T. Coleridge, Second Edition. To which are Now Added Poems by Charles Lamb, and Charles Lloyd*. Bristol: J. Cottle; London: Messrs Robinson, 1797.

———. *Fears in Solitude, Written in 1798, During the Alarm of an Invasion. To which are Added, France, An Ode; and Frost at Midnight*. London: J. Johnson, 1798.

———. *Sybilline Leaves: A Collection of Poems*. London: Rest Fenner, 1817.

———. *Christabel by Samuel Taylor Coleridge Illustrated by a Facsimile of the Manuscript*. Edited by Ernest Hartley Coleridge. London: Henry Frowde, 1907.

———. *The Complete Poetical Works of Samuel Taylor Coleridge Including Poems and Versions of Poems now Published for the First Time*. Edited by Ernest Hartley Coleridge. 2 vols. Oxford: Clarendon Press, 1912.

———. *Coleridge's "Dejection": The Earliest Manuscripts and the Earliest Printings*. Edited by Stephen Maxfield Parrish. Ithaca: Cornell University Press, 1988.

Cottle, Joseph. *Poems*. Bristol: the author; London: G. G. and J. Robinson, 1795.

———. *Reminiscences of Samuel Taylor Coleridge and Robert Southey* (1837). 2d ed. London: Houlston & Stoneman, 1847.

Cowper, William. *The Poems of William Cowper*. Edited by John D. Baird and Charles Ryskamp. 3 vols. Oxford: Clarendon Press, 1980–1995.

De Quincey, Thomas. *Recollections of the Lakes and the Lake Poets*. Edited by David Wright. Harmondsworth: Penguin, 1970.

Donovan, John, compiler. *Sublime Friendship Delineated*. Cork: J. Cronin, 1789.

Encyclopædia Britannica; or, A Dictionary of Arts, Sciences, and Miscellaneous Literature, on a Plan Entirely New. 18 vols. Dublin: J. Moore, 1790–1797.

The Gentleman's Magazine (and Historical Chronicle) (1731–1922).

Flagg, Jared. *The Life and Letters of Washington Allston*. London: Bentley, 1893.

Godwin, William. *An Enquiry Concerning Political Justice, and its Influence on General Virtue and Happiness*. 2 vols. London: G. G. J. and J. Robinson, 1793.

———. *Things as they are; or, The Adventures of Caleb Williams*. 3 vols. London: B. Crosby, 1794.

———. *Things as they are; or, The Adventures of Caleb Williams.* 3rd ed. 3 vols. London: G. G. and J. Robinson, 1797.

———. *The Enquirer. Reflections on Education, Manners, and Literature.* London: G. G. and J. Robinson, 1797.

———. *Memoirs of the Author of "A Vindication of The Rights of Woman."* London: J. Johnson, 1798.

———. *St. Leon: A Tale of the Sixteenth Century.* 4 vols. London: G. G. and J. Robinson, 1799.

Hartley, David. *Observations on Man, his Frame, his Duty, and his Expectations* (1749). 2 vols. Repr. London: J. Johnson, 1791.

Hayley, Eliza. *The Triumph of Acquaintance over Friendship: An Essay for the Times.* London: T. Cadell, Jr., 1796.

Hazlitt, William. *The Complete Works of William Hazlitt.* Edited by P. P. Howe. 21 vols. London: J. M. Dent, 1930–1934.

Hume, David. *A Treatise of Human Nature* (1739–1740). Edited by L. A. Selby-Bigge. 2d ed. Oxford: Clarendon Press, 1978.

Hunt, Leigh. *Juvenilia; or, A Collection of Poems: Written between the Ages of 12 and 16.* 2d ed. London: J. Whiting, 1801.

Johnson, Samuel. *A Dictionary of the English Language.* 2 vols. London: J. Knapton and others, 1755.

———. *Lives of the English Poets* (1779–1781). Edited by George Birkbeck Hill. 3 vols. Oxford: Clarendon Press, 1905.

Kant, Immanuel. *The Metaphysics of Morals* (1797). Translated and edited by Mary Gregor. Cambridge: Cambridge University Press, 1996.

Kegan Paul, C. *William Godwin: His Friends and Contemporaries.* 2 vols. London: Henry S. King, 1876.

Lamb, Charles. *The Letters of Charles Lamb to which are Added those of his Sister Mary Lamb.* Edited by E. V. Lucas. 3 vols. London: J. M. Dent & Methuen, 1935.

———. *The Letters of Charles and Mary Anne Lamb.* Edited by Edwin W. Marrs, Jr. 3 vols. Ithaca: Cornell University Press, 1975–1978.

Lloyd, Charles. *Poems on Various Subjects.* Carlisle: J. Richardson, 1795.

———. *Poems on the Death of Priscilla Farmer, by her Grandson.* Bristol: N. Biggs, 1796.

———. *Edmund Oliver.* 2 vols. Bristol: Joseph Cottle, 1798.

———. *Edmund Oliver 1798.* Facsimile reprint. Introduced by Jonathan Wordsworth. Oxford: Woodstock Books, 1990.

———, and Charles Lamb. *Blank Verse.* London: John and Arthur Arch, 1798.

Lovell, Robert, and Robert Southey. *Poems: Containing "The Retrospect," Odes, Elegies, Sonnets, &c.* Bath: R. Cruttwell, 1794.

Milton, John. *Paradise Lost* (1667). Edited by Alastair Fowler. London: Longman, 1971.

Montaigne, Michel de. *Essays* (1580). Translated and introduced by J. M. Cohen. London: Penguin, 1958.

The Monthly Magazine, and British Register (1796–1843).

Paine, Thomas. *Rights of Man: Being an Answer to Mr. Burke's Attack on the French Revolution.* London: J. Johnson, 1791.

———. *Rights of Man: Part the Second. Combining Principle and Practice.* London: J. S. Jordan, 1792.

Pastorella, Silviana. *The Cottage of Friendship, A Legendary Pastoral.* London: J. Bew and H. G. Pridden, 1788.

Pratt, Lynda. "'Perilous Acquaintance'? Lloyd, Coleridge and Southey in the 1790s: Five Unpublished Letters." *Romanticism* 6 (2000): 103–15.

Priestley, Joseph. *A Free Discussion of the Doctrines of Materialism, and Philosophical Necessity, In a Correspondence between Dr. Price, and Dr. Priestley.* London: J. Johnson, 1778.

Quarles, Francis. *Emblems, Divine and Moral; Together with Hieroglyphicks of the Life of Man* (1645). Repr. London: D. Midwinter and others, 1736.

Roberts, William. *The Looker-On, A Periodical Paper by the Rev. Simon Olive-Branch, A. M.* 3d ed. 4 vols. London: G. G. and J. Robinson, 1795.

Robinson, Henry Crabb. *Henry Crabb Robinson on Books and their Writers.* Edited by Edith J. Morley. 3 vols. London: J. M. Dent, 1938.

Sandford, Mrs. Henry. *Thomas Poole and his Friends.* 2 vols. London: Macmillan, 1888.

Shaftesbury, Third Earl. *Sensus Communis: An Essay on the Freedom of Wit and Humour.* London: Egbert Sanger, 1709.

Shakespeare, William. *The Riverside Shakespeare.* Edited by G. Blakemore Evans. Boston: Houghton Mifflin, 1974.

Shelley, Mary. *Frankenstein: or, The Modern Prometheus* (1818). London: Henry Colburn and Richard Bentley, corr. and rev. 1831.

Skelton, Abraham. *The Temple of Friendship.* York: W. Blanchard, 1792.

Southey, Robert. *Poems.* Bristol: Joseph Cottle; London: G. G. and J. Robinson, 1797.

———. *Poems.* Bristol: T. N. Longman and O. Rees, 1799.

———, ed. *The Annual Anthology. Volume I.* Bristol: T. N. Longman and O. Rees, 1799.

———, ed. *The Annual Anthology. Volume II.* Bristol: T. N. Longman and O. Rees, 1800.

———. *The Life and Correspondence of Robert Southey.* Edited by Charles Cuthbert Southey. 6 vols. London: Longman and others, 1849–1850.

———. *Selections from the Letters of Robert Southey.* Edited by John Wood Warter. 4 vols. London: Longman and others, 1856.

———. *New Letters of Robert Southey.* Edited by Kenneth Curry. 2 vols. New York: Columbia University Press, 1965.

———. *The Letters of Robert Southey to John May, 1797 to 1838.* Edited by Charles Ramos. Austin, TX: Pemberton Press, 1976.

Stevens, Frederick George, and Mary Dorothy George, eds. *Catalogue of Political and Personal Satires, Preserved in the Department of Prints and Drawings in the British Museum.* 11 vols. London: By Order of the Trustees, 1870–1954.

Thelwall, John. *Poems Written in Close Confinement in the Tower and Newgate, under a Charge of High Treason.* London: the author, 1795.

———. *Peaceful Discussion and not Tumultuary Violence the Means of Redressing National Grievance.* London: the author, 1795.

———. *The Tribune, A Periodical Publication, Consisting Chiefly of the Political Lectures of J. Thelwall.* 3 vols. London: the author, 1795–1796.

———. *Poems, Chiefly Written in Retirement.* Hereford: W. H. Parker, 1801.

———. *The Daughter of Adoption; A Tale of Modern Times. In Four Volumes. By John Beaufort.* London: R. Phillips, 1801.

———. "An Unpublished Letter from John Thelwall to S. T. Coleridge." Edited by Warren E. Gibbs. *Modern Language Review* 25 (1930): 85–90.

———. "John Thelwall's Marginalia in a Copy of Coleridge's *Biographia Literaria.*" Edited by Burton R. Pollin, assisted by Redmond Burke. *Bulletin of the New York Public Library* 74 (1970): 73–94.

———. "John Thelwall in Wales: New Documentary Evidence." Edited by P. J. Corfield and Chris Evans, *Bulletin of the Institute of Historical Research* 59 (1986): 231–39.

Turner, Rev. Daniel. *Sacred Friendship, Exemplified in the Case of Elijah and Elisha. A Sermon Preached [. . .] on the Death of Mrs. Eliza Turner.* London: G. G. J. and J. Robinson, 1786.

The Universal Magazine of Knowledge and Pleasure (1747–1800).

Warton, Thomas [the Elder]. *Poems on Several Occasions. By the Reverend Mr. Thomas Warton.* London: R. Manly and H. S. Cox, 1748.

Williams, Helen Maria. *Letters Written in France, in the Summer of 1790, to a Friend in England.* London: T. Cadell, 1790.

Wollstonecraft, Mary. *Original Stories from Real Life; with Conversations, Calculated to Regulate the Affections, and Form the Mind to Truth and Goodness.* London: J. Johnson, 1791.

Wordsworth, Dorothy. *The Grasmere Journals.* Edited by Pamela Woof. Oxford: Oxford University Press, 1991.

Wordsworth, William, and Samuel Taylor Coleridge]. *Lyrical Ballads, with a Few Other Poems.* London: J. and A. Arch, 1798.

——— [and Samuel Taylor Coleridge]. *Lyrical Ballads, with Other Poems, in Two Volumes.* London: T. N. Longman and O. Rees, 1800.

———. *The Prelude: 1798–1799.* Edited by Stephen Parrish. Ithaca: Cornell University Press, 1977.

———. *The Thirteen-Book Prelude* (1805–1806). Edited by Mark L. Reed. 2 vols. Ithaca: Cornell University Press, 1991.

———. *Poems, in Two Volumes.* London: Longman and others, 1807.

———. *The Letters of William and Dorothy Wordsworth: The Early Years 1787–1805.* Revised by Chester L. Shaver. 2d ed. Oxford: Clarendon Press, 1967.

———. *The Letters of William and Dorothy Wordsworth: The Later Years.* Edited and revised by Alan G. Hill. 2d ed. 4 vols. Oxford: Clarendon Press, 1988.

Wu, Duncan, ed. *Romanticism: An Anthology.* Oxford: Blackwell, 1994.

Yearsley, Ann. *Poems, on Several Occasions.* London: T. Cadell, 1785.

———. *Poems, on Various Subjects.* London: G. G. J. and J. Robinson, 1787.

———. *The Rural Lyre; A Volume of Poems: Dedicated to the Right Honourable the Earl of Bristol, Lord Bishop of Derby.* London: G. G. and J. Robinson, 1796.

SECONDARY TEXTS

Abrams, M. H. *The Mirror and the Lamp: Romantic Theory and the Critical Tradition*. New York: Oxford University Press, 1953.

———, ed. *English Romantic Poets: Modern Essays in Criticism*. 2d ed. London: Oxford University Press, 1975.

Aers, David, Jonathan Cook, and David Punter. *Romanticism and Ideology: Studies in English Writing 1765–1830*. London: Routledge & Kegan Paul, 1981.

Ashton, Rosemary. *The Life of Samuel Taylor Coleridge: A Critical Biography*. Oxford: Blackwell, 1996.

Baker, Felicity. "Rousseau's Oath and Revolutionary Fraternity: 1789 and Today." *Romance Quarterly* 38 (1991): 273–87.

Barth, J. Robert. *Coleridge and the Power of Love*. Columbia: University of Missouri Press, 1988.

Bate, Walter Jackson. *Coleridge*. London: Weidenfeld and Nicolson, 1969.

Beer, John, ed. *Coleridge's Variety: Bicentenary Studies*. London: Macmillan, 1974.

———. *Coleridge's Poetic Intelligence*. Basingstoke: Macmillan, 1977.

Bewell, Alan. "'Jacobin Plants': Botany as Social Theory in the 1790s." *The Wordsworth Circle* 20 (1989): 132–39.

Blatz, Berkeley Stevenson. "Romanticism and the Rhetoric of Friendship." Unpublished doctoral thesis. University of California at Long Beach, 1994.

Bloom, Allan, *Love and Friendship*. New York: Simon & Schuster, 1993.

Blum, Lawrence A. *Friendship, Altruism and Morality*. London: Routledge & Kegan Paul, 1980.

———. *Moral Perception and Particularity*. Cambridge: Cambridge University Press, 1994.

Bygrave, Stephen. *Coleridge and the Self: Romantic Egotism*. London: Macmillan, 1986.

Christie, William. "The Act of Love in Coleridge's Conversation Poems." *Sydney Studies in English* 7 (1981–1982): 12–31.

Coleman, Deirdre. *Coleridge and 'The Friend' (1809–1810)*. Oxford: Clarendon Press, 1988.

Colmer, John. *Coleridge: Critic of Society*. Oxford: Clarendon Press, 1959.

Crawford, Rachel C. "The Romantic Subject and the Poetry of the Bower: Coleridge, Wordsworth, and Keats." Unpublished doctoral thesis. University of Washington, 1989.

———. "Accident and Strange Calamity in 'This Lime-Tree Bower my Prison.'" *Romanticism* 2 (1996): 188–203.

Crawford, Walter B., ed. *Reading Coleridge: Approaches and Applications*. Ithaca: Cornell University Press, 1979.

Crosse, Cornelia A. H. "Thomas Poole." *Temple Bar* 87 (1889): 354–70.

Curran, Stuart. *Poetic Form and British Romanticism*. New York: Oxford University Press, 1986.

Deen, Leonard W. "Coleridge and the Sources of Pantisocracy: Godwin, the Bible, and Hartley." *Boston University Studies in English* 5 (1961): 232–45.

Dekker, George. *Coleridge and the Literature of Sensibility*. London: Vision Press, 1978.
Dowling, William C. *The Epistolary Moment: The Poetics of the Eighteenth-Century Verse Epistle*. Princeton: Princeton University Press, 1991.
Eager, Gerald. "Washington Allston's *The Sisters*: Poetry, Painting, and Friendship." *Word and Image: A Journal of Verbal/Visual Enquiry* 6 (1990): 298–307.
Ellison, Julie. *Delicate Subjects: Romanticism, Gender, and the Ethics of Understanding*. Ithaca: Cornell University Press, 1990.
Erdman, David. "Coleridge as Nehemiah Higginbottom." *Modern Language Notes* 73 (1958): 569–80.
Everest, Kelvin. *Coleridge's Secret Ministry: The Context of the Conversation Poems 1795–1798*. Hassocks: Harvester Press, 1979.
Fairer, David. "The Poems of Thomas Warton the Elder?" *Review of English Studies* 26 (1975): 287–300, 395–406.
———, ed. *Pope: New Contexts*. Hemel Hempstead: Harvester Wheatsheaf, 1990.
———. "Baby Language and Revolution: The Early Poetry of Charles Lloyd and Charles Lamb." *The Charles Lamb Bulletin* 74 (1991): 33–52.
———. "Organizing Verse: Burke's *Reflections* and Eighteenth-Century Poetry." *Romanticism* 3 (1997): 1–19.
Favret, Mary A. *Romantic Correspondence: Women, Politics and the Fiction of Letters*. Cambridge: Cambridge University Press, 1993.
———, and Nicola J. Watson, eds. *At the Limits of Romanticism: Essays in Cultural, Feminist, and Materialist Criticism*. Bloomington: Indiana University Press, 1994.
Fields, Beverly. *Reality's Dark Dream: Dejection in Coleridge*. Kent, Ohio: Kent State University Press, 1967.
Fulford, Timothy. *Coleridge's Figurative Language*. Basingstoke: Macmillan, 1991.
Garber, Frederick. *Wordsworth and the Poetry of Encounter*. Urbana: University of Illinois Press, 1971.
Gerdts, William H., and Theodore E. Stebbins, Jr. *"A Man of Genius": The Art of Washington Allston (1779–1843)*. Boston: Museum of Fine Arts, 1980.
Gravil, Richard, and Molly Lefebure, eds. *The Coleridge Connection: Essays for Thomas McFarland*. Basingstoke: Macmillan, 1990.
Gravil, Richard, Lucy Newlyn, and Nicholas Roe, eds. *Coleridge's Imagination: Essays in Memory of Pete Laver*. Cambridge: Cambridge University Press, 1985.
Griggs, Earl Leslie. "Robert Southey's Estimate of Samuel Taylor Coleridge: A Study in Human Relations." *Huntington Library Quarterly* 9 (1945): 61–94.
Hammond, Paul. *Love Between Men in English Literature*. Basingstoke: Macmillan, 1996.
Harding, Anthony John. *Coleridge and the Idea of Love: Aspects of Relationship in Coleridge's Thought and Writing*. London: Cambridge University Press, 1974.
Harris, Wendell V. *The Omnipresent Debate: Empiricism and Transcendentalism in Nineteenth-Century English Prose*. Dekalb: Northern Illinois University Press, 1981.
Henderson, Andrea K. *Romantic Identities: Varieties of Subjectivity, 1774–1830*. Cambridge: Cambridge University Press, 1996.

Hickey, Alison. "Double Bonds: Charles Lamb's Romantic Collaborations." *ELH* 63 (1996): 735–71.

Holmes, Richard. *Coleridge: Early Visions*. Sevenoaks: Hodder and Stoughton, 1989.

Humphreys, A. R. "'The Friend of Mankind' (1700–60)—An Aspect of Eighteenth-Century Sensibility." *Review of English Studies* 24 (1948): 203–18.

Hunt, Lynn. *The Family Romance of The French Revolution*. Berkeley: University of California Press, 1992.

Jones, Chris. *Radical Sensibility: Literature and Ideas in the 1790s*. London: Routledge, 1993.

Jones, Kathleen. *A Passionate Sisterhood: The Sisters, Wives and Daughters of the Lake Poets*. London: Virago, 1998.

Jones, S. Hester E. "Some Literary Treatments of Friendship: Katherine Phillips to Alexander Pope." Unpublished doctoral thesis. University of Cambridge, 1993.

Kearns, Sheila M. *Coleridge, Wordsworth, and Romantic Autobiography: Reading Strategies of Self-Representation*. Madison, NJ: Fairleigh Dickinson University Press, 1995.

Kelly, Gary. *Women, Writing, and Revolution 1790–1827*. Oxford: Clarendon Press, 1993.

Koestenbaum, Wayne. *Double Talk: The Erotics of Male Literary Collaboration*. New York: Routledge, 1989.

Kroeber, Karl. "Coleridge's 'Fears': Problems in Patriotic Poetry." *Clio: An Interdisciplinary Journal of Literature, History and the Philosophy of History* 7 (1978): 359–73.

Lankheit, Klaus. *Das Freundschaftsbild der Romantik*. Heidelberg: Carl Winter, Universitätsverlag, 1952.

Leask, Nigel. *The Politics of Imagination in Coleridge's Critical Thought*. Basingstoke: Macmillan, 1988.

Lefebure, Molly. *The Bondage of Love: A Life of Mrs Samuel Taylor Coleridge*. London: Gollancz, 1986.

Lewis, C. S. *The Four Loves*. London: Geoffrey Bles, 1960.

Lockridge, Laurence S. *Coleridge the Moralist*. Ithaca: Cornell University Press, 1977.

———. *The Ethics of Romanticism*. Cambridge: Cambridge University Press, 1989.

Lucas, E. V., ed. *Charles Lamb and the Lloyds*. London: Smith, Elder, 1898.

Magnuson, Paul. *Coleridge's Nightmare Poetry*. Charlottesville: University Press of Virginia, 1974.

———. *Coleridge and Wordsworth: A Lyrical Dialogue*. Princeton: Princeton University Press, 1988.

———. *Reading Public Romanticism*. Princeton: Princeton University Press, 1998.

Mangan, J. A., and James Walvin, eds. *Manliness and Morality: Middle-Class Masculinity in Britain and America 1800–1940*. Manchester: Manchester University Press, 1987.

Matlak, Richard E. *The Poetry of Relationship: The Wordsworths and Coleridge, 1797–1800*. Basingstoke: Macmillan, 1997.
Mavor, Elizabeth. *The Ladies of Llangollen: A Study in Romantic Friendship.* London: Michael Joseph, 1971.
Mayberry, Tom. *Coleridge and Wordsworth in the West Country*. Stroud: Alan Sutton, 1992.
McCarthy, Thomas J. *Relationships of Sympathy: The Writer and the Reader in British Romanticism*. Aldershot: Scolar Press, 1997.
McFarland, Thomas. *Romanticism and the Forms of Ruin: Wordsworth, Coleridge, and Modalities of Fragmentation*. Princeton: Princeton University Press, 1981.
Modiano, Raimonda. *Coleridge and the Concept of Nature*. London: Macmillan, 1986.
Mullan, John. *Sentiment and Sociability: The Language of Feeling in the Eighteenth Century*. Oxford: Clarendon Press, corr. ed. 1990.
Newlyn, Lucy. "Parodic Allusion: Coleridge and the 'Nehemiah Higginbottom' Sonnets, 1797." *The Charles Lamb Bulletin* 56 (1986): 255–58.
———. *Coleridge, Wordsworth, and the Language of Allusion*. Oxford: Clarendon Press, 1986.
———. "Coleridge and the Anxiety of Reception." *Romanticism* 1 (1995): 206–38.
Nussbaum, Felicity, and Laura Brown, eds. *The New Eighteenth Century: Theory, Politics, English Literature*. New York: Methuen, 1987.
O'Brien, Conor Cruise, and William Dean Vanech, eds. *Power and Consciousness*. London: University of London Press, 1969.
Olphin, H. K. *George Tierney*. London: George Allen & Unwin, 1934.
The Oxford English Dictionary. Prepared by J. A. Simpson and E. S. C. Weiner, 2d ed. Oxford: Clarendon Press, 1989.
Paley, Morton D. *Portraits of Coleridge*. Oxford: Clarendon Press, 1999.
Perry, Seamus. "Coleridge's Names." *The Coleridge Bulletin* 11 (1998): 37–47.
Potter, Stephen. *Coleridge and S.T.C.* London: Jonathan Cape, 1935.
Raiger, Michael. "The Poetics of Liberation in Imaginative Power: Coleridge's 'This Lime Tree Bower my Prison.'" *European Romantic Review* 3 (1992): 65–78.
Redford, Bruce. *The Converse of the Pen: Acts of Intimacy in the Eighteenth-Century Familiar Letter*. Chicago: University of Chicago Press, 1986.
Roe, Nicholas. *The Politics of Nature: Wordsworth and Some Contemporaries*. Basingstoke: Macmillan, 1992.
———. *Wordsworth and Coleridge: The Radical Years*. Oxford: Clarendon Press, 1988.
Ruoff, Gene W. *Wordsworth and Coleridge: The Making of the Major Lyrics 1802–1804*. London: Harvester Wheatsheaf, 1989.
Rzepka, Charles. *The Self as Mind: Vision and Identity in Wordsworth, Coleridge, and Keats*. Cambridge: Harvard University Press, 1986.
Shaffer, E. S. "'Infernal Dreams' and Romantic Art Criticism: Coleridge on the Campo Santo, Pisa." *Wordsworth Circle* 20 (1989): 9–19.
Sharp, Ronald A. *Friendship and Literature: Spirit and Form*. Durham, NC: Duke University Press, 1986.

St. Clair, William. *The Godwins and the Shelleys*. London: Faber and Faber, 1989.

Stelzig, Eugene L. "Coleridge in *The Prelude*: Wordsworth's Fiction of Alterity." *The Wordsworth Circle* 18 (1987): 23–27.

Stones, Graeme. "Charles Lloyd and *Edmund Oliver*: A Demonology." *The Charles Lamb Bulletin* 95 (1996): 110–21.

———. "The Ragged-Trousered Philanthropist: Coleridge and Self-Exposure in the Higginbottom Sonnets." *The Charles Lamb Bulletin* 100 (1997): 122–32.

Storey, Mark. *Robert Southey: A Life*. Oxford: Oxford University Press, 1997.

Sultana, Donald, ed. *New Approaches to Coleridge: Biographical and Critical Essays*. London: Vision Press, 1981.

Thompson, E. P. "Hunting the Jacobin Fox." *Past and Present* 142 (1994): 94–140.

Thompson, Judith. "An Autumnal Blast, a Killing Frost: Coleridge's Poetic Conversation with John Thelwall." *Studies in Romanticism* 36 (1997): 427–56.

Todd, Janet. *Sensibility: An Introduction*. London: Methuen, 1986.

Trott, Nicola. "The Coleridge Circle and the 'Answer to Godwin.'" *Review of English Studies* 41 (1990): 212–29.

Tucker, Susie I. *Enthusiasm: A Study in Semantic Change*. Cambridge: Cambridge University Press, 1972.

Welsh, John R. "An Anglo-American Friendship: Allston and Coleridge." *Journal of American Studies* 1 (1971): 81–91.

West, Shearer. "Libertinism and the Ideology of Male Friendship in the Portraits of the Society of Dilettanti." *Eighteenth-Century Life* 16 (1992): 76–104.

Whalley, George. "Coleridge and Southey in Bristol, 1795." *Review of English Studies* 1 (1950): 324–40.

———. "Coleridge's Debt to Charles Lamb." *Essays and Studies* 11 (1958): 68–85.

Wheeler, K. M. *The Creative Mind in Coleridge's Poetry*. London: Heinemann, 1981.

Woodring, Carl R. *Politics in the Poetry of Coleridge*. Madison: University of Wisconsin Press, 1961.

Wordsworth, Jonathan. "Lamb and Coleridge as One-Goddites." *The Charles Lamb Bulletin* 58 (1987): 37–47.

Wu, Duncan. "Coleridge, Thelwall, and the Politics of Poetry." *The Coleridge Bulletin* 4 (1994): 23–44.

Yarlott, Geoffrey. *Coleridge and the Abyssinian Maid*. London: Methuen,1967.

Yarrington, Alison, and Kelvin Everest, eds. *Reflections of Revolution: Images of Romanticism*. London: Routledge, 1993.

Index

Abrams, M. H., 31, 299
Addison, Joseph, 84
Advice, 109–15, 211, 280, 320–21, 336
Aeneas, 99
Aers, David, 45
Allston, Washington, 315–27; and accommodating differences, 323–26; and sympathy, 316–19; and virtue, 315–16. Poetry and prose works: "America to Great Britain," 324; "On Coleridge," 325–27; *Monaldi,* 324–25. Portraits: *Coleridge (unfinished),* 316–317; *Diana and Her Nymphs in the Chase,* 316–17; *Self-Portrait,* 316, 318; *The Sisters,* 325
Allston, Mrs., 323
Amicable Quixote, The; or The Enthusiasm of Friendship, 64, 84; and Platonic idealism, 56–57, 58; and enthusiam, 60–61, 63; and cross-rank friendship, 66–67; and utilitarian friendship, 232; and sympathetic friendship, 248–49, 252
Anchises, 99
Ansell, Charles or James K.: "An Irish Hug alias A Fraternal Embrace," 179, 181, 204; "Mutual Confidence in the Year 1799" 225–26; "Tears of Sensibility," 164–65
Anti-Jacobin; or The Weekly Examiner, 45, 46, 155, 165–76, 321, 340; "The Friend of Humanity and the Knife-Grinder," 158–60, 162–64, 341 n; "New Morality," 166–68, 228, 341 n; "The Soldier's Friend," 155–57
Ariès, Philippe, 303–4
Ashton, Rosemary, 66
Atkinson, Charles, 24; *The Mind's Monitor,* 17
Austen, Jane: *Love and Freindship,* 63–64

Austen, Lady, 77, 78
A. W., 153–54

Baker, Felicity, 150
Barbauld, Anna Laetitia: "To Mr Coleridge," 105–6
Barth, Robert J., 18, 28–29, 215, 269
Bate, Walter Jackson, 23, 38
Beaumont, Sir George and Lady, 250, 321
Bedford, Grosvenor, 35–36, 120, 131–32, 140, 142, 300, 304, 306; and Godwinian friendship, 353 n
Bedford, Horace, 119, 120, 131–32
Beer, John, 32, 290
Berkeley, George, 244
Bewell, Alan, 297
Bible, the: Acts, 235; 1 Isaiah, 143; 2 Kings, 91; 2 Samuel, 235
Blake, William, 185–213, 324; *The Marriage of Heaven and Hell,* 185–87. See also Friendship: and opposition
Blatz, Berkeley, 253, 261
Bloom, Allan, 46, 109
Blum, Lawrence, 121, 136
Boswell, James: *Life of Johnson,* 62, 192
Bowles, William Lisle, 38, 39, 190
Braithwaite, Guy, 213
Brotherhood. *See* Family: ideal of friendship; Fraternity
Burke, Edmund, 141, 173, 192–93, 201–3, 275, 340 n; *A Philosophical Enquiry,* 159; *Reflections on the Revolution in France,* 157, 167
Burnett, George, 126
Butler, Lady Eleanor, 72
Bygrave, Stephen, 22, 262–63

"Caius,": 271; "On Imprudent Friendship," 231–32, 269–70; "On Impru-

dent Friendships," 18–19, 58–59, 68; "On the Errors which arise from Friendship," 270. See also *Universal Magazine*
Caldwell, George, 244
Canning, George, 155; "The Friend of Humanity and the Knife-Grinder," 158–60, 162–64
Castle, Terry, 304
"C. C. C.": "Gleanings" 114. See also *Universal Magazine*
Chatterton, Thomas, 111, 128
Christ, Jesus, 90–91, 121, 125, 215–45
Christie, William, 38
Chubb, John, 203
Cicero: *De Amicitia,* 62, 73, 141
Coleman, Deirdre, 22, 29–30
Coleridge, George, 25, 26, 78
Coleridge, Samuel Taylor: and advice-giving, 109–15, 320–21, 327; and aspheterism, 128–29, 225; and associationism, 127; and attentions, 121–45, 161, 320; and bowers, 98–107, 219; and charity, 66, 92–93; childlike identity, 16–17, 26, 92–115, 295; and class, 65, 152, 160–61, 176; and contract, 88–89; and correspondence, 32–37; on cultural differences, 321–24; on egotism, 22–24; as "elect," 220–44; and enthusiasm, 56, 63–65, 73, 136, 327; and familial affection, 27–28, 47, 71, 124–45, 218, 267–68, 277; and "fantasy of continuity," 303, 307–13; and feminine friendship, 41–42, 87–115; on forces in friendship, 288–96; as friend to himself, 270–77; and friendship for humanity, 151–76; and Godwinism, 25, 120–42, 184–85; 184–85; and gratitude, 66, 92; and homoeroticism, 43–44, 96–97; and management, 81–82, 279–87, 296; and manly friendship, 40–43, 253, 87–115, 134–35, 137, 183–84, 189–90, 204, 253, 323; as mentor, 17; and mercantile friendship, 29–30, 225–36, 242; and "mingling identities," 37, 94, 259–60, 246–77; and "One Life," 18, 104, 254–56, 260, 264–65; and opposition, 177–213; and organic friendship, 30–32, 197–203, 297–306; and Pantisocracy, 116–45; and parental friendship, 26, 28; and physiognomy, 65, 194; and Platonic Idea of friendship, 30, 52–53, 86–87, 212, 310–12; and poetry, 38–40; and political conservatism, 201–04; and political radicalism, 45–48, 127–30, 151–213, 250; psychology of, 16–17, 25, 26, 247; and religious friendship, 28–30, 71–74, 78, 91–94, 124, 214–45, 254–55; and retirement, 194–204; and sensibility, 151–54; and sentimental friendship, 125; on symbol, 105; and sympathy, 20, 21, 99, 108–15, 136, 246–77, 283, 310, 316–21; and Unitarianism, 127, 129, 139, 215–45; and will/volition, 288, 293–96. *See also* Egotism; Family; Friendship; Pantisocracy; Sympathy
—. Friendships: with Allston, 315–27; with Godwin, 278–97; with Lamb, 214–45; with Lloyd, 214–45; with Poole, 87–115; with Southey, 116–45, 297–313; with Thelwall, 177–213; with Wordsworth, 246–77
—. Poems: "A Day-Dream," 267–68; "Address to a young Jack Ass," 125–26; "A Dialogue between an Author and his Friend," 287; "A Letter to—," 115, 268–69, 271; "An Effusion at Evening, Written in August 1792," 30; "Christabel," 277, 299–300, 302–3; "Dejection: An Ode," 272–73; "Effusion 10, to Lord Stanhope," 151–52; *Fears in Solitude,* 171; "Fears in Solitude," 45, 100, 171–73, 174, 201–3, 206; "France: An Ode," 173–74, 250; "Frost at Midnight," 23, 78, 206–9, 264–65; "Hexameters," 259–60; "Lines on a Friend who died of a Frenzy Fever," 136–37, 295; "Lines Written at the King's Arms, Ross," 121–22; *Lyrical Ballads,* (1798) 257; "Monody on the Death of Chatterton," 128, 227; "The Nightingale," 23, 40, 52–53, 78, 189–90, 255–56, 290; "Nil Pejus Est Caelibe Vitâ," 20; "Original Poetry. A Tale," 170–71, 341 n; "Pains of Sleep," 310; *Poems* (1797),

227–29, 237; *Poems on Various Subjects* (1796), 23, 38, 151, 182, 252–53; "Recantation Illustrated in the Story of the Mad Ox," 170–71, 341; "Reflections on Entering into Active Life," 184, 243; "Religious Musings," 38, 46, 187, 199, 216–17, 220–21, 223, 227, 240, 254–55, 322; "The Rime of the Ancyent Marinere," 43–44, 175, 225, 257, 277, 292–94; "The Soldier's Wife," 154–55; *Sonnets from various Authors*, 38–39; *Sybilline Leaves*, 324; "This Lime-Tree Bower my Prison," 78, 101–5, 173, 235–36, 258, 269; "The Three Sorts of Friends," 19–20; "The Triumph of Loyalty," 138–39; "To the Author of Poems Published Anonymously at Bristol in September 1795," 303–4; "To C. Lamb," 217–18, 227, 346; "To C. Lloyd, on his Proposing to Domesticate with the Author," 39, 224–25, 227, 230; "To a Friend Together with an Unfinished Poem," 217–28, 227, 346; "To an Infant," 294–95; "To John Thelwall," 183–84; "To Lord Stanhope on Reading his Late Protest in the House of Lords," 151; "To an Old Man," 90–91, 121, 115; "To One who Published in Print what had been Entrusted to Him by my Fireside," 239; "To the Reverend George Coleridge," 40, 94–96, 106–7, 133, 201; "To Simplicity," 41, 236–37, 299; "To a Young Lady with a Poem on The French Revolution," 60, 184; "Written at Shurton Bars," 252–53

—. Prose and Journalistic Writings: "Advice to the Friends of Freedom," 170; *An Answer to "A Letter to Edward Long Fox, M. D.,"* 153–54; *Biographia Literaria*, 21, 177, 204, 247, 275; *The Friend*, 22, 29–30, 275–76; *Lay Sermons*, 105; *Lectures, 1795* 74, 129, 139, 215; "Lecture on the Slave Trade," 152–53; "Lecture on the Two Bills," 178–79; "Modern Patriotism," 185; *A Moral and Theological Lecture*, 126–27; *Notebooks*, 15, 48, 82, 136, 271–22, 273, 289, 291, 298, 311–12, 316, 320; "On the Slave Trade," 152, 154; *The Plot Discovered*, 47, 179, 182; "Principles Not Titles," 174–75; *Table Talk*, 197, 276–77; "The Wanderings of Cain," 257; *The Watchman*, 41, 67, 92, 152, 185

Coleridge, George, 169, 174, 279
Coleridge, Hartley, 208–9
Coleridge, Sara (née Fricker), 88, 91, 95–96, 126, 137, 150–51, 195, 224, 247, 297, 308–9, 323
Collins, William, 327
Complete Letter-Writer, The, 35
Cook, Jonathan, 46
Cole, Lucinda, 54
Cornish, George, 121
Correspondence: 32–38, 210. *See also* Friendly and Corresponding societies
Cosgrove, Brian, 266–67
Cottle, Joseph, 225, 229, 241, 253, 348n; "Monody on the Death of John Henderson," 303
Cowper, William, 75, 79, 99; and gifts 79–80; and management, 80–81
Cowper, William. Poems: "Gratitude. Addressed to Lady Hesketh," 79–80; "On Friendship," 80, 81, 161, 280; "On a True Friend," 80; "A Poetical Epistle to Lady Austen," 75, 76–78; *The Task*, 78, 174, 206
Crawford, Rachel, 98
Crompton, Dr, 210
Cruikshank, Isaac, 192
Curran, John, 283–84
Curran, Stuart, 40

Dana, Richard Sr., 316
Danvers, Charles, 307, 308
Darwin, Erasmus, 282
Davy, Humphrey, 31, 249, 301
Dekker, George, 111
De Quincey, Thomas, 96, 277; *Recollections of the Lakes and the Lake Poets*, 257
Donovan, John: *Sublime Friendship Delineated*, 72–73, 75, 251, 336n
Donne, John, 34, 35
Dryden, John, 111

Eager, Gerald, 325
Egotism, 22–24, 39, 63–64, 240–41, 277–78
Elder, Thomas, 75
Elderton, Mr, "Friendship Defined. An Epistle," 83
Elijah, 91
Elisha, 91
Ellis, George: "The Friend of Humanity and the Knife-Grinder," 158–60, 162–64
Ellison, Julie, 41
Encyclopædia Britannica: "Fraternal," 71; "Friendship," 48–49, 65–66, 87–88, 93, 108, 128, 251–52, 257–58, 260
"Enjoying a Friend," 78–79
Erdman, David, 187
Erskine, Thomas, 164
Euler, Leonhard, 290
Evans, Mary, 133–34, 142, 184, 250
Evelyn, John: *Sylva, or a Discourse of Forest Trees,* 344n
Everest, Kelvin, 26–27, 47, 250

Fairer, David, 185–86, 189, 201–2, 353
Family: as conservative, 47, 131–34, 140–43; distinguished from friendship, 16, 27, 218, 251–52, 258–60; hierarchy of relationships, 75; ideal of friendship, 26–28, 71–72, 124, 262, 266, 267–68, 314, 325; as politically radical, 47, 124–25; religious significance of, 28, 218; sinister influence of, 135, 277
Fawcett, Rev. Joseph, 74
Fields, Beverly, 26, 331
Favret, Mary, 44–45
Femininity, 87–115, 134–35, 164, 243, 264. *See also* Coleridge: feminine friendship; Friendship: and femininity
Fitzgerald, Lord Edward, 164
Fox, Charles James, 164, 179, 192–93
Fox, Edward Long, 153, 180, 182
Fraternity, 71–72, 127, 150–51, 177, 324
French Revolution, 148–49, 157, 166–74, 177, 250
Frend, William, 215
Frere, John Hookham: "The Friend of Humanity and the Knife-Grinder," 158–60, 162–64
Fricker, Edith, 124, 131, 151, 247, 323
Fricker, Eliza, 151, 309, 323
Fricker, Martha, 151, 323
Fricker, Mary, 323
Fricker, Sara. *See under* Coleridge, Sara
Fricker, Mrs. (mother), 135
Friend: as adviser, 24, 109–15; candid, 168–70; of Humanity, 45, 112, 146–76, 321; to others, 269; as reader, 21–22, 262–63; to self 269–77
Friendly and Corresponding Societies: 44–45, 150, 163, 179
Friendship: accommodating difference, 191–213, 253–54, 263, 324–26; and advice-giving, 24, 109–15, 280, 285–87, 321; and amalgamation, 156–57, 273–74, 282, 284–85, 324, 340n; for animals, 125–26; and attentions, 26, 121–22, 138, 161, 320; Blakean model of and bowers, 94–107, 132–33, 219, 243, 264–65, 268; and candour, 168–69; and childhood, 59–60, 85; and the Church, 72–75; and class, 65–70, 149–52, 159–65, 175–76; and commerce, 225–245, 314; and communism, 46, 128–29; as contract, 60, 88–89, 229–32; and correspondence, 32–38; and croneyism, 75–76; definition, 18–19, 48–49; and drinking, 79, 214; and elegy, 301; empiricist conceptions of, 50–86; as English possession, 165–66, 172; and enmity, 167–72; and enthusiasm, 55–56, 61–65, 70–71, 124, 195–96, 319, 327; as exclusive, 167–71; and "fantasy of continuity," 303–14, 327; and femininity, 41, 87–115, 134, 243, 277; generation of, 33, 58, 63–65; and Germany, 72; and ghosts, 304–5, 312–13; and gift-giving, 79–80, 91–92, 98–99, 182, 235, 314, 342–43n; Godwinian model of, 25, 116–18, 353; and hierarchy, 24, 67, 75, 222, 234–37, 240, 253–54, 273, 319; and Hobbesian self-interest, 29–30, 228–45; and homoeroticism, 43–44, 96–97, 331;

and imagination, 306–9; and love, 20, 291; and magnetism, 290–93; and marriage, 72, 88–115; and masculinity, 40–44, 87–115, 134–35, 189–91, 314, 323; maternal mode of, 93–115; and natural forces, 16, 32, 279, 288–96, 313–14; and nature, 100–105; and opposition, 22, 33, 177–213, 324; as organic, 16, 30–32, 60, 77–78, 132, 167, 197–204, 268, 279, 296–314; and patriotism, 47–48, 74–75, 172, 182, 201–2; and physicality, 43, 161, 179, 181, 189–91, 211; and physiognomy, 62–63, 194; as Platonic Idea, 30, 50–86, 166–67, 212, 279, 311–14; and poetry, 38–40; and politeness, 279–87; and politics, 44–49, 116–213; religious significance of, 28–29, 49, 72–78, 91–93, 104–5, 124, 143, 214–45, 254–56, 294; and retirement, 133, 196–204; and sentiment, 117, 123–4, 146–76; and simplicity, 85–86, 236–339, 242; and sincerity, 81–82, 279–87; as spiritual brotherhood, 42–43, 88–93; and sympathy, 24, 108–9, 246–77, 316–21; and vows, 52, 58–61, 64; and virtue, 50–86, 116–45. *See also* Advice; Family; Love; Management; Sympathy; Virtue
Fulford, Timothy, 28

Garber, Frederick, 265
Gender. *See* Coleridge: and feminine friendship; Coleridge: and manly friendship; Friendship: and femininity; Friendship: and masculinity
Gerald, Joseph, 282
Gerdts, William H., 316
Gillman, James, 316
Gillray, James: "Copenhagen House," 179–80; "The Friend of Humanity and the Knife-Grinder," 158, 162–65, 341
Godwin, William, 26, 34, 35, 69, 82, 116–45, 184–85, 188–89, 263, 274, 278–97, 306, 311, 313, 322; and gratitude, 117; and "just affection," 25, 116–19; and magnetism, 290–92; and organic friendship, 296–97; and sincerity, 33, 279, 281–87.
—. Works: *Abbas, an Historical Tragedy,* 285–86; *Antonio,* 288–89; *The Enquirer,* 128–29, 282, 290; *An Enquiry Concerning Political Justice,* 116–19, 120, 127–30, 134, 136, 139, 140, 281–82; *Life of Chaucer,* 281; *Memoirs of the Author of "A Vindication of the Rights of Woman,"* 69; *St. Leon,* 278, 282, 291–92; *Things as they Are; or, the Adventures of Caleb Williams,* 120, 296–97 *Thoughts Occasioned by . . . Dr Parr's Spital Sermon,* 286
Golden, Maurice, 80
Gravil, Richard, 30–31
Green, Joseph Henry, 315
Grenville, Lord, 178
Griggs, Earl Leslie, 34, 302
Guardian Angel, The, 57–58

Hagstrum, Jean H., 53
Hammond, James, 85
Harding, Anthony, 17–18, 249–50
Hardy, Thomas, 210
Harper, George Maclean, 39–40
Hartley, David, 127, 134, 143, 220, 241; *Observations on Man,* 123–24, 215–16
Hayley, Eliza, 283; *The Triumph of Acquaintance over Friendship,* 82–85, 280–81, 334n
Hays, Mary, 298
Hazlitt, William: "My First Acquaintance with Poets," 101; "On the Pleasure of Hating," 341n
Henderson, Andrea, 232–33
Henderson, John, 303
Hesketh, Lady, 75–76, 99
Hickey, Alison, 227–28
Hobbes, Thomas, 230–31, 235; *Philosophicall Rudiments concerning Government and Society,* 228–29. *See also* Friendship: and Hobbesian self-interest
Holcroft, Thomas, 189
Holmes, Richard, 40, 97
Homer, 159
Horace, 180

Hume, David, 21, 249–76, 315; *A Treatise of Human Nature,* 247–48
Humphreys, A. R., 45, 289–90
Hunt, Leigh: "Remembered Friendship," 59
Hunt, Lynn, 150, 177
Hutchinson, Sara, 267–68, 269

Jackson, H. J., 32, 34, 36
Johnson, Samuel, 62, 82, 83, 85, 192, 237, 328; *Dictionary,* 16, 19; "Life of Pope," 81–82 "An Ode on Friendship," 55
Jones, Chris, 147, 153, 166
Jones, Kathleen, 96–97
Joseph, 215

Kant, Immanuel, 292; *Metaphysics of Morals,* 290–91
Kay, John, 75
Kearns, Sheila, 262
Kelly, Gary, 147–48
Kirwan, Richard: *Geological Essays,* 289
Koestenbaum, Wayne, 43–44
Kroeber, Karl, 45

Lamb, Charles, 22, 23, 25, 29, 31, 39, 78, 86, 214–47, 250; and commodified self, 233–36; disillusionment with friendship, 240–41; and drinking, 214; and mercantile friendship, 230–31, 234–36; and religious friendship, 220–22, 234–35; and simplicity, 236–37; and subordination, 222; and Unitarianism, 219–20; "To Charles Lloyd / an unexpected visitor," 233
Lamb, Mary, 218, 220
Leask, Nigel, 129, 139, 141, 196, 199–201
Lefebure, Molly, 17
Lépeaux, Louis La Révellière, 228
Leslie, Charles, 327; *Autobiographical Reflections,* 321
Lewis, C. S., 43, 48, 191
Lightfoot, Nicholas, 126, 160
Linnaeus, Carl, 297
Lloyd, Charles, 16, 17, 22, 23, 25, 28, 29, 30, 39, 58, 86, 214–45, 250, 285, 347n, 348n; commercial awareness of, 230, 347n; and disillusionment with friendship, 237–38, 241–44; and religious friendship, 222–24, 229–30, 238, 241–44; and speedy attachments, 238, 298
—. Poems: "Address to Wealth," 225; "Dedicatory Sonnet: *Ad Amicos,*" 27; "Lines Addressed to S. T. Coleridge," 39, 225–27; "London. A Poem," 243–44; *Poems on the Death of Priscilla Farmer,* 227, 347; "To C. Lamb," 233–34, 347; "To Coleridge," 222–23, 237, 346; "To the Same," 229–30, 237; "To ******. Written in Worcestershire, July 1797," 223–24; "Written at Burton in Hampshire, August 1797," 242–43
—. Prose: *Edmund Oliver,* 66, 214, 237–40, 299
Lloyd, Charles Sr., 227, 229–30
Lloyd, James, 347
Lloyd, Robert, 240–41
Lockridge, Laurence, 20, 24–25, 32–33, 154, 288, 293–94
Logau, Friedrichs von: "Freundschaft," 298; "Wahl eines Freundes," 270–71
Love, 25, 85, 143, 291; Burkean view of, 159; distinguished from friendship, 20, 300–01; linked to familial attachment, 20; as feminine, 42
Lovell, Robert, 142, 150; *Poems* (1794), 130, 301

Management, 80–81, 102, 278–87, 301, 310–11, 314
Magnuson, Paul, 45, 166, 171, 173, 260, 272
Manning, Thomas, 244
Mann, Peter, 178, 185
Martin, Henry, 151
Mary, 215
Masculinity, 40–44, 87–115, 134–35, 189–91, 253, 314, 323, 336n. See also Coleridge: and manly friendship; Friendship: and masculinity
Mathias, T. J., 197–98
Matlak, Richard, 247
Mavor, Elizabeth, 72, 97
McCarthy, Thomas, 34, 37, 87, 108

McFarland, Thomas, 16–17, 30, 31, 33, 41, 253
Melmoth, William, 73, 74
Mesmer, Anton, 290
Milton, John, 84, 97, 209, 220, 275, 276; *Paradise Lost,* 96, 108–11
Modiano, Raimonda, 274
Montaigne, Michel de, 46
Montagu, Elizabeth, 68
Monthly Magazine, The: "A Dialogue between an Author and his Friend," 287; "Reflections on Entering into Active Life," 184, 243; "To Simplicity," 236
"Moralis": "On the Fidelity of Friendship" 114
More, Hannah, 68
Morgan, J. J., 321, 322
Morganwg, Iolo, 205
Morning Post, The: "Dejection: An Ode," 272–73
Morse, Samuel, 323
Moses, 94
Mullan, John, 62, 248
Murdoch, Iris, 121–22

Newlyn, Lucy, 21, 252
Newton, Isaac, 220

O'Connor, Arthur, 179
Otway, Thomas, 111
Oxford English Dictionary, 116, 121, 156, 168, 333, 337, 340n
Olphin, H. K., 162–63, 341

Paul, 235
Paul, Jean, 15
Pantisocracy, 47, 58, 59, 71, 73, 116–45, 147, 167, 199–201, 214, 223, 297, 323, 340–41n; and aspheterism, 46, 66, 128–29, 227, 239, 322; and class, 68, 160–61
Paine, Thomas, 147, 149, 151, 156, 342–43n; *Rights of Man,* 340n; *Rights of Man: Part the Second,* 146
Paley, Morton D., 355n
Pastorella, Silviana: *The Cottage of Friendship,* 100–101
Patton, Lewis, 178, 185
Philanthrope, The, 67–68

Pitt, William (the younger), 152, 170–71, 178
Politics. *See* Coleridge: and political conservatism; —: and political radicalism; Friendship: and politics
Poole, Charlotte, 198
Poole, Thomas, 16, 23, 26, 28, 29, 32, 33, 36, 37, 43, 58, 60, 63, 71, 78, 80, 86, 87–115, 116, 133, 137, 175–76, 201–4, 229, 233, 250–51, 253, 263, 273, 277, 315, 321, 323; and advice-giving, 109–15; and contract, 33, 88–89; and enthusiasm, 61; and feminine friendship, 106–8; and homoeroticism, 96–97; and manly friendship, 89–90, 109–15; as mother figure, 93–99, 115; "Hail to thee Coldridge," 107–8
Ponsonby, Sarah, 72
Price, Richard, 221
Priestley, Joseph, 220, 224, 238; *A Free Discussion of the Doctrines of Materialism,* 221
Punter, David, 46

Quarles, Francis, 143–44

Raiger, Michael, 103
Redford, Bruce, 81
Richard, Jeffrey, 42
Roberts, William: *The Looker-On,* 31, 32, 41–42, 87
Robespierre, Isidore Maximilien de, 177
Roe, Nicholas, 127, 129–30, 140, 179–80, 182, 198, 203–4
Rousseau, Jean-Jacques, 236–37
Rzepka, Charles, 23–24

St. Albyn, Mrs., 203
St. Clair, William, 285–86
Sandford, Mrs. Henry, 92
Schelling, Friedrich, 247
Schliermacher, Friedrich, 21, 24, 36, 275
Seward, Edmund, 304–5
Shaffer, E. S., 21, 275, 316
Shaftesbury, third earl of, 73, 149, 150, 151, 152, 173; *Sensus Communis,* 147
Shakespeare, William, 275, 276; *Julius*

Caesar, 178; *King Lear,* 205; *The Winter's Tale,* 94
Sharp, Richard, 276
Sharp, Ronald, 29, 150, 219
Shelley, Mary: *Frankenstein,* 24
Sheridan, Richard Brinsley, 164, 171, 192
Skelton, Abraham, 55, 58, 82, 84; *The Temple of Friendship,* 50–52
Smerdon, Rev. Fulwood, 136–37
Smith, Charlotte, 39
Smith, Christopher, 131
Socrates, 319
Sotheby, William, 267
Southey, Margaret, 310
Southey, Mrs (mother of Robert), 124, 131, 135, 309, 323
Southey, Robert, 16, 23, 25, 26, 31, 35–36, 39, 41, 43, 44, 56, 60, 64, 65, 71, 74, 82, 101–2, 107–8, 111, 116–45, 147, 150, 155, 157, 162, 177, 178, 180, 185, 195–96, 218–19, 223, 228, 237, 238, 240, 247, 250, 254, 278–79, 281, 315; and class, 160; and domesticity, 130–33, 142–43, 298–99; and duty, 120, 138; and "fantasy of continuity," 303–7; Godwinian friendship of, 119–20, 126, 306; and management, 281; and organic friendship, 30, 132–33, 297–302, 304–5, 309–10; and Pantisocracy, 116–45; and radical sensibility, 154–57; and sentiment, 130–132, 140–41; as "sheet-anchor," 17, 142
—. Poems: *The Annual Anthology,* 298; "Beware a Speedy Friend, the Arabian Said," 298–99; "The Dead Friend," 304–5; "Metrical Letter, Written from London," 298; *Poems* (1794), 130, 301; *Poems* (1797), 154; "The Soldier's Wife," 154–55; "To the Fire," 130–31; "The Widow. Sapphics," 158
Spenser, Edmund, 105, 111, 301
Stanhope, Charles third earl of, 151–52
Stebbings, Theodore E., 316
Stelzig, Eugene, 23
Sterne, Lawrence, 148–49; *A Sentimental Journey,* 153
Storey, Mark, 131
Swartz, Richard, 54

Sympathy, 20, 22, 24, 98–100, 103, 107–15, 136–37, 152, 193, 314, 316–21; and correspondence, 34; Humean model of, 246–77; and magnetism, 290; and Schliermacher, 21, 274–75

Thelwall, John, 16, 22, 33, 40, 43, 44, 48, 56, 58, 71, 151, 156, 177–213, 250, 282, 315; disillusionment with friendship, 204–5, 209–10, 213; and enthusiasm, 195; as fighter, 183–84, 194; and Godwinism, 184–85; and oppositional friendship, 187–213; and retirement, 198–201, 205.
—. Prose: *The Daughter of Adoption,* 149, 175, 197, 211–12, 339; "Prefatory Memoir," 204; *The Tribune,* 149–50, 179, 342–43.
—. Poetry: "Lines, Written at Bridgewater," 198–201; "Ode I. The Universal Duty," 183; "On Leaving the Bottoms of Glocestershire," 207; *Poems, Chiefly Written in Retirement,* 204, 211; *Poems Written in Close Confinement,* 183; "To the Infant Hampden," 204–5, 207; "The Woodbine," 209
Thelwall, 'Stella,' 195, 209, 212–13
Themistocles, 117
Thompson, E. P., 195, 198
Thompson, Judith, 185, 206, 208–9
Tierney, George, 162–65, 170–71, 177, 341n
Todd, Janet, 41
Trott, Nicola, 130
Tucker, Susie, 70
Turner, Rev. Daniel: *Sacred Friendship,* 91–92

Unitarianism, 28, 106, 127, 215–19, 233, 238
Universal Magazine, 66; "Christianity Vindicated in not Particularly Inculcating Friendship and Patriotism," 74–75; "Gleanings," 114; "The Guardian Angel," 57–58, 62, 65; "On the Errors which arise from Friendship," 270; "On the Fidelity of Friendship," 109–10; "On Imprudent Friendship," 231–32, 269–70;

"On Imprudent Friendships," 18–19, 58–59, 68. *See also* "Caius," "C. C. C.," "The Guardian Angel," "Moralis,"

Virtue, 50–86, 116–45, 270–72, 315–16

Walsh, James, 198
Warton, Joseph, 133; "A Pastoral on the Death of Bion," 301, 353; "Retirement: An Ode," 338n
Warton, Thomas (the elder), 39, 133
Warwick, Henrietta, 33, 110
Watts, Alan, 188
Wedgwood, Tom, 107, 113
Weeks, Shadrach, 160
West, Shearer, 44, 166
Whalley, George, 299
White, James, 238
Wilkes, John, 162, 192
Williams, John, 283
Williams, Helen Maria: *Letters Written in France,* 148–49, 151, 152
Wimpory, J., 193
Wollstonecraft, Mary, 69; *Original Stories from Real Life* 125
Woodring, Carl, 47
Wordsworth, Dorothy, 75, 204, 255–60, 263–64, 302; *The Grasmere Journals,* 260, 267
Wordsworth, Jonathan, 238
Wordsworth, Mary, 267–68
Wordsworth, William, 16, 22, 23, 28, 38, 40, 41, 48, 71, 75, 82, 97, 111, 195–96, 198, 203–4, 208, 245–77, 285, 302, 319; and familial friendship, 258–60, 262; and "One Life," 256–60, 264–65, 315; and solitariness, 260–61, 264–67, 272, 276–77; uniqueness of, 253–54. *See also* Egotism; Family; Friend: to self; Friendship: accommodating difference
—. Poems: *An Evening Walk,* 252; "The Fountain, A Conversation," 265–66; "Lines Written a Few Miles above Tintern Abbey," 257–58, 260, 263; "Lines Written at Small Distance from my House," 256, 258; *Lyrical Ballads,* (1798), 257, 302; *Lyrical Ballads* (1800), 246, 264–65; *Lyrical Ballads* (1802), 277; "My Heart Leaps up," 275–76; "A Narrow Girdle of Rough Stones and Crags," 264–65; "Ode," 56; *The Prelude* (1799), 246, 260–63, 271; *The Prelude* (1805), 313–14; "The Recluse," 260, 262; "Resolution and Independence," 271–72
Wu, Duncan, 185

Yarlott, Geoffrey, 16, 17
Yearsley, Ann, 57, 58, 73, 77, 78, 80, 84; "Address to Friendship," 54–55; "On Being Presented with a Silver Pen," 55; "Remonstrance in the Platonic Shade, Flourishing on an Height," 54, 68; "To a Sensible but Passionate Friend," 70–71; "To Stella; on a Visit to Mrs. Montagu," 68–69

OHIO UNIVERSITY LIBRARY

Please return this book as soon as you have finished with it. In order to avoid a fine it must be returned by the latest date stamped below. All books are subject to recall after two weeks or immediately if needed for reserve.

CF